MW00843811

$32.76

Games User Research

GAMES USER RESEARCH

Edited by

ANDERS DRACHEN

Digital Creativity Labs, University of York

PEJMAN MIRZA-BABAEI

University of Ontario Institute of Technology

LENNART E. NACKE

University of Waterloo

OXFORD
UNIVERSITY PRESS

OXFORD

UNIVERSITY PRESS

Great Clarendon Street, Oxford, OX2 6DP,
United Kingdom

Oxford University Press is a department of the University of Oxford.
It furthers the University's objective of excellence in research, scholarship,
and education by publishing worldwide. Oxford is a registered trade mark of
Oxford University Press in the UK and in certain other countries

© Oxford University Press 2018

The moral rights of the authors have been asserted

First Edition published in 2018

Impression: 1

All rights reserved. No part of this publication may be reproduced, stored in
a retrieval system, or transmitted, in any form or by any means, without the
prior permission in writing of Oxford University Press, or as expressly permitted
by law, by licence or under terms agreed with the appropriate reprographics
rights organization. Enquiries concerning reproduction outside the scope of the
above should be sent to the Rights Department, Oxford University Press, at the
address above

You must not circulate this work in any other form
and you must impose this same condition on any acquirer

Published in the United States of America by Oxford University Press
198 Madison Avenue, New York, NY 10016, United States of America

British Library Cataloguing in Publication Data
Data available

Library of Congress Control Number: 2017958357

ISBN 978–0–19–879484–4

Printed and bound by
CPI Group (UK) Ltd, Croydon, CR0 4YY

Links to third party websites are provided by Oxford in good faith and
for information only. Oxford disclaims any responsibility for the materials
contained in any third party website referenced in this work.

FOREWORD

The field of Games User Research aims to provide data-informed feedback during game development to help the intended experience of the game, created during the design process, be realised by players.

The discipline is an important part of crafting the user experience of a game and one that is vital as companies put the player at the center of their experiences. Games User Research is also a science and as a science it thrives when data is shared, methodologies are followed and improved, and knowledge is passed on.

This book provides an excellent overview of approaches toward understanding and analysing game user experiences with its extensive coverage of topics. Written by experienced user researchers from across the industry, who have all worked on the development of methods and establishment of data-supported decision-making in game development.

All the contributors and the editors are members of the Games User Research Special Interest Group of the International Game Developers Association. A group founded by a small group of pioneering Games User Researchers with a desire to grow and support the discipline. Since then it has grown to include user research, user experience, and analytics topics in general. Our group thrives on sharing and improving the essential methodologies and vital concepts of our field.

The open, sharing, nature of the discipline is something we are proud of in the sometimes-secretive world of game development. We all have the desire to help games to be awesome and to share and support each other is the way forward to achieving this goal. As such, the heart of the group has always been a place to openly share knowledge, approaches, and methodologies. We view this book has an important extension of this ethos and we hope it will be a valuable asset for both existing researchers and newcomers interested in the area.

The role of the Games User Research Special Interest Group exists is to provide and support the community. As such, we endorse and support this book as a valuable resource both for our existing members and for others interested in the area. Furthermore, if you are not a member and the content of this book interests you, we welcome you to join us. You can find us online at http://game-suserresearchsig.org/ where you can join our LinkedIn group, take part in our Discord group, and access many additional resources put together by our members.

Please enjoy the book.
The Games User Research SIG Steering Committee

CONTENTS

AUTHOR BIOS

Anders Drachen, PhD, is a Professor at the Digital Creativity Labs, University of York and a veteran data scientist. His multiple award-winning work in the game industry as well as in data science is focused on game analytics, behavioral analytics, business intelligence, game data mining, user experience, industry economics, business development, esports and Games User Research. His research and professional work is carried out in collaboration with companies spanning the industry. He writes about analytics for game development on andersdrachen.com. His writings can also be found on the pages of trade publications such as Gamesindustry.biz and Gamasutra.com. His research has been covered by international media, including Wired, Forbes, The Independent, Techradar, Kotaku and broadly in the gaming press repeatedly over the course of his decade-long career. He is the most published experts worldwide on the topic of game analytics, game data mining and user profiling, having authored >100 research publications on these topics. He is an editor of the 2013 *Game Analytics: Maximizing the Value of Player Data*, a compendium of insights from more than 50 top experts in industry and research. He is a former Lead Analyst for SaaS provider Game Analytics and former member of the board of the IGDA SIG on Games User Research.

Pejman Mirza-Babaei, PhD, is an assistant professor for human-computer interaction and GUR at the University of Ontario Institute of Technology. He is also the User Research Director at Execution Labs, Montreal. He has been involved with the GUR community since 2009, publishing more than 50 articles and co-organizing workshops and courses at international conferences. He has contributed to more than 20 published commercial games, including award-winning titles such as PewDiePie: Legend of the Brofist, Crysis 2, and Weirdwood Manor.

Lennart Nacke, PhD, is the director of the HCI Games Group and an associate professor for human-computer interaction and game design at the University of Waterloo. He is a world-leading authority on the cognitive and emotional aspects of player experience in video games, with a special focus on physiological metrics and gameful design. He has authored more than 100 research publications on these topics, which have been cited more than 8,000 times. He can be found on Twitter (@acagamic) and is also working as a gamification and user experience consultant. He chaired the Computer-Human Interaction (CHI) PLAY 2014 and Gamification 2013 conferences, and is currently the chair of the CHI PLAY steering committee. He is an editor of multiple research journals and a subcommittee co-chair of CHI 2017 and CHI 2018. He has served on the steering committee of the International Game Developers Association Special Interest Group on Games User Research and loves the GUR community. His research group writes articles at http://www.hcigames.com, teaches a heuristics course at http://gamefuldesign.hcigames.com, publishes videos at http://youtube.com/hcigames, and they also tweet from @hcigamesgroup. He loves karaoke, chocolate, and beaches, not necessarily in combination.

Kati Alha, MSc, is a researcher and a doctoral student at the Game Research Lab, University of Tampere. She has been researching games from multiple perspectives, including playability evaluation, playful experiments, and hybrid experiences in play since 2008. She is interested in the design of free-to-play games and has recently studied player experiences and attitudes towards them.

James Berg is a Senior Games User Researcher at Electronic Arts Vancouver, where he has worked for nearly a decade. He has been proud to contribute to projects such as Dragon Age™: Inquisition, FIFA, NHL, EA Sports™ UFC, Mirror's Edge™ Catalyst, SSX™, NBA JAM, and many others. James is former chair of the IGDA

Games User Research SIG, and has been a contributor, speaker, and panelist at various conventions and conferences. He really, really likes talking about games research.He is currently leading the User Experience Research team's work for Bioware's new game, Anthem. He can be found on LinkedIn or Twitter (@ JamesBergCanada).

Björn Berg Marklund, PhD, is currently working at the interaction lab at the University of Skövde, where he researches games and their place in formal educational settings. His background is in game design and the development of serious games. In his current research, he argues for more realistic and sustainable ways of creating, discussing, and researching educational games and the people that use and play them. In his work, he frequently collaborates with developers and educators working with educational games, and he has experienced both successes and failures when it comes to creating games and applying them in classroom environments. By observing how games are perceived and played by such a wide range of players (developers, teachers, and students), his work also highlights the methodological challenges involved in studying gaming behaviours of heterogeneous audiences in various gaming environments.

Steve Bromley is a User Researcher, experienced with research for both software and hardware. He was lead researcher on many of PlayStation's top European franchises, and worked extensively on the PlayStation VR headset and virtual reality games. He helped create #gamesUR, the first European Games User Research conference and created and runs the Games User Research mentoring scheme. He currently leads the User Research team at UK's Parliament.

Florian Brühlmann is a PhD student at the HCI research group at the University of Basel, Switzerland. He is a trained psychologist with special emphasis on human-computer interaction. His research interests include player experience research, questionnaire development, and statistical methods for HCI research. Among others, he has worked together with Google/YouTube in the development and validation of questionnaires.

Pierre Chalfoun, PhD, is the biometrics project manager at Ubisoft Montreal's User Research Lab since 2012. His role is to establish methodologies, supervise overall biometric studies at the lab and drive actionable results for development teams. He has a PhD in computer-brain interaction and emotional intelligence from the University of Montreal. He has the privilege of doing novel biometric work for all the brands at the studio and is excited to be part of an immensely talented and generous GUR team.

Lysiane Charest is an experienced data analytics expert currently working at Outerminds as the lead data analyst and monetization manager. With a deep knowledge of analytics for games of all business models, she has collaborated with nearly 20 studios from playtesting to live ops. Previously working at Execution Labs, she has overseen the implementation and use of analytics in multiple F2P and premium games with various independent game studios. She has a rare expertise in utilizing analytics in playtesting for premium games. Previously she was the lead business intelligence analyst at Woozworld, a virtual world for teenagers. Lysiane holds a master's in business intelligence (BI) from HEC Montréal and a degree in mathematics from Université de Sherbrooke.

Shawn Connor is a manager for Data Insights, and has been doing game analytics in various capacities for over ten years, helping studios find value in all the data he keeps insisting they should collect. He has seen the entire data life cycle from instrumentation design through analysis, and has worked across a wide array genres and platforms.

Jonathan Dankoff is a passionate Games User Researcher with over 12 years' experience on more than 20 games ranging from huge AAA titles to educational children's games and everything in-between. He has developed many new methods and techniques to better understand and improve the player experience, and been privileged to be a part of exciting new endeavours in UX research such as enormous advances in telemetry and biometrics. During his tenure at Ubisoft Montreal, he shipped well over 100 million units on successful series such as Assassin's Creed and Rainbow Six. Jonathan is currently the senior research manager for Warner Brothers Interactive Entertainment, leading the research group and working on a wide variety of interesting projects.

Heather Desurvire, principal and founder of User Behavioristics Research, Inc., a user-player research company, through research objectively identifies barriers to optimal experience. This illuminates the truth and provides the knowledge for designers and producers to make optimal game and product design decisions.

Ms. Desurvire is a highly experienced Games User Researcher. Uniquely publishing work on user-player methodologies, having worked on AAA titles, with many highly regarded game publishers, studios and startups on all platforms and genres. She has contributed to the body of knowledge in the field. She is also a member of the University of Southern California (USC) faculty, in the interactive media and games department.

Ms. Desurvire works with Fortune 500/100 companies, top publishers, studios, start-ups, and the US government. Companies such as Electronic Arts, King, Disney, Sega, Gameloft, Blizzard, Survios, Microsoft, Flipboard and many more entrust their user and player experience to Ms. Desurvire for optimizing player enjoyment and creating user delight.

Her user and player research methodology work is published in Usability Inspection Methods (Wiley & Sons, eds Nielsen and Mack), 'Principles of Optimal Player Experience' and 'New Player Experience' published in Game User Experience Evaluation and Evaluating User Experience for Games (Springer, 2010, 2015, respectively). Principles of player experience in mobile games and virtual reality principles VR PLAY HCI, 2018. Her extensive academic research work—over 35 papers and articles—have been presented in journals and at conferences such as the HCI, INTERACT, IEEE, and CHI. She has served on the board and a co-founder of the special interest group GUR, a part of IGDA, co-organizer of the GDC Summit for GUR and co-chaired the SIGCHI game community. She mentors many budding game designers and game user researchers.

Johan Dorell, BSc, worked at Paradox Interactive (Stockholm, Sweden) as a user researcher focusing on usability and playability. He has worked on titles such as Leviathan: Warships, Cities in Motion 2, War of the Vikings, Magicka 2, and many others. He has been part of the genesis of Paradox's in-house quality assurance (QA) department, and has extensive experience constructing new QA processes and environments from the ground up. He has talked about this topic at several conferences, such as the game QA and localization conference. For a couple of years he worked on implementing tests focused on usability and playability, and on improving upon these processes. During this research, he discovered the field of GUR and has been studying it ever since. He focuses mostly on finding tools and methods that produce reliable answers to questions from project stakeholders. In 2015, he moved to EA DICE as an associate Games User Researcher working on Battlefield 1.

Nic Ducheneaut is a research scientist with more than ten years' experience combining data science with insights from sociology and psychology to better understand human behaviour. His studies have informed the design of computer systems ranging from desktop to mobile and web applications (resulting in 23 pending U.S. patents and more than 50 refereed publications). His research pioneered the use of large-scale, server-side data for modelling behaviour in video games. At Xerox PARC, he founded the PlayOn project, which conducted the longest and largest quantitative study of user behaviour in World of Warcraft (more than 500,000 players observed over five years). At Ubisoft, he translated his findings into practical recommendations for both video game designers and business leaders. Today, as the co-founder and technical lead of Quantic Foundry, he helps game companies bridge analytics and game design to maximize player engagement and retention.

Thomas Galati is a game developer and data scientist. He is interested in creating more accessible and affordable analytics and user research solutions for independent developers.

Kathrin Gerling, PhD, is an assistant professor at KU Leuven, where she is part of the e-Media Research Lab. Her main research areas are HCI and accessibility; her work examines interactive technologies with a purpose besides entertainment. She is particularly interested in how interfaces can be made accessible for audiences with special needs, and how interactive technologies can be leveraged to support well-being. Kathrin holds a PhD in computer science from the University of Saskatchewan, Canada, and she received a master's degree in cognitive science from the University of Duisburg-Essen, Germany. Before joining academia, she worked on different projects in the games industry.

Julien Huguenin is a User Research project manager at Ubisoft Montréal. He has been working as a Games User Researcher for Ubisoft since 2011, after graduating from a game design school. He worked in the HQ/Paris lab for more than 5 years, first as an analyst on AAA titles such as "Tom Clancy's Splinter Cell; Blacklist" or "Tom Clancy's The Division", then as a team lead and manager. In 2017, he joined the Montreal-based team to work on "Tom Clancy's Rainbow 6: Siege". You can find him on twitter @ JulienHuguenin.

Tom Knoll is a senior user experience consultant at Spotless (spotless.co.uk), a UX and service design agency based in central London. Tom's specific area of interest is in video games research, having worked on projects in many different areas within the gaming industry, including games usability testing, games for education, second screen experiences for broadcast TV, console hardware, and usability testing of console-based sales platforms (such as the PlayStation store). Tom has also co-authored several research papers on the subject of strategy use by different types of gamer within video games, which have been presented at major industry events such as CHI and CHI PLAY. He retains close ties with the academic world and is always on the lookout for further opportunities to be a part of original research.

Hannu Korhonen, PhD, has more than 18 years' experience in working with issues in both academia and industry. Although Hannu has worked in many different domains, mobile devices and services, including mobile games, have been the primary area for years. Hannu has developed playability heuristics which can be used to evaluate playability of all kinds of games. In addition, he is one of the developers of the playful experience (PLEX) framework which can be used for designing playfulness in different products. Recently, Hannu completed his PhD dissertation on playability evaluation of mobile games with an expert review method.

Elina Koskinen is a philosophy student at the University of Tampere. She wrote her bachelor's thesis on ethical issues in designing free-to-play games. Elina is interested in narratives and is currently working on her master's thesis on designing ethical experiences in video games.

Ben Lewis-Evans has a PhD in human factors psychology and works as a user experience researcher at Epic Games. In addition to games, his research interests include GUR, usability, human factors, human error, traffic psychology, and science in general.

Conor Linehan, PhD, is a lecturer in applied psychology at University College Cork, where he is a member of the People and Technology research group. He holds BA and PhD degrees in psychology from Maynooth University, and until recently worked as a lecturer at the Social Computing Research Centre at the University of Lincoln. Conor's research expertise lies in the design and evaluation of technology for the promotion of health and well-being, education, and behaviour change. He has worked on diverse research projects, investigating the design of educational games, pervasive games, vision therapy programmes, sleep monitors, and online mental health interventions.

Ian Livingston is the User Experience Manager for EA Canada, where he and his team provide user experience research and tools support for multiple franchises developed across Canada including FIFA, Plants vs. Zombies, and Mass Effect. Prior to EA, Ian worked at Ubisoft Montreal as the User Research Lead for the Far Cry franchise, working on titles including Far Cry 3 & 4. Ian has been working in the video game industry for almost 9 years, has published numerous academic articles in the field of HCI, and has presented work at a variety of conferences including GDC, and SIGGRAPH.

Sebastian Long works as a Games User Researcher at Player Research, the multi-award-winning playtesting and research studio based in the United Kingdom. With Player Research, Seb has contributed to hundreds of games and impacted billions of players, including many best-loved franchises and indie games. Seb is a '30 Under 30' and Develop Award winner, BAFTA member, GamesUR conference chair; he lives on the UK south coast with his partner Kathryn.

Guillaume Louvel is a UX/UR consultant and a former Games User Researcher at the Ubisoft Editorial UR Lab. At Ubisoft, he led user tests and research on several AAA titles, as well as smaller games for consoles, PCs, mobiles, and browsers. Besides video games, his user research work includes topics such as websites, apps, serious games, and automotive user interfaces.

Regan Mandryk, PhD, is a professor in Computer Science at the University of Saskatchewan; she pioneered the area of physiological evaluation for computer games in her award-winning Ph.D. research at Simon Fraser University with support from Electronic Arts. With over 200 publications that have been cited thousands of times (including one of Google Scholar's 10 classic papers in HCI from 2006), she continues to investigate novel ways of understanding player experience in partnership with multiple industrial and international collaborators, but also develops and evaluates persuasive games, games for health, games for special populations, and games that foster interpersonal relationships. Regan has been the invited keynote speaker at several international game conferences, led Games research in the Canadian GRAND Network, organizes international conferences including the inaugural CHI PLAY, the inaugural CHI Games Subcommittee, and CHI 2018, and leads the first ever Canadian graduate training program on Games User Research (SWaGUR.ca) with $2.5 million of support from NSERC.

Graham McAllister, PhD, is the founder and director of Player Research, an award-winning UX Research and playtesting studio based in Brighton, UK and Montreal, Canada. Player Research helps studios deliver successful games by challenging assumptions, validating design decisions, and providing evidence on the player experience throughout development. He has a PhD in Computer Science and was previously an academic in Human-Computer Interaction at the University of Sussex. Graham is a BAFTA Games member, a frequent conference speaker, and has written regular columns on UX Research for EDGE GamesIndustry.biz.

Michael C. Medlock is a Principal User Researcher at Oculus Rift with 20 years of industry experience in the field of Human-Computer Interaction. Early on he worked at Microsoft on Internet Explorer 4.0 and then at Boeing on internal airplane configuration software. He then helped found the Games User Research group at Microsoft in 1998. During 10 years in the games group, he worked on three Xbox console launches and many successful Xbox and PC games such as Project Gotham Racing, Age of Empires II, Dungeon Siege, Crimson Skies, Flight Simulator, Top Spin, Gears of War 3, Minecraft for Xbox, and Sunset Overdrive. While at Microsoft he has also worked on Windows Phone 6.0 – 7.0, Zune software, Xbox platform software, HoloLens & internal HR business systems. Additionally, he has worked on medical devices and software for Philips. He has documented and evangelized the Rapid Iterative Testing and Evaluation method (RITE) which is used worldwide, and UI Tenets & Traps, a heuristic system for evaluating user interfaces.

Elisa Mekler, PhD, is head of the HCI research group at the University of Basel, Switzerland. She holds a PhD in cognitive psychology from the University of Basel with special emphasis on HCI. Her research interests include motivational and emotional processes underlying the player experience. Her publications have won best paper and best paper honourable mention awards at the premier human-computer interaction conferences CHI and CHI PLAY.

Janne Paavilainen, MSc, is a games researcher at Game Research Lab, University of Tampere, Finland. For the last decade, Janne has been involved in research projects focusing on mobile, casual, and social gaming. Janne's research interests are in game usability, playability, and player experience. More recently, while finishing his doctoral thesis on Facebook games, he has studied the free-to-play revenue model, service design, and player experiences in social network games

Johanna Pirker, PhD, is a computer scientist focusing on game development, research, and education. She has lengthy experience in evaluating, designing, and developing games and virtual realities and believes in them as tools to support learning, collaboration, and solving real problems. In 2011–2012 she started developing virtual worlds for physics education at Massachusetts Institute of Technology. She specialized in games and environments that engage users to learn, train, and work together through motivating tasks. She started in the industry as QA tester at EA and still consults for studios in the field of GUR. At the moment she teaches game development at Graz University of Technology and researches games with focus on data analysis, HCI, AI, and virtual reality technologies. She has authored and presented numerous publications in her field.

Mirweis Sangin, PhD, is principal UX researcher at Sony PlayStation. Throughout his years at PlayStation, he has been responsible for helping improve the player experience of award-winning franchises such as LittleBigPlanet, Tearaway, Killzone, and Horizon: Zero Dawn. He has also worked extensively on improving the user experience and ergonomics of systems such as PlayStation Vita, DualShock 4, and PlayStation 4.

Mirweis holds a master's degree in cognitive science and a master's and PhD degrees in human-computer interaction. Prior to his position at PlayStation, he has worked as a freelance UX consultant and as co-founder and principal UX architect of a UX design agency in Switzerland.

Steven Schirra is the UX research manager at Twitch. He has led mobile user research on games and entertainment products at Zynga, the MIT Game Lab, and Yahoo. He received his master's in comparative media studies from MIT.

David Tisserand is a process manager at the Ubisoft Montreal User Research Lab, responsible for streamlining the testing process and ensuring top-quality findings. He also manages the international standardization of Ubisoft user research processes. Previously he was a process manager at Sony Computer Entertainment Europe where he led the international research effort on the PlayStation Vita and DualShock 4 ergonomics, and worked on games such as Heavy Rain and Beyond 2 Souls.

Brooke White is the senior director of UX research at Yahoo for all consumer products and advertising platforms. She started and directed user research practices for three different companies: Yahoo, Disney, and Volition/THQ. Brooke has decades of experience spanning research, marketing, and production in desktop, console, and mobile consumer games and entertainment.

Dennis Wixon, PhD, is an associate professor in the Interactive Media and Games Division at the USC School of Cinematic Arts, where he holds the Microsoft Professorship for user research. He has worked in user research since 1981. He has worked as an individual researcher and managed user research teams at Digital Equipment Corporation and Microsoft, including the Games User Research team at Microsoft Game Studios. He has worked closely with his teams to develop a number of applied research techniques including data logging, usability engineering, contextual design, RITE (rapid iterative testing and evaluation) and TRUE (tracking real-time user experience). Many of these techniques have been widely adopted and have become an industry-wide practice. TRUE was one of the first comprehensive descriptions of telemetry and analytics for game design and has been applied to well-known franchises such as Halo. Dennis has given talks on HCI and has co-authored over 50 articles and book chapters, and two books: *Field Methods Casebook for Software Design* and *Brave NUI World*. He has also served as papers co-chair, tutorials co-chair, posters and notes co-chair, and overall conference chair for SIGCHI. He was elected vice president of SIGCHI and focused on reforming the conference to broaden participation. He was also one of the founding members of the Greater Boston SIGCHI chapter, one of the oldest chapters in SIGCHI. Dennis has a PhD in experimental social psychology from Clark University. His current interests include research methods for game design and the application of data science to games research.

Nick Yee is the co-founder and analytics lead of Quantic Foundry. For over a decade, he has conducted research on the psychology of gaming and virtual worlds using a wide variety of methods. At Stanford University, he used immersive VR to explore how avatars can change the way people think and behave. At the Palo Alto Research Center (PARC), he applied social network analysis and predictive analytics to examine large-scale World of Warcraft data. He was a senior research scientist in Ubisoft's Gamer Behavior Research group where he combined data science and social science methods to generate actionable player insights for different game development teams. At Quantic Foundry, he leads the research and development of new tools and approaches for understanding the motivations of game audiences. He is the author of the book *The Proteus Paradox: How Online Games and Virtual Worlds Change Us—And How They Do not.*

Veronica Zammitto is a Director of UX Research at Electronic Arts. She focuses on strategic improvement of the UX research practice and building a world-class research team in the game industry. Veronica has extensive knowledge of research methodologies applied to video games. She has transformed how player experience is assessed at EA by introducing novel techniques, including eye tracking and mixed methods with telemetry, as well as setting processes and standards for impactful, high quality research. Veronica is passionate about corporate UX maturity, advocating user-centered practices that change the culture of the company, and building innovative research teams that drive the field. Veronica loves sharing her insights and vision of games user research. She frequently presents at top tier conferences like GDC, and has published book chapters and papers. Veronica's efforts have led games user research on multiple projects across all EA, including Battlefield, Plant vs Zombies Garden Warfare, Madden, FIFA, NBA Live, NHL, Star Wars: Battlefront.

CHAPTER 1

Introduction to Games User Research

ANDERS DRACHEN, *Digital Creativity Labs,*
University of York

PEJMAN MIRZA-BABAEI, *UXR Lab, University of*
Ontario Institute of Technology

LENNART E. NACKE, *University of Waterloo*

1.1 Focus on your players: Games User Research

Games User Research (GUR) is an interdisciplinary field of practice and research concerned with ensuring the optimal quality of usability and user experience (UX) in video games. This means that GUR inevitably involves any aspect of a video game that players interface with, directly or indirectly: from controls, menus, audio, and artwork to the underlying game systems, infrastructure, as well as branding, customer support, and beyond. Essentially, any aspect of a video game that influences the user's experience and perception of that game is of concern for an investigative GUR practice.

This makes GUR a field that interfaces with more or less every other area of game development. If game development were an ancient temple, the three biggest central pillars would be *design*, *art*, and *programming*. The majority of people working in games fit within one of these three wider areas. However, in-between these pillars would be dozens of smaller columns supporting the

Games User Research, Anders Drachen, Pejman Mirza-Babaei, Lennart E. Nacke (Eds).
© Oxford University Press 2018. Published 2018 by Oxford University Press

roof of our metaphorical temple, with columns denoting specific processes: from hardware to audio engineering, marketing and management, all the way over to legal and contracts handling, and for that matter even catering, to make sure teams have something to eat. All aspects of game development—to some degree—interface with various other aspects (e.g., system programmers interface with gameplay designers). However, our GUR column could rather be perceived as a strong vine that has its tendrils spread across the vast majority of columns, supporting each of them at the same time, providing evidence about how each column holds together, and how it is perceived by the players. The ancient temple-and-vine metaphor accurately describes GUR's role in contemporary game development: it supports, provides evidence to act on, troubleshoots, checks, and inspires. GUR is the field that helps us figure out if the experiences we hope to give our players are what we are indeed delivering, because GUR focuses on the players and their experience playing games, and this is at the heart of all games.

In practice, GUR production revolves around delivering evidence of what players experience in a game project and uses methods from many research fields, including human-computer interaction, human factors, psychology, design, graphics, marketing, media studies, computer science, analytics, and other disciplines to deliver robust tests to assess all aspects of UX in a game. In addition, Jakob Nielsen, a famous UX visionary, once observed when attending the GUR Summit (one of the GUR community's big events) that GUR includes testing multiple players at the same time that generate 'data at true scale'. This poses its own analytical challenges to user researchers in games. User researchers in games need a comprehensive and truly interdisciplinary skill set to be successful.

Contrary to the domains of QA and technical game testing—where errors in the game code are tracked and the error-free technological execution of the game is in the foreground—GUR is focused completely on evaluating players (based on observation of them playing or otherwise interacting with the game and its components, and analysis of the data they generate). GUR practitioners rely on experience analysis and on understanding player interaction. Their objective is not simply testing the player, but improving all aspects of a game's design through building empirical evidence via experimentation and testing. How to do this in practice is an interesting challenge—games are intricate, interactive computational systems, where engagement is an important factor. Over the past two decades, much work has been exerted adopting and extending the methodologies from other fields to develop appropriate tools for GUR.

We—the editors of this book—find GUR rewarding because it allows us to reflect on design, to iterate deeply on game mechanics, and to understand the components of a pleasurable UX. However, for over a decade, GUR in the game industry struggled to find the recognition it deserves, often because its outcomes are more subtly embedded in a final product than a game's assets, like its sounds, animations, and graphics. Moreover, designers often get the spotlight when a game mechanic is experienced as extremely polished, but the refinement can be the result of a long and elaborate iteration process that involves feedback about the quality of experience. One of our colleagues, industry veteran Jordan Lynn, once described GUR as the practice of 'telling designers that their babies are ugly'. Indeed, it is the user researcher's job to critically investigate elements in a game and find the parts that do not work well together or are detrimental to the UX.

Seasoned GUR professionals describe their job as well done when they can provide game designers and other stakeholders with insight about how their designs are being experienced by players. As our colleague Mike Ambinder, experimental psychologist at Valve Corporation, once noted, GUR can be seen as evaluating design hypotheses that are created during each development cycle in a game, which is similar to the scientific method. Thus, GUR is an evidence-driven, powerful process that helps designers create better gameplay experiences by finding weaknesses in the design and structure of games across all phases of their life cycle, from early designs, through prototypes, and after launch.

GUR methods are evolving constantly and user testing is now common-place in the games industry, which globally has an annual revenue of over US$100 billion (outselling the motion picture and music industries combined), with billions of players across any culture and demographic. With such a massive and diverse audience, to make this industry a success, users have become more and more integrated into game development. The steady increase in the size of the target audience for games, as well as its increasing diversification, has led to a stronger need for GUR. This has brought an opportunity for the industry to innovate on different forms of play, allowing different types of inter-actions and contexts, and the accommodation of different types of users of all ages, intellectual abilities, and motivations. Now, more than ever, it is necessary for designers to develop an understanding of the users and their experiences of interacting with games.

A lot of people from the GUR (#GamesUR) community worked hard for more than two years to make this happen. We hope you will enjoy it and find value among its pages. Thank you.

1.2 About this book

This book is focused on providing the foundational, accessible, go-to resource for people interested in GUR. It is a community-driven effort—it has been written by passionate professionals and researchers in the GUR community as a handbook and guide to everyone interested in user research and games. We aim to provide the most comprehensive overview from an applied perspective, for a person new to GUR, but which is also useful for experienced user researchers. We stress the term *overview*—GUR is a deep, interdisciplinary field with thousands of professionals working within it worldwide; hundreds of scientific papers are produced on the topic every year. It is not possible for one book to provide everything you need to know about GUR, but what a single book can do is provide the bird's-eye view, introduce the contexts and methods, and provide a pathway for further self-illumination. That is not to say that this book is not practical, as the various chapters not only describe high-level concepts, but also how to work in practice with GUR methods. This book contains practical guidelines on how to conduct user research across topics such as planning, methods, lab design, mobile games, accessibility, budgeting user research, and more. The book is grounded in the design and development process, and describes which methods we use at which stages, mimicking the glossaries used in the industry and academic research today, but putting everything into context. The connection between the wider context of GUR and the nitty-gritty details of work 'in the trenches' is perhaps the most valuable aspect of this book.

1.3 Overview of the book

We have structured this book into a couple of sections, each focused on a specific theme. Within each theme are several chapters that deal with particular topics, or treat the same topics from different angles.

Part 1: GUR in Production (Chapters 2–6). This part focuses on the practical context of GUR in game development, meaning how we work with our players in practice to test and evaluate games, and with our colleagues to put the knowledge gained into action.

In Chapter 2, Veronica Zammitto discusses the implementation of GUR in the production pipeline. It concerns itself with two aspects. Firstly, it discusses the challenges and pitfalls involved in the execution of GUR. Secondly, it outlines best practices for applying GUR in industry.

David Tisserand outlines the benefits of designing a GUR process adequately in Chapter 3. Chief among its contributions is that it addresses the necessary steps of designing, running, and analysing a testing method. The chapter concludes with a discussion of the proper maintenance of documentation for optimization of research efficiency.

Chapter 4 presents Ian Livingston's discussion of the potential benefits of post-launch GUR. Sources of post-launch data such as live data and benchmark studies are considered. The chapter takes an in-depth look at a powerful benchmark study method, review analysis, which can be used only after your game has been released.

In Chapter 5, Graham McAllister presents the different maturity levels that GUR can take depending on the studio. Given the wide variety of reactions to UX, it is important to understand where one is on that maturity scale. This understanding has the potential to help developers and user researchers focus on players.

In Chapter 6, Sebastian Long contributes processes for setting up functional lab environments. It outlines the process used by Player Research to set up their labs. In so doing it provides a range of elements to consider, including testing strategies, materials selection, and floor plans. Key lessons learned by Player Research along the way are discussed.

Part 2: Methods: Testing Things You Play (Chapters 7–19). This part focuses on the myriad methods used in GUR. From interviews to analytics, GUR professionals have a big toolbox of methods and techniques that are useful in various situations. Some of these, like think-aloud testing and observation, are time-honoured, flexible methods that can be picked up and used with little training and applied in a variety of scenarios. Others, such as psychophysiological measures, are more specialized and have a narrower focus, but are incredibly powerful for driving particular types of insights.

Chapter 7 functions as an index of common GUR methods. Michael C. Medlock gives small summaries of the methods and then discusses considerations for constructing and combining them. The chapter concludes with an exploration of how to match methods to the questions they can answer.

In Chapter 8, Graham McAllister and Sebastian Long give in-depth description of the eight most used methods in player research. Information is given about time frame, execution, and result delivery. Strengths and weaknesses of each method are discussed.

Chapter 9, by Florian Brühlmann and Elisa Mekler, is about surveys. It describes the qualitative method and presents practice-oriented guidance about when to use it. How to alleviate bias and make good questionnaires is also covered, with an emphasis on maintaining data quality.

Steve Bromley discusses player interviews in Chapter 10. Interview tips are provided as well as an exploration of the preparation of an interview as well as methods used in GUR such as interviews during the session and final interviews. The chapter ends with a discussion of data capture analysis and thoughts on the future of interview methods.

In Chapter 11, Mirweis Sangin talks about the player experience. It discusses methods applied in observing player behaviour to uncover usability problems. Furthermore, it provides an overview on how to capture usability events. Guidelines on tools and processes used to document and analyse observations are provided.

Tom Knoll describes the think-aloud protocol and its application to player experience in Chapter 12. It covers what the protocol is, when to apply it, how to conduct it, its pros and cons, and its variations. The chapter concludes with a discussion about think-aloud protocols with children and considerations necessary when using child participants.

Chapter 13 by Michael C. Medlock outlines the rapid iterative test and evaluation (RITE) method. At the heart of this method is the idea that if an issue is found, it should be fixed before the next tester plays the build. The chapter outlines the benefits and practical methodology of running RITE tests. It concludes with a discussion of the original 2002 case study which documented the method, Age of Empires 2.

In Chapter 14, Heather Desurvire and Dennis Wixon present PLAY and game approachability principle (GAP) heuristics for game design. It discusses the history of heuristics in games, including the research demonstrating their effectiveness, as well as describing the use of heuristics. The benefits of heuristics, such as revealing problems, fixes, possible enhancements, and effective current aspects are also discussed. Overall, heuristics have been found to be more effective than informal reviews.

Janne Paavilainen, Hannu Korhonen, Elina Koskinen, and Kati Alha talk about the heuristic evaluation method with updated playability heuristics in Chapter 15. It presents example studies identifying playability problems in social network games. Benefits such as cost-effectiveness and flexibility are also discussed. Finally, new heuristics for evaluating free-to-play games are proposed.

Chapter 16 summarizes a decade of Lennart Nacke's work on the use of biometrics for GUR, with attention given not only to the physiological justification for the different types of biometric data that are possible to capture, but also to some use-cases and caveats to be aware of.

In Chapter 17, Pierre Chalfoun and Jonathan Dankoff describe biometric procedures, particularly eye tracking, for GUR in production teams. It is divided into four sections and describes the ongoing efforts to incorporate biometrics into video game production. The challenges and benefits of these procedures are discussed. The chapter aims to make biometric data an accessible option in the toolbox of user researchers.

Pejman Mirza-Babaei talks about GUR reports in Chapter 18. It details the requirements of a GUR report, such as communicating the results accurately and motivating the team to make changes that increase quality. Its main message is that reporting findings is just as important as the finding themselves; the chapter describes pitfalls that arise when the reporting is inadequate.

Chapter 19 discusses game analytics. Anders Drachen and Shawn Connor describe what they are and how they can counteract weaknesses in traditional approaches. Game analytics can be deployed in any study size and are compatible with the various methodologies of GUR, making for a powerful method.

Part 3: Case Studies and Focus Topics (Chapters 20–30). This part presents a range of chapters that cover topics which are specific to particular types of games or situations or present case studies of GUR work in specific games, and show well the breadth and depth of GUR work. From leveraging analytics in indie studios, to dealing with the problem of bias imposed by lab settings, evaluating user experience in Dragon Age™, running user testing on a budget, involving players with special needs, and using GUR in VR and beyond, these chapters characterize many of the current front lines of user research.

Chapter 20 is aimed at small-to-medium-sized studios wanting to introduce analytics into their development process. Lysiane Charest focuses on concepts and techniques that are most useful for smaller studios and that require minimal skills. While money is always an issue, plenty of free analytics tools exist, whether they are third-party tools or simple in-house solutions. The chapter details how the most important factor is the availability of human resources.

In Chapter 21, Pejman Mirza-Babaei and Thomas Galati discuss user testing for indie studios. They describe how user testing often requires significant resources and expertise, but can be conducted in an affordable manner. The chapter explores the contributions of analytic techniques for existing GUR methods.

Guillaume Louvel talks about ecological validity in Chapter 22. He recognizes the biases inherent in user testing in lab conditions and prescribes remedies to increase validity. The duality between experimental conditions and ecological validity is discussed, with validity being most useful as it makes results meaningful.

Chapter 23 is a case study. James Berg describes the use of GUR in the development of Dragon Age: Inquisition. Challenges arising from the size of the game world, combat mechanics, and player classes and play styles are discussed. The chapter analyses the contributions of GUR to the game design.

In Chapter 24, Julien Huguenin discusses GUR on a budget. It provides a road map, from testing your game on the side with almost no resources to creating a dedicated lab space. Lessons are discussed.

Johan Dorell and Björn Berg Marklund continue the discussion about GUR on a budget in Chapter 25. Even when resources and prior GUR experience are low, small starts can be expanded to greatly impact the developer's working processes. Guidelines are provided for beginning to use GUR processes, including a step-by-step guide.

In Chapter 26, Steven Schirra and Brooke White present GUR for mobile games. They consider the context of gameplay for these types of games and prescribe methods which fit its mobile and touchscreen nature accordingly. This chapter considers the constraints of lab-based research in this context and explores field study methods such as diary studies.

In Chapter 27, Kathrin Gerling, Conor Linehan, and Regan Mandryk deal with the challenges involved in testing with special needs audiences. They describe three cases, focusing on young children, people with disabilities, and older adults. For each, playtesting challenges and user involvement in early design stages is discussed. Strategies to establish respectful and empowering methodologies with diverse audiences are explored.

Nick Yee and Nicolas Ducheneaut talk about the differences among gamers in Chapter 28. The model of gaming motivations is an empirically validated and accepted bridge between player preferences and in-game behaviours. Most importantly, engagement and retention outcomes can be calculated on the basis of the model.

In Chapter 29, Johanna Pirker discusses social network analysis. In the context of player and in-game data, network analysis can help researchers understand player behaviour in a social context. Key elements of network analysis and their benefits to user research are discussed.

Ben Lewis-Evans outlines GUR for virtual reality (VR) in Chapter 30. Recent interest in VR has led to studies and development around the game design issues unique to VR. Simulation sickness, for example, is a significant issue to be addressed. This chapter discusses the challenges for GUR posed by VR and makes practical considerations to minimize risks.

Finally, in Chapter 31, Anders Drachen, Pejman Mirza-Babaei, and Lennart Nacke discuss the rapid changes GUR has gone through as a domain of inquiry and as a community. Here, key areas of current work are identified and their potential and future are discussed. Areas of discussion include behavioural and physiological tracking, VR, and efforts to broaden target audiences. Challenges and opportunities for industry and academia are discussed.

1.4 About the editors

Anders Drachen, PhD, is a Professor at the DC Labs, University of York (UK) and a veteran data scientist. He is also affiliated with Aalborg University (Denmark) as an Associate Professor, as well as a game analytics consultant at The Pagonis Network. His work in the game industry as well as in data and game science is focused on game analytics, business intelligence for games, e-sports analytics, monetization, data mining, game user experience, industry economics, business development, and Games User Research. His research and professional work is carried out in collaboration with companies spanning the industry. Along the way he has supported the development of over a dozen games. He is one of the most published scientists worldwide on game analytics, virtual economics, user research, game data mining, and user profiling, having authored more than 100 research publications on these topics. He is also an editor of Game Analytics: Maximizing the Value of Player Data, a compendium of insights from more than 50 top experts in industry and research. He has served on the steering committee of the International Game Developers Association Special Interest Group on Games User Research. He is a former lead analyst for SaaS analytics solutions provider Game Analytics. He writes about analytics on andersdrachen.com and digital-creativity.ac.uk. His writings can also be found in the pages of trade publications such as gamesindustry.biz and gamasutra.com. His research has been covered by international media, including Wired, Kotaku, and Forbes. His research has won multiple awards. He can be found on Twitter @andersdrachen. He has been attacked by sharks three times and written a cooking book on ice cream.

Pejman Mirza-Babaei, PhD, is an Assistant Professor for Human-Computer Interaction and Games User Research at the University of Ontario Institute of Technology. He is also the User Research Director at Execution Labs, Montreal. He is a leading authority on GUR for independent game studios and champions the adoption of user research in game development. He has been involved with the GUR community since 2009, and has published more than 50 research articles and numerous other writings on GUR (most of them are available on his website: www.pejman.ca). He has co-organized workshops and courses in international conferences on user research. He has contributed to more than 20 published games, including award-winning titles such as PewDiePie: Legend of the Brofist, Crysis 2, and Weirdwood Manor. He loves rabbits (his rabbit Maple once got invited to serve as a conference program committee member) and has lovingly adopted several dogs.

Lennart Nacke, PhD, is the director of the HCI Games Group and an Associate Professor for human-computer interaction and game design at the University of Waterloo. He is a world-leading authority on the cognitive and emotional aspects of player experience in video games, with a special focus on physiological metrics and gameful design. He has authored more than 100 research publications on these topics, which have been cited more than 8,000 times. He can be found on Twitter (@acagamic) and is also working as a gamification and user experience consultant. He chaired the Computer-Human Interaction (CHI) PLAY 2014 and Gamification 2013 conferences, and is currently the chair of the CHI PLAY steering committee. He is an editor of multiple research journals and a subcommittee co-chair of CHI 2017 and CHI 2018. He has served on the steering committee of the International Game Developers Association Special Interest Group on Games User Research and loves the GUR community. His research group writes articles at www.hcigames.com, teaches a heuristics course at gamefuldesign.hcigames.com, publishes videos at youtube.com/hcigames, and they also tweet from @hcigamesgroup. He loves karaoke, chocolate, and beaches, not necessarily in combination.

1.5 Acknowledgements: advisory board and students

It took more than two years and more than 80 amazing people to make this book. GUR is not a topic to be taken lightly and the sheer variety of methods being used and the numerous ways in which we build and design games make it incredibly challenging to describe what GUR is within the pages of just one volume. Along the way, the GUR book was helped along by our stellar authors who contributed the chapters you find here, but also by our advisory board and supporting students.

The book would not have happened without our advisory board, a band of luminaries who have championed GUR for over a decade, some of them long-time friends, advisers, and mentors of the editors. We would like to thank, for their incredible support in helping us write a book with strong focus on GUR, Michael Medlock, David Tisserand, Ben Medler, Graham McAllister, Gareth R. White, Ian Livingston, Regan Mandryk, Dennis Wixon, Mirweis Sangin, Randy Pagulayan, Regina Bernhaupt, Christian Bauckhage, and Veronica Zammitto. Without this incredible team, this book would have not been possible. Thank you.

The book has also been helped immensely by an amazing group of GUR students from the Saskatchewan-Waterloo Games User Research Network and the University of Ontario Institute of Technology's UXR Lab (www.UXRLAB. ca), who supported the editors with the myriad practical details that go into collecting and editing material from dozens of people working across different fields, production sizes, and contexts: Colin Whaley, Giovanni Ribeiro, Karina Arrambide, Marim Ganaba, Melissa Stocco, Rylan Koroluk, Brianne Stephenson, Samantha Stahlke, Nelly Hamid, Alberto Mora, Gustavo Tondello, and Katja Rogers. Thank you.

Finally, we would like to acknowledge and thank the wider GUR community as represented by the International Game Developers Association Special Interest Group on GUR. This great community of over 1000 people across industry and academia forms a network for anyone interested in GUR, and has developed several initiatives towards supporting the field, including the yearly GUR summits, online knowledge repositories, and a highly active online form. For more information, please visit www.gamesuserresearchsig.org.

PART I

Games User Research in Production

CHAPTER 2

Games User Research as part of the development process in the game industry

Challenges and best practices

VERONICA ZAMMITTO, *Electronic Arts*

Highlights

Practising Games User Research (GUR) within a video game company possesses unique challenges, ranging from tight turnaround of findings to collaborating with the development team and incorporating the needs of the rest of company. This chapter describes processes and best practices for applying GUR in the industry while identifying and avoiding potential pitfalls.

2.1 Introduction

Games User Research (GUR) has become an established component in the making of video games. Major game developers and publishers such as Electronic Arts, Microsoft, Sony, Ubisoft, and Warner Brothers conduct GUR in-house. Smaller companies like Paradox and independent developer incubators such as Execution Labs also have dedicated staff for conducting research on

Games User Research, Anders Drachen, Pejman Mirza-Babaei, Lennart E. Nacke (Eds).
© Oxford University Press 2018. Published 2018 by Oxford University Press

players' experience. Although the actual organizational structure and specific needs vary across companies, the core responsibilities and execution is consistent (see also chapter 3).

This chapter provides the state of the art of GUR in the game industry, which has been evolving and optimizing itself over the last several years. This is relevant information for practitioners and academics alike serving as a guideline for:

- foundations of a business case for those researchers about to champion introducing GUR into a game company
- insights on organizational implications and how to structure a GUR team
- inspiration and comparison to optimize the practice of researchers already in the industry

2.2 Games User Research in the industry

Research efforts on understanding player experiences and game design implications have been present for most of the industry history; however, it has become properly formalized as a discipline—GUR—only within the last decade. The first associations, books, and venues solely dedicated to the field serve as landmarks. These include the first Digital Games Research Association's (DiGRA) conference in 2003, foundational books in 2008 and 2010 (Bernhaupt, 2010; Isbister and Schaffer, 2008), the first GUR Summit in 2010, and CHI PLAY in 2014.

There has been an increasing number of papers on user experience (UX) and GUR in key venues such as those under the Association for Computing Machinery (ACM) digital library and in particular the Special Interest Group on Computer-Human Interaction (SIG CHI). Papers across the whole ACM library that included 'user experience' as keywords started in the 1990s; from 1991 to 2000 there were a total of 167 publications, the following decade had 5,665 papers. All in all, the importance of UX across technological products has skyrocketed; the niche GUR community has provided up to 10% of the HCI contributions (Carter et al., 2014; Law, 2011).

The first integration of GUR within game development happened at Microsoft in 1997 when the first UX researcher for the gaming division joined the company as a contractor. Within seven years the team grew significantly, encompassing a total 35 people (Fulton, 2010). Other companies also started investing in GUR departments, and nowadays all major game companies have dedicated GUR

Table 2.1 *Subset of video game companies and their number of employees dedicated to GUR activities, including UX researchers, support staff, and managers, as of May 2016. (*) includes market research, analytics, and data science staff*

Company	Number of GUR staff
Electronic Arts	110 (*)
Microsoft	60
Paradox	5
Riot	70 (*)
Sony	23
Ubisoft	105 (*)
Volition	3

staff (see Table 2.1). Regardless of the specifics of investment on the number of employees and resources, this trend has impacted not only large companies but also small companies, as well as consulting firms solely dedicated to this field. Moreover, as the understanding of players matures within game companies, relevant related disciplines are consolidated within larger departments; as it is in the case of Electronic Arts, Riot, and Ubisoft where Games User Research, market research, analytics, and data science are part of an internal larger organization.

2.2.1 Who does GUR in a game company?

GUR practitioners come from a variety of backgrounds, although most commonly they hold a graduate degree (master's or doctorate) in one of the disciplines that the field draws from, such as psychology, computer science, and HCI. Such academic training provides a key understanding of research fundamentals, skills for defining hypotheses and variables, designing a study, and collecting and synthesizing data, all of which are at the core of the GUR practice.

Below are the two prototypical sets of responsibilities and associated roles that are carried out within a GUR group at a game company. It should also be noted that there can be multiple levels of seniority within them:

- Research: This covers all the aspects of performing a study, from requirements gathering, research design, creating test scripts, and conducting tests, to analysing data, producing reports, and delivering findings.
  - Moderator and Analyst: Involved in conducting tests, data collection, as well as helping with analysis.

    – Researcher: Responsible for the study design, ensuring that it's carried out properly, analysis, and reporting.
- Support: This encompasses all activities related to handling of resources employed for tests.
  - Recruiter: Handles the database of participants, screening, and inviting suitable candidates for each test.
  - Lab technician: Manages the lab equipment, ensuring all software and hardware functions properly for the tests.

Depending on the size of the company, all of the above roles can be carried out by different people or all of them by a single person. In many cases, researchers, beyond analysis and reporting, also have to do their own recruiting, setting up the lab, moderating, and taking notes. This happens more often in smaller companies and in early stages of GUR groups. When resources are available, these tasks and responsibilities are allocated among different people.

There are two clear advantages in having multiple people distributing the tasks: firstly, the development of expertise, which leads to a faster optimization of the process; secondly, and more importantly in the industry sphere, the activities can be carried out in parallel, which translates into achieving the same output in a shorter time. If participants can be recruited both while the lab is being set up and while the script of the session is developed, it can be best aligned with the timeline of production. In this way it would be possible to have a faster turnaround of results from the test, minimizing having development advancing without critical information.

In a nutshell, when GUR departments start, it is common that all activities are carried out by a single individual. However, as the team grows and the demand increases, it is almost essential to divide those roles among different people.

2.2.2 Organizational models: centralized, decentralized, and hybrid

There are three primary organizational models that a user research department within a game company can take. This is a strategic business decision that other fields in multiple industries have also faced, for instance, engineering and marketing. The two models used the most have been either centralized or decentralized within teams. However, recently there has been a new trend within game companies of employing a 'hybrid' approach (Figure 2.1).

This section covers each model, highlighting their advantages and shortcomings. Choosing a model should be based on the needs and resources of the company. Managers must keep a long-term vision for their teams and re-assess their model as the company continues evolving. In today's industry scene, it is necessary to remain competitive and to find optimizations, whether that means having an in-house GUR department or working with a third-party agency specialized in the field.

Decentralized   Centralized   Hybrid

Figure 2.1 GUR organizational models

2.2.2.1 CENTRALIZED

There is one single team across the organization that carries out the user research activities. Researchers work on diverse projects, distributing their time and effort based on prioritization according to the business goals. Most commonly, researchers are all located within their own desk space, grouped together, and separated from their stakeholders.

Among the positive aspects of having central teams are the following. First, it forges a strong, tight hub of experts, which allows easier sharing of best practices. It holds them accountable for ensuring uniform quality research, and dimin-ishes the likelihood of developers with no-research training having to over-see research activities. Second, the spectrum of projects and tasks tends to be broader and more varied, which in turn makes it more refreshing and appealing for researchers over long periods, and thus helps in retaining talent.

Moreover, the accumulation of knowledge across multiple projects and mul-tiple individual researchers in close collaboration can more easily support the advancement of their processes, offering more opportunities for optimization of research practice. It allows them to build on learnings from one project to another, and better able to answer questions that are more complex or larger in scope across projects.

Lastly, the economic benefits of centralized teams primarily manifest through shared resources and less duplication of effort and equipment. This encourages further investment because it results in higher Return On Investment (ROI). For example, building a lab for testing, which can be used for all projects; having an internal recruiter for participants that can be a full time employee because of the combined volume of testing; or the purchasing of software to facilitate analysis across all teams.

On the other hand, an unavoidable challenge with central teams is the rationalization of resources among all projects. This leads to a permanent re-prioritization exercise of the portfolio of a company or features and modes within a game, as well as the possibility that certain teams might not receive support. This is a delicate topic that leadership in any company needs to address, because it has direct implications on the vision for the products and the morale of the teams. Another shortcoming is that the relationship with stakeholders tends to be more at arm's length. The development team might perceive the researcher as an external agent, or the researcher might feel that they are an outsider to the project. This is due to rapid development cycles where a project can radically change over the course of a week. Therefore, a researcher on a central team is often having to catch up with the team. Of course, an experienced researcher leverages as much information as possible from multiple sources (such as internal wiki documentation, mailing lists, stand-up meetings), but this does not fully overcome the absence of the researcher from daily engagement within or sole attention to a single project team.

Microsoft's GUR division (called Studios User Research) operates in a rather centralized fashion. The headquarter is in Redmond (Washington, USA) where the vast majority of the team is located, with a few researchers at three remote locations (Vancouver, Canada; London, UK; Dublin, Ireland). This team engages with multiple game developers on a variety of projects, including the Halo and Forza series. Microsoft's Studios User Research has excelled on the titles launched. The company hosts world-class lab facilities include several rooms that accommodate different types of research approaches, such as multi-station playtesting rooms, to usability one-on-one rooms, and living-room-like set-ups (Microsoft Studios User Research, 2015a). These resources can meet the needs of the multiple researchers working with diverse projects. As a central team, they leverage on the constructed knowledge from the research done for different games, regularly synthesizing and publishing best practices (Microsoft Studios User Research, 2015b).

2.2.2.2 DECENTRALIZED

On the other end of the spectrum is the decentralized approach, where there are multiple independent GUR departments or individuals across the company. There is no organizational mandate to have them all aligned within a reporting structure, and they have the freedom to conduct processes differently as they see fit. These researchers are generally part of a development team to which they dedicate all their efforts.

The most advantageous aspect of decentralization is the high sensitivity to the needs of the specific group the researcher works with, which also leads to having a strong, positive impact on the perception of research as part of the development team. The researcher generally sits within the development area; this enables more channels of communication, particularly informal ones, and there is a constant dialogue. The researcher's level of knowledge about the game is deep and the design intentions are highly contextualized. Prioritization is not an issue in this model because the researcher is dedicated to the team they belong to, which in turn offers the utmost flexibility.

The shortcomings of the decentralized model are related to scalability, risk of comparable results, pacing for improving processes, and cost of resources. Having a researcher exclusively dedicated to each team means that a greater overall headcount is needed, which is a finite resource within any company. It also requires maintaining a full-time workload, and while there can always be research needs to satisfy (e.g., competitor evaluation, wireframe testing, playtesting, and post-launch analysis), it all depends on the production timeline and where the most impactful resource allocation is. When researchers practise their craft independently of one another, it is unavoidable that there will be differences in process and execution. Dissimilarities in practices can occur in the way that tests are conducted and in which measurement scales are used. For instance, in one playtest players fill out a questionnaire every 15 minutes, whereas in another they have an exit interview at the end after a full hour, and even though both of them answer questions on a 5-point scale, the anchors are completely different. The results of those two tests cannot be compared, missing an opportunity to benchmark against each other.

Because the single researcher does not have access to other projects, the opportunities for mentorship and learning from fellow researchers are not as present as in central teams. Therefore, the opportunities for iteration and refinement of processes are also less frequent, which can lead to a slower pace of advancement of research practice. Researchers in decentralized models require more effort to stay up-to-date in best industry practices via external resources such as engaging with community peers and reviewing presentations at key events like the GUR Summit (IGDA SIG Games User Research, 2015).

Lastly, acquiring resources in decentralized environments can also be more difficult because the costs cannot be spread out among multiple teams. This ranges from acquiring dedicated space and equipment for lab usage, to the purchase of software that can help to collect and analyse data. Compounding this issue would be duplicating equipment, resources, and efforts across the larger organization.

An excellent example of a decentralized GUR practice in the game industry is Ubisoft, because it has grown organically from within departments at multiple studios and they have actively worked to overcome all the shortcomings of this type of organizational model. Ubisoft GUR is distributed across 13 departments, which are located at different studios around the globe, including Montreal and Toronto (Canada), Montpellier (France), Malmö (Sweden), and also at the editorial division in Paris (France). Each department is autonomous, yet they have collaborated with each other over the years to achieve a consistency in their test instruments to make results comparable, sharing guidelines, tools, and labs space as needed (Debray and Wyler, 2015).

2.2.2.3 HYBRID

The latest trend in organizational models is a hybrid approach, where there is a single GUR department across the organization with a core at a central level, yet also having researchers embedded within the development teams. This way it tries to combine the best of both worlds. The focus is on maintaining a defined mandate on procedures and resources across the company while at the same time dedicating researchers to specific projects.

Positive aspects of this model are the unified best practices, the shared resources and technology, and deep integration with the development team. Similarly, as in central organizations, there is a shared knowledge on protocols and procedures. There is room for undertaking company-wide research and pushing the boundaries for new methodologies (see chapter 7 for an overview of GUR methods). Researchers do not need to waste time figuring out, for instance, which methodology to employ in a certain situation or what type of questions to ask to measure player experience. Additionally, everyone has access to technologies and resources such as lab space, survey software, and analytical tools. The distinction of this model is that on top of all these advantages, it also has the positive aspects of the decentralized model, where there are dedicated researchers as part of the development team. This has great implications for establishing long-term relationships with the team, more channels of communication, and increased sense of belonging.

The risks within this model are maintaining the relationship between central and embedded researchers, and sustaining tailored strategies while still keeping alignment with general processes. As embedded researchers spend all their time with the design team, circling back with the central team is less frequent. Scheduling activities for all researchers—such as mandatory check-ins, lunch and learn, peer review of documentation, and socially oriented team-building events—can help to minimize such potential disconnection.

Embedded researchers might also tend to feel a sense of urgency to over-tailor strategies for their development teams. This may generate a dissonance between established processes and alternate proposals. Such situations can lead to two non-ideal scenarios: (1) if the new proposal does not align with the central approach, the results can be isolated and non-comparable; (2) there might be a lost opportunity for a new idea that could have evolved into an established process.

Riot Games is a company that has been implementing a hybrid approach (Hsiung, 2016). The company has both central and embedded researchers. The central ones take care of initiatives such as regional variation studies, competitive analysis, and R&D. The embedded ones work directly with the development teams, ensuring they communicate across all the levels of the team, from those working on specific features (like a map) to whole sections of the game (like gameplay).

Electronic Arts is another company using a hybrid approach. The central component is strong even though the team is geographically distributed across eight locations, with researchers working on a myriad of projects ranging from Battlefield to NBA mobile. Best practices and guidelines are shared from a central level. Researchers who are embedded sit and work with specific game teams developing specific knowledge and relationships.

In conclusion, GUR teams at game companies can thrive in different organizational structures, whether centralized, decentralized, or hybrid. Each approach has its own strengths and risks, with an emphasis on either strong processes or a deep relationship with the development team—or trying to maintain a balance between the two. When adopting one or the other structure, an organization must be sensitive to the company-wide culture, the stage of growth of UX, and the resources available.

2.3 GUR planning and deliverables

Regardless of the actual organizational structure and size of a GUR team, researchers are responsible for planning and executing research, analysing data, and delivering findings. This section covers the different instances of designing research and how to convey results to the development team.

Across the game industry there are prototypical phases of development. They represent how much the content of the game is going to evolve at each stage (Novak, 2011). There are core parameters that are followed by all game companies; moreover, each organization elaborates detailed versions of these phases, creating clear guidelines for defining milestones and precise internal lingo. For instance, at Electronic Arts this plan is called the game development framework. Such documentation is part of the company culture and ensures everyone has the same understanding. GUR practice aligns with the development process, setting the foundation for long-term planning, then continuously executing research and bringing back findings to improve the player experience quality.

2.3.1 Long-term planning

It is possible to say that any commercial game has been developed following these phases. The exact length of the whole cycle varies depending on the scope of the game. Overall, it typically ranges from 12 months to 3 years. GUR is part of the full development process, and there are prototypical research questions at each of those stages. Researchers must work with the development team to further tailor the questions in terms of specific game characteristics and design intentions, as well as recommending the most appropriate techniques to carry out research. Over the last few years, the importance of a mixed-methods approach has been emphasized in order to properly understand the complexity involved in player experience (Ambinder, 2011; McAllister and White, 2010; Mirza-Babaei et al., 2013; Zammitto, 2011) (see also chapter 5).

Table 2.2 delineates the prototypical stages of game development along with the key research efforts.

2.3.2 Short-term planning

Throughout the development cycle, there will be a number of research tests; the exact number will be dependent on the organizational model of the company, the scope of the game, the resources available, and the overall time frame of development.

Regardless of the specific research question and methodology employed, it is a good practice to conduct at least one study every two weeks. This is applicable for an average usability session with eight participants in a one-on-one, think-aloud set-up, or for a playtest with twenty-four players and data collected through surveys. The main reason this length of time for each session is preferred

Table 2.2 *Stages of game development, its associated content, and GUR activity*

Stage		Content Scope	Key GUR undertakings
Pre-production	Concept	It is centred on the ideation of the game	Competitor evaluation
	Documentation	The core plan for features and game scope	Define overall UX vision and ideal player experience from game features
	Prototype	Initial implementations, like whitebox and user flows	Usability testing on basic interaction and core loop
Production	Production	This stage encompasses the main cycle of development, where content is added and the level of polish increases	Evaluation of usability, behavioural, and attitudinal aspects of the player experience at each milestone
	Alpha	Milestone reached when core gameplay features are implemented	Usability testing on features and player experience evaluation
	Beta	Milestone reached when a complete version of the game with full content is implemented	Usability on onboarding, full-playthrough testing
	Gold	Milestone reached when a version of the game is at quality and is ready to be launched for public release	Playtesting on final balancing and tuning
Post-production / Live Service		It covers all actions after the game has been released, including patches, expansions, and live content	Ongoing usability, balancing, and player experience evaluation as more content is released

is that the development team can have findings within days after the testing has occurred, which leads to the content evaluated staying relevant. Development continues to advance while research is being done. Therefore, when more than five days have passed, there is a very high risk that the content has evolved to a point where it is no longer comparable to its previous version due to the nimble adjustments to design. Thus, findings become obsolete; this has negative implications: not only does the team not have the needed information to iterate but the investment in resources for research has been wasted. The researchers' morale can also be affected, given that their effort is now inconsequential to the rest of the development team.

Researchers must learn to manage the scope of a session to fit within their development team's cycles and output findings with relevant content. It is a common mistake among junior researchers to set broad research questions or collect redundant data that slow them down in their analysis.

A default test can be divided into four steps: preparation, execution, analysis, and reporting.

1. Preparation: requirements gathering, defining the research question, recruiting participants, creating the script for the test. All tasks can be done within four days.
2. Execution: the players take part in the study; the session is conducted; data are collected. It is generally done within a day or two.
3. Analysis: the data are processed and conclusions are drawn. It is done within one to four days after the test.
4. Reporting: findings are conveyed into a shareable deliverable. The exact format and look varies from company to company (addressed in Section 2.3.3). Nevertheless, there is consensus that it must happen within one to five days after the test.

Involving the design team at each step is critical for the success of research. Stakeholders must be part of the discussion about a test's requirements and objectives. It is also very powerful to have the design team to watch the session as it happens; this can be done from an observation room or via livestreaming. Communicating findings to the stakeholders promptly is incredibly helpful in achieving a great product.

2.3.3 GUR deliverables

The purpose of a GUR department is to contribute towards the understanding of the player experience in order to be able to improve it. Reporting findings is the place where research and design meet, successes and failures of the design are highlighted, and recommendations for action are made. GUR deliverables can take multiple shapes. While there is common ground on foundations, each company makes variations and generates its own guidelines. Improving formats and efficiencies for reporting is an ongoing topic of interest among practitioners (Rebetez, 2012; Zammitto et al., 2014).

There are four primary forms a GUR deliverable can take:

1. Written report: This is by far the most common way that findings are conveyed to stakeholders, generally as a slide-deck or a document. A great written report will stand out by being concise yet fully informative. Data should be visualized for communicating insights at a glance. At Electronic Arts, there are two main instances when a written report is sent out: one is a 'top liner', which is delivered within one day after the test has been conducted; it contains a high-level analysis such as tracked key performance indicators (KPIs) and main qualitative trends or observations. This provides the game team with quick indications on where the main issues or gains are so they can continue allocating resources and changes accordingly. The second instance is the final report which gets delivered 3–5 days after the test, and contains a full analysis.

2. Debrief: This is a verbal delivery, generally in the form of a presentation and discussion by the time a full written report is ready. Debriefing with the development team has multiple benefits, including strengthening the relationship with stakeholders, helping them to unpack all findings, following up on specific leads, and diving into details that help them to understand better players' reactions.

3. Workshop: This approach was developed by Sony CEE (Rebetez, 2012). It was driven by the need to deliver results promptly while maintaining quality and confidence in the findings. It consists of conducting an analysis and meeting with the development team within two days after the test to review the issues and discuss potential solutions. After the meeting, time is allocated for further analysis of the agreed top issues and for writing a full report.

4. Ticketing issues: This format involves all identified UX findings being entered into an issue-tracking software such as JIRA or Hansoft, which are typical tools developers already use to manage their work. This is a recent trend that complements a full report, and has started being applied at Electronic Arts. Although the exact context of session details for each entered issue is less visible, there is a tremendous gain in providing access to findings to the whole development team. Moreover, it supports accountability by researchers and developers to raise issues, follow them up, assign owners to act on them, and easily track the impact of GUR on the development process.

2.4 Takeaways

Creating, growing, and leading a successful GUR department that is part of game development requires an organizational model that connects with the company culture and evolution. It also needs sound research processes that align with the pacing and production of game teams. Finally, it must produce outputs that are clear, actionable, and delivered in a timely manner. There are three keys to achieve these characteristics: scope, communication, and flexibility.

Scope determines how much work is needed within a company and for any given project, which in turn has a direct impact on the organizational model: for example, does every team need a fully dedicated researcher? Are there overarching research questions that should stay central? Scope is also essential for each test session, which is determined by the agreed research question; it must be big enough to shed light on the design and help to make a better experience, but small enough to be tackled within days in order to obtain findings in a timely fashion to stay relevant. Delivered results also need be scoped in order to make them easy to share, informing without overwhelming.

Communication in our practice is key. It is more than a transaction of information, it involves influence. On top of informing designers, researchers should have the right conversations that guide transformation for a better player experience. The organizational model of a GUR department will determine which channels are strongest. Researchers must engage in dialogue with the development team in a timely fashion, regardless of whether the organizational structure is centralized, decentralized, or hybrid. The trick is to balance the ongoing communication in person, via email, and through documentation. Leveraging existing channels where the information already flows—such as mailing lists, wikis, and stand-up meetings—will contribute to efficiency and good relationships. Communicating feedback on UX matters is the ultimate deliverable of a GUR team. Conveying those effectively will drive change for improving players' experience.

Flexibility must be exercised constantly. Keep taking the pulse of the company's evolution and adjust models as the needs of the business change. Revising priorities among and within projects is also part of the process for adaptation. Each project will present its own challenges that require updating the GUR action plan, as well as tailoring workflows and deliverables to best adjust to a specific game team. Ultimately, to achieve the best possible player experience, a successful GUR department must adapt based on the best interests of the company and of the game.

2.5 Further resources

Most GUR practitioners come from a strong academic background, therefore sharing knowledge and challenging ideas is part of our nature. A remarkable number of publications and presentations have been produced since the field was established just over a decade ago.

The number one recommendation for GUR within the industry is the series of presentations from the GUR Summit (IGDA SIG Games User Research, 2015), which is primarily driven by practitioners: http://gamesuserresearchsig. org/summits/gur-summit-presentations/.

For a broader spectrum across game studies and HCI, DiGRA's and ACM's digital libraries are also worthwhile sources: http://www.digra.org/digital-library/ and http://dl.acm.org/. Further information can be found in the References section.

References

Ambinder, M. (2011). Biofeedback in gameplay: how Valve measures physiology to enhance gaming experience. Presented at the Game Developers Conference, UBM, San Francisco, CA.

Bernhaupt, R. (ed.). (2010). Evaluating user experience in games: concepts and methods. Human-computer interaction series. London: Springer.

Carter, M., Downs, J., Nansen, B., Harrop, M., Gibbs, M. (2014). Paradigms of games research in HCI: a review of 10 years of research at CHI. In Proceedings of the first ACM SIGCHI Annual Symposium on Computer-Human Interaction in Play, CHI PLAY 14 (pp. 27–36). New York: ACM. doi:10.1145/2658537.2658708

Debray, J., Wyler, H. (2015). Building Ubisoft's games user research machine. Presented at the GamesUR Conference 2015, IGDA GUR SIG. London, UK.

Fulton, B. (2010). From 0 to 35 in 7 years: scaling up a games user-research group. In Games User Research Summit. Presented at the Games User Research Summit 2010, San Francisco, USA.

Hsiung, B. (2016). Riot Games' insights evolution: a journey to become more player-focused. Presented at the Games User Research Summit 2016, IGDA. San Francisco, US.

IGDA SIG Games User Research. (2015). #gamesUR Summit Presentations. Games User Research Summit Present. Retrieved from http://gamesuserresearchsig. org/summits/gur-summit-presentations/

Isbister, K., Schaffer, N. (2008). Game usability: advancing the player experience (1st ed.). San Francisco: Morgan Kaufmann.

Law, E.L.-C. (2011). The measurability and predictability of user experience. In Proceedings of the 3rd ACM SIGCHI Symposium on Engineering Interactive Computing Systems, EICS '11 (pp. 1–10). New York: ACM. doi:10.1145/1996461.1996485

Leroy, F., Long, S., Sangin, M., Odasso, S., Zammitto, V. (2016). Effectively communicating with development teams. Presented at the Games User Research Summit 2016, IGDA GUR SIG. USA.

McAllister, G., White, G. (2010). Video game development and user experience. In Evaluating user experience in games: concepts and methods, human-computer interaction (pp. 107–128). London: Springer.

Microsoft Studios User Research. (2015a). Studios user research facilities. Retrieved from http://gamesuserresearchsig.org/portfolio/microsoft-studios-user-research/

Microsoft Studios User Research. (2015b). Studios user research website. Retrieved from http://www.studiosuserresearch.com/

Mirza-Babaei, P., Nacke, L. E., Gregory, J., Collins, N., Fitzpatrick, G. (2013). How does it play better? Exploring user testing and biometric storyboards in games user research. In Proceedings of the 2013 ACM Annual Conference on Human Factors in Computing Systems, CHI '13 (pp. 1499–1508). New York: ACM. doi:10.1145/2466110.2466200

Novak, J. (2011). Game development essentials: an introduction. Boston, MA: Cengage Learning.

Rebetez, C. (2012). Rapid results. In Games User Research Summit 2012. Presented at the Games User Research Summit 2012, IGDA, San Francisco, CA.

Zammitto, V. (2011). The science of play testing: EA's methods for user research. Presented at the Game Developers Conference, San Francisco, USA.

Zammitto, V., Mirza-Babaei, P., Livingston, I., Kobayashi, M., Nacke, L. E. (2014). Player experience: mixed methods and reporting results. In CHI '14 Extended Abstracts on Human Factors in Computing Systems, CHI EA '14. (pp. 147–150). New York: ACM. doi:10.1145/2559206.2559239

CHAPTER 3

It is all about process

DAVID TISSERAND, *Ubisoft*

Highlights

This chapter points out the key benefits of a well-designed process in Games User Research. For example, the creation of templates and question databases can ensure that information is collected in a comprehensive, shareable manner. Maintaining this documentation can facilitate future optimization for increased research efficiency.

3.1 Introduction

Games User Researchers know exactly what needs to be done to produce a solid piece of research. They gather stakeholder needs, recruit users who represent the target audience, run studies, and deliver findings. All this work is done with the hopes of developing an improved experience for the end user. I have experienced this routine repeatedly, examining and testing the usability of products within the academic and commercial worlds, from mobile apps to websites. Studies are prepared carefully over the course of several weeks and about the same time is spent diligently writing reports. When I joined the so very appealing gaming industry, I realized one thing was different from other industries: the time pressure.

Before a game is announced, the team is often working on creating a representative slice of the experience (First Playable Prototype, FPP). When a game is announced around the alpha (early playable) stage, most of the game is implemented. From the alpha stage onwards, development teams will iterate on internal design in order to polish the experience. Major changes and innovation

Games User Research, Anders Drachen, Pejman Mirza-Babaei, Lennart E. Nacke (Eds).
© Oxford University Press 2018. Published 2018 by Oxford University Press

abound at this stage. With the announcement of a game's release date, development teams begin iterating very quickly on their *initial* design, aiming to have a finely polished game as soon as the timer rings. As a result, game developers tend to make changes very quickly in order to meet their deadlines (see also chapters 2 and 5).

Over the course of just a few weeks, they might rebalance the game's difficulty or redesign an entire gaming mechanic. A whole level might be removed or a brand new area added, bringing along a whole set of new challenges or puzzles. For this reason, development teams cannot spend a whole month conducting a study because it will always lead to outdated findings that will no longer be useful. In this industry, we (the user researchers) do not have the luxury of taking our time to plan every step of the research in detail. Tight scheduling pressures mean that the results must be delivered as soon as the last participant is out of the research facility. Of course, working at that pace is prone to error. For example:

- We might forget an important task that was key to ensuring the quality of the research.
- We can end up working extra hours because we are unable to evaluate accurately how long each step will take. We just get through them as quickly as we can.
- When something goes wrong, it is hard to identify which tasks should have been done differently because they all happened at the same time.
- We do not take the time to document best practices through templates, let alone update them!

How do we ensure we still deliver high-quality research results while under such intense time pressure? If you have not guessed it yet: it is all about process.

3.2 What is a process?

The word process comes from the Latin *processus*, which means 'progression' or 'course'. It is defined as 'a series of actions or steps taken in order to achieve a particular end'.

Within our discipline, processes are used to define each step of the research. They begin when a researcher first meets with a development team interested in conducting a study, up to and beyond the delivery of the study results.

Processes can take the form of a to-do list where the first item would be (1) meet the team to discuss their needs, … all the way through to, and beyond, (97) discuss the changes the team will implement based on the findings.

Along the way there are going to be many small tasks, all of which will contribute to increasing the quality of the research and maximizing its value for the development team.

3.3 Why do we need a process?

Processes in user research serve to ensure the quality of our work. From moderation techniques to interactions with a development team, all team members can benefit from a well-defined set of steps to follow. Of course, a process cannot replace researchers' analytical abilities, people skills, and innovative thinking. However, good processes can elicit even greater quality from the same researcher. Defining these processes well and sticking to them is beneficial to any research team regardless of size.

Some key ingredients researchers need in a process:

- Safety net: support researchers by helping them remember all the crucial steps of a study.
- Time saver: reuse what worked well last time and throw out what did not; this saves a lot of time in the long run.
- Time management: determine how long a study will take by assigning time estimates to each task. Effectively used time estimates will notify researchers when a deliverable is running late.
- People management: allow team managers to assign tasks to their staff, so they know when they will be freed again for the next one.
- Continuous improvement: enhance researchers' ability to pinpoint improvement opportunities in the research practice.
- Standardization: standardize methods so other researchers can run an identical study and get comparable results. This helps when transferring knowledge from one project to the next.
- Training: smoothen staff's induction. It helps new members of staff get up to speed much more quickly than if they were to shadow their peers alone.

3.4 So what is *the* process?

Every person, team, and company is different. No single process will be successful everywhere. However, the most successful research practices will follow similar approaches, all of which contain pre-test, test, and post-test tasks. Listing out these tasks is the first step towards putting in place effective processes that will increase the quality, efficiency, and consistency of a research team's work. Let us take a look at these key steps.

3.4.1 Gather information

When meeting a development team for the first time, it is crucial to make sure to cover all questions comprehensively. Information gathered at this stage defines each of the steps that follow. For those meetings, it is highly recommended to prepare a detailed template containing the standard list of questions and to follow it. I will refer to this template as the Research Brief for the rest of this chapter. A Word document that you can fill in as the meeting goes will often suffice. It should contain details such as:

- Profiles: what is the target audience?
- Objectives: what are the goals of the test?
- Dates: what is your deadline?
- Previous findings: if there was any previous research, what were the results?

Once you have designed this template you can share it with any researcher in your team; the most junior researcher shall then have access to the same information as the most senior one, efficiently supporting knowledge sharing.

3.4.2 Assess the suitability of the build

In an ideal world, you will have left the previous meeting (as discussed earlier) with a representative build (i.e., an executable of the game prototype) containing at a minimum the essential game mechanics to be tested. All other game elements could be placeholders at this point. However, it is quite likely that not all of the mechanics for immediate testing will be in the build at the time you meet the team. It is important to note that, with the increase in development teams' sizes, some of the game features will be implemented in just a few days. In this case, there should be design documentation available to explain how the mechanic will be implemented but might not be available at the time of the meeting. It is in this case important to ask for information on how such mechanics will be implemented and how players are expected to use them. You should ask for this information in order to understand what will be in the next build.

The next step is to play the game itself (or read the design documents if this is not possible) and assess whether you can answer all the questions that the development team has raised. For example, if the development team wants to know if players are able to learn and master the core mechanic with what they have implemented, but the tutorial itself is not yet available, you will not be able to answer this question. If the tutorial is not ready, you will not have a representative experience of the final product and the results will be erroneous. In this case, make a note in the Research Brief, take the information back to the development team, and ask them whether they will have the tutorial implemented in time for the test or if they have other plans on how to instruct players on the use of the game. If you need to fake the tutorial (e.g., by showing individual videos, pause the game, present some tutorial's key messages on sheets), you are not going to use the same research method as if you had the first hour fully implemented.

Before we move on, remember that not testing is also an option. Often when a development team proactively asks you to test their game, your first reaction will be to try to help and comply with their request. However, if the build is not yet suitable for answering the research goals, ask them whether something else could be tested. It might be that the core mechanic is not ready, but some of the menus are ready for examination. If nothing can be reliably tested at this stage, it is preferable to postpone the test rather than cancelling it. At least you will keep the dialogue open until the build is in a suitable state.

3.4.3 Design the overall testing method

At this stage, you do not need to know exactly which questions or scales you will use in your questionnaires, but you can certainly assess the overall testing approach. Typical questions you should ask yourself are:

- Number of participants: do you need to use a one-on-one method in order to know what participants are thinking at all times? Alternatively, can you let participants play the game at their own pace without interruption, allowing for testing with as many participants as you can accommodate at one time?

- Time: will two-hour sessions be long enough or do you need a longitudinal study over three weeks?
- Number of researchers: do you need one researcher per player to observe each participant or can you rely solely on telemetry?

You will find that development teams' questions are often very similar. For example:

- Usability: can players use the innovative mechanic easily?
- Appreciation: do players like their overall experience or the game?
- Clarity: do players understand what they have to do?
- Balancing: is the game too difficult or too easy?

Each of these questions should be addressed by the most reliable and efficient method to produce results. A simple table listing the questions along with the method, time required, and number of participants needed can help a researcher to assess quickly the best method(s) required to answer any goal.

3.4.4 Administrative planning

In a one-man-band research lab, some of the tasks in this section will be unnecessary, but as soon as you collaborate with another colleague, each of the steps becomes mandatory for the sake of research efficiency. Make sure you plan ahead by asking yourself the following questions:

- Is the testing room available on the day(s) you need it?
- Are any assistants or dedicated moderators available on the day(s) you need them?
- If you are planning to have your report reviewed, are the reviewers going to be available for the period needed to do this?
- Will your stakeholders be available when you intend to present the results to them?

The best way to get positive answers to all these questions is to plan ahead and book resources early. We are all extremely busy and live in a working world where calendars are often filled out weeks in advance. Ask your collaborators if they can attend a meeting the same day and their answer is often going to be 'no'. Ask them a week or so in advance and they will usually have some spare time for you.

Knowing your overall testing method, you also know how long you will be testing. With practice, you will even know how long it will take you on average to deliver the findings. With this information, you can book people weeks in advance and make sure everybody dedicates enough time for the research to be successful.

From this point on, you will find yourself becoming busier and busier, so you must ensure these administrative details are completed while you still have the time to do so.

3.4.5 Recruit the participants

I concede that it is unlikely that you will forget this step. However, the reason why it must be part of the process is twofold:

1. Timing: If you start recruiting too early, you may run the risk of having to do it all over again. For instance, this may occur when the study goals change because the build is not ready on time. If you start too late, you run the risk of struggling to find the right participants on short notice. Working backwards in your planning, i.e., retro-planning, will help you figure out the right time to recruit participants.

2. Recruitment interview templates: There are right and wrong questions to ask during a recruitment interview. It takes time to formulate good questions that do not give away the expected answers. In order to save time from one test to another, you must create a recruitment interview template. Once you have developed a recruitment template, you will be able to reuse it time and time again by only changing a few criteria (e.g., one game might be targeted at players with mobile games experience while the other could require PC players only; the question about platform used will remain the same but the criteria can easily be changed). If you realize later that a question did not produce useful results or was too leading, you can update the template accordingly.

3.4.6 Finalize the study design

You have the overall plan covered. Congratulations, now is the time to jump into the details! You need to plan carefully how the test will unfold and decide what exactly you will say to your participants. Here are some examples of questions you might ask yourself:

- Are you going to reveal the fundamental objective of the test to the participants or are you going to hide it and keep them unbiased? Both of these options have their pros and cons depending on what you are aiming to achieve with your study.

- How will you explain that you need participants to discuss verbally what they are thinking during gameplay?
- In what order and at what time will you communicate this information so participants are able to remember it?

You must make sure all participants receive the same instructions at the same time in order to remove any bias from your interactions with them. The only way to ensure your instructions are not biased is to write them down in what is called a Moderation Guide. This guide will not only be useful for your current research, but you can use it to update future test studies and smooth out any hiccups from the initial research. Once your discourse is set, you will never need to rewrite these standard instructions again. This will save you valuable time by allowing you to complete the research more quickly and dedicate more time to more useful research aspects.

One of the principal aims of the process is to ensure that the study objectives are answered in the most reliable way. To do this efficiently you will need to decide which measures are the most appropriate to gather sufficient data and which ones are simply not required. The most efficient way to approach this is to take each objective individually and associate it with the tools at your disposal that can deliver appropriate results. Tools like interviews, surveys, observation, data tracking, and biometrics all have their pros and cons. Once you have decided which ones suit your needs best, you can collaborate with the development team to set thresholds at which you consider the result to be a success or a failure. For example, if you were to assess the difficulty of a game, the logical way to prepare for the test could look like the diagram in Figure 3.1.

Figure 3.1 Example diagram to prepare for the test to assess the difficulty of a game

This approach will save you precious time when you will need it the most: during the analysis phase. Remember that designing templates will also save you time in the long run. Once you have written your first questionnaire, keep the questions and scales in a database for future reference. In this way, you can trace which question is best to answer a specific objective goal, and the exact question phrasing users understand best. If you discover an issue with one of these questions, you can update it within the database so all researchers will benefit from its improvement.

3.4.7 Prepare the lab

You have now completed the study design, and you will begin testing tomorrow or the day after. Now is the time to set up your lab and verify that each tool is working properly. An example list of tools might be:

- the game itself
- online questionnaires
- controllers and headsets
- video recording/streaming tools
- probe to gather in-game data

The importance of this step cannot be overstated. If you break one tool in the chain, you will likely find only incomplete data and less actionable results.

Issues with the testing protocol can often break the study and require you to make changes on the fly during the test, which makes the test prone to error. If you plan to conduct brief one-on-one sessions with participants, now is a good time to run a pilot. Try to recruit somebody within your company who has some spare time and who roughly corresponds to your target audience. Run the study as if they were real participants so they can tell you if the chain of tasks feels logical or if some questions are difficult to understand. After the pilot study, you will be able to update your study design and fix any issues before real users come in (chapter 6 talks more about lab setups, and chapter 22 about ensuring validity of lab-based work).

3.4.8 Run the test

Like recruitment, we might not always want to include this step on a to-do list as its presence is obvious. However, the way the test is performed can have significant consequences on the quality of the outcome. You have already set up your Moderation Guide, your questionnaires, and some other tools. Knowing in detail what you expect to happen on a typical testing day is mandatory to avoid improvisation in front of participants and the risk of making mistakes in the rush of it all. Some questions to ask yourself about include:

- When will you start the video recording?
- When and how will you debrief with the other researchers involved?
- At what point will you ask participants to fill out your questionnaire(s)?
- When will you give breaks to the participants?

Writing these tasks down and associating times at which they must be performed ensures you will not forget a critical step and will do each task at the right time (section 2 of this book covers a range of GUR methodologies, see chapter 7 for an overview).

3.4.9 Analyse the results

You have carefully prepared your study design and tests, which means that analysing the results should be fairly straightforward. Trained researchers with good preparation processes and efficient templates will be able to analyse results in less than a day. You have already designed your analysis tool during the preparation phase (see Step 6), so the first step will be to answer your questions and validate your hypothesis. For example:

- Did players rate the game under the minimum appreciation threshold you set with the development team?
- Did you observe the behaviour you were expecting at specific moments, e.g., 'when participants faced the boss in section four'?
- Did it take players longer than intended to complete a level?

You can answer these questions with simple yes or no answers. They will help you decide if there are any issues worth reporting or if there is good news to deliver. The time saved can be used to enhance your report by expanding your analysis or preparing a short video clip. These alterations can be used to convince a reluctant designer of a finding's reliability. When issues are flagged, you should check if the issue is relevant to any individuals on the project or if it is the result of a wider underlying problem. Here you must put your analysis skills to good use by digging deeper into the data and determining why you observed the behaviours you did.

3.4.10 Write the report

Any researcher can write a report. Writing a great report that is going to be useful and will motivate the development team to improve their game is something else. This is the outcome of all the hard work you have done up until now.

It would be a shame to waste the effort so far and see great research and issues go unnoticed because you have reported them badly. A good report template with embedded writing guidelines and mandatory sections to fill out (such as cause and impact) will help all researchers in a team to write their reports to the same high level of quality. Once created, you can update the template and reference documentation as your team discovers new best practices (chapter 18 focuses on reporting the results of user testing).

3.4.11 Present the findings

Depending on your preferences and your stakeholders' availability, you might be able to present your findings during a face-to-face debriefing session. I recommend you try to do this instead of or in addition to a written report. In terms of process, the same best practices apply to a presentation as they do to reports. Templates and presentation guidelines will help junior staff to learn more quickly—increase their skill set—than letting them start from scratch and discover best practices through trial and error.

3.4.12 Follow up

Depending on your company's set-up, you might not be physically co-located with the development team. If you are, you will be able to track what happens to your report and follow how the team intends to fix the issues found. If you work remotely from the development team, then you must make sure you follow up closely with all stakeholders, discuss which improvements they intend to make and when they will make these improvements. This will better prepare you for upcoming tests.

3.5 Miscellaneous

3.5.1 Folder structure

When you work with other people who need to access your deliverables, you must ensure your repository is organized in a consistent manner. If researchers organize their test folders differently, it will cause chaos for your research team. Disorganization makes finding a single file cumbersome, since you will need to wander through many folders and subfolders before you find the desired data.

If the data aggregation is not templated, you will also have to browse each file in order to find the piece of information you are looking for. The simple solution is to take the time to talk to your colleagues so you can agree on a single folder structure and ensure everybody follows it. If you really are process freaks, you can run a card-sorting test with all of those involved.

3.5.2 Continuous improvement

How can you actively look for ways to improve your practices? The answer is by putting time aside to do so. Through trial and error or by observing senior colleagues you will learn a few tricks to help you better moderate or stimulate reactivity from development teams. However, the quickest way to improve your practices is to reflect on each test together with your colleagues. This involves discussing what went well and not so well, so you can determine how you will improve your processes in the future. Some examples of lessons learned from user testing might be:

- Participants did not understand the framing of one of your questions, so they gave answers that were out of scope. Resulting action: rephrase this question in your questions database.
- The development team was supposed to deliver the test build on day X but actually did so two days later. This means the study had to be postponed by one week and recruitment had to be carried out again. Resulting action: put safeguards in place for next time.
- You tested a multiplayer game for the first time without considering the balance of the teams. This skewed the results drastically, since one team had an unfair advantage and won all of the matches. Resulting action: take the time to design a pre-test balancing method next time.

A key step of the process is to take one hour after publishing the report to determine what could be improved, streamlined, or just plain avoided. It will only take one hour to figure out what needs to be improved, but it saves countless hours from the time it will take to carry out all your future tests. Evaluation is vital as it helps continually improve and troubleshoot the process.

Researchers should be taking notes throughout testing for all of the issues raised with the process as they occur. It is important to note these details, or they will be forgotten. For example, you will not remember that the questionnaire tool created a typographical error for each question, and that it took five minutes on the day of testing to fix. If you do not make a note of this point, the next time you will spend another five minutes correcting the same error or, worse still, the next researcher might not even notice the error, leaving it to bias these next test results.

Once the meeting has taken place, you can make any corrections or improvements for the next tests. If some issues require a lengthier correction process, like reviewing the whole recruitment process or changing the questionnaire tool provider, then you must keep track of these more significant improvements and revisit the 'backlog' as often as you can. When this is completed, convert these improvements into concrete action items, which you can take care of yourself or delegate to colleagues.

Finally, it is important to remember what went well. You will need to fix the mistakes you made, but you will also need to reward yourself for good work and build on your successes. This can go a long way to help keep team members and researchers motivated. If a colleague tried something for the first time and it proved extremely successful, you will want to reuse it next time. If everyone works in silo mode and does not document their work, this successful approach would be lost and forgotten. On the other hand, if you write down the new method, template it, and place it visibly in a shared and structured folder, then all team members will be able to benefit from this useful innovation.

3.6 Conclusions

Processes and standards are often thought to be restrictive and to stifle creativity. In our discipline, processes and standards can actually enhance your innovation power. Processes and standards will save time on repetitive tasks, help you ensure you do not forget an important process step, give you more time to improve your methods, and more time to discuss developers' intentions. This can all be done with the comfort of a safety net, ensuring the tasks you repeat the most over time are bulletproof and as efficient as they can be.

To take this approach one step further (if your team has the resources to do so), you can automate a lot of these templates and processes:

- Your checklist can take the form of a collaborative online tool with links to the shared folder.
- The templates can be filled out automatically through a web interface, which inserts key information into several documents in one go.

- Your reports and presentations can be auto-populated thanks to specific macros which translate your analysis results into a formatted deliverable.

All these processes take time and effort to put in place and maintain, but the return on investment in the long term is invaluable for the researchers, the development team, and the company as a whole.

3.7 Takeaways

User research teams should think about standardizing and documenting their process:

- Create templates for each process step to avoid mistakes and ensure high-quality research across all teams.
- Automatize as much as possible.

CHAPTER 4

Post-launch in Games User Research

IAN LIVINGSTON, *Electronic Arts Canada*

Highlights

This chapter opens with a discussion of my personal thoughts and experiences post-launch in Games User Research (GUR). Its subsequent sections explore data sources that should be leveraged on a live title, and the importance and limitations of benchmark studies. The chapter concludes with a methodological example that can be implemented to kick-start your own post-launch analysis.

4.1 Introduction

Personally, I have always enjoyed the point when a project is wrapping up. That period when the end is visible and the struggles that were endured during development have faded, and all that remains is the satisfaction of a job well done. The end of a project is also my favourite time to both do research and reflect on the project as a whole. It is the moment when you can look back at all the research and analysis that was done and finally compare it to the game in the wild. It is tempting to think that there is not much user research to be done once a project has shipped, that our job stops when a game heads out the door, but that is untrue and a boring way to look at it.

While fundamentally different, classic box products and games that live on as a live service can be viewed with the same lens at this point. The only real difference, at least from my perspective, is the point at which you decide to close out

Games User Research, Anders Drachen, Pejman Mirza-Babaei, Lennart E. Nacke (Eds).
© Oxford University Press 2018. Published 2018 by Oxford University Press

a live service project. It is entirely possible that a project such as a mobile game with continuous content updates, or an MMO, will not reach a point where it will 'end'. In those circumstances it is best to just pick a moment and reflect. The rest of this chapter takes the stance that we are generally talking about a project with a defined end point. However, everything that I will discuss can be applied on a live project just as easily.

Some of the questions that I am often asked about user research in the post-launch period is: 'Why should a user researcher be involved? What's the value of the involvement?' I have always seen the reason and value as perfectly self-evident. However, if you do not agree, let me elaborate on what can be gained. A user researcher will often be involved with a project all the way through a production. They will have run many research sessions and will have a deep objective understanding of the players' behaviours and the user experience. The level of understanding is immensely valuable for contextualizing observed data patterns and player sentiment in a live environment. Additionally, there are numerous levels of comparative and exploratory research topics that can and should be explored (see chapters 2, 3, 5, and 7 for more on these topics).

The rest of this chapter covers three topics crucial to performing successful post-launch GUR. Firstly, I will describe some best practices for reflecting on the work done so far. Secondly, I will discuss data sources that should be leveraged on a live title. Thirdly, I will describe the importance and limitations of benchmark studies. I will wrap the chapter up with a methodological example that can be implemented on your project to kick-start your own post-launch analysis.

4.2 Reflections

I have always found self-reflection to be a highly worthwhile exercise. It is a great way to look at the work that I have done, see where I can make changes, and improve next time. When a project is ramping down, or just released, is a perfect time to do this type of exercise. In many cases, the ramping down period of time doubles as a planning phase for new projects, so learnings can be carried forward easily.

When I do this type of project reflection I will typically compile it into a post-mortem; a document which analyses the successful and unsuccessful elements of the project. This way I can ensure that there is use for both the research and game teams. The purpose of placing the reflection into a document is that it helps to ensure that the results of the post-mortem remain actionable. After all, it is important to ensure that the reflection drives learning and direct improvements to the work you do as a researcher.

The reflection should, at a minimum, include reflection on the following areas: communication, sessions and issues, and process.

4.2.1 Communication

So much of what I do as a user researcher comes down to effective communication. One day it is working with a designer to determine how best to answer a question, the next it's figuring out how best to present a finding. In all cases, communication is a crucial step in the research process. Reflecting on the effectiveness of your personal communication and the process by which that communication was carried out will help to ensure that you are able to identify best practices.

Another practice that I find useful is to do simple yet formal interviews with those whom you have worked most closely with on a project. Once you have got past that initial strangeness of asking 'How did I do?' the insight you gain from discussing your research with those you have worked with will give you a perspective that you could not find anywhere else. Some of the biggest growth moments I have had in my career have come from very candid discussions about how I could better communicate my work.

4.2.2 Sessions and issues

As a researcher, the vast majority of my work has revolved around the research project/sessions I am involved in, and the issues/problems I surface. Both of these topics are great for reflection, and will provide a wealth of information that will help you plan for your next project.

One of the first things I like to do is build a spreadsheet containing all the information about the research sessions. I like to include at least the following:

- date
- session type
- content focus
- number of new issues reported

- number of existing issues reported

As you look at this list, I am sure you can think of many other details you would like to track, but this is a good start. Additionally, if you are using an issue-tracking and project management tool such as JIRA by Atlassian to manage the user research issues on your project, you have an easy way to break down your issues into much greater detail by using the built-in tools.

Taking the time to deconstruct the details delivered from each session will provide you with a wealth of information. It is a really useful process that I have found helpful in identifying my personal, and my project's capacity to deliver and respond to user research findings.

4.2.3 Process

I have often found that when I am in the thick of a project it is almost impossible to see the forest for the trees. In contrast, the end of a project is the best time to look at how the overall research process could be improved. Taking the time to step back and find ways to improve the quality of the research you have been doing and to look for efficiency gains that can be made will help you and your team grow and will help you conduct better research on future projects.

It is hard to call out exactly what you should be looking for when reflecting on your processes, but try to consider three areas for improvements: cost savings, research quality, and session efficiency.

In all of these areas (communication, sessions and issues, and process) any amount of reflection will provide improvements and growth. Formalizing these findings into a post-mortem is just a best practice.

4.3 Live data

One of the most interesting and valuable parts of the post-launch process is the ability to finally see how a game will behave in the wild. I have always enjoyed seeing how all the different moving parts of a game's launch affect how a game is received by players and the media. I have also always found that this is the moment all the data I have collected thus far on a project can finally be compared with what goes on in the real world. If you have done your job well as a Games User Researcher, very little that is being said by players and the media at this point will be a surprise. However, inevitably there will be more to learn, and there is no better place to find it than in the live data.

I have chosen the term I am using here carefully. I am specifically not using the term telemetry because in truth that is only one type of live data. Live data can be any source of data that is available once a game has launched. These can be data that are scraped or collected from the usage of the game itself, like telemetry, it could be collected from publications such as reviews, found in player discussion forums, or collected in a research project such as a diary or ethnographic study.

Later in the chapter I describe a methodology called the review analysis, which walks through the process for conducting the analysis on a subset of live data. Where ever you collect your live data from it's worth analyzing and contextualizing it within the work you've already done. In many cases data sources are ignored while others are weighted too heavily. As a researcher it's your job to approach situations from every direction available to you.

4.3.1 Telemetry reporting

This might seem completely obvious, but one of the best sources of live data is in-game telemetry. The assumption here is that there is telemetry available in your game. If not, what are you waiting for? Data on simple details like how many players you have, when and for how long they play, and how much they spend on in-game purchases are too important to not be collected. There are books written on the subject, and if that is what you are interested in you will likely find more of value on the subject elsewhere.

Gameplay telemetry is special because it is valuable both after launch, and before launch in playtests, alphas, and betas. For example, in a game with a linear form of progression such as sequential missions, gameplay data can tell you things like how long people take to finish each mission, how many players reach those missions, and how many times they die or fail. When contextualized with the data collected during pre-launch sessions, a complete understanding of player behaviour and experience can begin to be formed (chapters 19–21 talk more about telemetry and analytics).

4.4 Benchmarking

With any benchmarking effort, it is important to remember why it is worth doing. At the most fundamental level, a benchmark will serve as a baseline for any future title you work on with your team. It helps with the understanding of where your team excels and where there is room for improvements. There are many different ways to benchmark a game. However, when you decide to approach the task, the only thing to remember is that consistency is key. For a benchmark to be valuable it needs to be comparable. For this reason, planning your benchmark is crucial.

I always prefer to focus my benchmark efforts on a set of high-level measures. When selecting the questions to use it is best to first identify those that can apply to the widest range of games. Topics such as usability, understanding, or enjoyment are a great place to start. Additionally, it can be easy to find existing and validated tools that might well suit your needs. The System Usability Scale (Brooke, 1996) or the Game Experience Questionnaire (Brockmyer et al., 2009) are good examples that can get you started.

When benchmarking it is also very important to remember that there will always be limitations. For example, much of a benchmark measure will rely on the circumstance around the launch of a game. When you benchmark, you are getting a snapshot of a game in time. The expectations of players will move with the state of the art, so you should expect that a game that measures well today would be comparable to a game that scores well five years from now regardless of how games grow or change. Additionally, it can be easy to assume that a lower value in your benchmark is always 'bad'. However, because each game is different, it is important to consider which areas your game was designed to excel at. Maybe that 'bad' value is perfectly justified given the design of your game. Whatever approach you take make sure you provide actionable findings in your benchmarking. Values by themselves are generally meaningless, and must be contextualized to be useful.

Now that we have established what should be done during post-launch, and how the data can be used, I will provide a specific example of a methodology that has proven to be immensely valuable as a standard practice: review analysis methodology.

I have always been fascinated by video game reviews. In fact, I based much of my thesis work on how the consumption of review content affected our overall player experience. What I discovered was that, objectively, it has no physiological effect on us. However, it does radically affect our perceived experience through a post-play cognitive rationalization (Livingston et al., 2011). This was different from a numerical anchoring effect because my work did not expose players to any values. It was a truly fascinating effect and supported the overall idea that text sentiment can have an impact on our experience. With this knowledge in hand, I set out to make use of the readily available and exceptionally rich source of live data that is professional reviews and player comments.

My first foray into the actionable use of reviews came in the form of a method I call 'critic-proofing' (Livingston et al., 2010). The method relies on the classic heuristic analysis process, but adjusts the severity of identified issues based on the effect that issue has on a critic's review. It helps to ensure that issues identified in the heuristic analysis are correctly prioritized. The great thing about the critic-proofing process is that it can be extended to work with any set of heuristics as long as the researcher is willing to conduct a baseline analysis on a set of video game reviews.

My fascination with video game reviews continued as I switched from academia to industry. While I was working on Far Cry 3, I had an opportunity to create a brand new approach. The goal was straightforward: we wanted to understand, in a broad and complete sense, how Far Cry 3 was being described by professional reviews. From this very simple request was born the Review Analysis methodology (RVA). RVA is a grounded theory process, which makes it slightly more complex to apply if you are not familiar with qualitative research methods, but ensures that I can capture all the nuance inherent in a rich data source like a video game review. Since its inception (and original presentation at the GURSIG Summit 2013), the method has been used continuously on titles at Ubisoft, and has seen adoption at companies around the world—a testament to the power and usefulness of the technique.

For the remainder of this section I will cover two important questions around the RVA. Firstly, I will discuss why it is important for the user research team to be conducting this work. Secondly, I will answer the question of how the technique should be executed to ensure a high degree of rigour in the analysis.

4.4.1 Why do an RVA at all?

Why do a review analysis at all? I have been asked this question so many times. Fundamentally, there are three main reasons to do this type of analysis: Firstly, reviewers are essentially highly articulate expert video game players; secondly, reviewers can and do tell us things about a game that players often cannot or do not have the industry perspective to do so; thirdly, and possibly the most important, everyone who is working on the game is already reading the reviews and forming opinions about why reviews are saying one thing or another. Let us look at each of these three points in a little more detail.

4.4.1.1 REVIEWERS ARE VERY ARTICULATE PLAYERS

If you are like me (and if you are reading this, then you likely are), I am going to assume that you are addicted to player feedback. In the most basic terms, knowledge is power, and the purest form of knowledge you can get while a game is in development will come from players.

When a reviewer writes a review, they are essentially providing a free-form description of their experience with a game. On top of this, they are also plugged into the marketing efforts that surround a title at launch, and will often include that experience (i.e., the hype and promise) along with their evaluation of the overall experience. The second advantage that they bring is the sheer amount of experience that they have with a wide variety of games, which enables them to comment and reference material that most of the gaming population will not have been exposed to. Additionally, speaking to the amount of experience that a reviewer brings to the table, they also explicitly care enough about that experience to share it with the world. Most importantly, they want to and will inform their audience about the game and thereby influence if they play the game at all, and as I demonstrated in my thesis they influence the degree to which the reader enjoys the experience.

4.4.1.2 REVIEWS CAN TELL US THINGS THAT PLAYERS CANNOT

It is easy to think of reviewers as just expert gamers, but that is doing a huge disservice to the entire profession. Game journalism is as old as gaming itself, and some of the best reviewers will not only describe their experience with a game, but also place that experience within the larger discourse that surrounds not just the title, but also the industry as a whole. They will often place a game within the context of culture or even social issues. It is absolutely crucial that we as researchers remember that games are an art form and as such do not exist in a vacuum of momentary experience.

When you consider how a review can tell you about an experience it becomes possible to understand how the experience is being described, or what it is best compared to. It also becomes clear what the individual author finds interesting or noteworthy. These are often areas where most playtesters I would bring into my lab will struggle, so a review becomes an incredibly rich live data source.

4.4.1.3 TEAMS ALREADY READ REVIEWS AND FORM OPINIONS

The single biggest reason to do this type of analysis is that if you do not, some-one else will, either in some formal manner, or informally in an ad hoc manner.

The reason that it is going to happen is because the data are just too attractive and accessible. Every person on the team is going to sit at their desk, or on their phone, and agonize over every new review that goes live. They will share them among themselves, they will take notes, and the strongest opinions will end up in presentations. I know, I have done it—it's fun.

However, at a basic level those who have invested in the development of the game are going to have the greatest difficulty staying objective when it comes to the analysis of these data. It brings to mind the three blind men and the elephant analogy, except the men are not blind: one is an expert on trunks, another is an expert on tails, and the third does not care about elephants at all and would prefer it to be a tiger. The point is, each has an agenda.

On top of a lack of objectivity in the analysis, most developers will struggle to apply a standard research procedure to their analysis. The truth is that most are just not trained in research practices and will often fall into many of the traps that new researchers fall into, such as dealing with personal bias or correct sampling techniques.

4.4.1.4 PROVEN TECHNIQUE

Finally, it is worth remembering that at the time of writing this chapter, the RVA technique has been used on almost a dozen titles (that I know of), across a wide range of genres, at many different companies and studios around the world. It is a proven technique that can provide real value to teams and researchers alike. We are not discussing hypotheticals here!

4.4.1.5 CONCLUSION

For the reasons already given, and many others that I am just not going to get into, the best candidate for conducting this analysis is a trained researcher. The researcher or research team for a project will generally be less implicated in the development process (though this is changing as researchers become more embedded with development teams). Additionally, they can contextualize the findings from the RVA within the research that was done before launch, which has immense value.

Ideally, it is best if the researcher is well versed in qualitative research techniques. If you are a researcher reading this and saying to yourself 'That doesn't sound like me', the best place to start will be in learning about grounded theory and qualitative coding techniques. The remainder of this chapter will provide an introduction to these topics; however, the best way to get better will be to practice and read deeply on the subject.

4.4.2 How do you do an RVA?

At the most simplistic level, conducting an RVA takes a raw review, codes it using qualitative techniques, and formats the output into actionable findings. To begin, we first need to understand grounded theory and how to conduct a study using the technique.

4.4.2.1 WHAT IS GROUNDED THEORY?

Grounded theory is a systematic qualitative methodology where a theoretical framework is developed through the analysis of a rich qualitative data source. As with other qualitative research methods, the value of the analysis is found in the 'how' and 'why' questions rather than the 'how many' or 'how much' frequency analyses. The goal of the analysis is to maintain and articulate the breadth and richness of the data found in the reviews. The richness is maintained by first breaking down the data via a coding process, and then building a research theory back up through the grouping of codes into concepts and categories. Finally, when the analysis is completed, the theory will capture the underlying structure of how and why a particular topic is described in a particular fashion.

The structure of the research is often counter-intuitive to many researchers who have been trained in quantitative research techniques. In the quantitative case, a researcher will start from a hypothesis and design a study to reject it. With grounded theory, the research ends with what is essentially a hypothesis (the theory) that fully describes the full breadth of observations. We will dive into each of these ideas in much greater detail later. For now, the best example I can provide is that this is the difference between knowing how often a feature (e.g., combat) is discussed, and knowing why it was important for reviewers to discuss the feature at all.

It would be impossible for me to go into a huge description of the history of grounded theory, how it was developed, its pitfalls, and its limitations. However, there are literally books written on those topics. I would suggest starting with the grandfather of the method, Glaser and Strauss's book *The Discovery of Grounded Theory* (Glaser and Strauss, 2009). You can also find more than you will ever need to know on the subject with a simple Internet search. I will do my best to provide you with what you need here, but there is so much more out there on the topic.

For our purpose, the RVA is an application of the grounded theory methodology to the data set of game reviews. It organizes the breadth of ideas they present into a stable theoretical framework which addresses the high-level questions of interest laid out by the development team.

4.4.2.2 WHAT IS A THEORETICAL FRAMEWORK?

The theoretical framework is the output from the RVA process. It is the articulation of the theory developed through the analysis of the reviews. It is the answer to the focus questions that were outlined at the beginning of the study (we will get to that soon). A good theoretical framework maintains the nuance of the data, while organizing it into an effective and consumable format.

The theories that make up the framework are developed not to 'prove' or 'disprove' an idea. Rather, they are the theories supported by the entire breadth of the data. Essentially, when looking at any review, any perspective or description should be captured in the presented theory.

4.4.2.3 THE PROCESS

I have covered the outcome from the RVA and the general idea that surrounds that grounded theory; now let us explore the steps for executing the procedure. There are four main steps to the process: planning, data collection, analysis, and reporting. The steps have remained constant over the years and have proven robust. I have experimented with adjusting how we conduct the individual steps to improve efficiency and repeatability. When you first start trying to execute the RVA method, I would not recommend changing the process. However, once you have mastered it, it is likely that customizations can be added that will add additional value for you and your team.

Step 1: Planning
The classic approach for conducting an RVA requires 2–6 researchers, takes 2–4 weeks, relies on 6–8 focus questions, and covers 20–30 reviews. Let's look at each of these in turn.

Researchers   At a minimum, it is important that you are not doing your research in a vacuum. Grounded theory is a complex method, and one of the most important checks that you need is to have one or more researchers doing the analysis with you. I have always found that it is important to not skip this step because it is crucial that you do not get trapped in your own analysis bubble. Having additional researchers looking at the data, building concepts, and sharing the outputs ensures that your theories will be much stronger.

---

continued

Time	2–4 weeks might sound like a long time to conduct a study, but with the sheer amount of analysis needed in the RVA as well as time to create a competent theoretical framework and the report, two weeks will fly by. When you are planning, it is best to assume that you will be able to code 3–5 reviews a day, and that it will take 3–5 days to create a reasonable theoretical framework that captures the analysis. Finally, allow for 3–5 days to build an actionable report. It is crucial that you give yourself enough time to fully develop the framework, as this is the primary value/output of the RVA process.
Focus Questions	The focus question is the device you use to provide the barest of direction to the initial coding effort. Some may argue that when conducting an open code there should be no direction at all as even a focus question may colour the output and prevent the development of a complete or correct theory. I do not subscribe to this notion. Without focus questions, it is far too easy for the analysis to go off track and possibly reduce the overall value of any findings.
	So what is a focus question? It provides a very high level direction to the areas of interest for the analysis. They function as the research questions, the overall research focus for the study. Some examples include: 'How was the gameplay described?', 'How was the narrative described?', 'How was the game described in relationship to the franchise?' You will notice that each of these questions is a 'how' question. You will also notice that in each case the term 'described' is used. We want our focus questions to remain as open as possible while still capturing the areas of interest for the team.
Number of Reviews	Common wisdom would suggest that 'more is better', but this is not the case in qualitative research. Thirty reviews would be great, but often a game may not even have that many reviews to look at. However, a larger number will often help support the work by satiating the common criticism about sample size in qualitative work. The correct answer to 'how many reviews should I use?' is 'until you reach saturation'. In qualitative work, saturation is the concept that new data sources should be added to a study until no new findings are identified, or until the developed theory remains stable, which in general will be 12–30 reviews. To capture this, it is important to look at conflicting data sources. Remember, we are doing a breadth analysis.

I know what you are thinking: 'This is a little extreme for my needs.' The numbers I have listed above are really the 'ideal', but as long as you are conducting your study in a controlled and rigorous manner, you can take some shortcuts. This will ensure that what you deliver will be done so in a timely manner, which is arguably the most important constraint that a user researcher must deal with. The fastest way to scope down the size of the research project is to bring down the number of focus questions and the number of reviews analysed. I would strongly suggest that you consider this during your planning.

Step 2: Data Collection

Once the planning has finished, it is time to begin collecting the data for your analysis. The best place to find reviews is on a review aggregate website. There are many to choose from, so I will not go into which to use. I like GameRankings.com, others like metacritic.com, but it does not really matter. Your goal is to find a collection of reviews that can be used for sampling.

The best approach when sampling the data is to take a sample from the top third, middle third, and bottom third based on the numerical rating. This helps to ensure that a breadth of opinions is analysed. Remember, we are not looking for agreement between the data sources; we want to explore many different ideas, so we need to collect reviews that are going to help us understand as many perspectives as possible.

Once the reviews have been selected they should be saved in a plain text format. This ensures easy analysis or integration into your qualitative analysis tool of choice. Once organized, you are ready to move on to the analysis.

Step 3: Analysis

The analysis is easily the most time-consuming part of the process; it is also the most important. The analysis process I like to use is broken down into six parts. Each step is not done in isolation, which is consistent with normal qualitative analysis practices. The general process has each review being coded and memoed, then the negative case analysis and the peer debriefing is carried out, and a theory is developed. Everything that is done in an ongoing process.

A frequency analysis is also always done as the final step after all data have been coded and theories have been articulated. The frequency analysis is an effective tool for communicating the weight of findings identified in the grounded theory analysis. I explore each of these parts in what follows.

Coding	Coding is the base process of analysis in most qualitative processes. It is the process of deconstructing a piece of data into the base constructs to address the underlying research and focus questions. In the review analysis, we make use of two types of coding: open and selective.
Open coding	Open coding is a technique that should be used at the start of the review analysis. The coding should use the focus questions as a tool to direct, but not limit the coding at the beginning of the process. Open coding at the start ensures that findings are not limited and allows for rapid theory iteration.
	When I first conducted the RVA, each researcher developed their own codes for all their reviews. Unfortunately, this led to a problem of similar concepts being coded slightly differently throughout. While this was not an issue for the development of theories, it did lead to some additional efforts during the frequency analysis part of the process. To remove this issue, we introduced frequent researcher debriefs to the process which I describe later.
Selective coding	Once approximately half of the reviews are coded, it is usually best to transition into a selective coding process. The codes that are consolidated during peer debriefing sessions are then used for the basis of the selective coding of the remaining reviews. The switch from open coding to selective coding helps to ensure that the process is efficient while maintaining data quality.

continued

The selective coding technique we use is slightly modified. Each idea that needs to be coded is limited to three codes, with the first set to relate the idea to a focus question. The second set to a conceptual label for the code. The third code is a positive or negative sentiment, which allow the researcher to quickly identify in which direction a comment was made when examined out of context during the frequency analysis. The change greatly improves coding efficiency with minimal effect on the quality of the research.

The memoing step is easy and serves multiple purposes. The memo allows the individual researcher to formulate an initial theoretical framework. It is a summary of the review that formulates the coded review into an initial set of concepts. It is primarily used during peer debrief, but also allows the researcher to articulate the primary ideas presented in the review.

Additionally, as each new review is coded and memoed, it enables the researchers to confront their current theoretical understanding of each focus question through negative case analysis (see below). Once the initial set of memoing is complete, it is time to move on to the peer debrief and sorting.

Peer debriefing and sorting

In any qualitative analysis procedure, it is important to perform peer debriefs. The reason that the RVA needs a minimum of two researchers is because of this step. The debriefing and sorting of findings is an ongoing process to ensure research rigour and consistency. The debrief is a crucial ongoing process that serves multiple purposes but fundamentally functions as the point to critique the emerging theories. The critique is crucial to ensure that the theory is robust.

Additionally, the debrief functions to ensure common coding practices between researchers. During the initial debrief, all codes currently used must be discussed and those that relate to the same conceptual idea are combined. After this initial debriefing session, the first set of coded reviews are reviewed and if they differ drastically from the combined coding set they are re-coded using the combined coding set.

The debrief also functions as an opportunity to expand the theoretical framework. During the debrief the initial theory is also developed. Memos are shared and theories are combined through the sorting of codes into logical concepts and then categories that address the focus questions. Generally, it is best if these debrief sessions take place after approximately 25%, 50%, 75%, and 100% of review coding and memoing has occurred. It is crucial that the debriefing sessions happen frequently, especially if you have more people involved. Doing so ensures that there is coding agreement between researchers and will produce a more complete theory.

Negative case analysis

Negative case analysis is a process whereby coding and memoing focuses on identifying specific cases that do not support, but rather contradict, the existing theoretical framework. The process helps the researcher reach saturation. The analysis also helps to ensure that the theoretical framework captures the full breadth of ideas surrounding the specific research question.

For example: Let us explore missions that some reviewers liked while others did not. In this case, perhaps there is consistency in what was liked, but not in what was disliked. In this form of analysis, our framework will capture this precise topic; that which was liked was generally consistent, but the factors that detracted from the experience were varied.

continued

| Theory development | It should be clear at this point that in reality the development of the theory began at the first review and continues throughout the analysis. Each researcher begins contributing to the theory in their first memo. In essence the first memo functions as the initial framework and each additional review expands the theory to capture the nuance from each additional review. During the debrief the frameworks are shared and combined between researchers. The combined framework is then challenged and expanded via the negative case analysis. Finally, the full theory is articulated by the lead researcher.

In practice I have generated the theory via the meetings and recorded them in a document we call the concepts and categories document. I originally did the organization and groupings via notes and then organized them in a text document. However, that is slow and inefficient. Now I do the organization in a spreadsheet to facilitate the final step of the process, which honestly makes sense if you can work that way. However, the key is to not let the tool limit your ability to group concepts or modify existing theories. Work with what you are most comfortable with. |
|---|---|
| Frequency analysis | The final step in the analysis is simultaneously the most and least important aspect of the analysis. Numbers are generally irrelevant to a grounded theory analysis; however, the communicative power that they provide should not be ignored, especially if dealing with individuals who do not have much experience with qualitative research. A simple frequency analysis, done to count the codes that relate to a concept or a specific focus question, can really illustrate theory if presented in context.

The 'counting' is never done before a theory is formed because people are predisposed to fixate on numbers as a measure of a topic's importance. Additionally, it can limit our analysis and bias the formation of theories. However, graphing the frequency of positive or negative sentiment around a category that is key to the underlying theoretical framework will be highly impactful. |

Step 4: Reporting

The final step is reporting the findings. The report should be presented in a manner that clearly indicates how the developed theory answers each of the focus questions. I have always found it best to frame the report so that the theory is supported with qualitative quotes from the reviews, and backed up with data collected during the frequency analysis. Regardless of how you decide to formulate the report, be sure that you are addressing the needs of your audience above all else. If you have done the analysis well, the story your presentation is communicating will be clear from your theoretical framework. Make sure your findings are actionable.

4.5 Conclusion

Post-launch is a huge opportunity for a user researcher to do some formative research work. I've only been able to scratch the surface of what can be done, and how to do it. There is no better time to compare the research conducted before launch to the game in the wild. Reflections about communication, issues, and processes used in the pre-launch research lead to more efficient and actionable research in the future. Benchmarking serves as a baseline for any future title you work on. One example of a benchmark is the review analysis method (RVA), which relies on grounded theory to provide a theoretical framework which answers the focus questions. Hopefully, by this point I have stimulated the creative juices and you are ready to start your own analysis! Most importantly, no matter what you decide to research, when you reach this point in your project's development, make sure that you constantly reflect on how your work is going to contribute to either the ongoing success of the launched title, or inform the development of future games. It is absolutely crucial that you focus on providing truly actionable research at all points in time.

References

Brockmyer, J. H., Fox, C. M., Curtiss, K. A., McBroom, E., Burkhart, K. M., Pidruzny, J. N. (2009). The development of the Game Engagement Questionnaire: a measure of engagement in video game-playing. Journal of Experimental Social Psychology, 45(4), 624–634.

Brooke, J. (1996). SUS: a 'quick and dirty' usability scale. Usability Evaluation in Industry, 189(194), 4–7.

Glaser, B. G., Strauss, A. L. (2009). The discovery of grounded theory: strategies for qualitative research. Piscataway, NJ: Transaction Publishers.

Livingston, I. J., Mandryk, R. L., Stanley, K. G. (2010, May). Critic-proofing: how using critic reviews and game genres can refine heuristic evaluations. In Proceedings of the International Academic Conference on the Future of Game Design and Technology (pp. 48–55). New York: ACM.

Livingston, I. J., Nacke, L. E., Mandryk, R. L. (2011, October). Influencing experience: the effects of reading game reviews on player experience. In International Conference on Entertainment Computing (pp. 89–100). Berlin and Heidelberg: Springer.

CHAPTER 5

User experience maturity levels

Evaluating and improving Games User Research practices

GRAHAM MCALLISTER, *Player Research*

Highlights

As user experience (UX) research in game development becomes more established, many studios are now incorporating UX practices within their studio. However, the maturity level of UX within a studio can vary widely, from those who are hostile towards UX up to those who embrace UX at all levels in the organization.

This chapter is for both game developers and Games User Researchers who are interested in assessing where they currently are on a UX maturity scale, and also keen to understand what more could be done to become more player-focused.

5.1 Introduction

While it is often the case that studios say they focus on the player experience, some studios focus on it more than others. After discussions with hundreds of game studios over the last five years about how much they focus on the player experience—which in this chapter I am taking to mean how much they engage in user research (or user experience, UX, research)—eight discrete levels of UX maturity have emerged which the majority of studios can fit into. Jointly, these eight levels or dimensions of UX practice provide a road map of how any

Games User Research, Anders Drachen, Pejman Mirza-Babaei, Lennart E. Nacke (Eds).
© Oxford University Press 2018. Published 2018 by Oxford University Press

company or research group can evaluate their current strengths and weaknesses in terms of Games User Research (GUR) practices, and consider how to
improve the specific or overall maturity of these practices.

These eight UX maturity levels represent studios of all sizes, and although it
is not necessarily true that the larger studios are at the higher end of the scale,
they are the ones who are most likely to be there today. This is often due to them
being early investors in user research, and as such their UX research departments have had time to mature. It is also worth stating that these larger studios
have enough resources available to make such investments. Of course, smaller
studios could also reach the higher levels, and in many ways it is easier for them
to achieve, as they may find it easier to adopt and integrate UX practices.

5.2 Why are the UX maturity levels useful?

Often when I am in discussion with studios I am told that they did 'all they
could' to deliver the best possible player experience. My response is usually
to ask them did they do any of the following user research methods, and I will
list a series of options, and the answer is usually 'No, we did not do any of that'.
These studios often did not seem aware that there were other user research
options available to them, and therefore if studios really are committed to putting the player experience first, it is useful to have a roadmap of what good user
research actually looks like and how to get there. The purpose of this chapter is
to provide such a roadmap in the form of a UX maturity model: this describes
the different dimensions of UX operations, and the levels of maturity within
each of them.

This chapter will help developers identify which level they are currently at,
and also how to progress to the higher levels, if indeed they want or need to be
there. These are some of the reasons to care about your UX maturity level:

- You want to improve the quality of games coming from the studio.
- You want to produce more successful games repeatedly (not just a
  one-off).
- You want to become a better designer (by understanding players better).
- The most successful studios tend to have more mature UX; what are
  they doing?
- You want to understand what to do next to become more player-focused.

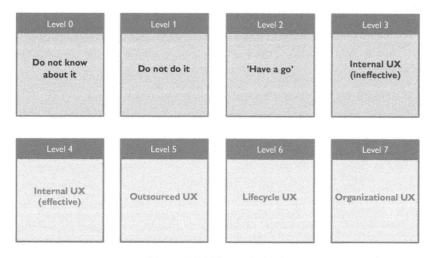

Figure 5.1 UX maturity levels

5.3 UX maturity levels: model overview

There are eight UX maturity levels in the model, ranging from 0 to 7 (listed in Figure 5.1), and they fall into two broad groupings. If you are currently in Levels 0–3, then your UX efforts could either be having no beneficial effect on your game, or potentially even making it worse. It is only at Levels 4–7 where the UX resources available are sufficient to reliably improve the player experience.

5.4 The variables

As we have eight discrete UX maturity levels, we will need a set of criteria so that studios can assess which level they are currently at. The five variables in Table 5.1 can be reframed as statements and used to assess a studio's commitment to getting the player experience right.

5.4.1 Staff/resources

What calibre of staff has the studio allocated to their user research needs? Staff at the lower levels of UX maturity may include anyone in the studio who has expressed an interest, but they may not have relevant background or training. Staff at the higher levels of UX maturity would hold advanced degrees (typically

Table 5.1 *Variables to take into account when assessing UX maturity level*

Variable	Description
Staff/resources	Staff are suitably qualified, real participants are recruited, dedicated space.
Dedicated budget	Each project gets a dedicated UX research budget.
Breadth of UX	UX research is across the whole game development life cycle.
Depth of UX	From the top of the company downwards, there is UX buy-in.
Games exhibit evidence of UX	The games that emerge are very well reviewed; no/little mention of UX problems.

a Masters or PhD) in a relevant discipline, such as human-computer interaction (HCI) or psychology.

In terms of resources, studios at the lower UX maturity levels would likely be using makeshift space in their studio, such as an unused meeting room or a quiet corner of the building. Conversely, studios at the higher UX maturity levels would have dedicated playtesting space with remote viewing rooms for the developers so participants can play without feeling observed. Studios at the higher end may also have dedicated player recruitment staff to handle the selection and logistics to ensure the right players arrive at the right time.

5.4.2 Dedicated budget

This refers to not only the amount of budget invested in UX research, but also how the budget is managed. Studios at the lower UX maturity levels will likely not have planned for UX research from the project outset, only realizing at some point that they need some form of UX feedback but have no budget. With little or no budget available, this can lead to informal guerilla UX testing, e.g., in coffee shops or even inviting friends and family into the studio to play the game. Studios at the higher UX maturity levels calculate the UX research budget alongside that for the rest of the game; it is an integral component of how games are made. This is important as it helps schedule the user research: the developers know what UX research is going to be conducted, and when.

5.4.3 Breadth of UX

UX research has available a toolkit of methods which span the entire development life cycle, from concept all the way through to release and live operations. Studios at the lower UX maturity levels may only be aware of playtesting, but studios at the upper levels will be applying UX research to their game at all stages. For example, they utilize player interviews to develop player personas, perform UX analysis of competitor titles, employ heuristic reviews of UI and gameplay, run diary studies to monitor long-term UX, among other methods (see chapter 7 for an overview of key GUR methods): Studios that utilize a wider range of methods can better assess a game from multiple viewpoints and also at various points in development. This helps the developers get feedback when they need it most.

5.4.4 Depth of UX

Depth of UX refers to how great is the influence of UX research felt in the studio. At the lower UX maturity levels, the top of the company may not read the reports, or even know about the UX research that is going on. It is also possible that many of the staff may never see the results of the user research. In contrast, studios at the higher end are fully onboard with the UX research. The studio head and C-level execs will be asking to read the UX research reports, the findings will be presented regularly at company meetings, and staff of all levels are reading the report (at least the parts that apply to them). The staff know when the latest reports will be available and how to access them. At the highest UX maturity level, UX research runs through the company culture.

5.4.5 Evidence

The reason for conducting UX research is that the game which emerges is experienced the way the designer intended—an enjoyable experience free from unintended friction. However, it is possible that studios could be investing in UX research, yet the games which result from development contain usability and UX issues. In such cases, it points to a problem somewhere within the studio's process, communication, or culture—I cannot say where—but the evidence shows a problem does indeed exist. The problem could also be that the rest of the studio does not have trust in the findings from the user researchers; regardless, I will not speculate as to where the problems are, but the evidence will show if issues exist.

Evidence of usability and UX issues could come from an analysis of game reviews—both from professionals and from players. There is no point investing in user research if the design team, artists, animators, programmers, producers, or management are not going to put the changes into action. If the changes are not being made, it could be because they were detected too late (a process problem), the right person did not know about them (a communication problem), or the right person did not want to make the changes (a trust problem).

While it is apparent that investing in UX research is no guarantee of a well-reviewed game, it will certainly increase your chances of doing so if fewer usability and UX issues are present in your game. In addition, player experience trumps usability, meaning that there are games where the overall player experience is excellent, despite usability issues persisting. However, this is rare, and most games which contain major usability issues would not be considered excellent (achieve very positive reviews).

Studios at the lower levels of UX maturity are more likely to be producing games of poor-to-average quality, meaning feedback from professional critics and real players would be commenting on gameplay elements which are confusing, difficult to use, or simply not satisfying. In addition, studios at the lower UX maturity levels would be quite consistent in their ability to produce poor-to-average games. Studios at the upper levels of UX maturity would likely be producing games free from usability issues; however, some minor criticisms on gameplay may still appear. Studios at these higher levels would also be consistent in their ability to produce games which review well by both professional critics and players.

The evidence variable is needed as some studios report that they have invested in user research, but the games that emerge deliver an experience which players may not enjoy. This variable identifies if your whole team is working together effectively, or if there is an issue somewhere in your game development process.

5.5 Overview—UX maturity levels and variables

What follows is an overview of all eight UX maturity levels and the level of effort invested with each variable per level (Figure 5.2). For each variable, there are four different amounts of effort possible, indicated by which column is shaded:

- Blank—no effort is invested by the studio.
- First column—a low amount of effort is invested.
- Second column—a moderate amount, but more is possible.
- Third column—the studio is investing as much as necessary in this area to achieve the desired results.

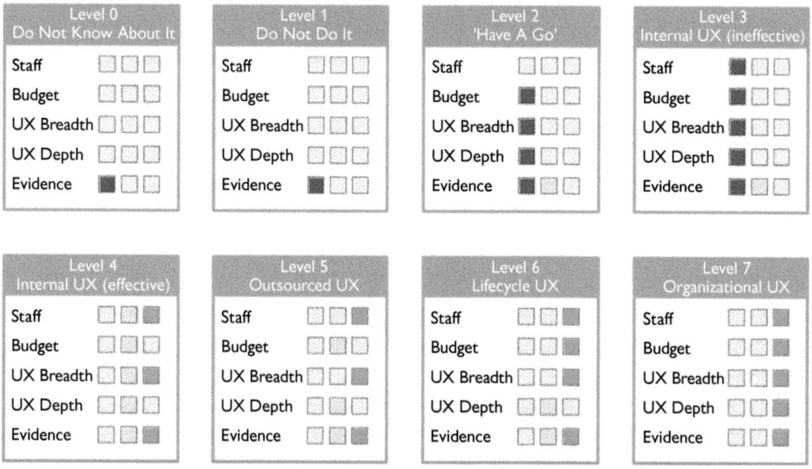

Level 0 — Do Not Know About It				Level 1 — Do Not Do It				Level 2 — 'Have A Go'				Level 3 — Internal UX (ineffective)		
Staff	□	□	□	Staff	□	□	□	Staff	□	□	□	Staff	■	□	□
Budget	□	□	□	Budget	□	□	□	Budget	■	□	□	Budget	■	□	□
UX Breadth	□	□	□	UX Breadth	□	□	□	UX Breadth	■	□	□	UX Breadth	■	□	□
UX Depth	□	□	□	UX Depth	□	□	□	UX Depth	■	□	□	UX Depth	■	□	□
Evidence	■	□	□	Evidence	■	□	□	Evidence	■	□	□	Evidence	■	□	□

Level 4 — Internal UX (effective)				Level 5 — Outsourced UX				Level 6 — Lifecycle UX				Level 7 — Organizational UX		
Staff	□	□	■	Staff	□	□	■	Staff	□	□	■	Staff	□	□	■
Budget	□	□	□	Budget	□	□	□	Budget	□	□	■	Budget	□	□	■
UX Breadth	□	□	■	UX Breadth	□	□	■	UX Breadth	□	□	■	UX Breadth	□	□	■
UX Depth	□	□	□	UX Depth	□	□	□	UX Depth	□	□	□	UX Depth	□	□	■
Evidence	□	□	■	Evidence	□	□	■	Evidence	□	□	■	Evidence	□	□	■

Figure 5.2 UX maturity levels and variables

The evidence variable is different than the others as it is not an indicator of effort invested, but rather of the relative game quality that emerges; that is, if the left-hand column is shaded, it may not necessarily indicate a bad game, but rather that the game could be significantly better from a usability and UX perspective, and therefore a better game overall.

5.6 UX maturity levels—breakdown

This section will detail each of the eight levels. For each level, a visual overview of the five variables will be presented along with key traits that your studio is at this level, followed by steps on how to progress to the next level up. Each section will conclude with a series of questions which act as gates—you should not progress to the next level until these conditions have been met.

5.6.1 Level 0—do not know about UX research

At this lowest level, the studio is not fully aware of what UX research is (Figure 5.3, Table 5.2). It is certainly possible that some people within the studio are familiar with some UX methods; however, as a studio there is no consistent understanding and communication of all methods and their benefits. In particular,

Figure 5.3 UX maturity Level 0

Table 5.2 *Signs you are at Level 0*

Signs you are at Level 0
• Think that UX=UI.
• Cannot distinguish UXD from UXR (UX design from UX research).
• Use 'focus group' but mean playtest.
• Cannot differentiate market research and user research.
• Not sure of the difference between talking to players and observing players (perception vs behaviour).
• Do not understand why six players are enough for a usability test.
• Think that usability/UX is about dumbing down the game.

the people who are the key decision makers are not likely to be fully aware or informed of UX research and how it could benefit their staff, game, and studio as a whole. It is also likely that some studios think they know about UX, but their understanding is incorrect.

5.6.1.1 WHAT TO DO NEXT

The most import area to focus on next is acquiring knowledge. Read articles, watch videos, or ideally find someone in the UX research area to speak to so you can arm yourself with the necessary information. Some useful resources:

- IGDA GUR webpage—http://gamesuserresearchsig.org
- LinkedIn group for GUR—https://www.linkedin.com/groups/1873014
- GDC Vault
- The six UX roles in games—I gave a talk at PocketGamer Connects on the different types of UX in the games industry—http://www.pocketgamer.biz/news/62327/game-ux-roles/
- Twitter, follow @GamesUR for UX research articles

5.6.1.2 WHEN ARE YOU READY TO MOVE ON?

You will be ready to move to the next UX maturity level when:

- You are aware of the key methods and approaches in UX research.
- You understand which type of UX research you need on your game, when it would be applied, and what the output of that research would look like.
- Overall, you can make informed decisions about UX research on your game.

5.6.2 Level 1—do not do UX research

At Level 1, the quality consistency of games being output from studios is the same as Level 0, mainly because there is the same amount of UX research being put in—none (Figure 5.4, Table 5.3). However, there is a major cultural difference between these two lower levels: studios at this level have knowledge of UX research but are actively deciding not to use it. There could be many reasons for this, but could include:

- The return on investment (ROI) value is not clear.
- Think they cannot afford to do it. However, studios should be thinking of value, not cost, so this is linked to their perception of ROI value.
- There is a blocker in the studio. Some people in the studio are convinced of the value, but key decision makers may not be. The studio has not reached a 'players first' maturity level.
- Not sure how to take the next steps; they have no one internal and do not know how to go external.
- They have had a bad experience with UX research in the past, mainly as it was done poorly, but the studios did not know it was poor research as they were not aware what good or bad UX research looks like.

Studios may do what they call informal playtesting by bringing their game to expos or asking friends and family to play their game.

5.6.2.1 WHAT TO DO NEXT

In order to improve your UX maturity level, address the following:

- Which issues does your game/studio currently experience? Could an improved approach to UX research help with this?
- Speak to all members of the team. Is there any resistance to doing UX research? Why?

Figure 5.4 UX maturity Level I

Table 5.3 *Signs you are at Level 1*

Signs you are at Level 1
• We make games with almost zero outside feedback. Leave us alone, we are artists!
• You are from the 'good old days'—we get feedback from sales data.
• You use the modern version of the 'sales data' approach—we use analytics during soft launch/launch. That is enough, right?
• Playtest at expos.
• Our friends and family play our game.
• We ask other developers.

5.6.2.2 WHEN ARE YOU READY TO MOVE ON?

You will be ready to move to the next UX maturity level when:

- Identify and list the specific reasons why you are currently not investing in formal UX research.
- Accept that your last game was not as well received as expected. What are you going to do about that?
- Accept that your last game had UX issues which should not have been present.
- You do not want to repeat previous mistakes. You are open to change.

5.6.3 Level 2—'have a go' approach

At Level 2, studios are motivated enough to try some aspects of UX research, most likely playtesting, but they are doing so with staff who are unlikely to have a suitable background or experience (Figure 5.5, Table 5.4). As such, all the various components of a playtest may be included—players playing the game, developers taking notes, players being interviewed—however, there is

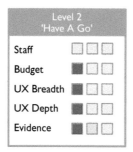

Figure 5.5 UX maturity Level 2

Table 5.4 *Signs you are at Level 2*

Signs you are at Level 2

- Various team members cobble together what looks like a playtest, but has no rigour. Think of Feynman's 'cargo cult science'.[1]
- Bringing players into the studio (probably known, or poorly chosen), stand behind them and watch.
- Poor planning and preparation, informal notes taken, little analysis of data.
- Asking bad questions in questionnaires or interviews.

[1] http://calteches.library.caltech.edu/51/2/CargoCult.htm

little rigour either in the planning, running of the sessions, or in the analysis. The result is unpredictable: some issues identified could improve the game; however, others could make the game worse, and other issues may go unreported altogether.

5.6.3.1 WHAT TO DO NEXT

In order to improve your UX maturity level, address the following:

- Assess if the team are getting value from the current playtests (or other area of UX research).
- Is there a desire to increase the quality of the UX research?

5.6.3.2 WHEN ARE YOU READY TO MOVE ON?

You will be ready to move to the next UX maturity level when:

- The Team is beginning to buy into the idea of scheduling and running playtests.
- You have allocated resources to a modest UX research department.
- You can see the ROI value of UX research.

5.6.4 Level 3—internal UX (ineffective)

Having an internal UX research resource is no guarantee of doing good UX research. At this level of UX maturity, studios can see the value in UX research and have appointed staff to lead that initiative, most likely from within the studio (Figure 5.6, Table 5.5). However, although dedicated staff have been appointed, the games that emerge from the studio will still not be of consistent high quality. The main reason for this is that the appointed staff may not be from a relevant background, and as such they are not suited to be running UX research (most likely just playtests at this level) and would not be aware of all possible methods and approaches to best help the team. In addition to not being suited to be running playtests, they will not be aware of the many other UX research methods available, limiting their impact on the game.

An additional problem that can occur at this level is that as the appointed staff are not qualified for the role, the rest of the development team are also aware of this and may not trust, or take notice of, the results. On a positive note, the studio has made the decision that UX research is worth investing in; however, their investment is not being used effectively.

Figure 5.6 UX maturity Level 3

Table 5.5 *Signs you are at Level 3*

Signs you are at Level 3
• Unqualified staff appointed to do the UX research (QA, producers, designers). Not aware what they are doing wrong.
• No/little structure to the playtests. Research questions/methods not well formed or alternatives evaluated.
• Output from playtests may not be trusted—lack of confidence from other team members.

5.6.4.1 WHAT TO DO NEXT

In order to improve your UX maturity level, address the following:

- Consider options for using your allocated budget more effectively, e.g., hire someone with a relevant background.
- Understand where the team need help most. Can using UX research earlier in development help?

5.6.4.2 WHEN ARE YOU READY TO MOVE ON?

You will be ready to move to the next UX maturity level when:

- Decide if you want to invest in a more effective internal UX team or outsource UX (or both).
- From a production perspective, plan for when you need UX research and make a budget.

5.6.5 Level 4—internal UX (effective)

Level 4 is the first level where UX research is likely to have a positive impact consistently on all games from the studio as there is now trained UX research staff on the team who can apply a range of methods across the development life cycle (Figure 5.7, Table 5.6). However, at this level it is still a modest investment, so the UX 'team' is likely only one person, which will limit the range of UX methods which can be applied across the game life cycle.

Figure 5.7 UX maturity Level 4

Table 5.6 *Signs you are at Level 4*

Signs you are at Level 4
• Small team of specialist UX people—Most likely one person.
• Staff may be relatively junior, e.g., just finished a Master's degree in relevant subject.
• Only getting input from one domain (e.g., psychology, HCI).
• Narrow range of UX research available to you, e.g., playtesting, heuristic review.

5.6.5.1 WHAT TO DO NEXT

In order to improve your UX maturity level, address the following:

- Do you need a broader range of UX research? Could UX research at other times in the development cycle add value?
- Do you need specialized research which needs UX research staff with a different skill set?
- Do you need an outside perspective? Perhaps to validate the internal findings?

5.6.5.2 WHEN ARE YOU READY TO MOVE ON?

You will be ready to move to the next UX maturity level when:

- You have identified where the risks/assumptions are in the game's design. Can UX research help address them?
- It is possible you do not know what you do not know; get some advice to ensure you are not missing out on any potential UX research methods.

5.6.6 Level 5—outsourced UX

For many studios, having an internal UX team may not be an option, what they want, or even what is best for them. Studios at this level of UX maturity are willing to invest in UX research, and an outsourced/external UX option best suits their needs (Figure 5.8, Table 5.7). Factors which influence this decision include:

- Want access to a team of UX researchers with a diverse range of skills.
- Want access to UX researchers who have experience of working on games from across the industry—not just one platform, genre, or developer/publisher.
- Do not want permanent staff; prefer to pay when needed.
- Do not have the space/budget to build an internal UX lab.
- Risk management—if the internal UX resource leaves, it would impact the project schedule and final player experience. Mitigate this risk.

However, there are issues too with only going external. The primary issue may be that the external UX resource has no control over who sees the report—there is no guarantee that it will reach everyone that it should. There is also the issue that the studio would not have an internal UX resource in the studio every day, which is something that they would benefit from.

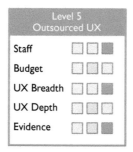

Figure 5.8 UX maturity Level 5

Table 5.7 *Signs you are at Level 5*

Signs you are at Level 5

- Do not want to, or does not make sense to, build an internal UX team. UX staff are expensive, lab space would may be not fully used, yet you would paying for it. Buy when needed.
- Want to get access to current UX knowledge across the whole games industry—genres, platforms, business models.
- Want an outside perspective. Does not have to please anyone, say it like it is.

5.6.6.1 WHAT TO DO NEXT

In order to improve your UX maturity level, address the following:

- Is the outsourced UX model working for you? Are there any downsides you want to address?
- Ask the team if an internal UX team would help them better in any way.

5.6.6.2 WHEN ARE YOU READY TO MOVE ON?

You will be ready to move to the next UX maturity level when:

- You have the go-ahead to invest significant resources (time and money) to build a strong in-house UX team.
- Decide whether the outsourced UX model could support internal Games User Research processes and approaches.

5.6.7 Level 6—life cycle UX

At this level, studios are heavily invested in UX research (Figure 5.9, Table 5.8). They have built-up a credible internal UX research team who have access to purpose-built playtesting labs, and the range of UX research being

Figure 5.9 UX maturity Level 6

Table 5.8 *Signs you are at Level 6*

Signs you are at Level 6
• You have heavily invested in UX (budget, effort).
• Dedicated staff, labs, player recruitment.
• Wide reach of UX services; span the life cycle.
• Games that emerge are getting average or good reviews, but not consistently good.
• Too many usability/player experience issues are making it into the final game.

conducted spans the entire development cycle. Studios at this level may also still be outsourcing UX research, perhaps so that players from other regions of the world can be used (cultural issues), or additional methodologies can be employed which cannot be done internally. As a result, the games produced by the studio are usually of high quality; however, they may not be so consistently.

It is difficult to speculate as to why the games are not consistently good given that such studios have access to UX researchers who are testing the game design assumptions and usability/player experience regularly throughout development. However, some possible reasons might include:

- Given that the UX research team is likely quite large, the quality of some researchers may not be as strong as others (as in any job role). Some people in this role should perhaps not be here. Is the UX research team made up of A players and B players?
- The reports are not being read by people who can take action.
- The feedback is happening too late; there is a problem with the UX research process.
- Resistance. The person who is in charge of making the change does not want to do it. Why? Do they not trust the research findings? Find out why.

Essentially, too many usability/player experience issues are making it into the final game. Is this because the UX research team are not finding them (weak team members), they are not being communicated (flow of information), or no changes are being made (resistance/trust)?

5.6.7.1 WHAT TO DO NEXT

In order to improve your UX maturity level, address the following:

- Are issues impacting player experience still getting through into release? Read a broad range of reviews from your last game (professional and from players). Do they mention any usability/player experience issues? Why could this be happening?
- Are all UX researchers of the right quality? Is this an issue?
- Are the UX reports being read by the necessary people? All the team?

5.6.7.2 WHEN ARE YOU READY TO MOVE ON?

You will be ready to move to the next UX maturity level when:

- You understand why all the team and management are not reading the report. Why are they not engaged in learning about how their game is progressing from a player perspective?
- UX research reports are mainly concerned with design and the player experience. But the UX of your game is related to your business success. Ensure management understand this point.

5.6.8 Level 7—organizational UX

At the top UX maturity level, the whole studio, from the C-level board downwards, is invested and interested in UX (Figure 5.10, Table 5.9). This means everyone is actively reading the latest playtest reports, and top findings from the UX research reports are presented in company meetings, supported by video highlights of these issues in action. Everyone knows the current state of the game from the players' perspective, and the team are actively working on those issues which are impacting most on the player experience. Findings from the UX research department are integrated with findings from the business intelligence and market research teams, and there is a very good understanding of both the game and players throughout the studio.

You are a 'players first' studio. By this I mean that when decisions are made in the studio the first question asked is 'Is this better for the player?', rather than a question about budget, logistics, etc. The player is put first and foremost when making any decision relating to the player experience.

Figure 5.10 UX maturity Level 7

Table 5.9 *Signs you are at Level 7*

Signs you are at Level 7

- You have heavily invested in UX, and can see the return on investment.
- Dedicated staff, labs, player recruitment.
- Wide reach of UX services; span the life cycle.
- The UX reports reach the full depth of the studio—C-level down to all those who implement the findings.
- Integration with analytics, BI, market research.
- Games that emerge get good reviews, consistently.
- You are a 'players first' studio.

5.6.8.1 WHAT TO DO NEXT

You are at the top UX maturity level; however, there is still room for improvement. Address the following:

- Improve your processes. Where are the opportunities to refine what you are doing?
- Add UX services where new opportunities exist. Platforms, genres, and business models change all the time—look for new ways to assess the player experience.
- Apply learnings across other games/platforms. If you are making a console game, are there lessons from mobile games that could help you (and vice versa)?

5.6.8.2 HOW CAN YOU KEEP IMPROVING?

To stay at the top level of UX maturity, you need to keep doing what you are doing, but also learn from mistakes made:

- Analyse all reviews of your game post-release. If issues exist, how did they slip through your process? What needs to change to prevent them happening next time?

5.7 Conclusion

These eight levels of UX maturity are based on real interactions with a wide variety of studios worldwide, but you should treat them as a guide. Your studio may not fit exactly into one level completely. It is possible you have traits across several, so for such cases you should consider your studio to be in the lowest level where you can identify signs of your own studio's behaviour.

The aim here has been to show the UX research qualities of the studios that are making the best games, and can consistently do so. UX research is not a guarantee of making a great game, but having a rigorous UX process in place across the game development life cycle should be providing the team with timely feedback leading to the systematic identification and resolution of negative usability and player experience issues. At the higher UX maturity levels, research should be starting even before game design begins, understanding and bringing in successful UX patterns and practices from other games to ensure your game's UX is starting on solid foundations.

All of this does come at a cost, but the studios at the top do not talk about cost—they talk about value. Is the investment in improving their game's usability and player experience worth it? Their answer is a clear 'yes'. These companies have assessed the ROI of UX from both a business and game quality perspective, and continue to invest heavily in putting the players first. Happy players are good for business.

5.8 Takeaways

This chapter introduced and explained UX maturity levels which aim to help with the following:

- Developers and games user researchers can assess their level of UX maturity based on current behaviours within the studio.
- A road map is provided showing how to improve UX maturity. Each level is broken into key variables showing which areas need improving.

CHAPTER 6

Designing a Games User Research lab from scratch

SEBASTIAN LONG, *Player Research*

Highlights

Towards informing the development of new playtesting labs, this chapter outlines the process we used at Games User Research studio Player Research for setting up our labs. Setting up a functional lab environment requires a range of considerations—across floor plans, materials selection, technology choices, testing strategies and more—and in this chapter we describe some of the key lessons we learned along the way.

6.1 Introduction

Following a year of planning and installation, Player Research—a playtesting and user research studio based in Brighton, UK—completed work on their bespoke playtesting lab in May 2015. The new research space comprises of a 12-player concurrent playtest lab and a single-player/family testing room, both with private observation suites for the Games User Researchers and attending developers to remotely observe play. The lab is designed for video game playtesting on all formats and genres, including PC, console, smartphone, tablet, VR, and both massively multiplayer and single-player games. The completion of the lab in 2015 included months of research and development into audiovisual solutions, as well as designing the physical layout of the 2000-sq.-ft open-plan space. With a view to informing the development of future playtesting labs, this

Games User Research, Anders Drachen, Pejman Mirza-Babaei, Lennart E. Nacke (Eds).
© Oxford University Press 2018. Published 2018 by Oxford University Press

chapter outlines our process, the lessons we learned in designing the lab floor plan and selecting materials, the reasoning behind our technology choices, and more.

6.2 Starting from scratch

At the time the work on the current lab set-up began, Player Research had been running small- and medium-scale playtesting for a number of years, typically inviting between 1–4 concurrent players to their research labs, totalling 6–24 players per study—suitable numbers for game usability and understandability research. Game development teams, however, were at the time beginning to bring to us questions that necessitated greater player numbers to address their inherent subjectivity, or to offer broader research that could cover entire narrative trees or full-game playthroughs. As such, the need for a larger and more configurable research space was clear, and Player Research began the hunt for a new office space that would eventually result in our current labs.

There were a large number of criteria entertained when considering office space. Among basic legal and financial concerns (price, lease length, etc.) building a playtest lab required a building that

- offered a city-centre location with ease of public transport access
- was not a ground floor office for security purposes
- was wheelchair-accessible, step-free from the street
- offered high-speed Internet connectivity for playtest streaming
- had sufficiently professional but not grandiose appearance
- was eligible for complete internal refit of partition walls and soundproofing

After more than a year of property hunting, Player Research successfully leased Claremont House, a 2000-sq.-ft office in Brighton, UK.

6.3 Divide and conquer

After finalizing the property lease, our first challenge was the division of the new open-plan office space and layout design with walls, making the internal rooms. The process of designing and developing the space began with an open discussion: 'What research facilities do we need to best answer game developers' questions?'

Consideration was needed towards rooms required and the room arrangements that would best serve both developers' needs and our own, while also respecting the constraints of the premises at Claremont House. Every member of the research team was provided with a digital scale model of the floor plan which included a range of to-scale furniture and a series of requirements, such as the inclusion of certain room types (given below), as well as guesses towards the number of developers and researchers that should be accommodated in each room (Figure 6.1). Our design process might be considered as 'design by attrition': individually designing many alternative layouts and solutions for the space, then putting them into competition with one another to reason out the most effective floor plan proposal as a group.

The team was charged with designing floor layouts for the research space, with the inclusion of these seven rooms:

- single-player playroom and observation room (SPPR, SPObs)
- multiplayer playroom and observation room (MPPR, MPObs)
- waiting room
- storage room
- office
- any other rooms deemed valuable enough, given the space constraints

As well as existing features informing the layout (such as the location of the existing front door and access points for telephony and air conditioning), we endeavoured to learn as much about the quirks of the building as possible. One of the most insightful experiments was to spend an afternoon in the empty office; it quickly became clear that one side of the office had much higher ambient noise levels than the other. Despite having roads on three sides, the road to the west (at the bottom of

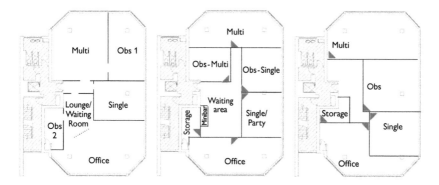

Figure 6.1 Three alternative floor plans of more than 50 generated by the team, shown without furniture. Only the hashed area and outer walls (glazed on three sides) had immovable walls

the floor plans in Figure 6.1) was significantly busier during the day, which we factored into our design by eventually allocating the western corner to the multiplayer playroom, within which players would be wearing headphones much of the time, oblivious to any road noise. We also learned a little about how warm the rooms were likely to get across the course of the day, which later influenced a rethink of the air conditioning vent layout and investment in specific types of blinds.

With the team members each generating templated designs, we totalled more than 50 alternatives, which the whole team compared and whittled down to a shortlist and an eventual single hybrid design. Final tweaks to this design were made by marking out the floor plan using wooden battens, allowing us to nudge walls and corridors a few inches in order to better accommodate the existing light fittings and immovable features.

This templating and comparison process not only bettered our final design (see Figure 6.2), but was also an effective team-building exercise, leaving each staff member proud of the space we had researched, designed, and reasoned out together.

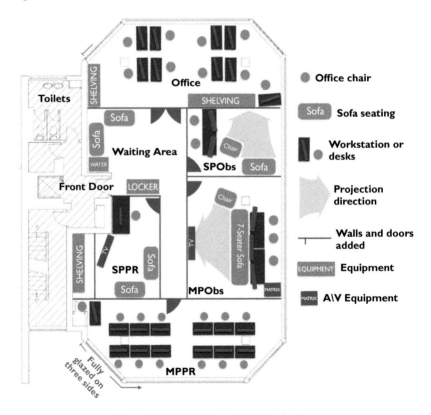

Figure 6.2 The final layout including furniture

6.4 Two playrooms, two designs

The two playrooms were designed with differing needs and research questions in mind. The single-player playroom (SPPR) needed to accommodate 1–6 players in a social and dynamic setting for many different game formats. The multi-player playroom (MPPR) needed only to facilitate seated experiences, but was optimized to accommodate as many players as was practical from both a space and AV technology perspective.

6.4.1 Single-player playroom

Our single-player playroom is designed for players to play in one of a number of different formats, including usability playtesting with a single participant (our most common format) on smartphone, tablet, or PC; focus groups (~5 players being interviewed by a single researcher); 'couch co-op' playtesting (~4 players facing a single television); room-scale VR; dancing; music games with peripherals; future technologies that require whole-body control or locomotion; and so on—a significant design challenge.

The room was deliberately designed, laid out, and decorated to resemble a typical family lounge, absent excessive branding or posters (Figure 6.3). It includes two sofas in an L shape, allowing 4–6 players to be equidistant from the central TV or a researcher, depending on the research needs. A separate area with a gaming PC allows for a desk-format playtesting, with the PC dual-purposed as

Figure 6.3 Photo of the SPPR

a compositing and capture device for camera, device video, and audio feeds. To remain dynamic for alternative research formats, all the furniture can be removed from the room as required, including both sofas. A woollen rug prevents wear to the carpet, and also lessens echo when capturing sound during a playtest.

Having dynamic observation camera positions is perhaps the defining and most important feature of a SPPR. This can be achieved with a roaming camera ('pan tilt zoom'; PTZ), and/or by the use of small, movable static cameras. Player Research opt for the small movable camera approach, utilizing two cameras at once in some combination of the three most common views: over-the-shoulder (seeing hand placement on a touchscreen), face camera (used during interviews, for some indication of expression, and for security purposes), and room capture (allowing the player to move around, or to capture multiple players). Having the ability to fully and freely place cameras around the room has been paramount for projects including guitar game projects (pointing the camera at the guitar body and guitar neck), augmented reality projects (requiring a camera pointed at the floor), and on many other occasions. Consider this when designing your cable layouts and camera mounting points in your SPPR, as a rigid and inflexible design could restrict your ability to capture and observe absolutely vital video data. Microphones ought to be similarly dynamic, although a single high-quality cardioid condenser boundary microphone can capture room audio from almost any position in the room.

6.4.1.1 OBSERVING SINGLE-PLAYER SESSIONS

For capturing and compositing the various media streams—including the two cameras, device video, device sound, room sound, and button input—Player Research employ an open source compositing software called Open Broadcaster Software (OBS), using HDMI, USB, and HDSDI capture cards to transfer video, and XLR cables to transfer audio. In the single-player observation room (SPObs), the composited video signal (Figure 6.4) is projected onto a white wall to a screen size of ~65 inches for observation by the attending development team.

In our previous labs, the developers and researchers shared a single viewing format: the high-definition projection. To better serve the researchers, the researchers' view was shifted to dedicated 24-inch HD monitors in the new premises, which aided in seeing the rich detail in PC-format games (Figure 6.5). The quirks and specifics of individual game genres should be taken into account if the prospective lab is likely to have a specific genre or platform research focus; for example, a team making a PC-based multiplayer online battle arena could consider having an observer screen completely dedicated to a minimap or scoreboard.

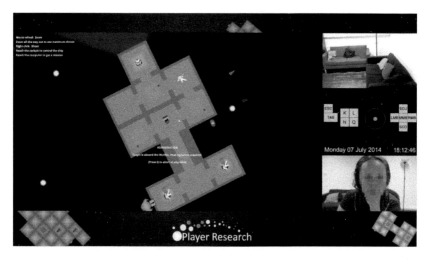

Figure 6.4 A composited image from the SPPR showing gameplay, mouse and keyboard inputs, face camera (blurred here), time and date, and the interview space. Screenshot from Heat Signature, a game from developer Tom Francis, www.heatsig.com

Figure 6.5 The SPObs with two 24-inch monitors and a large projection, all of which show the composited image from the SPPR (Figure 6.4)

6.4.2 Multiplayer playrooms

For several years Player Research were served well by a SPPR and combination observation/office space. To facilitate answering research questions that required larger-scale research with greater participant numbers, a second playroom was included in the Claremont House lab design. The multiplayer playroom (MPPR) provides private individual booths for 12 players to playtest games concurrently, equipped with testing equipment for PC, mobile, and console games. The individual booths have a technical set-up very similar to the SPPR, duplicated 12 times, once for each booth.

The fundamental layout of this room began by defining the size of the single basic unit: the desk and chair at which an individual player would play. We appreciated the range of sizes of IKEA's relatively inexpensive table tops, which afforded us a wide variety of options. From this basic unit of a single booth we could structure the room using the same template tool that we had employed during the design of the internal walls (Figure 6.2). Our approaches were grouped into two differing design philosophies: lining the outer walls with booths, or having a cluster of booths in the centre (Figure 6.6). Among several pros and cons, the former allows a moderator to have a more effective view of the screens of multiple players when walking around the room, while the latter

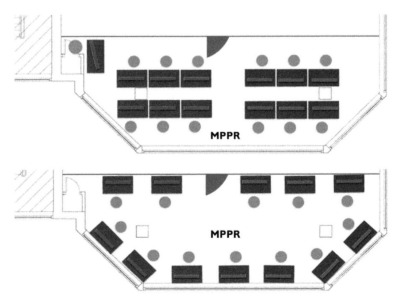

Figure 6.6 The two alternative arrangements for desks in the MPPR: clusters or lining the walls

affords easier cabling and better prevents players seeing other players' screens. The two clusters of desks was the eventual layout we opted for, along with a moderation desk (as shown in Figure 6.6).

When laying out a MPPR, consider the size and shape of your walkways, ensuring that the smallest walkway allows enough room for wheelchairs to enter, turn, and exit. If opting for a cluster arrangement in the centre of the room, invest in high-quality cable tread to protect fragile AV cables underfoot.

To allow remote observation of gameplay, the gaming PCs on each desk generate a real-time composite of footage. The PC captures an HDMI signal, which is the output format for all current- and previous-generation consoles as well as both Android and iOS devices. For PC games, the composite is altered to show a duplicate of the PC screen itself. Gameplay is composited using OBS on the gaming PC, along with a USB face camera for each player, as well as a readout of the time, date, and player number, for a total of 12 composited video signals (one from each booth) at 1080-pixel resolution and 60-Hz refresh rate as an HDMI output of the gaming PC (similar to Figure 6.4, with the addition of a player number graphic).

6.4.2.1 MOVING AWAY FROM HDMI

Using the HDMI cable format presents a number of issues for playtest lab design:

- HDMI suffers from signal distortion beyond 30 m length (30 m 'run-length').
- The behind-the-scenes communication between devices ('handshaking') can cause reliability issues.
- Duplicating or splitting signals from one source to multiple destinations in HDMI format, which is often a requirement in a playtest lab, is technically complicated, unreliable, and can be expensive.

These limitations in combination suggested that moving away from HDMI as the fundamental transmission standard for the lab. The alternative cable formats were limited to serial digital interface (SDI; a well-established transmission format used for television broadcast and cameras), fibre optic (a new and expensive format at the time of research), and IPTV, or video over ethernet (inexpensive cabling but proprietary and expensive equipment). SDI was chosen for its reliability and sheer range of compatible and standardized equipment.

To convert the composited output of the gaming PC to SDI, a conversion device was used at each individual booth. There is a large range of these devices available at differing price points and with differing feature sets, including frame-rate conversion and duplicate inputs/outputs. SDI can also carry multiple audio signals, either embedded in the HDMI, or as separate audio inputs on some converter models. Individual research labs' needs will vary.

The SDI video signals are brought together in a bundle of HDSDI cables and routed through to the multiplayer observation room (MPObs) into a 'matrix' routing device which can duplicate and route signals using electronic switching.

6.4.2.2 A MULTIPLAYER OBSERVATION CHALLENGE

The observation room that accompanies the 12-player MPObs presented a far more significant technical and logistical challenge than any other aspect of the playtest lab development. This was a result of our desire to rethink and re-examine the traditional multiplayer observation format, as well as accommodate a wide range of game genres. Our eventual design was the result of reviewing our own experiences, critiquing the design of other multiplayer playtest labs, and discussing with other Games User Researchers and developers.

As identified in the design of the single-player observation room, researchers and developers have subtle but differing needs in observing players at play. In order to facilitate behavioural observation in the MPObs (using sampling methods or observing a subset of players at once), researchers must be able to read text and see small UI elements in detail, thereby requiring an HD resolution (1920 × 1080 pixels). It is also important that researchers quickly gain an overview of all players at once, perhaps to ensure no game has crashed (often a black screen or error message) or to see if players had completed a survey (demarcated with a red stop sign in our survey designs).

To provide the HD view, 12 high-definition HDMI monitors were mounted on adjustable mounting arms at a desk large enough to seat a maximum of four researchers. While SDI monitors are available, they were prohibitively expensive, such that buying significantly less expensive HDMI monitors and the SDI-to-HDMI conversion equipment was the obvious course of action. The addition of HDMI convertors in the observation room to convert signals to displays has introduced some delay when switching between sources, caused by the HDMI handshaking process, and also some issues with frame-rate incompatibility. Ideally, budget permitting, the observation room would have been completely SDI-based, without conversion back to HDMI.

Game developers are often present for playtests but, unlike the researchers, would not undertake structured observation of players during play, instead preferring to split their attention between them. We provided a long row of

Figure 6.7 The bank of 12 monitors and developer seating. The overview projection is beamed onto the wall behind the camera in this image

comfortable seating facing a large projection of all 12 players' video feeds to accommodate this, which also facilitates the same overview to the researchers, who can see past their individual player screens to the overview projection on the wall in front (Figure 6.7).

Developers' familiarity with the game structure often allows them to quickly identify individual players exhibiting behaviour that does not meet their intent, and also to quickly identify areas or menus of the game that are of particular interest for the research study. To allow developers to focus on an individual 'player of interest', we also situated a 48-inch television under the projection image, along with a digital controller that allows developers to choose a single player from the 12 above to view in high definition and at a larger size. This process can facilitate useful discussion between the developers as they choose a shared focal player, allowing discussion of his or her behaviour in the game. Developers' feedback on this set-up has been extremely positive, particularly concerning their feeling of autonomy and control, as well as the value of the conversations that the developer overview and singular focal player encourages.

Neither of Player Research's observation rooms contain a one-way mirror. There are a great number of pros and cons towards the use of one-way mirrors, chief among them being the cost and the drawbacks for the comfort of observers in the observation rooms. One-way mirrors require that the observation rooms are kept dark and quiet, which impacts the viewing experience of the researchers and developers in many ways. One-way mirrors are also expensive to install, so the choice was made to utilize inexpensive digital CCTV cameras integrated into the existing observation technology, allowing developers to switch the 'focus TV' to a room camera if they desire.

6.5 Support rooms and office space

The playrooms and observation suites are the heart of the Games User Research lab, but there are many other supporting areas and facilities that need to be considered and designed. These include the waiting area for players, storage and device charging facilities, and the toilets.

6.5.1 Waiting area

Offering a comfortable place for players to wait at the beginning and end of the sessions is extremely helpful. The waiting area (Figure 6.2) contains two large sofas, seating six, as well as stacking chairs to seat a further 10 people. This maximum of 16 is sufficient (given the 12 seats in the multiplayer area), except in cases where children under 16 attend the labs accompanied by parents, which unfortunately necessitates uncomfortable standing. Our office design does suffer from having only one entrance, situated in the waiting room. This entrance is used by players and attending developers, and therefore presents a slight inconvenience at busy times. Developers are given strict attendance times to minimize developers' and players' arriving at the same time.

Player Research's entire research lab is deliberately devoid of branding or video game art. One of the challenges faced by studios building in-house playtesting areas is the often ostentatious and heavily branded studio environment. Research that examines players' emotions and requires honest and frank feedback does not benefit from players that are overawed by their surroundings. This is particularly important for the waiting room, in which players are forming their first impressions.

The waiting area also features lockers for players' personal items during the playtest; the use of lockers with transparent doors allows researchers to quickly see if items have been left behind (Figure 6.8). The locker keys are fitted with wristbands for convenience of the players. A water fountain provides self-serve drinks for players, which lightens the workload of the research staff.

6.5.2 Storage and device charging

Our storage needs for the office were underestimated by about one third, specifically due to large items like computer cases and spare computer peripherals. For mobile device testing, it is important that devices can be kept charged before the test, without compromising their security. As such, when considering

Figure 6.8 Numbered lockers with see-through panels make for great temporary storage that researchers can quickly scan for items left behind

a location for your storage area, try to identify somewhere with sufficient power cabling to allow charging of devices. Paying players in multiplayer tests also requires a large amount of cash (or a cash equivalent), so consider the location and type of security safe you will require, and how it might be bolted to an immovable object.

When considering your SPPR, remember that furniture may need to be completely removed from the room to open the space. This furniture will need to be stored while the tests are in progress, so ensuring there is space allocated for temporary storage is also a consideration.

6.5.3 Temperature and sound management

The transmission of sound and heat through the research lab are closely linked. Both require specific materials to be used when building the lab structure, and also require additional investment.

Sound transmission is a significant challenge for studios wanting to section off a part of their studio for guerilla playtesting. The issue is exacerbated when relying on think-aloud protocols (where players are asked to speak their mind while playing, see Chapter 12 for more details), and moderated playtesting (with a moderator present in the playroom at all times asking questions). Both of these formats—commonly used in guerilla-style playtesting rely on a quiet environment. Preventing the transmission of sound in Claremont House began with the design of the layout, ensuring that as few single-thickness walls as possible separated researcher and player spaces; corridors were used instead. We utilized double-thick interior walls using specific sound-deadening foam in internal walls. To protect against sound through the suspended ceiling, we invested in sound-deadening pads which lay on top of individual ceiling tiles.

Temperature is also a key factor, especially in the waiting room area where players gather between sessions, so air conditioning is essential. Other factors to consider include offering self-service chilled drinks for players, situating the multiplayer rooms in the coolest areas of the building, and researching materials such as heat- and glare-reflective film for windows.

6.5.4 Security arrangements

In addition to the device and cash security already discussed, there are factors of intellectual security to consider as part of the lab design. Consideration for the position of security cameras should be factored into the initial lab design, particularly if the space has no suspended ceiling for CCTV cabling to be discreetly and securely run. Most CCTV systems also require a secure recording device which is recommended to be separate from storage of equipment. The replacement of locks with key card–based access; the inclusion of PIR sensors for intrusion detection (perhaps as part of a larger security system); as well as metal detectors, personnel barriers, and manned reception desks should also be factored in, depending on your needs. These security procedures will need to be scaled according to the size of building and the significance of the research projects; the list provided here is certainly not exhaustive.

The design and arrangement of internal doors is a factor that was underthought in our lab design. Avoiding direct line of sight between doors prevents lab visitors from seeing confidential data. Internal doors should also be hung counter to the standard opening direction, thereby *blocking* the view of as much of the room as possible to prevent persons from seeing into rooms when moving between them. Consider also that some doors may legally require windows for fire safety, and that this could compromise security in some arrangements, so local code should be consulted. The use of blackout curtains over doorways and the addition of extra doorways can help with intellectual security and also with soundproofing.

Consider the players' journey right from the front door to the waiting room, and then from playroom to the toilets. This is particularly important for studios retrofitting playtesting areas into existing spaces. Will players need to be escorted, and if so, whose responsibility that will be? Which meeting rooms will the players pass, and how will developers know to hide confidential information on playtest days? Role-play the part of the thief: what could be easily stolen on a walk around the research lab? Do players pass the area designated for postal deliveries? Award cabinets? Game collections? At what points are players not covered by security cameras? Installing door auto-closers can help prevent unauthorized passage between rooms and restricting passage to designated areas.

One must not forget that the playtester's own property security should be considered too; we have had players arrive with suitcases, skateboards, bicycle wheels, and even children (!). Where can their property be cared for securely throughout the playtest?

Cross-site security is also a risk, and research labs particularly benefit from not being overlooked and from not being situated on the ground floor. The aforementioned anti-glare film can prevent windows from becoming a security risk, as well as simply facing observation and gameplay monitors away from windows with overlooking buildings or passers-by.

6.6 Summary

Player Research's lab design process was an incredible experience. Our choice to design the lab completely in-house has led to a much greater understanding of the capabilities of the space, allowing us to run more dynamic research and to better understand the capabilities and future-proofing of the space. Our innovation in the format of multiplayer observation has led to a unique observation experience not only for the researchers, but also for the attending game developers. While there are still bugs to iron out and mistakes to correct—you are never done designing a user testing lab—the lab development project was ultimately a great success.

Takeaways

- This chapter outlines the design, development, and decision making that led to the development of Player Research's third and largest playtest lab. Designed in-house from the ground up by the author, this chapter outlines the many choices, mistakes, and successes encountered during the playtest lab development process.
- This included a complete re-thinking of the traditional gameplay observation format, ultimately eschewing one-way mirrors, single-format observation for observers and developers, and many other traditional features and format choices, all towards the advancement of the playtest observation experience, and a more comfortable experience for visiting playtesters.

Acknowledgements

The author wishes to thank Player Research staff including Director Graham McAllister; office fit-out contractors, Rocket Projects; Dr Ben Lewis-Evans; the numerous suppliers and advisers to the technical design; and the US #GamesUR Conference Committee for inviting the presentation that inspired this chapter.

Further reading

Goodman, E., Kuniavsky, M., Moed, A. (2012). Observing the user experience: a practitioner's guide to user research (2nd ed.). Burlington, MA: Morgan Kaufmann Publishers.

http://www.gamesuserresearchsig.org: the website of the Games User Research Special Interest Group. On the website you can find a variety of resources, including a panel on lab design in the videos section.

PART II

Methods: Testing Things you Play

CHAPTER 7

An Overview of GUR Methods

MICHAEL C. MEDLOCK, *Oculus Rift*

Highlights

This chapter provides bite-sized summaries of the most common methods of the Games User Research (GUR) field. It then focuses on the questions to be considered when constructing and combining GUR methods. It concludes with a discussion of what methods best address what questions.

7.1 Introduction

A skill that a Games User Researcher should have is the ability to design high-quality methods and measures to answer questions about human behaviour and attitudes with games. Games User Researchers should have a thorough understanding of the limits of different methods and measures as well. Another skill should be guiding teams to focus on the most appropriate questions—because while all questions are interesting, not all are equally useful to making a game better.

Picking or devising a method to answer questions is just like a sport or any skill-based endeavour. You get better at it the more you do it. So the more you try, the better you get (just like playing games). Engaging in method selection is

Games User Research, Anders Drachen, Pejman Mirza-Babaei, Lennart E. Nacke (Eds).
© Oxford University Press 2018. Published 2018 by Oxford University Press

as much driven by practice as it is by theory. This introduction to GUR methods will focus on both the theory and practice that come up most commonly for Games User Researchers.

Many excellent overviews have been written about research methods and measures. They tend to fall into two organizing principles:

1. Cookbook approaches. Each method is listed with its pros and cons. This approach is excellent for giving an overview. It gives a holistic look at methods. However, in practice things tend to be messy. Rarely does a method fit as described. In the real world, researchers often have to tailor research methods to the situation; for example, see Shadish et al. (2002).

2. Structural approaches. The atomic elements of methods are listed and users are encouraged to construct methods from them. In this approach there are no set 'named' methods; there are parts that can be recombined to form any number of methods. This approach is excellent for the more seasoned researcher. It also more closely models the real world. However, it is difficult to use as a starting point. It is hard to holistically grasp for those newer to the research discipline; for example, see Boruch (1975).

This overview will mostly focus on a cookbook approach and end with a sprinkling of 'structuralist'-style advice with a focus on types of study questions that Games User Researchers often get.

7.2 The GUR method cookbook

Figure 7.1 shows the most common GUR methods and how they align to five different questions. (1) Does the method apply to behaviours or attitudes? (2) Which phase of the game life cycle is the method best used in? (3) Is the method quantitative or qualitative? (4) What is the 'uber' question the method answers? (5) How long does it take to implement the method?

Table 7.1 lists all the methods in the figure with a brief definition, pros, and cons.

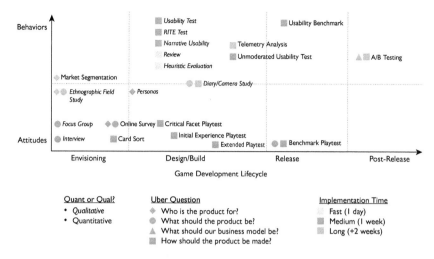

Figure 7.1 Visualization of GUR methods

Table 7.1 *GUR Methods*

Method	Description	Pros	Cons
A/B Testing	A controlled experiment in which two or more alternatives for a design are randomly assigned to users of the product 'in the wild'. Then the behaviour of interest is measured via telemetry to see which design performed better.	Definitive answers to usage questions around the designs in question. Quantifies the impact of a design compared to another design. One of the few true experiments.	Difficult and expensive to set up. All alternatives have to be designed, coded and working. Does not tell the researcher why the winning design 'won'.
Benchmark Playtest	A standardized attitudinal test run with a larger sample size (e.g., 35+ participants). Used to compare against other standardized attitudinal tests run in the exact same way on other products.	Standardized way to compare how much things are liked or disliked. Allows for meaningful comparisons if a game or game facet is 'liked' or 'disliked'. It gives meaning to measures taken in the future.	Since it is self-report data it does not accurately tell the researcher why participants felt the way they did. Also, since the benchmark happens at the end of development, it does not help the game it is used for. Instead it helps other games that come after the benchmark as a reference point.

continued

Table 7.1 *Continued*

Method	Description	Pros	Cons
Card Sort	A group of participants organize topics into categories that make sense to them and label these groups. Alternatively a group of participants place topics into groups that have already been created for them to see if the groupings make sense to them, or if there is similarity between individuals in understanding of the groups.	Gives insight into how users think about how the information in a space relates to each other. Gives an excellent starting point for organizing menus or other hierarchical structures.	Does not give definitive answers to questions of grouping or hierarchy. Often final navigational behaviour is different from what users claim their navigational behaviour will be. Is a starting point, but does not completely finalize decisions around information architecture.
Critical Facet Playtest	A survey technique which assesses attitudes and perceptions about very specific core experiences (e.g., the aiming model in vertical levels, the camera for 3D platformers, the steering control in turns for a racing game).	Gives quantified insight into user's attitudes about specific core game experiences.	Does not indicate if these core experiences are ultimately important to the overall enjoyment of the game. Since it is self-report data, it does not accurately tell the researcher why participants felt the way they did.
Diary/Camera Study	A qualitative technique in which participants are provided with the materials and structure to record daily events, tasks and perceptions around a game in order to gain insight into their behaviour and needs over time.	A relatively cheap qualitative way to track some behaviours and attitudes over time.	Not good for quantification. Can have some loss due to reliance on participants to consistently fill out the diary and take pictures.
Ethnographic Field Study	A holistic qualitative observational study of users in the context of their actual environment over a period of time.	Deep qualitative observational insight into user behaviour. Gives a good idea of why the participants do what they do.	Does not allow for quantification and generalization of the behaviours and attitudes to others.
Extended Playtest	A survey technique which assesses the attitudes and perceptions users have of a game in development over an extended period of time. Often run across 2 days and 16 hours of testing.	Gives quantified insight into user's attitudes about the game experience over time. Can be especially good at highlighting differences between 'levels' of the game.	Since it is self-report data it does not accurately tell the researcher why participants felt the way they did.

continued

Table 7.1 *Continued*

Method	Description	Pros	Cons
Focus Group	A qualitative research technique in which a group of people are asked about their perceptions, opinions, beliefs, and attitudes about a game or game experience. Questions are asked in an interactive group setting where participants are free to talk with other group members.	Good for generating new ideas and getting participants to generate ideas by interacting with one another.	Poor at getting accurate behavioural or attitudinal data on how users either use or feel about games (since their interaction with other participants influences their answers).
Heuristic Evaluation	One or more evaluators examine a game or prototype and judge its compliance with recognized game usability principles (the 'heuristics').	Fast to implement. Can catch known problematic issues quickly. Often a good starting point.	Does not give actual behavioural or attitudinal data from participants. Will not catch all the important issues. Often only as good as the reviewer or the heuristics.
Interview	A 1:1 technique in which an interviewer asks participants questions about their perceptions, opinions, beliefs, and attitudes about a game or game experience.	Good at understanding what each individual believes about their game experience. Can help augment the understanding of why users do what they do.	Poor at getting accurate behavioural data on how users use a game. Does not quantify a user's attitudes about a game experience.
Initial Experience Playtest	A survey technique which assesses the attitudes and perceptions users have of a game in development over the first 2 hours of use.	Gives quantified insight into user's attitudes about the initial game experience.	Since it is self-report data it does not accurately tell the researcher why participants felt the way they did.
Market Segmentation	A survey technique usually combined with cluster analysis used to divide the market for a product into groups of customers with identifiable needs and characteristics.	Can be good for quantifying how portions of a market self-report as feeling or behaving. A good starting point combined with ethnographic work for understanding users.	If the questions used are poor, or not focused on the correct things then the needs and characteristics that segments are divided into can be meaningless or misleading. Relies on self-report, so can be incorrect about actual behaviour (especially purchasing behaviour).

continued

Table 7.1 *Continued*

Method	Description	Pros	Cons
Narrative Usability	A 1:1 observational technique in which participants attempt to understand the narrative, from beginning to end, with a prototype of the narrative before it is implemented in the game.	It can help identify areas of confusion, misaligned expectations, genre interactions, and gaps in logic allowing the designer to either correct or embrace these beliefs. It does so early in development before changes are costly.	It does not tell the researcher if the users will "like" the narrative. Or otherwise provide meaningful data on how the user feels about the narrative.
Online Survey	A flexible survey technique which allows researchers to assess the attitudes and perceptions users have on a wide variety of topics. Can be qualitative or quantitative.	Can give quantified insight into user's attitudes about many things. Very flexible.	Since it is self-report data it does not accurately tell the researcher why participants felt the way they did. Also the stimulus is rarely controlled.
Personas	Fictional characters created to represent the different user types that might use a game in a similar way.	Gives a team someone concrete to focus on when making a product. Can build team empathy for users and help with some fast decision making.	Can become over generalized or overused when the underlying data for the persona do not support the decisions being made based on it.
Review	One or more evaluators examine a game or prototype and judge if there will be issues based on their experience watching other users use similar games.	Fast to implement. Can catch known problematic issues quickly. Often a good starting point.	Does not give actual behavioural or attitudinal data from participants. Will not catch all the important issues. Only as good as the reviewer used.
RITE Test	A 1:1 observational technique in which participants attempt to perform a variety of tasks with a prototype or game in development, while observers note what each user does and says. Performance data are recorded. After each participant the game or prototype may be changed to see if the change solves the issue previously observed.	Good at identifying issues that keep users from playing a game well. Good at getting insight into why users are not able to accomplish tasks or meet the usability goals of a game. Good at seeing if a change actually solves an issue previously observed. Excellent at getting teams in a 'fix' mentality.	Requires more buy-in from team to set up. Poor at understanding or quantifying attitudes. For example, if the game or game facet is 'liked' or 'disliked'.

continued

Table 7.1 *Continued*

Method	Description	Pros	Cons
Telemetry Analysis	Automatic collection of behavioural data from users of the product. This can be on any behaviour that the system can 'count' (e.g., deaths, collisions, levels completed, time taken to do thing).	Excellent at quantifying behavioural data. When done well gives an unparalleled assessment of 'what' the participant did.	Takes a long time to set up. If the wrong kind of data is collected it can be unhelpful. Can be very hard to analyse. Does not tell the researcher why the user engaged in the behaviour.
Unmoderated Usability Test	A 1:1 observational technique in which participants attempt to perform a variety of tasks with a prototype or game in development while an automated system notes what each user does and says and performance data are recorded.	Good at identifying issues that keep users from playing a game well. Good at running something fast, at scale.	Poor at understanding or quantifying attitudes. For example, if the game or game facet is 'liked' or 'disliked'. Also because the sessions are unmoderated it is hard/impossible to follow up with questions to understand why participants did what they did in the moment.
Usability Benchmark	A standardized 1:1 observational test run with a larger sample size (e.g., 20+ participants). Focused on tasks and task completion. Used to compare against other standardized observational tests run in the exact same way.	Standardized way to compare how users perform with products. Allows for meaningful comparisons of observable behaviour on a game or game facet. It gives meaning to behavioural measures taken in the future.	Since it is often focused on task or task completion it does not holistically quantify attitudes well. Also, since the benchmark happens at the end of development, it does not help the game it is used for. Instead it helps other games that come after it as a reference point.
Usability Test	A 1:1 observational technique in which participants attempt to perform a variety of tasks with a prototype or game in development. Observers note what each user does and says and performance data are recorded.	Good at identifying issues that keep users from playing a game well. Good at getting insight into why users are not able to accomplish tasks or meet the usability goals of a game.	Poor at understanding or quantifying attitudes. For example, if the game or game facet is 'liked' or 'disliked'.

7.3 Considerations when constructing a GUR method

In real life, all methods and measures must be adjusted to fit the purpose they will be put to. It is rare that some aspect is not changed or fitted to the purpose. What follows are the basic steps a researcher might need to follow to think through or adapt a method.

7.3.1 Consideration 1: what are the questions?

All research starts with the question to be answered and framing that question in such a way that an answer can be found. The questions that need to be answered are the primary determinant of the method and measures that the researcher will use. There is rarely just one question, and this is the first challenge because different kinds of questions often require different kinds of methods. Additionally, some methods do not combine gracefully with others because it violates their underlying assumptions. Usually this means that the researcher and the people needing the answers have to make choices; specifically, which questions are more important to answer than others. Teams have to make choices between questions due to time and resource constraints—few teams have an unlimited amount of time or resources in the games business. Of course, if you are on a well-funded team there is always the possibility of running more than one study—but that is another matter.

The most common questions that a Games User Researcher gets asked are shown in Table 7.2. While this list is not exhaustive, it is a large percentage

Table 7.2 *What are the questions?*

Uber Question	Detailed Question
Who is the product for?	• Who are the users? • Who should the users be?
What should the product be?	• What kind of experience should we build? • Why will users buy this product? • What do our users do? • What do our users wish they could do? • How do we generate new ideas that we have not come up with before?
What should our business model be?	• At what rate should we give out X? • What should X cost? • When and where should we place pay walls or payment opportunities? • Who will convert? • Who is buying what? • How is our business model doing?

continued

Table 7.2 *Continued*

Uber Question	Detailed Question
How should the product be made?	• Is X fun? • Are there any issues with X? • How much do users like X? • Is X appropriately challenging? • Is X 'good enough'? • Is X or Y better? • We have both X and Y, but which is more important? • How often does X happen? Or how often does Feature X or Thing X get used? • I expect users to do X with this thing I made. Do they? • Does X work the way users expect it to? • Does the game narrative make sense? Do users like it? • How do all these options 'group' together? • Does X belong in the same group as Y, or is it more like Z?

of what Games User Researchers have to be proficient at designing methods and measures for.

7.3.1.1 CONSIDERATION 1A: WHAT *SHOULD* THE QUESTIONS BE?

While all questions are interesting, not all are profitable. It is not uncommon for teams to focus on two kinds of questions that have little to no benefit.

1. 'Curiosity' questions. These are questions which you cannot do anything with. There is no action to take after finding out the answer to them.
2. Questions that are always a leap of faith or whose answers are dubious at best.

Practically, what this means is that skilled Games User Researchers guide teams to the questions they should be answering or that can be answered via research. They should also help teams understand which questions will likely never have satisfactory answers.

The user researcher should always be asking themselves, 'Once we get our answer, what might we do with it?' For example, the question might be: 'How often are users using the sniper rifle?' Let us say the answer is 10% of the time, or 50% or 70% of the time. Would the team change anything as a result of this answer? If the answer is 'no', why are you pursuing this question? In fact, sometimes it is good to pose potential fake answers to the team directly. Often as a result, the team will adjust to focusing on a different question, or a different version of the question that they might take action on. For example, the question instead might be, 'In matchups with other weapons, how often does the holder of the sniper rifle win?' Now if your answer ends up being 10%, 50%, or 70%, you could see a team potentially taking action on that. A sniper rifle winning 70% of the battles on a short-range map with shotguns … clearly something needs to change about the sniper rifle, the shotgun, or something else. This is an extreme example, but hopefully the point is made.

In Table 7.3, I have indicated which questions tend to be more actionable in **bold**. This does not mean that the other questions are worthless, or not ever

Table 7.3 *What* should *the questions be?*

Uber Question	Detailed Question
Who is the product for?	• **Who are the users?** • **Who should the users be?**
What should the product be?	• What kind of game should we build? • Why will users buy this game? • **What do our users do with our game?** • **What do our users wish they could do?** • How do we generate new ideas that we have not come up with before?
What should our business model be?	• **At what rate should we give out X?** • **What should X cost?** • **When and where should we place pay walls or payment opportunities?** • Who will convert? • Who is buying what? • **How is our business model doing?**
How should the product be made?	• **Are there any issues with X?** • **Is X fun?** • **How much do users like X?** • **Is X appropriately challenging?** • **Is X 'good enough'?** • **Is X or Y better?** • **We have both X and Y, but which is more important?** • How often does X happen? Or how often does Feature X or Thing X get used? • **I expect users to do X with this thing I made. Do they?** • **Does X work the way users expect it to?** • **Does the game narrative make sense? Do users like it?** • **How do all these options 'group together'? Does X belong in the same group as Y, or is it more like Z?**

actionable, just that the researcher should be wary and dig deeper for where the true value will be before agreeing or pushing for answers.

7.3.1.2 CONSIDERATION 1B: WHAT METHOD IS BEST FOR WHAT QUESTION?

The short answer to this question is, 'It depends'. However, there are some clear methods that are better than others for the questions listed. Conversely, some methods are just downright inappropriate to use. Figure 7.2 highlights which methods tend to be best for which questions. Additionally, the viewer can see which methods might also work (even if they are less powerful). The darker the highlight, the better the method for that question.

7.3.2 Consideration 2: will you need to quantify attitudes?

The moment you deal with questions regarding the quantification of attitudes, larger sample sizes become important, and therefore the time to run a study becomes a potential issue. The reason is that attitudes are rarely (if ever) interesting in isolation. To have meaning, they need a point of comparison. For example, if you have a 3-point scale (Not Fun, Somewhat Fun, and Very Fun) and 70% of your participants chose 'Very Fun', is this great or just OK? You will not know until you compare it to another game using the same method and scale.

Once a point of comparison is needed, all the needs of standard statistical analysis come into play; specifically, effect size, power, the level of significance, and the level of measurement (which dictates the type of statistical test). All these affect the sample size, in general, driving the sample size up to 25 participants and higher at the least. In turn this affects the time or resources needed to run the study. A full discussion of these topics is beyond the scope of this chapter. I highly recommend Sauro and Lewis's (2012) *Quantifying the User Experience* for an excellent dive into this material that will not leave you completely confused. I also highly recommend the free tool G*Power from the University of Düsseldorf http://gpower.hhu.de/ for calculating effect sizes and power.

Note that if you are using attitudes as purely qualitative data, then this does not matter. For example, if you ask participants open-ended questions about why they like a game, these data cannot be quantified, so the preceding discussion does not apply.

Question	A/B Testing	Benchmark Playtest	Card Sort	Critical Facet Playtest	Diary/Camera	Ethnographic Study	Extended Playtest	Focus Group	HE/Review	Interview	Initial Experience Playtest	Market Segmentation	Narrative Usability	Online Survey	Personas	RITE Test	Telemetry	Unmoderated Usability Test	Usability Benchmark	Usability Test
Who are the users?	No	No	No	No	No	Yes	No	No	No	Yes	No	Yes	No	Yes	Yes	No	Yes	No	No	No
Who should the users be?	No	No	No	No	No	Yes	No	No	No	Yes	No	Yes	No	Yes	Yes	No	No	No	No	No
What kind of game should we build?	No	No	No	No	No	Maybe	No	Maybe	No	Maybe	No	No	No	No	No	No	No	No	No	No
Why will users buy this game?	No	No	No	No	No	Maybe	No	Maybe	No	Maybe	No	No	No	No	No	No	No	No	No	No
What do our users do with our game?	No	No	No	No	Yes	Yes	Yes	No	No	No	Yes	No	No	No	No	Yes	Yes	Yes	Yes	Yes
What do our users wish they could do?	No	No	No	No	Yes	Yes	No	Yes	No	Yes	No	No	No	Yes	No	No	No	No	No	No
How do we generate new ideas that we have not come up with before?	No	No	No	No	No	Maybe	No	Maybe	No	Maybe	No	No	No	No	No	No	No	No	No	No
At what rate should we give out X?	Yes	No	No	No	No	No	No	No	No	No	No	No	No	No	No	No	Yes	No	No	No
What should X cost?	Yes	No	No	No	No	No	No	No	No	No	No	No	No	No	No	No	Yes	No	No	No
When and where should we place pay walls or payment opportunities?	Yes	No	No	No	No	No	No	No	No	No	No	No	No	No	No	No	Yes	No	No	Yes
Who will convert?	No	No	No	No	No	No	No	No	No	No	No	No	No	No	No	No	Maybe	No	No	No
Who is buying what?	No	No	No	No	No	No	No	No	No	No	No	No	No	Yes	No	No	Yes	No	No	No
How is our business model doing?	No	No	No	No	No	No	No	No	No	No	No	No	No	No	No	No	Yes	No	No	No
Are there any issues with X?	No	Yes	No	Yes	No	No	Yes	No	Yes	No	Yes	No	No	Yes	No	Yes	No	Yes	Yes	Yes
Is X fun?	No	Yes	No	Yes	No	No	Yes	No	No	No	Yes	No	No	Yes	No	No	No	No	No	No
How much do users like X?	No	Yes	No	Yes	No	No	Yes	No	No	No	Yes	No	No	Yes	No	No	No	No	No	No
Is X appropriately challenging?	No	Yes	No	Yes	No	No	Yes	No	No	No	Yes	No	No	No	No	No	Yes	No	No	No
Is X "good enough"?	No	Yes	No	Yes	No	No	Yes	No	No	No	Yes	No	No	Yes	No	No	No	No	Yes	No
Is X or Y better?	Yes	Yes	No	Yes	No	No	No	No	No	No	No	No	No	No	No	No	No	No	Yes	No
We have both X and Y, but which is more important?	No	No	No	Yes	No	No	No	No	No	No	No	No	No	No	No	Yes	No	No	No	Yes
How often does X happen? Or how often does X feature/thing get used?	No	No	No	No	No	No	No	No	No	No	No	No	No	Yes	No	No	Yes	No	No	No
I expect users to do X with this thing I made. Do they?	No	No	No	No	Yes	Yes	No	No	No	Yes	No	No	No	Yes	No	Yes	Yes	Yes	Yes	Yes
Does X work the way users expect it to?	No	Yes	No	Yes	No	Yes	Yes	No	No	Yes	No	No	No	Yes	No	Yes	No	Yes	Yes	Yes
Does the game narrative make sense? Do users like it?	No	No	No	No	Yes	Yes	No	No	No	Yes	No	No	Yes	No	No	No	No	No	No	No
How do all these options "group" together?	No	No	Yes	No	No	No	No	No	No	No	No	No	No	No	No	No	No	No	No	No

Figure 7.2 Which methods are best for the most common GUR questions?

7.3.3 Consideration 3: consider the practicalities of time, resources, capabilities, and political willpower

Regardless of the situation, the four practical considerations of the apocalypse tend to affect study design more than anything else. They are time, resources, capabilities, and political willpower.

- Time: Generally, any method that requires a lot of participants has challenges with time constraints. Most methods that need quantification cannot be done in one week's time (or less). Depending on your set-up, you may have challenges even at two or three weeks' time. Likewise, any question that looks at longitudinal behaviour will be challenging unless done via a cross-sectional method instead.
- Resources: Who is available to do the work? Do you have the funds needed to pull off the method? The materials?
- Capability: Be honest with yourself: can you really execute this method you are cooking up? Can you pull off a log-linear multivariate analysis (or whatever crazy statistical method is needed to do this right)? In general, the more complex the research method, the less likely it will be pulled off well by people who have not done it before. Likewise, if it is an unstructured or qualitative method, then the quality is almost wholly dependent on the ability of the person running it to make good observations. People who have done this a lot make better observations than those that have not. Back to the gameplay analogy: practice makes perfect.
- Politics: Sometimes it does not matter what your method is, because the decision makers have already decided what method will convince them and what method will not. The most common misconception is when decision makers (erroneously) believe that they need much larger sample sizes than they really need (because they do not understand sampling and sampling error). The more senior you become, the better you will get at persuading them otherwise. However, even the most senior and persuasive of researchers sometimes has to do a method in a non-optimal way to get buy-in. Buy-in is the ticket to change, and change is why we do what we do.

7.3.4 Consideration 4: can you combine methods and reuse the same participants?

In general, the best insights are gleaned from triangulation of data. Unfortunately, it is difficult to run studies simultaneously in order to triangulate data. If you have enough resources, you can run as many studies as you like simultaneously. But this is a luxury many cannot afford.

So then the question is, can you reuse the same participants and run two (or more) studies with the same set of participants? Figure 7.3 quickly shows which kinds of studies might be able to reuse participants (if the conditions are arranged correctly) and which cannot reuse participants.

Sometimes even though methods can be combined, they must be combined in a very particular way. When you use different methods with the same participants, it is a type of within-subjects design. This has one big disadvantage, namely, that participation in one condition will affect performance in another (even if only a little bit). So, for example, somebody might do better in a second memory test simply because they have had the chance to practice the first time

	A/B Testing	Benchmark Playtest	Card Sort	Critical Facet Playtest	Diary/Camera Study	Ethnographic Field Study	Extended Playtest	Focus Group	Heuristic Evaluation	Interview	Initial Experience Playtest	Market Segmentation	Narrative Usability	Online Survey	Personas	Review	RITE Test	Telemetry Analysis	Unmoderated Usability Test	Usability Benchmark	Usability Test
A/B Testing																					
Benchmark Playtest	No																				
Card Sort	No	No																			
Critical Facet Playtest	Yes	No	No																		
Diary/Camera Study	No	No	No	No																	
Ethnographic Field Study	No	No	No	No	Yes																
Extended Playtest	No	No	No	No	No	No															
Focus Group	No	Yes	No	Yes	No	Yes	Yes														
Heuristic Evaluation	No	No	No	No	No	No	No	No													
Interview	No	Yes	Yes	Yes	Yes	Yes	Yes	No	Yes												
Initial Experience Playtest	No	Yes	No	No	No	No	Yes	Yes	Yes	Yes											
Market Segmentation	No	No	No	No	No	Yes	No	No	No	No	No										
Narrative Usability	No	No	No	No	No	No	No	No	No	Yes	No	No									
Online Survey	Yes	No	Yes	No	No	Yes	No	No	No	No	No	Yes	No								
Personas	No	No	No	No	Yes	Yes	No	No	No	Yes	No	Yes	No	Yes							
Review	No	No	No	No	No	No	No	No	Yes	No	Yes	No	No	No	No						
RITE Test	No	No	No	No	No	No	No	No	Yes	Yes	No	No	Yes	No	No	Yes					
Telemetry Analysis	Yes	Yes	No	Yes	Yes	Yes	Yes	No	Yes	No	Yes	Yes	No	Yes	No	Yes	Yes				
Unmoderated Usability Test	Yes	No	No	No	No	No	No	Yes	No	Yes	No	Yes	No	Yes	No	Yes	Yes	Yes			
Usability Benchmark	No	No	No	No	No	No	No	No	Yes	Yes	No	No	No	No	No	No	Yes	No	Yes		
Usability Test	Yes	No	No	Yes	No	No	Yes	No	Yes	Yes	Yes	No	Yes	No	No	Yes	Yes	Yes	No	No	

Figure 7.3 Which methods can be combined to reuse participants?

	Current State	Comparison	Affinity	Needs	Generative
A/B Testing	No	Yes	No	No	No
Benchmark Playtest	Yes	Yes	No	No	No
Card Sort	No	No	Yes	No	No
Critical Facet Playtest	Yes	Yes	No	No	No
Diary/Camera Study	Yes	No	No	Yes	Yes
Ethnographic Field Study	Yes	No	No	Yes	Yes
Extended Playtest	Yes	Yes	No	No	No
Focus Group	Yes	No	No	Yes	Yes
Heuristic Evaluation	Yes	No	No	No	No
Interview	Yes	No	No	Yes	Yes
Initial Experience Playtest	Yes	Yes	No	No	No
Market Segmentation	Yes	No	No	No	No
Narrative Usability	Yes	No	No	No	No
Online Survey	Yes	No	No	Yes	Yes
Personas	Yes	No	No	Yes	No
Review	Yes	No	No	No	No
RITE Test	Yes	No	No	No	No
Telemetry Analysis	Yes	Yes	No	No	No
Unmoderated Usability Test	Yes	No	No	No	No
Usability Benchmark	Yes	Yes	No	No	No
Usability Test	Yes	No	No	Yes	No

Figure 7.4 Which methods best address which research need?

around. This is what is known as 'order effects' or 'carryover effects'. These kinds of effects have more impact on some kinds of studies than others.

There tend to be five things you may need to do to answer the questions we have listed (Figure 7.4):

1. Measure the 'current state' of something. For example, how many times do people get lost? Do people make mistakes or get confused using our inventory system? How many of our game players are female? Who is our audience?
2. Compare one thing to another. Does button mapping X make gamers more successful than button mapping Y?
3. Find affinity between things. What should be grouped with what? Should the armour be in the same place as the magic potions in the store?
4. Discover the needs and requirements that users have. This is both conscious and unconscious.
5. Generate new ideas.

Most of what Games User Researchers do falls into the bucket of measuring the current state of things. But GUR researchers also make comparisons, and

Table 7.4 Comparison and affinity studies

	Current State	Comparison	Audience	Generative	Affinity	Needs
Current State		X				
Comparison	X		X	Comparison goes 1st	X	Comparison goes 1st
Affinity		X		Affinity goes 1st		Affinity goes 1st
Needs		Comparison goes 1st			Affinity goes 1st	
Generative		Comparison goes 1st			Affinity goes 1st	

when they do, order effects are important. They are so important that they often block the reuse of participants from comparison-type studies. Table 7.4 shows that comparison and affinity studies suffer from order effects (marked with an X). In general, if comparison or affinity studies reuse participants, it is important that the comparison or affinity portion of the study goes first.

7.4 Final takeaway

The better the researcher understands the rules behind methods, the more likely they are able to artfully break the rules. Learn the rules so that you can break the rules. In the end, be creative and look to see where methods and measures can be combined. Do not be afraid to adopt new technologies and experiment with them to see if they provide viable extra insight. Likewise, be appropriately sceptical of these new technologies. Are they really saving you time or money, or answering your questions in a more valid way? Do not be lured to something simply because it is new. Instead, adopt things that are better in some tangible way.

References and suggested readings

Boruch, R. F. (1975). Coupling randomized experiments and approximations to experiments in social program evaluation. Sociological Methods & Research, 4(1), 31–53.

Campbell, D. T., Stanley, J. C. (1966). Experimental and quasi-experimental designs for research. Chicago: Rand McNally College.

Cook, T. D., Campbell, D. T. (1979). Quasi-experimentation: design and analysis issues for field settings. Chicago: Rand McNally College.

Desurvire, H., Wiberg, C. (2009). Game usability heuristics (PLAY) for evaluating and designing better games: the next iteration. In Online communities and social computing (pp. 557–566). Berlin, Heidelberg: Springer.

Drachen, A. (2012, 27 February). Ten great game telemetry reads—GameAnalytics. Retrieved 4 July 2016 from http://blog.gameanalytics.com/blog/10-great-game-telemetry-reads.html

Federoff, M. A. (2002). Heuristics and usability guidelines for the creation and evaluation of fun in video games [doctoral dissertation]. Indiana University.

G*Power. (2007, 1 December). Heinrich-Heine-Universität Düsseldorf RSS. Retrieved 4 July 2016 from http://gpower.hhu.de/

Henderson, D. (2014). Using User Research to Improve Game Narratives. Talk at Game Developers Conference 2014.

Kirk, R. E. (2012) Experimental design: procedures for the behavioral sciences. Thousand Oaks, CA: Sage Publications.

Kivikangas, J. M., Chanel, G., Cowley, B., Ekman, I., Salminen, M., Järvelä, S., Ravaja, N. (2011). A review of the use of psychophysiological methods in game research. Journal of Gaming & Virtual Worlds, 3(3), 181–199.

Kruschke, J. K. (2011) Doing Bayesian data analysis: a tutorial with R and BUGS. Burlington, MA: Academic.

Lazzaro, N., Keeker, K. (2004). What's my method? A game show on games. In CHI '04 Extended Abstracts on Human Factors in Computing Systems (pp. 1093–1094). New York: ACM.

Medlock, M. C., Wixon, D., Terrano, M., Romero, R., Fulton, B. (2002). Using the RITE method to improve products: a definition and a case study. Usability Professionals Association, 51.

Nunnally, J. C., Bernstein, I. H. (1994). Psychometric theory. New York: McGraw-Hill.

Pagulayan, R. J., Keeker, K., Wixon, D., Romero, R. L., Fuller, T. (2003). User-centered design in games. In J. A. Jacko A., Sears (eds.), The human-computer interaction handbook: fundamentals, evolving technologies and emerging applications (pp. 883–906). Mahwah, NJ: Lawrence Erlbaum Associates.

Rohrer, C. (2014, 12 October). When to use which user-experience research methods. Retrieved 21 March 2016 from https://www.nngroup.com/articles/which-ux-research-methods/

Sauro, J. (2013, 12 March). What UX methods to use and when to use them. http://www.measuringu.com/blog/method-when.php (accessed 21 March 2016).

Sauro, J., Lewis, J. R. (2012). Quantifying the user experience. New York: Elsevier.

Shadish, W. R., Cook, T. D., Campbell, D. T. (2002). Experimental and quasi-experimental designs for generalized causal inference. Boston, MA: Houghton Mifflin.

Trochim, W., Land, D. (1982). Designing designs for research. The Researcher, 1(1), 1–6.

UsabilityNet: Methods table. (n.d.). Retrieved 21 March 2016 from http://www.usabilitynet.org/tools/methods.htm

CHAPTER 8

A framework for player research

GRAHAM MCALLISTER, *Player Research*

SEBASTIAN LONG, *Player Research*

Highlights

This chapter describes each of the eight methods for player research we have used, and covers why the method is used in the context of player research, how it is executed, the time taken, and what is delivered as a result. Each of the methods has been refined over the years to reflect the balance between time and budget required and accurate and actionable results delivered. The strengths of each of the methods with respect to understanding player appeal, understanding, usability, experience, and successful monetization are presented.

Intro to Player Research

Player Research is an independent Games User Research (GUR) studio based in Brighton, UK. Being independent allows us to work not just on games belonging to one studio or publisher, but on the full spectrum of games in the industry—from the smallest of indie studios to AAA blockbusters. The games we work on cover all platforms (mobile, desktop, console, VR), audience types (casual through to core), and revenue models (free-to-play, premium, and hybrids of both).

Working with such a broad range of developers and games has resulted in our being subjected to a wide range of user research challenges over the years, increasing the range of services we offer from initially only one (usability testing), to eight today. These eight core services cover the full-game development life cycle, from initial

Games User Research, Anders Drachen, Pejman Mirza-Babaei, Lennart E. Nacke (Eds).
© Oxford University Press 2018. Published 2018 by Oxford University Press

concept through to post-launch—user research can, and should, be applied at all stages of game development.

8.1 Layered models of game evaluation

There are two key reasons why it is critical to apply different user research methods throughout game development. The first is so that developers can get feedback regularly throughout development, and the second is that each method offers a different lens on what is being evaluated. These lenses are just as important as the methods themselves, as they help our clients understand why we need to use different methods. In addition, the lenses also help explain the strengths and weaknesses of each method. Together we refer to these lenses as the five-layer model of game evaluation, and we use it to bind all the methods together. The model can apply to both free-to-play (F2P) games and premium, although the structure differs slightly between them.

8.1.1 The five-layer model—F2P game evaluation

The five-layer model was originally derived from the data we were seeing while working on F2P games. For clarity, a F2P game is one where the game itself is free to download and the developer hopes to generate revenue via in-app purchases (IAPs) and/or advertising. When F2P started to become popular in 2011, some developers were surprised when their games did not generate as much revenue as expected. The cause for this, many developers believed, was that they did not balance their in-game economy correctly: they had made a good game; however, the new F2P business model was new to them, so that must be where the problems lay.

In many cases however, it was not the business model that was the issue—it was issues with the game itself. The new F2P business model had exposed weaknesses with developers' games that were always there, but in the past, with a premium model, the effect was somewhat hidden as players had to pay upfront. F2P changed that completely. Now players were only likely to pay if the game offered an enjoyable player experience. This was the initial seed from which the five-layer model began—F2P game developers needed their game to success-fully monetize; however, this was only likely to happen if the player experience was good enough (Figure 8.1).

We sometimes refer to these top two layers as the success layers: moneti-zation is financial success and player experience is critical success. The next

Figure 8.1

logical question is what then makes a good player experience? From the data we observed based on the games we worked on, one of the most important factors impacting good player experience was usability, that is, could the players do the things which the designer intended them to do? (See Figure 8.2.)

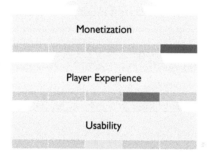

Figure 8.2

Breaking this down further, a key factor which affects usability is player understanding—does the player actually know the rules of the game world, and what is available to them? (See Figure 8.3.)

Figure 8.3

However, all of this assumes that the player has somehow managed to get as far as actually downloading the game. Therefore, it is also critical to understand why a game appeals to players to begin with (Figure 8.4).

It is easier to understand the model from the top down. Game developers are running a business, so they need to generate revenue (monetization layer), and this is more likely to happen if the game is enjoyable (player experience layer). One of the key reasons why games are not enjoyable is that players are not able to do what the designers want them to do (usability). One of the key factors impacting on usability is player understanding—do they know what to do in the game world and what is available to them? None of this can happen however, if the player does not find the game appealing enough to download in the first place.

This model shows that a studio's ability to generate money is directly related to all layers, and the source of the problem may in fact be far from where the effects are seen. So if the overall effect is that no revenue is being generated, it is possible that a significant cause of that is that players are not fully understanding the rules of the game world. What the five-layer model is good at, then, is helping to explain to developers the types of issues that are possible in their game, and also how these underlying issues can eventually make their way up to the surface layers—player experience and monetization.

Monetization

Player Experience

Usability

Understanding

Appeal

Figure 8.4

8.1.2 The four-layer model—premium game evaluation

For most premium games, the monetization layer is not required, as payment happens upfront, in which case we use a four-layer model to evaluate premium games (Figure 8.5). (Of course, some premium games do offer IAPs, in which case the five-layer model would apply to them also.)

Player Experience

Usability

Understanding

Appeal

Figure 8.5

Now that the five-layer model has been introduced, let us see how it is used in conjunction with each user research method in the game development process.

8.2 Methods and lenses

Each user research method is at its most efficient when it is used at a specific point in time to answer specific questions. Our user research process arranges the methods into a schedule which is best for most games, but of course exceptions always arise. We map the methods onto the following key game development phases:

- concept—generation of game ideas, identifying audiences and platforms
- prototype/design—exploring game ideas, designs, and prototypes
- production—iterative development from prototype to full game
- soft launch/launch—release to public (limited or otherwise), analytics data typically available

The methods themselves are as follows:

Concept phase

1. concept test
2. UX competitor analysis

Prototype/design phase

3. collaborative design
4. usability expert analysis

Production phase

5. usability playtest
6. large-scale playtest

Soft launch/launch

7. engagement diaries
8. analytics-driven playtest

Combined, these methods allow us to assess factors relating to a game's UX, including attitude, perception, understanding, interaction, behaviour, and player experience. (Note that some clients may not choose to do all of them; they will just select the ones which best answer their questions or point in the development life cycle.)

Let us now consider each method in more detail.

8.2.1 Concept test

8.2.1.1 WHAT IS A CONCEPT TEST? WHY SHOULD YOU DO IT?

A concept test is a method which aims to answer questions such as:

- Which art style do players prefer?
- Which features would players prefer?
- Why do players play games in a certain genre?
- Why did players make/not make IAPs?
- What do players expect a certain object to do?

8.2.1.2 WHEN IS IT USED?

The concept test is often conducted towards the very beginning of game development, as you want to understand players' general attitudes towards the style of game that is being made, and their perceptions of early artwork, game setting, and potential features (among other aspects). Ideally, any disparities between how the designers expect players to react and how they actually react can be caught quickly, and changes made easily.

8.2.1.3 TYPICAL ASSETS REQUIRED

- concept art
- mock-up of store images and copy
- story (text)
- previous games or competitors' games.
- concept video

8.2.1.4 HOW DO YOU DO IT?

As the questions being asked are often subjective, you need a reasonable sample size to draw any meaningful conclusions. We use two main approaches—either players submit their individual responses to stimuli using a questionnaire, or we use a focus-group approach if group discussion is considered more appropriate. For the individual questionnaire approach, we typically recruit 36 players organized into three groups of 12. Each session is typically 1.5 hours long, making it possible to elicit responses from all 36 participants in one day.

For the focus-group approach, we typically run eight groups, with each having five participants (40 participants total). Each group discussion lasts around 1.5 hours, allowing us to run four groups per day (20 participants), therefore taking two days to run all eight sessions. We also need two days beforehand to prepare for these sessions, and around 3–4 days to analyse and report the findings. During the actual concept tests or focus groups, we require three staff— two user researchers and one support person to help with note taking.

8.2.1.5 DELIVERABLES

The output of a concept test or focus group is a report detailing findings of any quantitative questions along with an analysis of any qualitative questions (grouped by theme or other analysis method). Presentation of results needs to consider any segmentation, for example, age group, or game experience.

8.2.1.6 WHICH OF THE FIVE LAYERS A CONCEPT TEST POLISHES

- Appeal (high)—you will obtain feedback on proposed store images and copy: do they motivate players to buy or download the game? You will also receive feedback on potential art styles and features.

- Understanding (low)—obtaining insights into what players think of other games in this genre or this new game being developed can help ensure that any early assumptions are validated.
- Usability (low)—players may comment on any frustrations they have experienced with similar games.
- Player experience (low)—what do players enjoy about previous games? Why is that? Did they complete the game? If not, why?
- Monetization (medium)—players may report previous experiences of whether or not they made any IAPs, and if so, how they felt as a result.

Figure 8.6 shows how and when the concept test method contributes to the player research framework.

Figure 8.6

8.2.2 UX competitor analysis

8.2.2.1 WHAT IS A UX COMPETITOR ANALYSIS?

What do your competitors do well and where could they improve? The aim of a competitor analysis is to answer these questions by identifying both good and bad UX implementations from games which you will be competing against. The intention is to understand what those games are doing well, so those principles can be factored into your own game design, and also where they are weak, as these are opportunities for your game to offer a better experience. It is worth stressing that this is not about copying game design features, but rather the UX principles upon which the features are built. The UX competitor analysis, then, is an ideal complement to a design/mechanics competitor analysis that studios would typically perform internally.

A competitor analysis is a method which aims to answer questions such as these:

- Which game has the best onboarding experience?
- What is the best way of presenting a push notification? (important for retention)
- What is the best way to present a 'for sale' item in the store?
- What is the best way to signal to the player that the game has more depth in future levels?

8.2.2.2 WHEN IS IT USED?

A competitor analysis is most effective if used at the concept stage, as you want to base some of your own design decisions on the findings from this analysis. By utilizing user research like this from the very earliest stages, it can contribute to reducing development time, project spending, and risk, while also improving the player experience.

8.2.2.3 TYPICAL ASSETS REQUIRED

- List of competitors' games. If it is a sequel, it could also consider previous games in the series.

8.2.2.4 HOW DO YOU DO IT?

We always have two user researchers assess each game, and we would normally recommend 2–3 titles to evaluate. The titles could be competitor titles of interest, or, if your game is sufficiently complete, then it is possible to do a competitor analysis on your game and two others. Evaluating more titles is certainly possible, but three is a balance between time taken, budget, and results. In terms of the analysis itself, the questions would typically come from the client: they may suggest a defined list of criteria for comparison (e.g., first-time user experience, store usability, controls), or they may just ask for an unguided analysis (no prompting at all). In terms of the analysis itself, the researchers would not use a specific heuristics list, but instead evaluate the game based on the game components, for example, UI (diegetic and non-diegetic), interaction design, teaching of game rules, dialogues, in-game feedback, presentation of progression systems, character customization, and so on. In addition to each game component being assessed, the researchers also consider higher-level analysis of how these components fit together to structure gameplay, including second-to-second gameplay, minute-to-minute gameplay, and any longer-term meta-game.

8.2.2.5 DELIVERABLES

The deliverable is a report typically around 100 pages. The structure of the report will vary depending on the style of games being evaluated, but for each component of interest, there would be a discussion of which game succeeded in implementation, why that is, and, if possible, how it could be improved even further.

8.2.2.6 WHICH OF THE FIVE LAYERS IT POLISHES

- Appeal (low)—it is possible to assess the copy and images/video on the store. Are they an accurate representation of the game, or are they misleading the player? Are the game's most interesting features being clearly communicated?
- Understanding (high)—analysis of the introduction of new concepts. Is the player learning correctly how to play and enjoy the game?
- Usability (high)—analysis of well-understood UI principles, interaction design (IxD), and information architecture (IA).
- Player experience (medium)—exploration of issues relating to moment-to-moment gameplay and meta-game.
- Monetization (medium)—assessment of factors impacting IAP behaviour, and in communicating value to the player.

Figure 8.7 shows how and when the UX competitor analysis method contributes to the player research framework.

Figure 8.7

8.2.3 Collaborative design

8.2.3.1 WHAT IS COLLABORATIVE DESIGN?

One of the biggest UX issues we repeatedly see is not with gameplay itself, but everything else around the game (the meta-game). This includes the user flow and various UIs (particularly store UI), most of which are likely to confuse the player and hinder them from experiencing the game the way the designers intended. We help studios by getting involved at the design stage, often reviewing their UI/wireframes when at mock-up stage where it is cheap and quick to change. Waiting until production often means it is too late to make significant changes.

8.2.3.2 WHEN IS IT USED?

Our user researchers either co-design (assist in the creation) or give feedback on existing designs during the game's design phase.

8.2.3.3 TYPICAL ASSETS REQUIRED

- wireframes (low-fidelity mock-ups of UI and user flow)—could be physical sketches or made with software (Photoshop, Sketch, etc.)
- game design document
- prototype—some studios prefer to design by making a working prototype

8.2.3.4 HOW DO YOU DO IT?

This involves two of our user researchers being on-site with the development team for two days, or we can work from our offices. If on-site, the first day is spent listening to the intentions of the design team, then working collaboratively to critique and redesign the wireframes. This will continue into the second day, and there may be periods when the user researchers will work separately from the design team, for example, if they need time to consider alternative solutions. The UI/wireframes will be evaluated from a usability and understanding point of view, and we bear in mind the expectations and abilities of the target audience. The designs are evaluated against usability principles and frameworks while also factoring in observational data which we have seen from playtests. The two-day period would finish with a presentation of the findings and planning of next steps.

8.2.3.5 DELIVERABLES

The output will be an evaluation of the current wireframes, which would include recommendations for improvements and also redesigns. If on-site, a presentation is part of the deliverables.

8.2.3.6 WHICH OF THE FIVE LAYERS IT POLISHES

- Appeal (low)—the user researchers and designers are not best positioned to comment on the game's appeal; however, they can add some insight by making sure the game is applying best practices to communicate its key features.
- Usability (high)—catching usability, interaction, and user flow issues early can lead to significant benefits later in the development. Major redesigns of the UI are less likely. Factoring in the abilities and expectations of the player into the project from the earliest stages helps to ensure a player-centric design process.
- Understanding (high)—having user researchers and game designers work together to design how game concepts are introduced should lead to an improved first-time user experience (FTUE) or tutorial.
- Player experience (medium)—factors contributing to the meta-game (retention) can be discussed and co-designed at this early stage.
- Monetization (low)—store UI and user flow for IAPs can be wireframed from very early stages.

Figure 8.8 shows how and when the collaborative design method contributes to the player research framework.

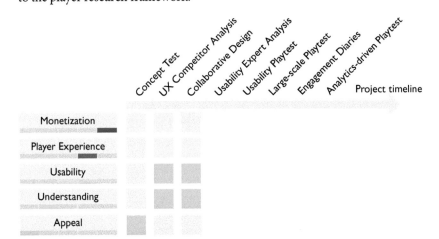

Figure 8.8

8.2.4 Usability expert analysis

8.2.4.1 WHAT IS A USABILITY EXPERT ANALYSIS, AND WHY DO IT?

Before putting your game in front of real players, it is advisable to ensure that as many potential barriers to enjoyment are identified and removed as possible. Ideally, real players should be informing you about issues which were previously unknown, not getting caught up on issues which could have been identified early in development by expert evaluation. This is the purpose of the usability expert analysis.

8.2.4.2 WHEN IS IT USED?

We typically perform the expert analysis either during the design phase (on wireframes) or during production (once an early prototype is ready). The main purpose is to identify and remove any issues before playtesting with real users. In some cases, studios give us their game to assess either when it is very close to release, or even after it has been released. The aim here is to see if we can improve their key performance indicators (download numbers, retention figures, income).

8.2.4.3 TYPICAL ASSETS REQUIRED

- UI mock-ups (lo-fi/hi-fi mock-ups of UI and user flow)—could be physical sketches or made with software (Photoshop, Sketch, etc.)
- prototypes—most likely to be on the core mechanic of the game but could be on any other segment also

8.2.4.4 HOW DO YOU DO IT?

Two user researchers evaluate the game against the five key layers: appeal, understanding, usability, player experience, and monetization. For each layer, the researchers would use their knowledge of existing usability principles and lessons from observing playtests to assess the game components. The researchers would assess separate sections of the game to cover as much as possible within the tight time frame; however, they would also both assess key sections of the game—sometimes two viewpoints are critical. For smaller mobile games, the period of play usually lasts one day and the reporting takes one further day. Larger games may take one day longer; however, it is usual for the expert analysis to focus on a particular section of the game rather than evaluate everything. For mobile games, the FTUE is the most commonly requested section to assess.

8.2.4.5 DELIVERABLES

The deliverable is a 30–50 page report detailing specific issues which will impact on the player experience. One issue is usually reported per page, in the following format: priority, description of issue, screenshot of issue, and suggested action.

As for turnaround time, most mobile games can be evaluated in two days.

8.2.4.6 WHICH OF THE FIVE LAYERS IT POLISHES

- Appeal (low)—evaluation of appeal, which could include store description, store screenshots, and analysis of expectations players may form based on how the game is presented/positioned. The intention here is to identify any potential miscommunication or missed opportunities to resonate with the target audience.
- Understanding (high)—is the game effective at teaching the player how to play the game? Which methods does it use to introduce concepts and reinforce them?
- Usability (high)—apply known principles of UI/IA/IxD to the game. Also compare with approaches from other games.
- Player experience (medium)—although it is impossible to assess if someone else will like the game, there are aspects of the player experience which can be assessed, such as, Is a clear motivation presented? Are the game mechanics fair? Are the retention mechanics reinforced and understandable?
- Monetization (low)—all aspects of the game which relate to real currency are evaluated against our lowest three layers—appeal, understanding, and usability.

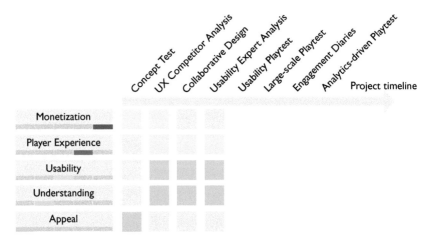

Figure 8.9

Figure 8.9 shows how and when the usability expert analysis method contributes to the player research framework.

8.2.5 Usability playtest

8.2.5.1 WHAT IS A USABILITY PLAYTEST, AND WHY DO IT?

A usability playtest should typically be used to answer questions such as:

- Are the controls suitable for the target audience?
- Will users navigate through the game the way that was intended (user flow)?
- Are we onboarding players effectively?
- Are players able to make an IAP?

8.2.5.2 WHEN IS IT USED?

A usability playtest could be conducted as soon as a prototype is ready. The playtest could be run on a core game mechanic, or perhaps later on the game's tutorial.

8.2.5.3 TYPICAL ASSET REQUIRED

- a playable build

8.2.5.4 HOW DO YOU DO IT?

Real players are recruited to play the build; normally six is a reasonable balance between reliable results and cost/time. Session times are usually one hour (can be more) and split into 40 minutes of play and 15 minutes of interview; the remaining five minutes is for signing non-disclosure agreements and briefing the player. After the briefing, the player is left alone with the game; two user researchers would observe from a remote room. All video is recorded and streamed to the client if necessary. Each researcher makes their own notes on the player's behaviour, which can be compared at a later stage. Questions asked during the interview would be structured around questions from the developers and also with the intention of exploring what caused the players to behave as they did.

8.2.5.5 DELIVERABLES

The deliverable is 30–50 page report and video recordings of all sessions. In some cases, a presentation to the developers may also occur, allowing them the chance to ask follow-up questions.

8.2.5.6 WHICH OF THE FIVE LAYERS IT POLISHES

- Appeal (medium)—as this method involves players who are represent-ative of the target audience, we can ask them questions directly around initial impressions and expectations. It is worth stressing, however, that as the usability playtest typically involves low numbers of players, such results may not be considered reliable.
- Understanding (high)—having the ability to directly ask players how specific aspects of the game work gives a reliable insight into their understanding of the game.
- Usability (high)—are the UI, controls, and user flow effective at allow-ing a successful gameplay experience? These can be directly observed and evaluated during the playtest.
- Player experience (medium)—players will be able to comment on how the gameplay feels. As before, there is only a small number of players, so be careful about drawing conclusions from the responses.
- Monetization (low)—players could be asked how they think the game monetizes. Did they notice how to make IAPs? Do they understand the relationship between the various currency systems? Do they see why they should spend in the game?

Figure 8.10 shows how and when the usability playtest method contributes to the player research framework.

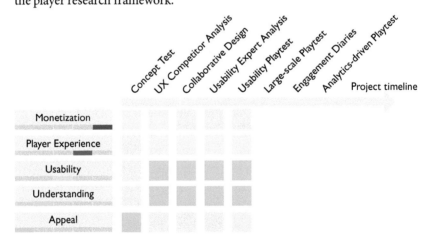

Figure 8.10

8.2.6 Large-scale playtest

8.2.6.1 WHAT IS A LARGE-SCALE PLAYTEST, AND WHY DO IT?

Are players enjoying the designed experience of your game? This is the core question that a large-scale playtest is intended to answer.

8.2.6.2 WHEN IS IT USED?

A large-scale playtest is typically conducted during the latter half of production. All usability issues should ideally have been removed by this stage so that the focus is now on assessing the player experience.

8.2.6.3 TYPICAL ASSET REQUIRED

- a playable build complete with as many features as possible;

8.2.6.4 HOW DO YOU DO IT?

As we are trying to answer a subjective question—Do players like the designed experience?—we need to recruit a reasonable number of players in order to draw meaningful conclusions. As a minimum, we playtest with 36 players, but more are possible. Using our large-scale playtest lab, which seats 12 users at a time, the group of players play the build, then complete a carefully designed questionnaire. Sessions would typically be 1.5 hours long, split into one hour of gameplay and 25 minutes of answering questionnaires, and in some cases a sample of players may be invited for a group interview. Using this approach, it is possible to playtest with 36 players in one day (three groups of 12).

8.2.6.5 DELIVERABLES

The deliverable is a report structured by the questions from the developer. In most cases the questions are a mixture of quantitative and qualitative; analysis time for the qualitative responses is much higher, as it needs to be treated before analysis. The typical time required to run a 36-player UX playtest is six days (two days' preparation, one day UX playtest, three days' analysis and reporting).

8.2.6.6 WHICH OF THE FIVE LAYERS IT POLISHES

- Appeal (high)—players can be presented with a questionnaire directly following the playtest and subjective questions asked about the game's art style, features, core mechanics, etc.
- Understanding (low)—using the questionnaire, it may be possible to capture players' thoughts on how the game works, but follow-up questions are not possible, of course.

- Usability (low)—it is difficult to observe the behaviour of 12 players at once; however, some usability issues can often be observed or captured with the questionnaire.
- Player experience (high)—the questionnaire is the primary method for capturing players' perceptions of the game, although interviews are also possible.
- Monetization (medium)—are players aware of what they can buy? Do they understand the benefits of IAPs?

Figure 8.11 shows how and when the large-scale playtest method contributes to the player research framework.

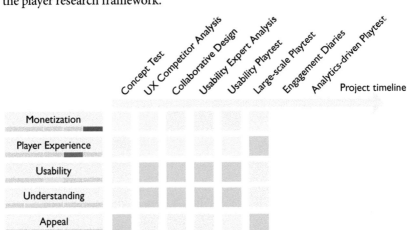

Figure 8.11

8.2.7 Engagement diaries

Whereas in-lab user testing is ideal for understanding how users are interacting with your game for short periods (typically 1–10 hours), developers often want to know how players feel over longer periods of time—weeks or even months. To answer these sorts of questions, another approach is needed.

8.2.7.1 WHAT ARE DIARY STUDIES, AND WHY DO THEM?

A diary study method is a longitudinal approach to assessing specific aspects of a game over longer periods, which for us would typically mean anywhere from one week to one month. This is ideal for F2P games in particular, as developers are keen not only on the early experience (in-lab methods can answer these questions), but also on the longer-term retention issues. For example, developers may want to know what players think about specific aspects of their game after playing for a few days compared to when they first play it. Retention figures in F2P games would typically be assessed on Days 1, 7, and 30, and although analytics will capture the raw numbers, they will not explain what is the cause of the figures, that is, *why*. A longitudinal diary then can be thought of as an ideal complement to analytics—metrics can identify where the problem is and diary studies can help explain why the issue is happening.

8.2.7.2 WHEN IS IT USED?

We typically use engagement diaries (diary studies) during the soft-launch period or just before—the game should be reasonably complete. For some games, we have conducted diary studies long after a game has been released with the aim of understanding why players are leaving. Once the underlying causes are identified, solutions are provided to the developers, who then make the changes; then metrics can measure how much of a difference has been made.

8.2.7.3 TYPICAL ASSETS REQUIRED

The game should be as feature-complete and polished as possible, especially if you are asking player experience questions. You will also need to design a questionnaire for players to fill out every day.

8.2.7.4 HOW DO YOU DO IT?

The process begins by identifying which questions you want to answer. These questions could come from analytics (e.g., you already know you have a retention problem) or they could be a list of concerns the developers already have. You should also think carefully about the style of question: should it be quantitative (e.g., rate these specific features of a game) or qualitative, where you need players to describe how they feel about various aspects. Qualitative questions will likely provide you with more insights; however, the data will take much longer to analyse.

Once the questionnaire is designed, you need to recruit a panel of users. We normally recruit around 24 users, expecting four to drop out, leaving 20 to fully participate in the engagement diary. Players are provided with a build of the game and asked to complete the survey each time they play the game. As players may play a few sessions a day for up to 30 days, you could expect 100 responses per participant, or up to 2000 in total. This is why it is advisable to keep qualitative questions to a manageable minimum: when it comes to analysis, trying to group the qualitative responses into themes can be time-consuming. Our survey software can flag if a player does not play for a few days, at which point a researcher will phone them up to understand why that is.

8.2.7.5 DELIVERABLES

The output of this method is a report identifying how the target audience feels about specific aspects of a game over a longer period of time. The report would be rich in detail, focusing on how players felt, and what contributed to them feeling that way. If they did not make a purchase on Day 5, why is that? Are they feeling bored after Day 1? Can they see why the game would be engaging one month in? The report would provide developers with such answers.

8.2.7.6 WHICH OF THE FIVE LAYERS IT POLISHES

- Appeal (medium)—players can comment on their initial impressions of the game and if this has changed over time.
- Understanding (medium)—players often comment on what is confusing them. Does this resolve itself over time? If so, how did they resolve these issues—was it from the game's feedback or an external source (e.g., YouTube)?
- Usability (medium)—engagement diaries can capture feedback on issues with UI, controls, and other usability issues. Do these issues disappear over time as the player becomes familiar with the interface, or do they remain issues?
- Player experience (high)—are players enjoying the game? Does this feeling remain or does it change over time? What are the causes of this?
- Monetization (high)—did players make a purchase during the diary study period? If so, why? Do they feel it was worth it? If they did not spend, why not?

Figure 8.12 shows how and when the engagement diary method contributes to the player research framework.

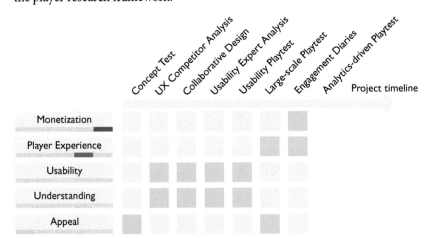

Figure 8.12

8.2.8 Analytics-driven playtest

8.2.8.1 WHAT IS AN ANALYTICS-DRIVEN PLAYTEST?

An analytics-driven playtest follows the same process as a usability playtest except the areas to focus particular attention on are identified by analytics. For example, analytics could have identified that many players are dropping out of the game, but they would not reveal why. Therefore, the main purpose of an analytics-driven playtest is to identify why issues are occurring and arrive at solutions to resolve the issues.

8.2.8.2 WHEN IS IT USED?

This method is typically used during soft launch or post-launch, as the gameplay should be complete and polished.

8.2.8.3 TYPICAL ASSET REQUIRED

- polished gameplay

8.2.8.4 HOW DO YOU DO IT?

This is the same process as a usability playtest, except the areas to pay particular attention to are identified by analytics. What you want to happen during the playtest is for the offending issues to be replicated, so ideally the analytics should narrow down the scope of gameplay as much as possible. For example, it would be better if you could identify that players are dropping off or are hindered by a certain screen rather than just knowing that players drop off on Day 3.

8.2.8.5 DELIVERABLES

The deliverable is 30–50 page report and video recordings of all sessions. The underlying causes of issues identified with analytics should be identified and potential solutions presented.

8.2.8.6 WHICH OF THE FIVE LAYERS IT POLISHES

- Appeal (medium)—data should provide some insight into which areas of the game players are enjoying. If a choice of eight characters is available, which are the most frequently selected—do you know why?
- Understanding (high)—analytics will have identified *where* the problem is occurring; the key focus of the analytics-driven playtest is to uncover *why* it is occurring. Being able to observe player behaviour and then interview them is essential to providing the understanding which leads to resolving issues.

- Usability (high)—directly observing player behaviour at sections of the game which analytics indicate are an issue allows user researchers to focus their attention on resolving usability issues.
- Player experience (medium)—data could indicate features of the game which are performing well, or not. Playtesting at these points can provide insights into why this is the case.
- Monetization (medium)—data will show which IAPs are successful and which are not performing well. Running a playtest which focuses on the store and IAP user flow can help reveal the underlying issues.

Figure 8.13 shows how and when the analytics-driven playtest method contributes to the player research framework.

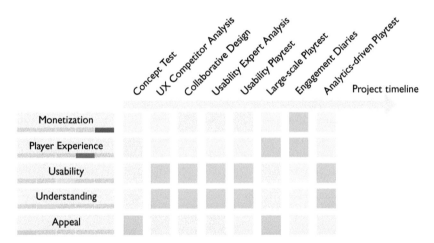

Figure 8.13

8.3 Summary

One of the key mistakes we often see developers make is that they should be seeking feedback earlier in development. The user research process we have outlined here shows developers that they can receive feedback from the very earliest stages of their project. The extension to this is the five-layer model. The five-layer model was designed to communicate the benefits of using research at all stages of development, and in particular, to show that in order to add sufficient polish to all five layers, a range of methods is needed—no one method is enough. The five-layer model was derived from evidence—it emerged from the results of the games we worked on, yet it is sufficiently simple that clients can easily remember it and use it in conversation among their team.

Game developers are of course very familiar with software development processes; however, many have a very low awareness that a UX process is also possible. By mapping our services to the software development life cycle, developers can easily understand how and where user research can help them. Additionally, the five-layer model shows the value of using each user research service—which layers of the game it polishes.

Finally, the resulting matrix of user research methods and which layers they polish (Figure 8.13) visually communicates to developers how many opportunities they have to improve their game. No matter which development stage your game is at today, user research can help to improve the player experience.

CHAPTER 9

Surveys in Games User Research

FLORIAN BRÜHLMANN, *University of Basel*

ELISA MEKLER, *University of Basel*

Highlights

Surveys are an essential method of data collection that can deliver generalizable and actionable insights about the player's experience. In this chapter, we present practice-oriented guidance about when the method is appropriate, what constitutes a good questionnaire, and how to alleviate possible biases and issues with data quality.

9.1 Introduction

One of the main goals of Games User Research (GUR) is to evaluate the player-game interaction with the objective of using the results to improve the player experience. Surveys are a methodology that can help us achieve these goals. They are used to gather data from a subset of the population being studied. The results of the survey can then be generalized to the larger population. Surveys can capture players' opinions and self-reported gaming habits. They are a quick, easy, and cost-effective way to generate a sizeable amount of data to reveal more about the subjective experience of playing a game. This might make it seem relatively easy to put together a survey, but there are seemingly minor oversights that can severely limit the utility of your survey data. There are many different types of surveys, different ways to sample a population, and various

Games User Research, Anders Drachen, Pejman Mirza-Babaei, Lennart E. Nacke (Eds).
© Oxford University Press 2018. Published 2018 by Oxford University Press

ways to collect data from that population. Surveys can be administered via mail, telephone, or in person, as well as online. They have consistently been used in psychology, marketing, and HCI research to help answer a variety of questions related to people's attitudes, behaviours, and experiences (Müller, Sedley, and Ferrall-Nunge, 2014).

Drawing from our own work in player experience research, this chapter outlines the benefits and drawbacks of using surveys. In addition, this chapter provides a 'how-to' guide and best practices for practitioners and academics interested in applying surveys in GUR. We begin by outlining the types of research questions that are best addressed by surveys. We then review points that need to be considered when designing a survey, such as sampling and question types, followed by steps to be taken to ensure data quality.

9.2 What to research with surveys

The goal of a survey is to provide statistical estimates of the characteristics of the target population. Because surveying the whole population (e.g., all potential players of Dark Souls III) is usually impractical or even impossible, data from a sample of the population are collected instead. One central premise of survey research is that if you can provide a description of the sample, you can describe the target population (Fowler, 2013). The second premise states that the answers given by the participants in the sample accurately describe the characteristics of the respondents (Fowler, 2013). To retain these premises, researchers need to be aware of possible sources of error and bias and take measures to limit their influence. Only then can well-designed surveys provide insights into players' attitudes, experiences, motives, demographics, and psychographic characteristics.

Overall, there are two main categories of questions a researcher can ask respondents about: objective facts and subjective states. Objective facts are directly observable and can be verified by other people. For instance, objective facts can include demographic characteristics such as age and gender, as well as the number of hours spent playing games. In contrast, subjective states such as attitudes and emotions are not objectively verifiable. For instance, identification of a player with the protagonist of a game cannot be directly observed. Overall, surveys are very flexible when it comes to the research questions they can address: They can be used to assess characteristics of your player base, measure the differences between groups of players or different iterations of a design, and identify changes in players' attitudes and experiences over time. Surveys can be administered anytime during the game development cycle, depending on your research question.

Surveys in GUR can be useful to assess the following:

1. *Player attitudes and experiences.* Surveys can accurately measure and reliably represent attitudes and perceptions of a population. When assessing quantitative data, surveys provide statistically reliable metrics, which allow researchers to benchmark attitudes towards a game or an experience, to track changes in attitudes over time, and to tie self-reported attitudes to actual behaviour (e.g., via log data). Collecting qualitative data about player experience can also be used to understand players' interaction with a game or inform game design improvements.

2. *Motives.* Surveys can collect players' motives for playing a game at a specific time or in a specific situation. Unlike other methods, surveys can be deployed while a person is actually playing a game (e.g., an online intercept survey), minimizing the risk of imperfect recall on the players' part. It is important to note that the specific details and the context of one's intent may not be fully captured in a survey alone. For example, 'Why did you play Canabalt?' can be answered in a survey, but interviews may be more appropriate for determining a player's underlying motivations to engage with this game.

3. *Player characteristics.* Surveys can be used to understand a game's player base and to better serve their needs. Researchers can collect players' demographic information, their genre savviness or overall gaming expertise, and psychographic variables such as personality traits. Such data enable researchers to discover segments of players who may have different needs, motivations, attitudes, preferences, and overall player experiences (e.g., Nacke, Bateman, and Mandryk, 2014).

4. *Comparisons.* Surveys can be used to compare players' attitudes, perceptions, and experiences. These comparisons can be made across player segments, time, competitor games, and between different iterations of game design aspects, such as interfaces. This allows researchers to explore whether or not players' needs and experiences vary across countries, assess a game's strengths and weaknesses among competitors, and evaluate potential game design improvements to make informed decisions.

Survey research is even more valuable when used in conjunction with other GUR methods. Players can be asked to self-report their behaviours, but gathering this information from log data (if available) will always be more accurate. This is particularly true when trying to understand precise behaviours, as players will struggle to recall their exact sequence of in-game actions. Combining surveys with more objective measures of player behaviour (see Chapters 16 and 19) helps to paint an even more detailed picture of the player experience. For instance, game analytics (see Chapter 19) might show that players are more likely to succeed in one version of the level, but the survey data may reveal that players were less challenged and experienced boredom (Hazan, 2013). Physiological measures (see Chapters 16 and 17) may be another complement to survey data. For example, player experience researchers have combined surveys of fun and immersion with measures of facial muscle and electrodermal activity (e.g., Nacke et al., 2010).

9.3 How to design a survey

As with all GUR methods, a survey is only as useful as its design. Before starting to write survey questions, researchers should first think about what they want to find out (Ambinder, 2014), what kind of data needs to be collected, and how the data will be used to meet their research goals. An overarching research goal may be to understand how challenging players find each portion of the game. Once research goals are defined, there are several other considerations to help determine whether a survey is the most appropriate method and how to proceed:

- Do the survey questions focus on the results, which directly address research goals and support informed decisions, or do they only provide informative data? An excess of questions increases the survey length and the likelihood that respondents will drop out before completing the questionnaire, diminishing the effectiveness of the survey results.
- Will the results be used for longitudinal comparisons or one-time decisions? For longitudinal comparisons, researchers must plan on multiple survey deployments without exhausting available respondents.
- What is the number of responses needed to provide the appropriate level of precision for the insights needed? Calculating the number of responses needed (as described in the following section) will ensure

that key metrics and comparisons are statistically reliable. Once the target number is determined, researchers can then decide how many people to invite.

9.3.1 Determining the appropriate sample and sample size

The key to effective survey research is determining who and how many people should participate. The first thing that needs to be determined is the survey *population*—usually the target audience or the player base of a specific game or franchise. Depending on your research question, this may also encompass any set of individuals that meet certain predetermined criteria (e.g., novice players) and to whom you want your findings to apply to (e.g., what do novice players think of the new tutorial?). This is the population from which the *sample* for your survey should be drawn. Reaching everyone is typically impossible and unnecessary. However, if the sampling systematically excludes certain types of people (e.g., very disengaged players), the survey will suffer from *coverage error*, and its results will misrepresent the population.

While random sampling is the gold standard in scientific research, GUR is chiefly interested in capturing the attitudes and behaviours of relatively 'small' populations (i.e., the player base). Hence, it is acceptable to resort to *non-probability sampling* methods, such as volunteer opt-in panels, self-selected sur-veys (e.g., links on blogs, gaming forums, and social networks), and *convenience samples* (e.g., undergraduate psychology students). However, non-probability methods are prone to high selection bias and will reduce the representativeness of the results in comparison to random sampling methods.

It is important to carefully determine the target sample size for the survey. If the sample size is too small, findings from the survey cannot be accurately generalized to the entire player base or may fail to detect differences between groups. Therefore, calculating the optimal sample size becomes crucial for every survey.

There are many factors influencing the necessary sample size such as the frequency of a characteristic, the research question, effect size, the desired margin of error, and how accessible a certain demographic is. In general, a larger sample has less margin of error for an estimated characteristic of the population (e.g., enjoyment). However, it is important to remember that representativeness is related but not equal to sample size. This means it is not just small samples that are affected by sampling biases. Sampling bias can reduce the representativeness of even very large samples with small margins of error. There are various formulas for calculating the target sample size (see Müller et al., 2014, for an extended discussion of sampling in HCI surveys), but there is no one-size-fits-all recommendation, as it depends on the specific situation.

As a rule of thumb, when a sample needs to be representative of a large population (e.g., the player base), we recommend a sample size of at least 500 survey respondents. Estimating a population parameter with this sample size would yield a margin of error of less than 5% at a 95% confidence level (Müller et al., 2014). Similarly, if you plan on conducting statistical significance testing (e.g., to compare two different game versions using an independent samples t-test), it is recommended to have at least 20–30 survey respondents per group to be able to properly assess the distribution of a statistic and have the necessary probability (statistical power) of detecting a true difference. However, estimates of sample size based on a priori power calculations (e.g., with the GPower program by Faul et al., 2007, which is available free of charge at http://www.gpower. hhu.de/) while taking the research context into account are preferable to rules of thumb.

9.3.2 Mode of survey invitation

There are four basic survey modes used to reach respondents: mail or written, phone, in-person, and online. These survey modes may be used independently or in combination with other modes. The survey mode needs to be chosen carefully, as each mode has its own advantages and disadvantages. For instance, surveys have different response rates, introduce distinct biases, require resources and costs, represent different scales of audience that can be reached, and offer respondents various levels of anonymity.

Today, many game research–related surveys are conducted online, as benefits often outweigh their disadvantages. Online surveys have the following major advantages:

- Easy access to large geographic regions (including international reach).
- Simplicity of creating a survey by leveraging easily accessible commercial tools.
- Relatively cost-effective to distribute (e.g., no paper and postage, simple implementation, insignificant cost increase for large sample sizes) and quickly analysed (returned data are already in electronic format).
- Short fielding periods (i.e., time required to collect the answers), as the data are collected immediately.

- Lower bias due to respondent anonymity, as surveys are self-administered with no interviewer present.
- Ability to customize the questionnaire to specific respondent groups using skip logic (i.e., asking respondents a different set of questions based on the answer to a previous question).

9.3.2.1 CROWDSOURCING

A promising mode for survey invitation are crowdsourcing platforms, such as CrowdFlower[1] or Amazon Mechanical Turk.[2] On these platforms, individuals, enterprises, and research institutions can post 'jobs', which may range from categorizing images, writing summaries of articles, to filling in surveys. The so-called crowd workers can then complete these jobs for a monetary payment set by the employer (Kittur et al., 2008). These platforms have the advantage of providing a large pool of readily available participants with a variety of backgrounds and interests. Crowdsourcing has been found to be reliable for behavioural research and user studies (Mason and Suri, 2012). Crowdsourced surveys are a low-cost avenue, even for small and indie game developers. People generally like to engage in crowdsourced micro-tasks, as fun and passing time are the main motivations for participation rather than monetary rewards (Antin and Shaw, 2012). This makes crowdsourcing platforms an ideal resource for participants when comparisons of interface variants or adjustments of difficulty settings are needed.

A few guidelines on what to keep in mind when distributing your survey over crowdsourcing platforms:

- Reduce the pool of participants to your target audience.
- Combine quantitative measures with qualitative data for a more detailed understanding of the collected data (e.g., have respondents explain in their own words why they rated the game as 'very easy').
- Include one or more control questions to reduce careless responses and identify fraudulent survey respondents. For example, include a control question such as 'Respond with "strongly agree" to this item' or ask for self-report of data quality (e.g., 'In your honest opinion, should we use your data?'; refer to Curran, 2016, and Meade and Craig, 2012, for an extensive review of careless response detection methods).

---

[1] www.crowdflower.com
[2] www.mturk.com

- Pay respondents only a small amount for completing the survey, but provide respondents who answered the questions carefully with a reward, and mention this in the job description.
- Examine data quality by combining objective measures such as completion time to identify outliers with reported technical difficulties.

Providing incentives is often effective for encouraging survey responses. As exemplified by crowdsourcing platforms, monetary incentives tend to increase response rates more than non-monetary incentives. If the crowdsourcing incentives are unavailable—for example, when social media is used as a means of recruitment—a lottery of monetary rewards or other prizes can be useful as an alternative.

9.4 The art of asking questions—questionnaire design

Once the research questions and the appropriate sampling methods are established, researchers can begin designing the survey questionnaire. Questionnaires allow researchers to gain information in an objective, reliable, and valid way:

Objectivity means that respondents' answers should not be influenced by who is conducting the survey. This is less problematic in online surveys but can have an influence in lab studies. For example, a respondent may answer survey questions overly positive so as to appeal to the researcher.

Reliability refers to the accuracy and consistency of the questionnaire. For example, a respondent's answer to a question about gaming habits should not drastically change from one day to the next. Reliability is more difficult to achieve when internal processes or attitudes are the focus of the study. While reliability is a concern for researchers that develop their own surveys, it is of special importance when measuring psychological phenomena (see deVellis, 2012, for an in-depth discussion).

Validity refers to the extent that the collected data represent the phenomenon of interest. A measure is valid if it measures what it is supposed to and not some other factors. Several aspects of validity are important for survey research:

1. *Content validity* refers to the degree to which a survey or a question in a survey captures the phenomenon of interest in a representative manner. This means that all aspects of the phenomenon are somehow represented in the questionnaire. For example, asking participants how

often they played a game in the last two weeks might not give the full picture of their behaviour, since the question does not capture how long these game sessions were.

2. *Criterion-related validity* refers to the association of a survey or a question in a survey with another characteristic or behaviour of the respondent. For instance, players who enjoy a particular game may be more likely to recommend the game to their friends. In this case, enjoyment can predict the likeliness of recommendation, and thus features criterion-related or, in another term, predictive validity.

3. *Construct validity* concerns the theoretical foundation of a facet measured by a questionnaire. A questionnaire shows construct validity if the answer behaviour of the respondent can be linked to the phenomenon of interest. For example, this means that a questionnaire for presence in games actually measures feelings of presence rather than feelings of enjoyment. Establishing construct validity is a complex process and beyond the scope of this chapter (but please refer to deVellis, 2012, for an in-depth discussion). Nevertheless, researchers should take content, criterion-related, and construct validity into account, and think about how participants' answers to the survey questions relate to their real-life behaviour. This can help with refining and selecting survey questions as well as identifying possible problems with question wording.

For most surveys there is only one opportunity for deployment, with no possibility for requesting further clarification or probing (cf. interviews, see Chapter 10). It is therefore important for researchers to carefully think through the design of each survey question, as it is fairly easy to introduce biases, which can have a substantial impact on the reliability and validity of the data collected. Survey questions should minimize the risks of measurement error that can arise from the respondent (e.g., lack of motivation, comprehension problems, deliberate distortion) or from the questionnaire (e.g., poor wording or design, technical flaws).

9.4.1 Types of survey questions

There are two main types of survey questions, open- and closed-ended. Open-ended questions (e.g., 'Please describe a recent outstanding experience with a digital game'; see also Figure 9.1) require the respondents to produce their

Please bring to mind **an outstanding positive or negative experience** you had **in your** __most recent__ __game-session__ **in Dark Souls III:**
• Try to describe this particular experience as accurately, detailed and concrete as possible.
• What were your thoughts and feelings?
• How did you respond emotionally to this event in the game?

You can use as many sentences as you like (at least 50 words).

This was my experience:

Figure 9.1 Example of an open-ended question (used for the study described in Petralito et al., 2017)

How long ago did the experience take place?

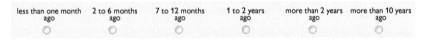

less than one month ago	2 to 6 months ago	7 to 12 months ago	1 to 2 years ago	more than 2 years ago	more than 10 years ago
○	○	○	○	○	○

Figure 9.2 Example of a single-choice question (used for the study described in Bopp et al., 2016)

own answer in a text-based format, a video, or a mind map (e.g., Hillman et al., 2016). Closed-ended questions provide a set of predefined answers to choose from (e.g., multiple-choice or rating questions; see also Figure 9.2). The question type format that is the most appropriate for the research study is dependent on the research question. In general, open-ended questions make sense when not much is known about the phenomenon of interest and for discovering more about a topic in exploratory studies. In one of our own surveys, for instance, the use of open-ended questions allowed us to identify several game design aspects related to players' emotional experience (Bopp et al., 2016). Open-ended questions are also valuable for studies where the research question is clear, and validated scales exist. These types of questions can help researchers understand why respondents answered questions in a certain way. For instance, it can make sense to ask participants to explain why they rated the aspect 'control' so low for a specific game.

Open-ended questions are appropriate when:

• The range of possible answers is unknown (e.g., 'What is your favourite game?').
• Measuring quantities with natural metrics (i.e., constructs with an inherent unit of measurement, such as age, length, or frequency). For instance,

when researchers are unable to access information from log data, such as time, frequency, and length, they might ask open-ended questions to acquire this information (e.g., 'How many times do you access Steam in a typical week?'; using a text field that is restricted to numeric input).

- Measuring qualitative aspects of players' experience (e.g., 'What do you like best about this game?').

It may be tempting to use large text field entries throughout your survey, but it is important to note that these text fields may intimidate respondents and cause higher dropout rates. In one of our own surveys, we experienced a substantial dropout on the page that featured two large text fields. Nevertheless, the data quality was excellent for participants who persevered until the end of the survey (Bopp et al., 2016).

Closed-ended questions are appropriate when:

- The range of possible answers is known and small enough to be easily provided (e.g., 'Which devices do you use for gaming?'; the answers provided could include 'PC' and 'consoles').
- Rating a single object on a 7-point scale from 'Not fun at all' to 'Extremely fun' (e.g., 'Overall, how fun was the game?').
- Measuring quantities without natural metrics, such as importance. For example, 'How important is it to have your smartphone within reach 24 hour a day?' (on a 5-point scale from 'Not at all important' to 'Extremely important').

There are four basic types of closed-ended questions: single-choice, multiple-choice, rating, and ranking questions.

1. *Single-choice questions* work best when only one answer is possible for each respondent.
2. *Multiple-choice questions* (Figure 9.3) are appropriate when more than one answer may apply to the respondent. Frequently, multiple-choice questions are accompanied by 'select all that apply'.
3. *Ranking questions* (Figure 9.4) are best when respondents must prioritize their choices or express their preferences.
4. *Rating questions* (Figure 9.5) are appropriate when the respondent must judge an object on a continuum on either a unipolar or a bipolar scale.

Rating questions should include midpoints to avoid having respondents, who actually feel neutral, end up making a random choice on either side of the scale. Also, include (optional) open-ended questions to encourage respondents

What kind of game do you usually like?
Choose all that apply.

☐ Casual Game	☐ First-Person Shooter
☐ Role-Playing Game	☐ Multiplayer Online Battle Arena
☐ Action-Adventure	☐ Visual-novel
☐ Simulation Game	☐ Massively Mutiplayer Online Role-Playing Game
☐ Strategy Game	☐ Action Role-Playing Game
☐ Real-Time Strategy	☐ Adventure

Figure 9.3 Example of a multiple-choice question (used for the study in Bopp et al., 2016)

Please rank these Game genres from your favorite to your least favorite, 1 = favorite, 5 = least favorite.
Please rank the questions by clicking on them in order.

Action Game	
Adventure Game	**1**
Strategy Game	**3**
Simulation Game	
Role-Playing Game	**2**

Figure 9.4 Example of a ranking question

Thinking about your **most recent Dark Souls III game-session**, please indicate to what extend you agree with each of the following statements. Please rate these statements from 1 (strongly disagree) to 7 (strongly agree).

	Strongly disagree (1)	(2)	(3)	(4)	(5)	(6)	Strongly agree (7)
The game provided me with interesting options and choices.	○	○	○	○	○	○	○
I felt very capable and effective when playing.	○	○	○	○	○	○	○
When I accomplished something in the game I experienced genuine pride.	○	○	○	○	○	○	○
Learning the game controls was easy.	○	○	○	○	○	○	○
I could always find something interesting in the game to do.	○	○	○	○	○	○	○
I didn't feel close to other players.	○	○	○	○	○	○	○

Figure 9.5 Example of a Likert-type scale rating question. Note the midpoint (4) on a scale ranging from 1 to 7

to comment on any points of confusion during the survey or to clarify their responses. These questions can be added at the end of each page or at the end of the entire survey.

9.4.2 Questionnaire biases and other pitfalls

After writing the first survey draft, it is crucial to check the phrasing of each question for potential biases. Consider the following:

- Avoid complex, difficult to understand questions.
- Avoid answer options such as 'no opinion', 'do not know', 'not applicable', or 'unsure', since respondents with actual opinions will be tempted to select this option to avoid spending time on thinking about their

opinion. A good survey question should be answerable by all respondents. Moreover, the analysis and interpretation of these 'no opinion' answers is often not straightforward.

- Instead of giving options that allow participants to opt out of responding, include an optional text entry field for respondents to justify and explain their answer at the bottom of each page.

- Avoid using the same rating scale in a series of back-to-back questions (e.g., 'How fun was X?', 'How fun was Y?').

- Be wary of cramming many questions into a single survey, as respondents will become bored or fatigued. This will increase your dropout rate, or worse, participants will rush through the questionnaire without paying attention to their answers. Both of these outcomes limit your data's usefulness and should be avoided.

- Social desirability occurs when respondents (e.g., fans of a franchise) answer questions in a manner they feel will be positively perceived by others (e.g., the game designers and developers). For example, respondents might give a more positive evaluation for popular publishers/ studios or under-report unfavourable opinions (Ambinder, 2014). To mitigate these effects, respondents should be able to answer the survey anonymously. In addition, the survey should either be conducted by a third party or the survey should be self-administered.

- Halo and placebo effects by mentioning (allegedly) new game features can influence survey responses (Denisova and Cairns, 2015). Consider disclosing information about specific game features only sparingly.

- *Broad questions* lack focus and can be interpreted in different ways. For example, 'Describe the way you play on your smartphone' is too broad, as there are different games, motives, and situations for mobile gaming. These questions are too general and usually yield few actionable insights. A more focused set of questions for the example above include 'Which games did you play on your smartphone over the last week?' and 'Describe the locations in which you played on your smartphone last week.'

- *Leading questions* may introduce unwanted biases in the data by manipulating respondents into giving a certain answer. For example, 'This game has a Metacritic score of 93. How much fun did you experience with the game?'. The same holds true for questions that ask the respondent to agree or disagree with a given statement; for example, 'Do you agree or disagree with the following statement: I use my smartphone more often than my tablet for gaming.' Questions should be asked in a neutral way without examples or additional information that may bias respondents towards a particular response.

- *Double-barrelled questions* ask about multiple items while only allowing for a single response, decreasing the reliability and validity of the data. These questions can usually be detected by the existence of the word 'and'. For example, when asked 'How fun is it to play on your smartphone and your tablet?', a respondent with differing attitudes towards the two devices will be forced to pick an attitude that either reflects just one device or the average across both devices. Questions with multiple items should be broken down into one question per construct or item.

- *Prediction or hypothetical questions* ask survey respondents to anticipate or imagine future behaviours or attitudes in a given situation. Examples include 'Over the next month, how frequently will you access the PlayStation store?'; 'Which of the following features would make you have more fun with this game?'. Even if respondents have clear answers to these questions, their response may not predict actual future behaviours or experiences.

9.5 Established questionnaires in GUR

An alternative to constructing a new questionnaire is to employ a well-established questionnaire. Ideally, these questionnaires have been previously validated, which allows researchers to compare the results to other studies that have used the questionnaire. An existing questionnaire can be adapted to the specific study context as needed; however, this reduces the comparability between different studies. GUR is a relatively new field in comparison to other disciplines; therefore some questionnaires in GUR have not been extensively validated, and should be employed with caution (Brühlmann and Schmid, 2015). Some of the most commonly used GUR-related questionnaires are the following:

- Game Experience Questionnaire (GEQ). The GEQ by IJsselsteijn and colleagues (IJsselsteijn et al., 2008) incorporates seven different dimensions of player experience: sensory and imaginative immersion, tension, competence, flow, negative effect, positive effect, and challenge. The GEQ is a self-report measure for a rather multifaceted investigation of game experience and is yet to be validated.

- Player Experience of Need Satisfaction Scale (PENS). The PENS is a proprietary questionnaire investigating the 'motivational pull' of video games (Ryan et al., 2006). It is based on self-determination theory and focuses on the three basic human needs: autonomy (volitional aspects of an activity), competence (experience of control and mastery), and relatedness (connection to others).
- Immersive Experience Questionnaire (IEQ). The IEQ was developed by Jennett et al. (2008) and measures the *player-related* factors cognitive involvement, real-world dissociation, and emotional involvement, as well as the *game-related* factors challenge and control.
- Positive and Negative Affect Schedule (PANAS). The PANAS is widely used as a measure for *strong* positive and negative affective reactions in a variety of contexts and was developed by Watson et al. (1988).
- Self-Assessment Manikin (SAM). The SAM measures the dimensions pleasure, arousal, and dominance of affective reactions nonverbally. It is composed of three rows of pictograms assessing the dimensions on a 5-point scale (Bradley and Lang, 1994).
- Intrinsic Motivation Inventory (IMI). The IMI is a multidimensional measurement device developed to measure different aspects of an experience (Ryan, 1982). It includes a subscale for interest/enjoyment that was originally intended as a measure for intrinsic motivation, but is also widely used as a measure of enjoyment in GUR (Mekler et al., 2014).
- Player Experience Inventory (PXI). Similar to the GEQ, the PXI aims to measure the player experience broadly and is conceptually linked to the MDA framework (Hunicke et al., 2004). The PXI measures functional consequences (dynamics) and psychosocial consequences (aesthetics) with various subscales as well as overall enjoyment from playing the game. The measure is still in development and soon to be validated (Vanden Abeele et al., 2016).

9.6 Conducting surveys

9.6.1 Survey implementation

There are several online survey tools available for implementing online surveys. Most of them can be used for free (with limited features), such as Google Forms, LimeSurvey, Questback, SurveyGizmo, and SurveyMonkey. When deciding on the appropriate survey platform, the functionality, cost, and ease of use should be taken into consideration. Depending on your study, the questionnaire may require a survey tool that supports functionality such as branching and conditionals, the ability to pass URL parameters, multiple languages, and a range of question types. Of course, there is always the option of preparing your online survey in-house and hosting it on your own servers.

In addition, the survey's visual design should be taken into account, since specific choices may unintentionally bias respondents. For example, progress bars can be misleading and intimidating in long surveys, resulting in increased dropout rates. In short surveys, progress bars are likely to increase completion rates, since substantial progress is shown between pages.

When launching a survey, check for common dropout points and long completion times, examine data quality checks, and review answers to open-ended questions. High dropout rates and completion times may point to flaws in the survey design, while unusual answers may suggest a disconnect between a question's intention and respondents' interpretation. Other survey data worth monitoring include the devices from which the survey was accessed and how many respondents dropped out on each page. It is important to monitor such metrics, so that improvements can be quickly applied before the entire sample has responded to the survey.

9.6.2 Data quality checks

Data quality checks have become a staple in empirical research, as they ensure a certain quality of respondents' answering behaviour and filter out responses that do not meet these standards. These qualities include attentiveness, honesty, and carefulness. Attentiveness refers to respondents reading all instructions and questions, without skipping over possibly important parts or missing a word. As there is no investigator present during online surveys, it is impossible to know whether or not respondents actually read the questions before answering without resorting to *attention-check questions*. These typically consist of bogus items, hidden within the main survey questions, which have only one correct answer. Example items include 'Yesterday while watching TV I had a fatal heart attack' and 'I read instructions carefully. To show that you are reading these instructions, please leave this question blank.' However, note that many survey respondents, particularly on crowdsourcing platforms, have learned to easily spot and circumvent these questions. Hence, we additionally suggest implementing a *seriousness check* at the end of the survey, which consists of a question asking respondents whether or not they seriously filled in all questions

(Aust et al., 2013). For example: 'It would be very helpful if you could tell us at this point whether you have answered all questions seriously, so that we can use your answers for our analysis, or whether you were just clicking through to take a look at the survey.' Respondents were able to choose one of two following answers: 'I have answered all questions seriously' or 'I just clicked through the survey, please throw my data away.'

9.7 Data clean-up and next steps

9.7.1 Preparing and exploring the data

When exploring the collected survey data, you should always look for signs of low-quality responses. Low-quality survey data can either be left as is, removed, or presented separately from trusted data. If the researcher decides to remove poor data, there are three options: (1) Remove individual respondents' data when of poor quality (i.e., listwise deletion), for instance, when they are identified as speeders or straight-liners (see following). (2) Remove individual questions or variables if the responses are of consistently poor quality (i.e., pairwise deletion), for instance, because respondents did not fully understand the question. (3) Exclude data beyond a certain point in the survey where respondents' data quality has declined. The following are signals to look out for at the survey response level:

- *Duplicate responses.* Respondents might be able to fill out the survey more than once. Respondent information such as name, email address, or any other unique identifiers should be used to find and remove duplicate responses.
- *Speeders.* Respondents that complete the survey faster than what is expected under normal circumstances. Speeders may have carelessly read and answered the questions, resulting in arbitrary responses. Even if attention-check questions were implemented, examine the distribution of response times and remove any respondents that were suspiciously fast.
- *Straight-liners.* Respondents that always, or almost always, pick the same answer option across survey questions are referred to as straight-liners. Grid-style questions (see Figure 9.5) are particularly prone to respondent straight-lining. Straight-liners tend to pick the first answer option when asked to rate a series of items or alternate between the first and second answer options across questions. If a respondent straight-lines

through the entire survey, consider removing the respondent's data entirely. If a respondent starts straight-lining at a certain point, consider keeping the data up until that point.

- *Missing data and dropouts.* Some respondents may finish a survey but skip several questions. Others may start the survey but break off at some point. Both result in missing data.
- *Low inter-item reliability.* When multiple questions are used to measure a single construct, respondents' answers should be consistent across this set of questions. Respondents that give inconsistent or unreliable responses (e.g., selecting 'very fast' and 'very slow' for separate questions assessing the construct of speed) may not have carefully read the questions and should be considered for removal.
- *Outliers.* Answers that significantly deviate from the majority of responses are considered outliers and should be examined. For questions with numeric values, we typically calculate outliers as anything outside of two or three standard deviations from the mean. Determine how much of a difference keeping or removing the outliers has on variables' averages. If the impact is significant, the researcher may either remove such responses entirely or replace them with a value that equals two or three standard deviations from the mean. Another way to describe the central tendency while minimizing the effect of outliers is to use the median rather than the mean.
- *Inadequate open-ended responses.* Open-ended questions may lead to low-quality responses due to the amount of effort required to answer these questions. Remove obvious nonsense answers, such as 'asdf'. After this, examine all of the other answers from the same respondent to determine whether all their survey responses warrant removal.

9.7.2 Data analysis and reporting

Data analysis and interpretation should be as objective as possible. Games User Researchers usually have the benefit of not being as emotionally invested in the development of the game. This allows GUR to play the role of the player's advocate, who might have very different views than the developers. Nevertheless, it is beneficial to think about whether a different researcher would have come to the same conclusions.

To analyse closed-ended responses, *descriptive* and *inferential statistics* may be employed. Descriptive statistics describe the existing data set and help identify emerging patterns. They include measures such as the frequency distribution, central tendency (e.g., mean or median), and data dispersion (e.g., standard deviation). Inferential statistics can be used to draw inferences from the sample (your survey respondents) to the overall population (e.g., your player base). A comprehensive overview of statistical analysis methods is beyond the scope of this chapter, but we wholeheartedly recommend Andy Field's *Discovering Statistics* series on the topic. There are several packages available to assist with survey analysis: Microsoft Excel and certain survey platforms, such as SurveyMonkey and Google Forms, allow for descriptive statistics and charts. More advanced software such as SPSS, R, SAS, and Matlab can be used for complex modelling, calculations, and charting.

Analysing open-ended responses contributes to a more holistic understanding of the phenomenon being studied, as it reveals important insights that cannot otherwise be extracted from closed-ended responses. To do so, the qualitative data are analysed by applying a coding scheme established with regard to the objective of that survey question. We recommend Johnny Saldaña's (2009) book for a comprehensive overview and description of different coding approaches. After analysing all respondents' comments, researchers may begin to summarize the key themes of the data. These themes can be exemplified with representative quotes.

Once the question-by-question analysis is completed, findings need to be synthesized across all questions to address the goals of the survey. These findings will help identify larger themes and answer the initially defined research questions. Finally, these findings are translated into recommendations and design implications as appropriate.

Acknowledgements

Special thanks to Lena Aeschbach for assisting with the literature review and providing feedback on earlier drafts of this chapter.

References

Ambinder, M. (2014). Making the best of imperfect data: reflections on an ideal world. In Proceedings of the 2015 Annual Symposium on Computer-Human Interaction in Play (pp. 469–469). New York: ACM.

Antin, J., Shaw, A. (2012). Social desirability bias and self-reports of motivation: a study of Amazon Mechanical Turk in the US and India. In Proceedings of the SIGCHI Conference on Human Factors in Computing Systems (pp. 2925–2934). New York: ACM.

Aust, F., Diedenhofen, B., Ullrich, S., Musch, J., 2013. Seriousness checks are useful to improve data validity in online research. Behavior Research Methods, 45(2), 527–535.

Bopp, J. A., Mekler, E. D., Opwis, K. (2016). Negative emotion, positive experience? Emotionally moving moments in digital games. In Proceedings of the 2016 CHI Conference on Human Factors in Computing Systems (pp. 2996–3006). New York: ACM.

Bradley, M. M., Lang, P. J. (1994). Measuring emotion: the self-assessment manikin and the semantic differential. Journal of Behavior Therapy and Experimental Psychiatry, 25(1), 49–59.

Brühlmann, F., Schmid, G. M. (2015). How to measure the game experience? Analysis of the factor structure of two questionnaires. In Proceedings of the 33rd Annual ACM Conference Extended Abstracts on Human Factors in Computing Systems (pp. 1181–1186). New York: ACM.

Curran, P. G. (2016). Methods for the detection of carelessly invalid responses in survey data. Journal of Experimental Social Psychology, 66, 4–19.

DeVellis, R. F. (2012). Scale development: theory and applications. Thousand Oaks, CA: Sage Publications.

Denisova, A., Cairns, P. (2015). The placebo effect in digital games: phantom perception of adaptive artificial intelligence. In Proceedings of the 2015 Annual Symposium on Computer-Human Interaction in Play (pp. 23–33). New York: ACM.

Faul, F., Erdfelder, E., Lang, A. G., Buchner, A. (2007). G* Power 3: a flexible statistical power analysis program for the social, behavioural, and biomedical sciences. Behavior Research Methods, 39(2), 175–191.

Fowler Jr, F. J. (2013). Survey research methods. London: Sage Publications. ISBN: 978-1-4522-5900-0.

Fowler Jr, F. J. (2014). Survey research methods. Thousand Oaks, CA: Sage Publications.

Hazan, E. (2013). Contextualizing data. In M. S. El-Nasr et al. (eds.), Game analytics (pp. 477–496). London: Springer.

Hillman, S., Stach, T., Procyk, J., Zammitto, V. (2016). Diary methods in AAA games user research. In Proceedings of the 2016 CHI Conference extended abstracts on Human Factors in Computing Systems (pp. 1879–1885). New York: ACM.

Hunicke, R., LeBlanc, M., Zubek, R. (2004, July). MDA: a formal approach to game design and game research. Proceedings of the AAAI Workshop on Challenges in Game AI, 4(1).

Jennett, C., Cox, A. L., Cairns, P., Dhoparee, S., Epps, A., Tijs, T., Walton, A. (2008). Measuring and defining the experience of immersion in games. International Journal of Human-Computer Studies, 66(9), 641–661.

Kittur, A., Chi, E. H., Suh, B. (2008). Crowdsourcing user studies with Mechanical Turk. In Proceedings of the SIGCHI Conference on Human Factors in Computing Systems (pp. 453–456). New York: ACM.

Mason, W., Suri, S. (2012). Conducting behavioural research on Amazon's Mechanical Turk. Behavior Research Methods, 44(1), 1–23.

Meade, A. W., Craig, S. B. (2012). Identifying careless responses in survey data. Psychological Methods, 17(3), 437–455.

Mekler, E. D., Bopp, J. A., Tuch, A. N., and Opwis, K. (2014). A systematic review of quantitative studies on the enjoyment of digital entertainment games. In Proceedings of the SIGCHI Conference on Human Factors in Computing Systems (CHI '14) (pp. 927–936). New York: ACM.

Nacke, L. E., Bateman, C. Mandryk, R. L. (2014). BrainHex: a neurobiological gamer typology survey. Entertainment Computing, 5(1), 55–62.

Nacke, L. E., Grimshaw, M. N. Lindley, C. A. (2010). More than a feeling: measurement of sonic user experience and psychophysiology in a first-person shooter game. Interacting with Computers, 22(5), 336–343.

Petralito, S., Brühlmann, F., Iten, G., Mekler, E. D., Opwis, K. (2017). A good reason to die: how avatar death and high challenges enable positive experiences. In Proceedings of the 2017 CHI Conference on Human Factors in Computing Systems (pp. 5087–5097). New York: ACM.

Ryan, R. M. (1982). Control and information in the intrapersonal sphere: an extension of cognitive evaluation theory. Journal of Personality and Social Psychology, 43, 450–461.

Ryan, R. M., Rigby, C., Przybylski, A. (2006). The motivational pull of video games: a self-determination theory approach. Motivation and Emotion, 30(4), 344–360.

IJsselsteijn, W., van den Hoogen, W., Klimmt, C., de Kort, Y., Lindley, C., Mathiak, K., …, Vorderer, P. (2008). Measuring the experience of digital game enjoyment. In Proceedings of Measuring Behavior (pp. 88–89). Maastricht, The Netherlands.

Vanden Abeele, V., Nacke, L. E., Mekler, E. D., Johnson, D. (2016). Design and preliminary validation of The Player Experience Inventory. In Proceedings of the 2016 Annual Symposium on Computer-Human Interaction in Play Companion Extended Abstracts (pp. 335–341). New York: ACM.

Watson, D., Clark, L. A., Tellegen, A. (1988). Development and validation of brief measures of positive and negative affect: the PANAS scales. Journal of Personality and Social Psychology, 54(6), 1063.

Further reading

For an excellent, more in-depth overview of survey research in HCI, make sure to check out this paper, which also served as a template for this chapter:

Müller, H. Sedley, A., Ferrall-Nunge, E. (2014). Survey research in HCI. In J. S. Olson and W. A. Kellogg (eds.), Ways of knowing in HCI (pp. 229–266). Springer.

For all your statistics needs, we recommend any of the Andy Field 'Discovering Statistics' books, for instance:

Field, A., Miles, J. Field, Z. (2012). Discovering statistics using R. Thousand Oaks, CA: Sage Publications.

For a comprehensive overview of qualitative analysis and description of different coding approaches, we recommend:

Saldaña, J. (2009). The coding manual for qualitative researchers. Thousand Oaks, CA: Sage Publications.

CHAPTER 10

Interviewing players

STEVE BROMLEY, *Parliamentary Digital Service*

Highlights

Interviews provide direct insight into the player's behaviours, motivations, and understanding of how the game works. This chapter will explore the preparation of an interview, interviews during the session, final interviews, and interview tips. It concludes with a discussion of data capture and analysis, as well as thoughts on the future of the method.

10.1 Introduction

Interviews are a key part of a successful qualitative user test session. They offer one of the only ways to understand players' motivations, their understanding of mechanics or features in the game, and why players act in weird ways! In this chapter, we will explore how to use interviews to extract rich and useful data from playtests, and cover techniques to ensure that the findings from interviews are relevant, true, and will provide actionable data to development teams.

One of the most common forms of playtesting is one-to-one sessions, where a single moderator watches a single player (or single group of players for multiplayer games) play through the game. The moderator's role in these sessions is to observe the session, noting any usability issues, and probing to understand why the observed usability issues occurred.

Unfortunately, researchers do not have the technology to look inside people's brains and understand what they are thinking (yet!). Instead we have to ask players what they are thinking, what they are doing, and why they are thinking

Games User Research, Anders Drachen, Pejman Mirza-Babaei, Lennart E. Nacke (Eds).
© Oxford University Press 2018. Published 2018 by Oxford University Press

or doing it. By asking the player questions during or after a session, researchers can check comprehension and understanding of the game or mechanics within the game. They can also ask for opinions about the game, although, as we will see, caution must be taken when dealing with opinion data.

There are also some topics that interviews are not suitable for, despite the temptation to ask, such as coming up with new ideas, or understanding how players would use the game in the future. This chapter will also look at what areas researchers should avoid asking about, and why this is the case.

10.2 Preparing an interview

A successful interview requires preparation before the session. Most qualitative tests will use a semi-structured format in which the questions are prepared beforehand, but the moderator is free to divert from them with follow-up questions, or to help tease out answers from participants.

The first thing to decide when preparing an interview is what to ask about. There are some questions that are almost always relevant to ask at the end of a session. Some good ones include the following:

- Overall, what did you think about the game?
- What did you like about the game?
- What did not you like about the game?
- Was there anything more difficult than you expected in the game?
- Was there anything more confusing than you expected in the game?

These questions fall into two categories. Some are asking opinions, which are typically not reliable enough to report with the limited number of users that will be seen in a qualitative test. However, they are easy to answer, which helps put the participant at ease, and can lead to discussions about the problems with the game—which are often caused by usability issues.

The questions about difficulty and confusion are more directly targeted to usability issues. If the player talks about not being able to understand what they should do, this is a good clue that there is an issue here, and follow-up questions should be used to understand what the confusion is and why it occurred.

In addition to asking the preceding generic questions, the moderator should review the goals of the test to identify if there are any other areas of the game that should be asked about in the final interview. In many cases, each of the goals can directly translate to a question—for example, if the developer's question is 'Do players understand the dodge mechanic?', a question should be asked about the dodge mechanic.

When writing questions, it's important to imagine how the player may answer, and whether that information would be useful for answering the test's objective. The dodge mechanic objective centres on understanding, so care needs to be taken to ensure the question is phrased in a way that will find out whether the player *understands* the mechanic, not just their thoughts on it. 'What do you think about the dodge mechanic?' is too vague, and may not get actionable data.

The question should also verify the player's understanding, because they may not realize they do not understand aspects of the game. Players may answer the question 'Do you understand the dodge mechanic?' with 'Yes', but it is not possible to tell from their answer if they do, truly, understand how it works. A better form for this item would be 'Explain to me how the dodge mechanic works', which can then be compared to the development team's definition of how the dodge mechanic works for validation. Follow-up questions may be needed to fully probe the player's understanding, which will be covered later.

A printed script should be prepared for the interview, to remind the moderator about the topics that they need to cover. Because this interview format is semi-structured, the moderator should be prepared to deviate in how they actually ask the questions and what they follow up on. As long as all of the topics are covered at the end of the session, the interview was a success!

10.3 Interviewing during the session

It's important that researchers identify the appropriate time for asking questions during the research session. When observing tests, moderators will usually ask 'probing' questions to help uncover what players are thinking while playing (as covered in Chapter 11). However, interviews do also have their place during the research session.

A very common technique is to start the test with a pre-session interview. This serves two purposes: not only does it help put the participant at ease, but it can also be used to validate that they are an appropriate user for this session. Typically, these will start with broad, easy questions, and then follow up with questions that home in on the recruitment criteria. So, for example, if a test was looking for someone who plays online competitive multiplayer games, the moderator may ask the following:

- 'What game are you currently playing at home?' [participant responds]
- 'And what do you think about that game?' [participant responds]
- 'And do you ever play games with people online?' [participant responds]
- 'Which games do you play online against other people?' [participant responds]
- 'And what is it you look for in an online game?' [participant responds]

In this example, the questions were easy to answer, which should help put the participant at ease. The participant may be worried about what will happen in the session, or whether they will be 'good enough', so these questions will help them realize that they can contribute. By asking them to reflect on their experiences, this also helps frame the session for them, so that they understand that their opinions are of interest (even if the moderator is really watching their behaviour!). These questions will also verify whether the participant does play online games and that they can speak articulately about their opinions and experiences—which will help decide if they are an appropriate user or a mis-recruit.

Once the player starts playing, there are other times in the session when an interview may be appropriate. For studies which compare two alternate versions of something (A/B testing), such as alternate control schemes or alternate HUDs, the moderator will likely want to interview the participant on their impressions of the first version before swapping to the second, before the user forgets. Interviewing them about their experience then will influence their opinion of the second variation of the study, though, so remember to alternate the order between subjects.

In some studies, the moderator may also want to perform 'skill-check' interviews, which ask players to describe specific abilities or mechanics and how they work (e.g., 'What attacks do you have? And how does each one work?'). For skill-check interviews, the moderator should agree with the developers on a time in the game by which the players should have learned all of the mechanics. Skill-check interviews can then be run at the designated point in the session with each participant. By checking players' understanding using this technique during the session, it is possible to assess the success of the tutorials, and then correct the player's understanding so that other usability issues (other than the problems with the tutorial) can be cleanly identified.

10.4 Final interview

Throughout the session the moderator may have observed behaviours or potential issues, but will not yet fully understand what they are or why they are happening. For example, a player might have consistently displayed an odd behaviour, such as consistently reloading twice in a row. The moderator may have noticed this behaviour in the session, but from observation alone the moderator has no idea why it is occurring. The final interview is the appropriate time to validate observations, to ensure that the moderator has understood them correctly, and to discover why the issues occurred.

It is common practice to start the final interview with a very broad 'What did you think about the game?' question. This question is open enough that it would not lead players into a specific subject matter, and will allow them to discuss the things that they feel are most pertinent about the game, which may include major usability issues. This is best followed up with a question about the best and worst aspects of the game ('What did you like best about the game? What did you like least about the game?') which ensures the moderator can capture the unprompted positive and negative aspects of the game from the player. These will often be opinions, rather than usability issues, but that's okay—this can be checked, and disregarded if not appropriate during analysis.

As covered earlier, the questions should then move onto specific topics, usually prompted by the objectives of the test. For example, if a test was focused on understanding different game modes, the moderator should ask about each directly to assess the player's understanding of each game mode and its rules. Hopefully, this list of questions related to mechanics will cover many of the observations noted in the session, but additional questions can be added on the fly as required.

Because the interviews are semi-structured, it's okay to deviate from the script if the participant is not giving up the goods! Players often talk about things unrelated to the question, and the moderator's task will be to bring them back on track or ask them to explain a previous point in more depth.

Having covered all of the points that are relevant to the test's objectives, there are some standard questions that are good to finish the session with. One is 'If you could change one thing about the game, what would it be?'. This should hopefully be a repeat of a point that has already been discussed in the interview, but it also serves as a good sanity check to make sure that the moderator has fully probed the player's thoughts. I also like to follow this up with 'And anything else you'd like to say about the game that I have not given you the chance to?', to ensure that the player has had the chance to fully express themselves, and nothing has been missed.

Having completed the interview, the session is over and the participant can go free!

10.5 Interviewing tips

There are lots of challenges with interviewing, and techniques for dealing with them that moderators should be aware of. Here are a few!

10.5.1 Repeating questions

Be aware that asking questions will change player behaviour. If a player is asked about their understanding of a mechanic or a feature before the end of the session, they will be more aware of that feature from then on, which can affect how they play. Because of this, repeating questions throughout a session can be dangerous—the moderator will only get their true understanding the first time, and after that the question will have influenced their behaviour and potentially how they understand the mechanic. Moderators should ensure that they are ready for the player's behaviour to be altered before asking questions, and ask at an appropriate point so as not to impact the data.

10.5.2 Repeating answers

When the player responds to a question, it can often be useful for the moderator to repeat their answer back to the player, rephrasing it slightly to ensure it sounds like normal conversation. This has a few advantages. If the player has been ambiguous in their answer, it helps ensure that the moderator has correctly understood the player's point. It also may prompt the player to explain their answer deeper, or add clarifying points. Finally, it will give the note taker additional time to write down the response!

10.5.3 Answering questions

Players will sometimes ask questions, either about the game or whether they have understood something correctly. A good technique when players are asking about the game is to turn it back on them, and ask about their expectations.

For example, when responding to 'Oh, I think this game is only for two play-ers. Is that right?', the moderator should say 'What would you expect?' or 'How would you expect it to work?'. The question then becomes another source of information about the player's current understanding of the game (in this exam-ple, whether the menus and game modes made the number of potential play-ers explicit). If players persist with their question or are asking if they have got something right, best practice is to defer—'Unfortunately, I'm not going to be very helpful right now, so I will leave that with you. If it's still unclear at the end of the session, we can talk about it then.'

10.5.4 Leading questions

Be very careful about not leading players with the phrasing of the question. A common mistake is to give away that they have not understood something by phrasing the question with a negative connotation—asking 'What made you think that?' indicates that the player was wrong, which can make them defensive or change their view. 'How do you know that?' is a better way of getting them to explain their thinking without giving away that they have misunderstood something.

10.5.5 Opinions

Opinions are not very useful in themselves in qualitative user tests. However, they can be the start of another source of information. When players report that they did or did not like something, by probing further ('What makes you say that?'), the moderator may discover that a usability issue is the cause. It can therefore be worth asking opinion questions, even if the opinion is not reported to the development team directly. During analysis, the researcher should be careful not to start including opinion data or reporting it as an issue. Due to the low sample size, these data are not as reliable as the usability feedback, and put-ting the two together can confuse development teams, or cause them to reject the usability findings because they do not agree with the opinion findings.

10.5.6 Unreliable answers

Because interviews happen after gameplay has finished, players may have for-gotten what they were thinking or doing earlier in the session. However, play-ers will still want to answer the questions, and so will try and think of a logical answer when asked—they may be too embarrassed to say they have forgotten or do not know. This means that there is a risk that players will come up with explanations that are inaccurate or do not reflect their behaviour or opinion while they were actually playing. When asking questions about events earlier in the session, watch out for unintentional lies—often it can be better to probe the player during the session soon after the issue occurred rather than waiting until the end. When interviewing at the end of the session, being aware of the risk of false/unreliable memories will help moderators know when to validate the interview data with other information sources such as observations.

10.5.7 Getting more information

A challenge when interviewing is knowing when the moderator has understood a player's answers fully, and when it is time to move on to the next topic. This can be difficult to recognize, but a good rule of thumb is to imagine explaining the issue to the game developer. For example, if the player describes the controls as 'rubbish', consider whether that would be useful for the developer to help fix it. In this case, it would not—there is no explanation of why the player believed the controls were rubbish, or how that impacted their experience when playing. If the player has not yet explained the root of the problem, the moderator should probe further by asking questions such as 'Why is that?', 'What caused that?', and 'How did that effect you playing the game?', until they have actionable information.

10.5.8 Do not let players project

A common problem to watch out for in sessions is when players stop describing their own opinions and experiences, and instead project to another. For example, they may say 'Well, it was not confusing for me, but it could be for kids.' This can mean two things. The first is that it was confusing for them, and they are embarrassed. This could be a usability issue. The second is that it was fine for them, but they think others may struggle, which would not be a usability issue yet. When this occurs, best practice is to verify whether it was confusing for this player or not ('How was it for you?'), and ignore the point about kids—if the researcher wanted to discover whether the game was confusing for kids, they should test kids directly. Another way in which players can be encouraged to project is by asking them what they would do in the future or in another hypothetical situation. Because the player is not being observed, and the situation is not real, this becomes opinion data and not suitable for a usability test. Do not ask those questions!

10.6 Data capture

It is difficult to hold a conversation while writing, and so ideally the session will have a separate moderator (speaking to the participant) and a note taker (hidden, writing down what was said). This allows the moderator to focus entirely on the player, rather than having to take time to write things down, which can impact the conversation and the participant's willingness to share. Two researchers are not always possible, though. In those cases, it is best to be upfront with the player and apologize: 'I'll be taking notes today, which may mean I'm sometimes slow, or will ask you to repeat things. Sorry about that, please bear with me!' It would also be possible to avoid taking notes at all during sessions with only one researcher, and then to watch the videos after to take notes on a second pass. This would, however, double the amount of time it takes to analyse the sessions, and so is often not practical in an active development environment where quick turnaround times are valued.

Regardless of whether the moderator will be taking notes, preparation will reduce the time it takes to analyse the results. Using the script for the interview as a guide, a note-taking template can be prepared which has different areas for each subject that will be covered. When taking notes during the session, the note taker can then write the notes directly into the relevant section. When it comes to analysis, this means the notes will be pre-sorted into categories, reducing time copying and pasting the notes.

Whether the notes from each session should all go into one document or several is up to the researcher. A single document will save analysis time later combining the notes, but increases the difficulty of removing 'dud' participants or mis-recruits. Despite this, in a busy development environment, speed is usually essential, which leads me to recommend all notes going into one document.

10.7 Analysis

Using the session design and tips above, the moderator will end a test with a lot of notes capturing what each player said during the session. After running a typical test with 5–10 users, these notes will be extensive. As recommended earlier, categorizing the notes during the session into sections provides a helpful shortcut in analysis and can greatly reduce the turnaround time for reporting.

Our team advocates using mind-mapping tools for capturing notes during user test sessions, which allows all of the sessions to be aggregated on the same map and moved around easily. Regardless of the method used to capture notes, time spent combining all of the responses into one document will save time later, if the notes were not originally captured on one document. For each topic covered in the interview, put all of the interview data into its relevant section (e.g., scoring, difficulty, controls).

Then run through all of the data, starting at the top of the first session to the end. Usability issues are typically either comprehension issues (e.g., misunderstandings, did not discover aspects of the game), or performance issues (e.g., when the player describes something as difficult or impossible to perform, and that was not the designers' intent). When data are encountered that indicates a potential usability issue, write the issue in a second 'usability issues' document, and copy the data from the interview into it (this is where using mind-mapping tools saves a lot of time). This list of issues will be supplemented by additional sources, such as observation and questionnaires which should also be sorted and added to the usability issues document, either as new issues or as additional data for the issues identified in interviews. Triangulation between different data sources is extremely important for ensuring that the usability issues are comprehensive and representative; therefore interviews should be used in conjunction with other methods, such as observation.

After integrating the data from all the sources into a list of issues, a second pass of the issues will allow the researcher to extract the *cause* and *impact* of each issue. The cause is what about the game made the issue occur, and will help developers identify what they should be altering to fix the issue. The impact of the issue will indicate what the consequence of not fixing the issue will be. Interview data are particularly suited for identifying cause and impact because the moderator should have explicitly asked the player to describe the cause of any problems and what impact they had—so some of the analysis is already done (although the player's thoughts will need to be validated by the researcher's understanding of the context).

Once all of the issues are fully explained and their relative severity identified, interview data can also be used to pull indicative quotes from the session, which can help convince stakeholders of the severity and impact of the issues. Video clips from interviews can also help with this.

After analysis, the researcher will now have a list of issues, their causes and impacts, and helpful quotes related to each. This is now ready for presenting to the development team.

There are also tools available that can help explore the data further through techniques such as keyword analysis or relationship mapping. They can be useful for deeper investigation of patterns or common themes in the responses. However, they will add significant time to your analysis, so should be saved for after the initial debriefing to the development team.

10.8 The future

Interviews continue to play a key role in understanding players' behaviour and motivation because of the direct insight they provide to the player's understanding of how the game works. Interviews are a primary method for researchers to see what is going on inside the player's head.

With the resurgence of interest in VR, the importance of interviews is only going to increase. VR headsets introduce methodological challenges to a traditional one-to-one user test due to the difficulties communicating with a player wearing a headset, which can make probing during the session difficult. This makes interviews and observation the primary way of collecting data during VR testing.

Interviews will also continue to be relevant for moderated one-to-one testing, as the key method of validating observations related to understanding and performance, and during larger-scale playtests as a method of getting a deeper understanding of the player's experience than can be revealed by surveys. With an awareness of the potential risks of interviewing covered in this chapter, researchers can combine interview data with other data sources such as observation and surveys to create a holistic view of the player's understanding and behaviour. Interviews are therefore a key part of uncovering and understanding usability issues, and ultimately help make games better!

CHAPTER 11

Observing the player experience

The art and craft of observing and documenting Games User Research

MIRWEIS SANGIN, *Sony PlayStation*

Highlights

This chapter covers applied methods to uncover usability problems and concrete guidelines on how to plan for capturing usability events. An overview of tools and processes that can help to document and analyse observations made by the researchers is also presented.

11.1 Introduction

Games User Research (GUR) is a field rich in methodologies used to investigate players' experience with games. These methods rely on a variety of different techniques to collect and document data on player experience. This data can be put into two main categories: behaviours (the actions players take in the game) and attitudes (players' opinions on what they play).

Direct observation of player behaviour is an extremely powerful tool researchers have at their disposal. It provides direct and objective insights into players' behaviour. As researchers, we have developed a great intuition for observing

Games User Research, Anders Drachen, Pejman Mirza-Babaei, Lennart E. Nacke (Eds).
© Oxford University Press 2018. Published 2018 by Oxford University Press

others' behaviour and making educated assumptions about players' knowledge and intentions. Observation of player behaviour is usually less prone to subjective biases compared to self-report methods such as interviews and contextual probing. However, they can still be prone to researcher biases such as the interpretation bias, observer-expectancy bias, and confirmation bias. There is a risk of jumping to conclusions and making unverified assumptions about players' intentions and the thought processes behind their behaviour.

Observing player experience can also be very demanding. It can put a heavy burden on the observer who needs to capture and document a constant flow of cues about players' behaviours, feelings, and thoughts.

In this chapter, we will walk through a series of concrete considerations about observing and capturing player experience in the context of GUR. We will cover methods to plan observation protocols and cover tools and processes to observe and document usability events. We will identify ways to avoid some of the pitfalls of observing and documenting player experience.

11.2 Planning for observation

As for every aspect of GUR, effective observation of player behaviour heavily relies on preparation. In a fast-paced industry such as game development, time is often of essence when it comes to turning around results. User research is often a race against the clock. The best way to save time on analysis and reporting is to spend as much time as possible on planning and preparing.

Planning games usability testing boils down to identifying areas where the player experience does not match the intended experience. When preparing for observing the player experience, you need to consider two main elements: (a) have a clear idea of what you need to observe, and (b) have a clear idea of how you will document your observations.

To do so, you need to consider three main components:

- Collect and clarify research objectives and business needs.
- Develop a thorough understanding of the game content and the player experience.
- Identify the key events where the content is not experienced as intended.

An important aspect of planning usability observations is the level of complexity of the player experience you want to observe. Factors such as depth of the gameplay mechanics, broadness of the game environment, and intricacy of the game's rules can add to the complexity of the observation and make the planning phase a daunting experience. Varying degree of complexity in the testing content requires careful preparation in order to break down the content and use the appropriate observation and documentation techniques to avoid the pitfalls of overly relying on pure intuition.

One helpful trick is to visualise how to best report the findings, and walk your way backwards. Ask yourself: 'Is my data likely to benefit from a presentation following a form of narrative? How can I best convey the context players are involved in when the problem occurred? How much detail do I need to supply to convey my findings? Do I need visual supports to persuade the stakeholders? How important is it to report the space and time where the event took place?' But it all starts with clarifying the study objectives and business needs.

11.2.1 Clarify study objective and business needs

The starting point of any user research is to clearly define objectives and ask yourself why you are doing the research in the first place. Research objectives allow you to identify the relevant events to observe and capture (target events), but also what is out of scope and should not be a captured (distracters). Time is of essence when it comes to observing player experience, and any time spent on capturing unnecessary information risks missing out on more relevant data. Clarifying the study objectives and business needs—what your company or client wants to get out of the research—is paramount to ensure that your observations are relevant and focused.

Clearly stating the usability goals should enable you to identify elements of the player experience you need to cover during your observation. If it is your first contact with the project, it is important to spend as much time as necessary to fully understand what the intended design is by talking to as many stakeholders possible.

Once you have listed the study objectives, it always helps to rephrase them as questions. Whenever possible, break down each research question into subquestions. For each sub-question, assess if it relates to *clarity* (can players work out what to do and how to do it?), *way-finding* (can players work out where to go?), and *difficulty* (are players able to perform what is required of them?). When planning your sessions and observation methods, make sure that you stick to the objectives agreed with the stakeholder.

Lastly, ask yourself:

- How much detail do I need to answer the main objectives?
- Do my stakeholders expect the main issues or a detailed report of high- and low-priority problems?
- Are they likely to take my word for it or are they likely to need some convincing?

11.2.2 Understanding player experience

Once you have clarified study objectives and research questions, it is time to have a clear understanding of the content players have to play: the player experience. Start with the categorisation of the objectives in terms of 'knows what to do', 'knows how to do it', 'is able to do'.

'Knowing what to do' is subject to game instructions and clarity of objectives. In your game, identify the instructions and prompts that are designed to help players understand the game objectives and rules.

'Know how to do' is related to on-screen clues on how to control the game. You need to compare the inputs used by the player and the inputs required by the game (e.g., Is the player pressing the correct button to jump? Is the player tapping the appropriate element on-screen?).

'Is the player able to do' is related to game difficulty. This usually implies looking out for failure states such as deaths, crashes, or failing to complete a level or mission in time. Repeated failures need to be captured as well as signs of frustration (e.g., sighs, swearing) as symptoms of an imbalanced game.

There are two major aspects of the player experience you need to consider when preparing your observation and note taking: *time* and *space*. First, you need to assess how the game experience unfolds over time. Is your experience linear? Linear games control how the various challenges and events unfold for the players. Linear events follow a sequence and can be put in a timeline. Often, for linear games, the places where the events occur are less relevant.

Non-linear games are focused on player freedom, empowering players to do what they want and in the order they want. Open-world and Sandbox games fall into this category. As the order of experiencing the events is usually up to the players, the relevant criterion is usually the place where these events are occurring, such as specific quests or areas.

11.2.3 Preparing data capture strategy

There are three main approaches to note taking: free-form, structured, and semi-structured.

A *free-form* approach has no pre-established structure. It usually relies on you to capture events relevant to the study. Both the content and the form are left open so that you have the freedom to capture the information as best fits. The advantage of a free-form approach is that it usually does not require much preparation. You are free to capture usability events at your discretion and with the tools you are most comfortable with. The downside is that it is likely to be labour-intensive during the session and lead to capturing more detail than really necessary. It can take some significant mental bandwidth to write notes, because in the absence of a clear structure and guidelines, you will have to handle both the content and the form of your notes on the fly. If too much of your attention is taken by this process, you may miss important observations.

The *structured* approach requires careful preparation of a note-taking protocol and template. The purpose of a structured approach is to establish a clear observation grid on which all relevant events are laid out in advance. The researcher only needs to tag a specific event on the grid when it occurs (often with specifically assigned codes and shortcuts). A structured approach frees up a lot of mental bandwidth for observing. The drawback is that it can be often constraining and does not enable the freedom to capture events that fall outside the established structure.

A *semi-structured* approach is a happy middle ground where you prepare a global structure for your notes but still allow enough freedom to adapt on the fly. Typically, you should have an idea of how to group events in meaningful buckets. However, the form and level of details can vary from one note to another.

11.2.4 Structuring the note-taking guide

According to Wurman and his 'five hat-racks' LATCH model, there are five main ways of organising and displaying information: location, alphabet, time, category, and hierarchy.

Location is mapping the information in a XY space where geographical organisation gives the most meaning to your data. Location works great when you need to convey the *where* of your usability events. Structuring and organising your notes spatially such as 'geo-tagging' events on a level map can be a powerful way of communicating coordinates of problems related to level design, for instance.

Time is the best way to organise events that occur during a set timeline and over fixed durations. The sequence in which events unfold can offer major insights into the causes and impacts of a usability event. Capturing events on a timeline is the most efficient technique when your gameplay follows a linear structure where events unfold in the same order.

Categories and *hierarchies* allow you to sort information into meaningful buckets. Pre-established categories such as 'onboarding', 'balancing', and 'way-finding' are useful to save time on reporting and ensure that usability events are reported in a meaningful way.

Alphabet is best used when you have a lot of issues to refer to that cannot be organised in any of the four other ways (e.g., dictionaries, phonebooks). This is probably the least effective way of organising usability events, unless you are building a large library of usability problems or a findings log.

11.2.5 Note-taking tools

When making notes, you have many tools at your disposal, each with their strengths and weaknesses. Here is a brief summary of the main type of note-taking tools.

Pen and paper. Handwritten notes represent the most basic way of capturing usability events. This should come naturally to pretty much everyone. They also do not require any complicated set-up and offer a great deal of freedom to use the space on a sheet of paper to structure your notes to your liking and mix up written words and sketches to best capture the player experience.

The downside is that it can be a slow process. You might miss events if you are caught up in writing. If you work as a team of moderator and note taker, legibility of handwriting can also become an issue. Finally, you will most certainly need to digitise your notes, which can add extra time to the time-sensitive phase of analysis and reporting. (Note-taking tip: Use different colours of sticky notes. Write one event at a time. These will make the aggregation and analysis process easier and more efficient.)

Word processing and spreadsheets. Word processing and spreadsheet programs are probably the most common tools used for capturing observations. They have many advantages, the most notable being that they are ubiquitous. Chances are that you know well your way around them. Plus, they are easy to share and edit. They are perfectly suited to capture notes in a sequential order.

The downside is that they usually do not support very well note-taking guides organised by space, categories, and hierarchies. They do not offer much flexibility in terms of structuring and grouping on the fly. It can become quite time-consuming to move events around, as often you will need to copy and paste or add lines to a spreadsheet.

Event-logging software. A more advanced alternative to traditional note-taking tools is to use specialised software to log events. Audio or video logging software such as OVO or Morae enables you to add markers and annotations to a video capture of your session. You can review the videos later and use the markers as quick access to specific points of interest. These usually also come with a handy functionality to generate clips to send to your stakeholder.

Mind-mapping tools. Mind-mapping is a method to organise information in a radial diagram created around a central concept, to which items as keywords, sentences, or images are added (Figure 11.1). The top categories are represented radially. The sublevels are branched out in a tree-like hierarchy. These simple rules make mind-mapping an extremely powerful tool to collect and organise your usability events. Here are a few advantages among many more:

- Common mind-mapping tools allow you to input your observation events as unique objects, making them easy to (re)organise via simple drag and drop.
- Information can be grouped in categories (Level 1), or hierarchies (Level 2 and above), as a timeline (used as an outline to parse info from top to bottom) or spatially (by dragging and dropping each branch in the 2D space).
- The spatial and hierarchical representation helps improve thinking, and highly facilitates the parsing of information.
- The ability to open and close branches allows you to better manage your attention, improve focus, and minimize scrolling.

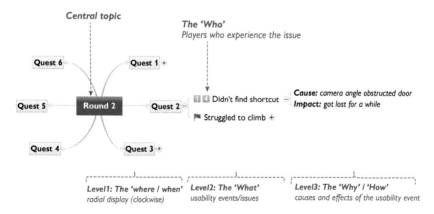

Figure 11.1 Example of a mind-map layout

For these and many other reasons, I highly recommend you consider mind-mapping as a tool to collect, organise, and analyse observations.

11.3 Observing player experience

In traditional lab-based research, there are many types of events you can observe and document. They are listed below in order of priority.

11.3.1 In-game events

In-game events are the most common and insightful type of observables. You will probably be spending most of your time observing and capturing these.

11.3.2 Control inputs

Inputs on gamepad, keyboard, mouse, or touchscreen are the means for players to interact with the game. Often, there is no need to focus on controls, as the in-game events are a direct reflection of player actions. But these are occasionally helpful to identify misconceptions, where players use the wrong input to perform a specific action.

11.3.3 Spontaneous player comments

Spontaneous comments and verbal expressions of frustration or annoyance such as sighs and swearing can also be good opportunities to jump in and unpack a usability problem that players are encountering.

11.3.4 Players' body language, facial expression, and posture

Non-verbal indicators can tell a lot about what players are going through. These metalinguistic cues are out of the scope of this chapter. Remember that your intuition can mislead you. It is always worth validating with players any assumption you make. Highly immersed players can often display signs of frustration even when they are having fun and are engaged with the game.

Some games require specific set-ups and settings and cannot be solely tested in a lab. They are best tested in context, or a setting as close as possible to how they are to be experienced in the wild. They usually take advantage of innovative techniques such augmented reality (e.g., Invizimals™, Wonderbook™), geolocation (e.g., Pokémon Go™), motion-based interfaces, and VR. These games have additional observation needs. Here are the key factors to keep in mind when making observation in situ.

11.3.5 The play space

Do not limit your observation to players' behaviour and comments. Try to capture as much detail about the physical space where the play takes place. When visiting participants' homes, it is for instance worth taking pictures of the space where players are likely to experience your game.

11.3.6 The set-up

When researching first-time player experiences in context, it is often also important to carefully observe and document how players set up the space and technology. This is especially important for player experiences taking advantage of full-body motion such as motion gaming and VR. You may also want to capture specifics about players' existing setting and set-up, such as lighting conditions and cabling capability.

11.3.7 The social context

Games can be complex social experiences. If your game is likely to be played with friends and family, it is paramount to capture as much detail you can about the social dynamics and rituals during play. These include, but are not limited to, dynamics between siblings, the role of parents, and turn-taking rituals. Observing social play is a complex and intricate effort requiring a full chapter of its own. The good news is that social play inherently elicits social interaction that brings to light players' inner thoughts and feelings without requiring much moderation effort.

11.4 Separating moderation and observation

In a moderated usability test, it can get very difficult to run the session and take notes at the same time. Moderation on its own can be overwhelming, as you have to take care of many aspects of the research: introducing the session to players, setting their expectations, guiding them through various tasks and objectives, keeping them on track, asking them questions when they fail or behave in an interesting way, and keeping the sessions on time.

Whenever possible, it is highly recommended to work in pairs, with separate roles as moderator and note taker. The moderator can focus on managing the session, probing when necessary, and unpacking usability problems. The note taker can focus entirely on observing and documenting player behaviour. This greatly improves the quality of the data gathered and saves time in analysis and reporting. You will get the most value when both the moderator and the note taker are equally involved in the preparation and analysis phases. Having two brains on the same project can save you a lot of time and greatly improve the quality and rigour of your research.

If you cannot afford to separate these two roles and need to take notes while moderating, there are a few pitfalls worth bearing in mind. If you are present in the same room as the player, taking notes can have many undesirable effects on the player. While taking notes, you will have to compromise on important aspects of good moderation:

- You may not be able to maintain eye contact as frequently when players are sharing insights with you.
- You may not be able to allocate as much attention to maintaining a friendly and welcoming posture to elicit feedback.
- Your note taking can make players feel under scrutiny and self-conscious.

Based on the timing of your note taking, players can build assumptions on what you are expecting. They may adapt their behaviour by trying to please you and supply you with feedback that they think you are interested in.

There are ways of avoiding intrusive note taking during moderated sessions, each with their advantages and drawbacks.

Audio and video recording the sessions allows you to focus on moderation. You can go back to the footage for notes. However, this significantly increases the time to analyse and report the findings.

If your lab is equipped with a one-way mirror, sitting behind it and using voice-of-god type of techniques to communicate with the player can help you avoid giving away too much on the desired feedback. But bear in mind that this can make players feel even less comfortable.

Remote usability testing is a good compromise to make players feel at ease (as they play from home) and limit metalinguistic contact. But be mindful of the confidentiality risks involved in the process, as you are not fully in control of who can and cannot see your game's content.

Using two researchers on the same project is a tremendous advantage when observing and capturing player experience. If you do not have the luxury, put extra effort in preparation to make up for the limitations of wearing both the moderator and note taker hats.

11.5 Capturing the player experience

When you are taking notes, you are probably not observing. It is important to write as little as possible when capturing usability observations in order to leave as much time and attentional resources as possible to observing. Here are various techniques to reduce the time spent on capturing observations and increase time spent on actually observing the player experience.

One of the classic mistakes that novice researchers make is to capture everything. This can be a waste of time, as a significant proportion of events and comments produced in a session are likely to be irrelevant to your study objectives and to your stakeholders. Try to avoid capturing anything that does not align with your study objectives. One tip is to keep in mind *what* you are going to report. Here are tips about taking lean and streamlined notes:

- Remove as many unnecessary words as you can. You probably do not need to write 'user' or 'player' every time you report their action.
- Whenever possible just use a keyword (e.g., 'died', 'lost'). You would be surprised how often just one or two words convey the same meaning as a full sentence.
- If a key word is not enough to convey context, use key phrases rather than full sentences (e.g., 'failed to take shortcut', 'struggled to open door').
- Avoid using adverbs and adjectives. If you need to convey severity, use a severity key or tag.
- Do as much of the analysis work as you can without having to compromise on observation by also capturing the causes and impacts of a usability event.

Remember, you will probably have to commit time later to (re)write beautifully crafted sentences in your report. During the session, focus on capturing the content rather than being distracted by the form.

11.5.1 Anatomy of a usability observation

As a researcher, when observing and reporting player events, you act in a similar way to a journalist reporting on a news event. Therefore, the famous 'five Ws' of journalism is a good model to define the anatomy of a usability event. According to the model, a report can only be considered complete if it answers these five questions:

- *Who* was involved? Who was responsible for the event and whom else did it affect? (e.g., player, the NPC).
- *What* happened? Player behaviour/decision/comment/expression.
- *Where* did it happen? In a specific area of the game, the map, or the screen.
- *When* did it happen? At a specific time or a specific step in a sequence of events.
- *Why* did it happen? What was the cause or the rationale behind the action?
- *How* did it happen? In what way and by what means? This is where you add more contextual information such as objects or power-ups used. Note that the *how* can often be extrapolated from the 'what', 'where', and 'when'.

The 'why' and 'how' of a usability event are usually insights into its cause(s). They are extremely important to capture, and deserve to be grouped under their own tag: *cause*. Finally, alongside causes, it is crucial to capture the effects of an event on the player experience. Assign them the tag *impact*.

It is crucial to distinguish observations (the what) from assumptions about causes (the why) and player comments (subjective statements). This can be achieved in many ways. You can use different methods such as colour or text format (e.g., bold, italic). If your favourite note-taking software allows tagging and icons, these can be handy to tag assumptions. When you have access to the player, park your assumptions for when you get the chance to ask them during the final interview or a break in gameplay (e.g., loading time).

11.6 Analysing observations

Once you have finished running all sessions, it is time to analyse the results. In a fast-paced environment such as video game development, it is crucial to make this process as streamlined and efficient as possible. As we saw in the preparation section, the best way to reduce the time spent analysing and reporting is to spend more time carefully planning your observations. Typically, the analysis of observations follows these main steps:

- *Collating* data: This is where you group observations from all players that may have been scattered across multiple sheets or files into a single consolidated one.
- *Organising* data: In this phase, you group events thematically. If you have been writing observations on individual sticky notes, a good technique is to apply a closed card-sorting method to group issues into categories defined by your research objectives or business needs.
- *Aggregating* data: Aggregating observation events boils down to transforming all single usability events observed into general usability problems. A general usability problem is a rewrite of your events where you describe the what, the why, and the how of the problem, and, if relevant, shedding light on the 'when' and 'to whom' they happened.

If you follow a reasonably structured approach and apply the guidelines supplied in the preceding sections, you may have captured observations in a global note-taking template where all events are in one place and organised in meaningful way. The analysis phase should be reasonably fast, allowing you to focus your time and energy on reporting the usability problems to your stakeholders in a clear, concise, and impactful manner.

11.7 Conclusions

This chapter aimed at providing a summary of concrete considerations when observing and capturing player experience. We covered methods to plan your observation protocols as well as tools and processes to observe and document usability events. Here are the key takeaways:

- Plan and prepare for observing and capturing the usability events that your players may encounter. Make sure that your observation and note-taking guides take into account the research questions and the intended player experience.
- Build a thorough understanding of the player experience in your game to list key usability events where the players' experience may not match the intended experience.

- Build a clear template to structure and organise usability events that you capture in terms of time, space, categories, or hierarchies.
- Make sure to optimise the time you spend observing by reducing the time you spend taking notes. Use key words or phrases when taking notes and avoid capturing events that are irrelevant to your research questions.
- Whenever possible, have a sidekick who can take notes when you moderate sessions.
- Use the appropriate tools that allow you to save time both during capturing and analysing. Consider using a mind-mapping tool as it gives you flexibility to organise and structure your data in various appropriate ways.

My hope is that these simple and proven tips and guidelines will allow you to sharpen your art and craft of observing player experience, one of the most powerful tools in our toolbox as Games User Researchers.

Reference

Richard Saul Wurman, Peter Bradford, *Information Architects*. Graphis Press Corp, Zurich, Switzerland, 1996.

CHAPTER 12

The think-aloud protocol

TOM KNOLL, *Spotless*

Highlights

This chapter is about the think-aloud protocol and its application to player experience. It covers what the protocol is, when to apply it, how to conduct it, its pros and cons, and its variations. The chapter concludes with a discussion about the think-aloud protocol with children and the considerations necessary when using child participants.

12.1 Introduction

The think-aloud protocol is one of the most popular methods in usability research (Desurvire and El-Nasr, 2013). In fact, the Nielsen Norman Group have even referred to it at the "*#1 usability tool*" (Nielsen, 2012). The basic premise of the think-aloud protocol is to ask a research participant to verbalize their thoughts as they attempt to complete a task. This provides the researcher with an insight into the cognitive processes that go into using a product or service. The researcher can then use these insights to make recommendations to the designer for the product or service to be improved. The overall aim of the think-aloud protocol (as it is used in non-game-related research) is to make products and services as intuitive and effortless to use as possible.

The think-aloud protocol has also been used extensively in the research of player experience with video games. However, in contrast to non-game-related products, when it is applied to player experience, thinking aloud is a useful way to understand whether a player is engaging with a game in the way the

Games User Research, Anders Drachen, Pejman Mirza-Babaei, Lennart E. Nacke (Eds).
© Oxford University Press 2018. Published 2018 by Oxford University Press

developers intended (Schell, 2008). For example, this author has used the think-aloud protocol in collaboration with several game development studios to determine whether a player is following the narrative of the story, has mastered the controls as expected, or understands the basic mechanics of the game world.

In this chapter, the use of the think-aloud protocol and its application to evaluating player experience will be explored. We shall discuss the following:

- the basics of the think-aloud protocol and when to apply it
- how to conduct a think-aloud session with research participants
- the pros and cons of the think-aloud protocol
- variations of the think-aloud protocol (such as retrospective think-aloud)

The chapter will conclude with a discussion about using the think-aloud protocol with children. Due to the high proportion of games that are targeted directly at children, it is essential that the needs of this user group are addressed, while considering the unique challenges and considerations associated with using child participants for research.

12.2 What is the think-aloud protocol?

Throughout several years of conducting usability studies with research participants (both game- and non-game-related), the majority of the author's one-to-one research sessions have involved the use of the think-aloud protocol. It is a methodology that does not require any specialist equipment, it can be used across most platforms, at any stage of development, and it provides powerful and convincing feedback to product stakeholders—hearing multiple research participants consistently report the same problems is difficult to ignore. In addition, it is very easy to learn how to conduct sessions using the think-aloud protocol.

The overall objective of the think-aloud protocol is to identify the cognitive processes responsible for a participant's behaviour. As participants interact with a product or service under test conditions, they are asked to continuously verbalize their thoughts. Within game user research, this allows the researcher to determine why participants encounter issues and perform certain actions. The insight provided by a participant's monologue allows researchers to identify pain points and difficulty spikes which can then be passed on to the game designers to consider whether adjustments to the game are necessary.

There is one major element that makes using the think-aloud protocol for Games User Research (GUR) unique from all other types of usability research.

Traditionally, when used for non-game-related research, the think-aloud protocol has been used to eradicate all sources of challenge and difficulty. This is certainly not the case when it is applied to player experience (Desurvire and El-Nasr, 2013; Hoonhout, 2008). Players expect a certain level of challenge from games; otherwise there would be little intrinsic reward in playing them. One of the elements that make games both enjoyable and immersive is a balanced difficulty curve. The role of a researcher using the think-aloud protocol for player research is to consider the need for balance in order to provide an adequate level of challenge, but without letting that challenge turn into frustration and loss of immersion. There is a thin line between a game that is cognitively stimulating and one that is frustrating.

It should also be noted that thinking aloud is not necessarily limited to what the participant is consciously saying. A lot of useful information can be gained from behaviours that participants may not have intended to display. For example, an angry grunt may be an indication that a participant is becoming frustrated with the difficulty of the game. Similarly, a reduction in the amount of thinking aloud that a participant is providing might be an indication that they are becoming more immersed in the game.

12.2.1 Why use the think-aloud method for Games User Research?

Many of the larger game development studios rely entirely on observation, post-session interviews, and the experience of their research team to determine when a player is encountering issues within a game. Observation is a great way to determine how well a participant understands how to play a game, but it can only tell you *what* a participant did, not *why* they did it.

Consider a situation where a player is unable to proceed in a game. Simple observation will tell you that there is a problem. But without an insight into the player's state of mind, it can be difficult to determine the cause of this problem. Has the player misunderstood or forgotten instructions given to them within the game world? Are the controls too challenging? Has the player failed to learn a vital game mechanic? By relying on observation alone, it would be down to the researcher to infer the cause of the problem and their assumptions could be open to misinterpretation. Even when a post-session interview is used, it might be difficult for participants to remember exactly what they were thinking when they encountered a specific issue after several hours of gameplay.

In comparison to observation alone, the think-aloud protocol can provide richer data about player experience in the context of when critical incidents occur. Providing a real-time commentary also reduces the risk of participants misrepresenting their experience (Rouse, 2005). As an example, Nielsen et al., discussed that players in testing conditions are often very sensitive about their gaming ability (Nielsen et al., 2002). If players encounter a problem within the game world, often their first instinct is to make excuses for their perceived poor performance, which also has the effect of reducing their level of confidence. Given time to consider their responses (such as during a post-session interview), they may misrepresent their experience of the game in order to portray their gaming proficiency in a more positive light. For this reason, having players think-aloud during gameplay is more likely to capture a true representation of their thought processes. However, due to the self-reporting nature of the think-aloud protocol, it would be very difficult to remove the effect of misrepresentation entirely.

12.3 How to conduct a think-aloud study

12.3.1 Who should run the sessions?

In order to save costs, it might be tempting for a game development team to try to conduct think-aloud sessions themselves with representative users. Although the think-aloud protocol is an easy method to learn, this is generally a bad idea due to the emotional investment that game designers are likely to have in their product. Whether intentionally or not, anyone who has been involved in the creation of the game may influence the decision making of the participant through the use of language or an over-willingness to help when they become stuck (Desurvire and El-Nasr, 2013; Schell, 2008). It is worth hiring a professional and independent user researcher to conduct the sessions on your behalf. They will be able to maintain an impartial stance throughout the data collection process, which will improve the reliability of collected data and make the findings more robust.

12.3.2 Preparation

As with all user research studies, think-aloud sessions should start with the recruitment of representative participants (for information about the recruitment of good research participants, see Section 12.8, Additional Resources).

The environment where the research takes place is also important. For example, it is unlikely that a participant will feel completely comfortable thinking aloud in a developer's branded lab surrounded by other people (Schell, 2008). This is likely to result in participants trying to please the researchers by telling them what they think they want to hear. Also, if they believe that they are in the presence of the people who have created the game, they may be reserved in the feedback that they give, for fear of causing offence. In addition, and as already noted, players tend to be quite sensitive about their gaming ability. If they feel like they are being closely watched by both researchers and gaming peers, they will likely feel uncomfortable. For this reason, it is best to try to arrange a private setting, where only the participant and a single researcher are present. It would be worth using an independent testing facility that is set up for games research such a testing room that looks like a living room. For an even more realistic setting, researchers should consider conducting sessions in participant's own homes (see Chapter 22 for more information).

At the end of the gaming session, make sure that you have prepared some questions for a short post-session interview. This will focus on participant's overall feelings towards the game, as more specific data will have been captured as part of the think-aloud protocol.

12.3.3 Procedure

Once research participants have signed consent form, any necessary non-disclosure agreement and are ready to begin the session, it is important that the researcher briefs the participant in a way that covers the following points:

1. Let the participant know that you (as the researcher) have not been involved with the creation or development of the game that they will be playing (whether this is the case or not), as this will reassure them that they can be honest without the risk of causing offence.

2. Tell participants that you would like them to 'think out loud' as they play the game to give you an insight into their thought processes. Give them some examples of the types of things that you are interested in, such as things they like or dislike, anything that they do not understand, or anything that they find frustrating. Do not be too specific though, let them know that they should feel comfortable saying whatever comes into their head and that there are no right or wrong answers.

3. Once the session is underway, it is common for participants to forget that they should be thinking aloud, especially if they start to become immersed in the game. This can happen for a few reasons: either the

participant has forgotten that they are supposed to be thinking aloud, they do not think that there is anything worth thinking aloud about, or the difficultly level of the game means that they need to dedicate all of their cognitive resources to the game and their ability to multitask has diminished. Whatever the reason, try not to interrupt participants with questions about what is happening. Instead, use very brief and neutral prompts to remind them to speak, such as 'Please keep talking.'

Running a think-aloud session takes practice, but your technique will improve once you get a feel for how best to elicit player feedback. If it is your first time using the think-aloud protocol, then it would be beneficial to run a pilot session prior to the real research to ensure that your instructions feel natural. This will also allow you to refine the instructions and any questions you may ask.

12.3.4 Capturing think-aloud data

You will need to record the session to ensure that you can code the data at a later time. For this, there are many software packages that allow you to capture a TV or monitor output and overlay it with a separate audio track (in this case the participant's voice as they think out loud). Some of the software packages that the author has used in the past are Morae and XSplit (see the Additional Resources section for further details). Ensure that a good-quality microphone is used to capture participant's commentary and that the volume of the game being played is not too loud to obscure the participant's voice. If a retrospective think-aloud is being used (to be discussed later), then make sure that the video output file does not require heavy rendering time and can be immediately available for playback.

12.4 Limitations

Despite the many benefits of using the think-aloud protocol as a research tool for GUR, it does involve risks and limitations. For a start, thinking aloud in a simulated gaming environment is not a natural experience; it is likely to cause discomfort in some participants, especially at the start of a session.

The act of having to continuously verbalize their thoughts is cognitively demanding for participants (Fierley and Engl, 2010). It requires them to multitask, where they would not be doing so in a real-life situation (Branch, 2000; Preece et al., 2002). It's like watching a movie while simultaneously trying to explain what is happening in that movie to another person who is not watching.

Most games are designed to be immersive experiences where the player dedicates their entire attention to the game. This leaves few cognitive resources available for other things. As a result, thinking out loud may have a detrimental effect on player performance within the game world. Constantly disturbing players through prompting them to think aloud pulls them out of any immersive experience they may be having (Nielsen et al., 2002).

Speed of articulation is also an issue. Most people think faster than they can speak. For this reason, it may be the case that participants choose to play the game in a way that is easier to explain, rather than how they would play it in real life. For example, an in-game scenario may require multitasking such as driving, shooting, and solving puzzles at the same time. It would be difficult to comment on all of these activities at once, which may lead to participants offering a filtered or cut-down version of their thought process so that they are able to keep up. Thinking aloud could also change the way a game is played, such as playing in a more linear way, playing at a slower pace to enable them to think-aloud more easily, or playing in a more mindful way, as the act of thinking aloud forces them to consider their actions more carefully. In addition, it may be the case that a participant is unable to articulate what they are thinking, especially if the game involves a fantasy setting that is difficult to put into words.

When a player encounters a challenging section or element of a game, it is common for them to stop verbalizing their thoughts as they focus all of their available cognitive resources on the game (Nielsen et al., 2002). This is particularly problematic for researchers, because it is these challenging sections of the game that provide the richest information about player experience. While prompting players to continue talking is a useful way to keep data flowing, it is likely to be distracting to players and affect the way they play.

As well as limitations that can affect the reliability of collected data, there are also limitations to the think-aloud protocol from a researcher's perspective. First of all, think-aloud data take a long time to analyse. For example, a 60-minute gameplay session will take several hours to transcribe. The rate at which data can be collected is also an issue. For example, earlier it was mentioned that many large game developers rely heavily on observation rather than the think-aloud protocol. These observation-based sessions often take place with multiple participants (often between 10 and 20) who all interact with the game simultaneously. In many facilities, researchers sit behind a one-way mirror, watching the feeds of numerous players and noting critical incidents (Rouse, 2005). On the other hand, the think-aloud protocol requires one-to-one interaction between a researcher and a player, which means that the collection of data is a lot slower.

12.5 Retrospective think-aloud

One way to overcome the limitations of the think-aloud protocol while still retaining the benefits is to use a variation called retrospective think-aloud. This method leaves the player alone during a research session to interact with the game in their own way. The researcher does not sit with them and they are not asked to continuously verbalize their thought processes as they play. Instead, a recording is made of the gameplay session, which is played back to the participant as soon as they finish playing. At this point the researcher will ask the participant to think aloud and provide the commentary for their thought processes as they played the game.

By leaving participants to play the game on their own, they are no longer having to divide their cognitive resources between playing and commentating on their gameplay. Instead they can focus all of their attention on the game without interruption from the researcher. This should reduce the potential negative effects discussed in Section 12.4 (Fierley and Engl, 2010; Hoonhout, 2008).

In spite of the benefits of asking the participant to verbalize their thoughts retrospectively, there are still some limitations to this method. First of all, the length of research sessions increases dramatically. Not only does the participant have to sit and play the game (which can take several hours), but they then have to sit through their gameplay session for a second time in order to provide the necessary commentary. This means research sessions are at least twice as long. Secondly, providing participants with the time to consider their responses may lead to them misrepresenting their experience of the game, either to please the researcher or to portray their gaming abilities more favourably. There is also a risk that participants may find it difficult to remember their exact state of mind when trying to recall a critical incident that happened some time ago during gameplay.

12.5.1 Using the think-aloud protocol with additional methodologies

So far this chapter has shown the think-aloud protocol and its variations as both a robust and convincing user research tool that is not without its faults. But as any professional researcher will tell you, it is not ideal to rely on a single method, especially as the think-aloud protocol works very well in combination with other methodologies (Nielsen et al., 2002).

A change in body language, unprompted utterances, and facial expressions are usually good indications that a player is experiencing a strong emotional reaction to a game (Schell, 2008). These critical incidents are good points of focus for the observing researcher, and once the participant has overcome (or given up on) the scenario causing this response, follow-up questions or a request for a detailed review of the incident by the participant can provide an excellent insight into their experience.

A post-session interview is also a good way to gauge a player's overall impression of the gameplay experience (Rouse, 2005). It could be the case that the player experienced a few frustrating incidents, but their experience of the game overall was highly positive. In such cases, designers need to carefully consider whether the game needs to be adjusted, as removing too many pain points could change a player's overall perceptions of the game: it could be the case that overcoming a very challenging portion of the game resulted in feelings of accomplishment that contributed to their positive experience. It should be noted that post-session interviews are best used to gain an overall understanding of a player's enjoyment of the game rather than detailed information about specific issues that they encountered (Hoonhout, 2008).

12.6 Special case: using the think-aloud protocol with children

Although more and more games are targeted at an adult market, a large proportion are still aimed exclusively at children. As a result, their input into the design of games is vital. There are many potential design issues that can only be uncovered by involving children in the design process. Some examples include their ability to manipulate the game controller (due to having smaller hands) as efficiently as is required by the game and their tolerance and understanding of copy-based instructions. Such issues would be difficult to anticipate if player experience research were based entirely on adult participants. Children offer a unique perspective when it comes to the evaluation of interactive media. Anyone under the age of around 15 is of a generation that have always been surrounded by digital media, therefore their experiences are likely to be different to someone who played their first game later in life. The think-aloud protocol is a useful tool for understanding the experiences of children as they engage with interactive media. However, particular care needs to be taken in order to ensure the reliability of collected data.

As noted by Baauw and Markopoulos (2004), most usability testing methods were designed with adult participants in mind, and the think-aloud protocol is no exception. As mentioned earlier, adult participants often find it challenging to verbalize their thought processes as they play games, and this is even more the case for child participants (Donker and Reitsma, 2004). Children need to be prompted more than adults to think aloud, which suggests that they find it more difficult to do so. In addition, Baauw and Markopoulos (2004) found that asking child participants to continuously verbalize caused them to report many non-issues for the sake of trying to please the researcher. This study also found that children are generally not as articulate as adults. This can be an issue because children generally pick up the mechanics of a game quickly, but are unable to keep up a commentary with their rate of play, which can lead to gaps in data.

Children, especially those under the age of 10, are highly sensitive to leading questions. If they detect that a researcher is trying to elicit a particular response from them, they are likely to say what they think the researcher wants to hear. For this reason, instructions and prompts must use entirely neutral language to ensure that an accurate reflection of their experience is captured.

Despite the additional care that needs to be taken, several studies have shown that important findings can come from using the think-aloud protocol with child participants. For example, Blumber and Randall (2013) found that think-aloud data provided by child participants helped the researchers to identify issues that had not been previously anticipated when using adult participants. Also, persistence and severity of these issues were evident from a combination of think-aloud and observational data. Donker and Reitsma (2004) also found that the think-aloud protocol was a useful method for uncovering usability issues with children, but commented that thinking aloud should be used in combination with other methods, such as observation and post-session interviews.

12.6.1 Talk aloud rather than think aloud

One alternative suggested by Donker and Reitsma (2004) is to get child participants to *talk aloud* rather than *think aloud*. Talking aloud requires the participant to verbalize what they are doing rather than what they are thinking. This puts less strain on their available cognitive resources, while still uncovering useful insights due to the different ways that children approach in-game challenges compared to adult players.

12.6.2 Spontaneous utterances and behaviours are as important as prompted utterances

Compared to adult participants, children are far less concerned about social etiquette during research studies. This is an excellent trait to exploit when it comes to usability testing. For example, if a child is restless, looking around the room, or shifting position in their seat, then this is usually a good indication that they are not very engaged with the game. Similarly, the author has also experienced several instances of children asking questions during research sessions such as 'Can we play another game now?' or 'How much of the game is left?' These questions give the impression that a participant's interest in the game is starting to wane.

When it comes to verbalizing their in-game experiences, some researchers (e.g., Donker and Reitsma, 2004) place strong emphasis on utterances that are made by child participants when not specifically prompted to do so. Generally speaking, child participants tend to remain fairly silent when engaging in single-player games. Therefore, verbalization tends to indicate that a critical incident (whether positive or negative) has occurred. Again, due to their reduced level of restraint when it comes to social etiquette, spontaneous utterances of excitement or frustration are more frequent with child participants. Rather than prompted verbalization, spontaneous utterances are more likely to be a true reflection of the child's current state of mind rather than the somewhat forced nature of the think-aloud protocol.

While a traditional think-aloud may not always be appropriate for child participants (especially younger children), when combined with other methodologies such as observation, valid data can still be obtained. Additional emphasis should be placed on observed behaviour changes and unprompted utterances during gameplay, as these provide clues to critical incidents, which can be discussed further in post-play interviews or retrospective think-aloud sessions.

12.7 Conclusions

The purpose of this chapter has been to provide an introduction to using the think-aloud protocol to assess player experience, while highlighting some of the key factors that must be considered if the collected data is to be trusted. As noted by Hoonhout (2008), games differ from regular digital products because they are designed to be entertaining rather than useful. Therefore, the focus of the think-aloud protocol when applied to games is to maximize playfulness rather than efficiency.

Considering some of the main limitations of the think-aloud protocol can help researchers determine the best use for this method in research. For example, due to the cognitive strain placed on participants by the think-aloud protocol during periods of high challenge, it may be best suited to casual, slower-paced, or strategy-based games that do not have time-critical elements (Fierley and Engl, 2010). This will allow participants sufficient time to focus fully on the game while thinking aloud, and reduce the negative impact on having to provide a commentary at the same time. In addition, aside from actual gameplay, most games feature menus, options, and in-game UI systems that can be evaluated using the think-aloud protocol in a more traditional and 'function-focused' way to ensure that they are easy to use as well as easy to navigate.

Relatively speaking, player experience is still an emerging area of research. Although it is a popular method, the think-aloud protocol is not necessarily the best data collection tool for this medium, especially when used in isolation. At the very least, the think-aloud protocol should be used in combination with other methodologies such as observation in order to capture reliable data. As technology improves, other research tools such as eye tracking and game metrics (although each have their own limitations) should become more viable for researchers. These tools could be used with the think-aloud protocol to identify pain points within games and help to take the cognitive strain off of the participant.

12.8 Additional resources

12.8.1 Introductions to the think-aloud protocol

A great introduction to the think-aloud protocol as it is used in non-game-related research can be found on the Nielsen Norman Group website:

Nielsen, J. (2012). Thinking aloud: the #1 usability tool. Retrieved 12 April 2016 from https://www.nngroup.com/articles/thinking-aloud-the-1-usability-tool/

For a detailed introduction to the think-aloud protocol and its application to player experience, Henriette Hoonhout has written a very informative chapter in the Game Usability book:

Hoonhout, H. C. M. (2008). Let the game tester do the talking: think aloud and interviewing to learn about the game experience. In K. Isbister and

N. Schaffer (eds.), Game Usability: advice from the experts for advancing the player experience (pp. 65–77). Amsterdam: Elsevier/Morgan Kaufmann.

12.8.2 Conducting research with child participants

The UX Matters website provides an informative guide to working with child participants:

http://www.uxmatters.com/mt/archives/2013/07/5-things-to-remember-when-conducting-ux-research-with-children.php

12.8.3 Recruiting representative participants for research projects

An extremely detailed resource is provided by the Nielsen Norman Group for recruiting research participants:

https://www.nngroup.com/reports/how-to-recruit-participants-usability-studies/

Another article from the UX Matters website that details the recruitment of representative research participants:

http://www.uxmatters.com/mt/archives/2015/09/recruiting-the-right-participants-for-user-research.php

References

Baauw, E., Markopoulos, P. (2004). A comparison of think-aloud and post-task interview for usability testing with children. Proceedings of the 2004 Conference on Interaction Design and Children: Building a Community, 1(1), 115–116.

Blumberg, F. C., Randall, J. D. (2013). What do children and adolescents say they do during video game play? Journal of Applied Developmental Psychology, 1(34), 82–88.

Branch, J. L. (2000). Investigating the information seeking processes of adolescents: the value of using think alouds and think afters. Library & Information Science Research, 22(4), 371–392.

Desurvire, H., El-Nasr, M. S. (2013). Methods for game user research: studying player behavior to enhance game design. IEEE Computer Graphics and Applications, 4, 82–87.

Donker, A., Reitsma, P. (2004). Usability testing with young children. Proceedings of the 2004 Conference on Interaction Design and Children: Building a Community, 1(1), 43–48.

Fierley, R., Engl, S. (2010). User experience methods and games: lessons learned. BCS'10 Proceedings of the 24th BCS Interaction Specialist Group Conference, 204–210.

Hoonhout, H. C. M. (2008). Let the game tester do the talking: think aloud and interviewing to learn about the game experience. In K. Isbister and N. Schaffer (eds.), Game usability: advice from the experts for advancing the player experience (pp. 65–77).Amsterdam: Elsevier/Morgan Kaufmann.

Lewis, C. H. (1982). Using the 'thinking aloud' method. In Cognitive interface design [technical report]. IBM. RC-9265.

Nielsen, J. (2012). Thinking aloud: the #1 usability tool. Retrieved 12 April 12 2016 from https://www.nngroup.com/articles/thinking-aloud-the-1-usability-tool/

Nielsen, J., Clemmensen, T., Yssing, C. (2002). Getting access to what goes on in people's heads?—reflections on the think-aloud technique. NordiCHI 2002, 1(1), 101–110.

Preece, J., Rogers, Y., Sharp, H. (2002). Interaction design: beyond human-computer interaction. New York: John Wiley & Sons.

Rouse III, R. (2005). Playtesting. In Game design: theory & practice (pp. 483–497). Piano, TX: Wordware Publishing.

Schell, J. (2008). Good games are created through playtesting. In The art of game design (pp. 389–396). Boca Raton, FL: Taylor & Francis Group.

CHAPTER 13

The Rapid Iterative Test and Evaluation Method (RITE)

MICHAEL C. MEDLOCK, *Oculus Rift*

Highlights

This chapter begins with a discussion of the philosophy and definition of the RITE method. It then delves into the benefits of this method and provides practical notes on running RITE tests effectively. The chapter concludes with an overview of the original case study behind the 2002 article documenting this method.

13.1 Introduction

This chapter is about the Rapid Iterative Test and Evaluation Method (RITE). There are two parts to the RITE method: the method itself and the philosophy of RITE, which can be applied to many methods. RITE is a discount usability test in which changes can be made after each participant. The essence of the philosophy is: find a problem, fix a problem. Historically, the method and the philosophy have been used long before the original article documenting it (Medlock et al., 2002)—in all truth, probably since the beginning of tool making. But since the publication of the article, RITE's use has greatly spread, particularly in the making of products that can change rapidly (e.g., game, web, or cloud products). RITE is now regularly used in game companies that engage in user research. In fact, in some gaming companies it is the most used method. For example, I first

Games User Research, Anders Drachen, Pejman Mirza-Babaei, Lennart E. Nacke (Eds).
© Oxford University Press 2018. Published 2018 by Oxford University Press

worked with Insomniac Games in 2013 and discovered that *all* their usability testing was done RITE style and had been for years.

At the time the original RITE article came out, user research in general had been going through a decades-long change. Starting in the 1980s, user research was emerging from its rigid methodological underpinnings and slowly embracing design techniques. Research was moving from focusing on issue finding to focusing on issue fixing. In this respect, the philosophy behind RITE is what feels most enduring and inspiring . . . rather than the specific method itself.

13.2 Philosophy of RITE

The philosophy behind RITE is simple:

1. Once you find a problem, solve it as soon as you can.
2. Make the decision makers part of the research team.

With this philosophy, RITE straddles the research/design divide. It is as much a design technique as a research technique. Philosophically, it has as much in common with the philosophy of participatory design (Rudd and Isensee, 1994, 1996; Squires and Bryne, 2002) as it does with usability testing.

These simple statements of the RITE philosophy have profound implications for methods. If followed to their logical conclusions, it forces researchers to change methods in ways that challenge traditional definitions of reliability and validity. Specifically, it puts the onus of validity (e.g., if an issue is a 'real' issue worthy of attention) and reliability (e.g., would the issue show up again given the same circumstances) *wholly* in the judgement of the researcher and the team. This makes research and academic audiences squirm, but for most business audiences it has the opposite effect—it delights them.

For research and academic audiences, reliability and validity are mechanisms for establishing truth. There are philosophical and mathematical norms that are followed. In the usability space, these philosophical and mathematical norms have been excellently researched and explained by Jim Lewis and Jeff Sauro (Lewis, 1990, 1991, 1993, 1996; Sauro and Lewis, 2012). However, these philosophical and mathematical norms are not how games businesses regularly make decisions. It is important to remember that making judgements about the validity of issues based on limited information is standard operating procedure for game creators (or software creators of any stripe). Most changes to games and game UIs happen *without ever having watched a single user*. Testers file bugs daily, and the bugs get fixed daily. The judgement of the 'validity' of the bug is wholly up to the tester and the team. The primary reasons for this are the focus and way the business model works.

In an academic setting, 'truth' is usually the focus. In a business setting, 'profit' is usually the focus. In an academic setting, money comes in at a regular cadence—students pay to come, grants are applied for at certain times of year, and there are fund drives. In the games business, money usually only comes in when a product is launched, when a product is out in the wild, or when there is a change to a product in the wild. Therefore, there is great financial pressure to 'ship' fast. A games business audience is less concerned about ultimate or scientific truth. People in the games business are instead concerned about effectiveness and efficiency and the costs related to both. Consequently, validity in a business context is established through observation, anecdotes, examples, clarity of presentation, the credibility of the messenger, and most importantly, the immediate perception of the relevance of the information to the goals of the business. It is not that businesses do not care about 'truth'—it's that they are willing to sacrifice it if it gets them 80% there quickly.

13.3 Definition of RITE

The RITE method is a discount usability test conducted in a fast and highly collaborative manner (Medlock et al., 2002; Medlock et al., 2005). As a general rule, it can often be used in situations as an alternative to a discount usability test. A RITE test shares the same initial four basic principles of usability tests as outlined by Dumas and Redish (1993), specifically:

1. The goal is to improve the product.
2. The participants are real users.
3. The participants do real tasks.
4. You observe and record what participants do and say.

However, RITE differs from a 'standard' usability test in the following three ways. Firstly, the data are analysed after each participant, or at least after each day of testing. Secondly, changes to the user interface get made as soon as a problem is identified *and* a potential solution is clear. In situations in which the issue and solution are 'obvious', the change may be after one participant. Finally, the changed interface is tested with subsequent users to see if the changes solve the issues previously uncovered without introducing new problems.

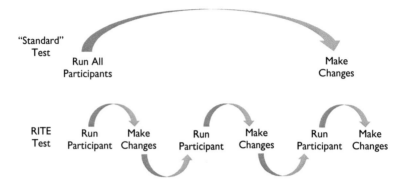

Figure 13.1 RITE testing versus standard usability testing

In order for the RITE method to work successfully, the user interface has to be able to change—and often change rapidly. In order for changes to the interface to be possible, two things usually have to be true: firstly, there need to be resources to make changes; and secondly, there needs to be enough political/ organizational will to make changes. When we talk about 'resources' in this case, it is usually someone who has the *ability* to make a change to the user interface. For example, a developer, or designers with access to the actual game code. When we say 'political will', we are usually talking about a person or group of people with decision-making *authority*. Identifying the minimal set of key decision makers is an important and necessary step when doing RITE testing. As a general rule of thumb, these key decision makers must observe the participants with the user researcher if success is to be achieved. To see a visual representation of RITE compared to a 'standard' discount usability test, refer to Figure 13.1.

13.4 Using RITE effectively

When used in an appropriate context, a RITE-style usability test has been found to result in a number of advantages (Medlock et al., 2005) over a 'classic' usability test. Firstly, more issues get fixed in a shorter period of time, and sometimes more issues are found. Secondly, RITE can build team morale and dynamics via the deep collaboration of the rest of the team (Terrano, 1999).

Users of RITE should adapt the method to their needs and context. In many ways, the philosophy behind RITE is more important than following the defined method exactly. There are ways that the classic RITE test can and has been adapted successfully. For example, combining RITE with a playtest at the same time, extending the number of days between fixes, changing the number of sessions a day . . . these are all possible. Be creative and understand the limitations of the methods you are using. Educate yourself enough to know when doing something creative violates some critical aspect of the method.

Having said this, the RITE method can fail if certain conditions are not met. The 'real' decision makers must be identified for inclusion. If the people you have with you do not have the authority to make changes, then the enterprise is destined for failure. The decision makers of the development team must participate to address the issues raised quickly. Note that this is more than a commitment to attend and review. This is a commitment to actually make decisions and changes during the time the test is being run. The user researcher must have experience both in the domain and in the problems that users typically experience in that domain. Without this experience, it is difficult to tell if an issue is 'reasonably likely to be a problem'.

For someone who is inexperienced with a domain, a more traditional usability test is more appropriate. The design team and user researcher must be able to interpret the results rapidly to make quick and effective decisions regarding changes to the prototype or whatever is being tested. There must be the ability to make changes to the system or prototype very rapidly (e.g., in less than two hours to test with the next participant, or before the next day of testing, depending on context). This means that development time and resources must be scheduled in advance to address the issues raised during testing, and the development environment must allow for those rapid changes to be made. There must be enough time between participants to make changes that have been decided upon. How long this time is depends upon how quickly teams can make decisions and implement them. For example, text interfaces can be changed very quickly (minutes), whereas changes to the behaviour of an underlying game system can take days.

It should be noted that often the set-up for a RITE-style test costs more time and energy upfront compared to standard usability testing—paying off in all the things listed in previous sections. To give the reader some idea of the revised timeline for a RITE-style test, consider Figure 13.2. It should be noted that this schedule works well for many different games that the author has worked on.

There are a number of things that should be done during the planning phases that will make everyone's tasks much easier during a RITE test. Firstly, set expectations for the decision makers on what a RITE test is and what their roles

Monday	Tuesday	Wednesday	Thursday	Friday	Saturday	Sunday
1 Plan	2 Plan + Schedule Participants	3 Plan + Schedule Participants	4 Schedule Participants	5 Schedule Participants	7	8
9 Run Participants + Analyze Data	10 Fix Issues	11 Run Participants + Analyze Data + Fix Issues	12 Fix Issues	13 Run Participants + Analyze Data + Fix Issues	14	15
16 Run Participants + Analyze Data	17 Fix Issues	18 Run Participants + Analyze Data + Fix Issues	19 Fix Issues	20 Run Participants + Analyze Data + Fix Issues		

Figure 13.2 Example of timeline for RITE testing

will be. A good way to do this is to give the decision makers a 'script' of what a RITE test is and what their role in it will be. Secondly, have someone on the team keep a record of the changes made and when they were made. It is very difficult for a user researcher to accomplish these tasks during testing. Make sure this record is easily accessible so that all team members can see it. Thirdly, do not schedule too many participants per day and allow for plenty of time between participants. Sometimes four participants a day can push everyone's boundaries when making changes between participants. In other situations, four participants a day may be fine—or one participant every two days. This *entirely* depends on the situation the user research and game team is in. Fourthly, have a dedicated place for the people making the prototype or coding changes to view the testing, or have a remote viewing stream. The ideal situation is where the people making the changes can both observe the participants and comment on the observations with the researcher in real time. Do not underestimate the importance of being able to talk about what the participant has done in real time, or at the very least do not underestimate how disruptive it can be when there is a lag between what different observers see. While remote viewing technologies have greatly helped with observation, there is often a lag that makes discussing things the participant has done in real time challenging. Fifth, consider saving full versions of the application between changes, so previous versions could be examined, or reverted to if problems are encountered with 'fixes'. Finally, set up a format for recording issues that can instantly be translated into a report format to assist turnaround time of the final results. We have provided an example of an Excel recording template, along with an example of how we have used it.

Figure 13.3 is a fictitious example of tracking the effectiveness of a RITE study. The columns represent participants and the rows represent issues.

Issue/ Participant	P1	P2	P3	P4	P5	P6	P7	P8	P9	P10	P11	P12	1st Change	2nd Change	3rd Change
Issue 1: Player doesn't know how to select a unit	X												Note fix		
Issue 2: Player doesn't understand fog of war				X		X				X					
Issue 3	X	X	X			X							Note fix		
Issue 4	X	X		X	X								Note fix	Note new fix	
Issue 5							X	X	X				Note fix		
Issue 6	Fail	Fail	X										Note fix		
Issue 7				Fail	Fail	Fail	X	X	X				Note fix	Note new fix	
Issue 8	X	X		X		X		X	X				Note fix	Note new fix	Note new fix

Figure 13.3 Sample RITE table: fictitious issues and fixes' history

The participants are numbered in the order they were tested. To make this into a blank template, simply erase all the shading and text.

In the fictitious example of Figure 13.3 we have run 12 participants. This is an idealized example and illustrates possible outcomes of a RITE test. However, in practice it is not far from the actual outcome of a RITE test. The issues listed are also fictitious—and only the first two have descriptions.

- For Issue 1, the problem was very clear and very severe: the participant could not select a unit and could not play the game as a result. The team felt they understood it well enough to make a fix after just one participant. The team made the fix and the next 11 participants did not experience the problem.
- For Issue 2, the problem did not get fixed during this test, either because the team did not feel it was that serious or it was too difficult to attempt a fix in the given time frame of the test.
- For Issue 3, the problem was experienced by the first three participants, but the team could not agree on a fix or thought that the problem might not be seen again. They waited until after Participant 6 and then fixed the problem, and it was not experienced by users again.
- For Issue 4, a fix was tried after the first three participants and it was not successful, that is, the problem recurred. A new fix was tried after Participant 6, which appears to have been successful.
- Issue 5 did not surface until Participant 7, but was noted for three participants. It showed up because fixing Issues 1 to 4 allowed users to complete more tasks.

- Issue 6 caused failures and was fixed successfully after three participants.
- Issue 7 showed up with Participants 4–6 and caused failures. The fix reduced its severity but did not eliminate it. A new fix was tried after Participant 9 and eliminated the problem entirely.
- Issue 8 required three fixes before it was eliminated.

13.5 Original case study: Microsoft Age of Empires II tutorial

Age of Empires II is a game created by Ensemble Studios and published by Microsoft Game Studios in 1999 (Terrano, 1999). The overall goal in Age of Empires II was to build a civilization and conquer the other civilizations that opposed you (Figure 13.4). You gather resources which you then use to create military or technological advances to achieve your goals. It is part of a genre of games known as real-time strategy games. In many ways it is a bit like the classic board game chess, but there is no turn-taking. It is a complex game that requires users to understand new rules and master new skills to be effective.

The original Age of Empires, published in 1997, was a successful game—but the game designers wanted to expand their demographic, and this meant going

Figure 13.4 Age of Empires II screenshot

after people who did not play real-time strategy games or did not normally play games. To achieve this goal, the game designers could have chosen to change the complex rules by which the game is played. However, after some experimentation, the rules were deemed to be the very thing that made the game fun—so the challenge became teaching new users how to play the game in a fun way. A teaching mechanism was needed, and an interactive tutorial was deemed to be the solution by the designers.

Prior to testing the tutorial, the user researcher and the team developed a list of tasks and concepts that participants should be able to do and/or understand after using the Age of Empires II tutorial. Issues were identified for which there would be zero error tolerance, for example, learning how to move units or gather resources. Once testing ensued, at least one decision maker on the development team, authorized to make changes, was present at every session (e.g., the program manager, game designer, or development lead). After each participant, the team would quickly meet with the user researcher, go over issues seen, and do one of the following:

1. Attempt a fix, and then use the new prototype with the remaining participants.
2. Start to work on a fix; use the new prototype with the remaining participants as soon as it is available.
3. Collect more data (e.g., more participants run) before any fix is attempted.

The results of the case study are summarized in Figure 13.5, which is a record of failures and errors over time (as represented by the participants) on the Age of Empires II tutorial. Failures were things that stopped the participant

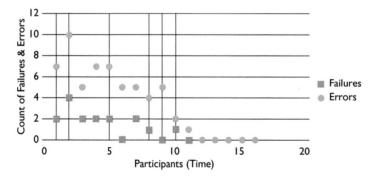

Figure 13.5 A record of errors over time as changes to the Age of Empires II tutorial were made using the RITE method

from completing the tutorial. Errors were things that caused confusion, irritation, or time wastage, but did not stop the participant from completing the tutorial. In addition, the graph indicates that less errors and failures accrued as the tutorial was revised and improved. Changes were implemented after Participants 1, 2, 5, 8, 9, and 10 (six iterations over approximately two and a half weeks' time).

The prototype was changed after the first participant. It is instructive to examine an issue that caused the team to make a fix after having observed so few instances of an issue. In the tutorial, participants are supposed to gather resources with their villagers. One of the resources that they are instructed to gather is wood by chopping trees. However, initially there were no trees on-screen, and as a result the first participant spent a long time confused as to what to do. The problem was clear and so was the solution—place some trees within view and teach users how to explore to find trees off-screen. Both of these were done and the issue never showed up again in the next 15 participants.

It is also clear in Figure 13.5 that the number of failures and errors generally decreases over time as iterations occur, and eventually go down to one error after the final iteration. Sometimes there were 'spikes' after a revision. This appeared to be caused by participants being able to interact with more of the game by removing previous blocking issues. For example, once the woodchopping issue was removed after the first participant, subsequent participants were able to move further into the tutorial, thus encountering other issues along the way that otherwise may not have been found.

Often the RITE method allows researchers to uncover fixes that need re-fixing. Here is an example of a re-fix. Participants had problems with terminology in Age of Empires II that required repeated fixes. Specifically, participants thought that they needed to convert their villager units into swordsmen units when in fact the two types of units were completely unrelated. When the tutorial directed the user to 'Train five swordsmen', participants would move their villagers over to the barracks (a building that creates swordsmen) assuming that the villagers could be *converted* into swordsmen. In fact, swordsmen had to be *created* at the barracks using other resources (e.g., food, gold). When this issue manifested itself, there were inconsistencies in the terminology used in the product; in some places, the user interface said 'Train units' and in others it said 'Create units'. After watching six of eight participants fail to produce new units, the team decided that the text inconsistency was the problem, and chose to use the term 'Train units' throughout the user interface. When the next participant was run, the problem reoccurred in the exact same way. As a result, the team changed the terminology to 'Create unit' throughout the rest of the user interface. Once it was re-fixed, this problem was not seen again after seven participants.

13.6 Takeaways

The example of the re-fix is a good one to close on. It is instructive when thinking about reliability, validity, the goal of user research in general, and the philosophy of RITE. No matter what technique or method gets used, sometimes the solution to an issue will be wrong. The general assertion of the literature is that more data are always better than less data when it comes to finding and understanding issues (Nielsen and Turner, 1994, 2002; Sauro and Lewis 2012; Spool and Schroeder, 2001; Virzi, 1992; Woolrych and Cockton, 2001). This is true. However, *finding* issues is not the goal of user research; *fixing* issues is the goal of user research (Wixon, 2003). It is debatable if more data make for better fixes. What makes for better fixes (apart from more skilled designers) is the chance to see if the fixes worked. It is more important to focus on the fix than on the failure. It is more important to spend your statistical power on seeing if a fix worked than wringing your hands philosophically if you have found all the issues or understood them perfectly.

As time passes, there are more and more creative ways in which researchers are combining methods and measurement techniques. In general, the techniques that seem to stick best are those that lead the teams making products to believe that their products are getting better. They tend to be methods focused on *fixes*. As such, the philosophy behind the RITE method is alive and well.

References and suggested readings

Dumas, J., Redish J.C. (1993). A practical guide to usability testing. Norwood, NJ: Ablex.

Lewis, J. R. (1990). Sample sizes of observational usability studies: tables based on the binomial probability formula. Technical Report 54.571. Boca Raton, FL: International Business Machines, Inc.

Lewis, J. R. (1991). Legitimate use of small samples in usability studies: three examples. Technical Report 54.594. Boca Raton, FL: International Business Machines, Inc.

Lewis, J. R. (1993). Sample sizes for usability studies: additional considerations. Technical Report 54.711. Boca Raton, FL: International Business Machines, Inc.

Lewis, J. R. (1996, May). Binomial confidence intervals for small sample usability studies. In Proceedings of the 1st International Conference on Applied Ergonomics. Istanbul, Turkey.

Medlock, M. C., Wixon, D., Terrano, M., Romero R., Fulton B. (2002, July). Using the RITE method to improve products: a definition and a case study. Usability Professionals Association (UPA2002), Orlando, FL.

Medlock, M., Wixon, D., McGee, M., Welsh, D. (2005). The Rapid Iterative Test and Evaluation method: better products in less time. In R. Bias and D. Mayhew (eds.), Cost-justifying usability, an update for the Internet age (2nd ed.) (pp. 489–518). Burlington, MA: Morgan Kaufmann.

Nielsen, J., Lewis, J. R., Turner, C. W. (2002, July). Current issues in the determination of usability test sample size: how many users is enough? Usability Professionals Association (UPA2002). Orlando, FL.

Nielsen, J., Landauer, T. K. (1994). A mathematical model of the finding of usability problems. In Proceedings of ACM INTERCHI'93 Conference. Amsterdam, The Netherlands (24–29 April 1993) (pp. 206–213).

Participatory design. Wikipedia. Retrieved 16 March 2016 from https://en.wikipedia.org/wiki/Participatory_design

Rudd, J., Isensee, S. (1994). Twenty-two tips for a happier, healthier prototype. Interactions, 1(1), 35–40.

Rudd, J., Stern, K., Isensee, S. (1996). Low- vs. high-fidelity prototyping debate. Interactions, 3(1), 76–85.

Sauro, J., Lewis, J. R. (2012). Quantifying the user experience. Amsterdam: Elsevier.

Squires, S., Bryne, B. (2002). Creating breakthrough ideas: the collaboration of anthropologists and designers in the product development industry. Westport, CT: Berwin and Garvey.

Spool, J., Schroeder, W. (2001). Testing websites: five users is nowhere near enough. In Proceedings CHI 2001, Extended Abstracts (pp. 285–286). New York: ACM.

Terrano, M. (1999, October). Age of Empires II: designer diary. Retrieved 6 January 2004 from http://firingsquad.gamers.com/games/aoe2diary/

Virzi, R. A. (1992). Refining the test phase of usability evaluation: how many subjects is enough? Human Factors, 34, 457–468.

Wixon, D. (2003). Evaluating usability methods: why the current literature fails the practitioner. Interactions, 10(4), 29–34.

Woolrych, A., Cockton, G. (2001) Why and when five test users aren't enough. In J. Vanderdonckt et al. (eds.), Proceedings of IHM-HCI 2001 Conference, Vol. 2 (pp. 105–108). Toulouse, France: Cépadèus Éditions.

CHAPTER 14

Heuristics uncovered for Games User Researchers and game designers

HEATHER DESURVIRE, *University of Southern California*

DENNIS WIXON, *University of Southern California*

Highlights

This paper presents a set of heuristics (PLAY and GAP) for game design and discusses the history of heuristics for games, describes the use of these heuristics, summarizes research demonstrating their effectiveness, and describes a hypothetical model that reviewers use when evaluating a game. The usage by designers and evaluators when reviewing two released games is also compared. Overall heuristics were found to be much more effective than informal reviews and their use led not only to problem identification, but to suggested fixes, possible enhancements, and effective aspects of the existing designs.

14.1 Introduction

Heuristics have been widely recommended for commercial digital products. Their effectiveness has been repeatedly demonstrated and the factors which contribute to this effectiveness have been analysed (Nielsen and Molich, 1990; Rodio et al., 2013). The research on heuristics for video games is not as extensive but is growing.

Games User Research, Anders Drachen, Pejman Mirza-Babaei, Lennart E. Nacke (Eds).
© Oxford University Press 2018. Published 2018 by Oxford University Press

This chapter describes a comprehensive set of heuristics for games, reviews their origin, and discusses the process used by game evaluators. The evaluators fall into two groups: student designers and student game researchers. Each group was given two sets of heuristics (PLAY and GAP, described later) to use when evaluating player experience. The chapter briefly reviews both experimental and case study evidence which supports the effectiveness of these heuristics.

In addition, a quantitative analysis of heuristic player experience reports (reports) shows that when using heuristics, reviewers found more issues, suggested more design enhancements, and reported more successful aspects of existing player experiences than reviewers who were using an informal approach to evaluate games. A qualitative analysis focused on the relationship between the evaluator's review comments on the game, the heuristic itself, and the game content. Overall, these findings demonstrate the usefulness of a thorough set of heuristics and suggest that the use of heuristics promotes a more thorough review of the game.

In addition to this empirical approach, we discuss a set of case studies which demonstrate the effectiveness of heuristics in an applied context. We also review the process of applying them and the background required of those conducting the review.

14.1.1 What is player experience?

Player experience is complex and not simple to identify, much less evaluate. Starting with the digital product world, user experience utilized and categorized heuristics as a way to understand and evaluate it. The Mitre Corporation published 200 elements that go into a good user experience (Smith and Mosier, 1986). This was a precursor to Nielsen and Molich's work on developing the ten heuristics that make up good user experience/usability, widely used in digital design. Nielsen has modified these several times to be more understandable and more up-to-date with changing technology. Heuristics developed into a method of evaluating the usability, then expanded to focus on the overall user experience of digital products. User experience has evolved from considering usability to usefulness, and then towards engagement and delight.

How does player experience differ from user experience? Some basics of user experience still apply, such as not relying on excessive documentation or help to play the game, making player status and game score easy to find and use, but beyond these and a few other basics, it's clear that other elements must not be so easy that they compromise the fun and challenge of the game. Finding the balance between challenge and approachability makes designing play experience for games more complex than user experience for productivity products. Player experience is similar to user experience, but takes into account the unique elements that make a gameplay experience enjoyable: challenge, immersion, sense of flow, mechanics, story, and characters. All these elements make the gameplay experience a good one and different from user experience with traditional productivity products and tools (Pagulayan et al., 2002).

To address these unique needs of games, we have created categories to structure the understanding of player experience (Desurvire and Wiberg, 2008, 2009, 2015; Desurvire et al., 20045). There are five categories: (1) gameplay, (2) engagement immersion, (3) game usability/mechanics, (4) new player experience, and (5) game story immersion (if applicable).

14.1.2 Origins of PLAY and GAP heuristics

Heuristics for video games evolved to address the interface and player experience challenges created by more complex, sophisticated, and interesting designs. When considering digital products, another motivation was to develop and use heuristics and assess their efficiency and effectiveness compared to various forms of user testing. In contrast to user testing, heuristics typically offer teams more opportunities to design and evaluate a game design before it is translated into a playable build. User testing usually requires a playable build or prototype. The early assessment provided by heuristics can save teams time and money by positioning evaluation earlier in the development cycle.

When games were first designed to be played on computers, their interfaces were relatively simple both in terms of visual design and fundamental game mechanics. The very first games were relatively straightforward imitations of real-world games with direct controls (e.g., Pong) or presented clear challenges (e.g., destroy approaching enemy spaceships). Many of these early games used readily understood approaches to make the games progressively difficult. For example, they gradually increased the number of enemies and the pace of their attack. The result was that optimal game designs could be easily learned but were difficult to master (e.g., 'Wolfshead').

As hardware capabilities increased, game designs became more complex and delivery methods more diverse. Game designers incorporated sophisticated story lines, graphics capabilities, character development, and sound design. The diversity of controls and playable hardware (e.g., consoles) increased and their performance dramatically improved. Designers developed more intricate game mechanics. In parallel with these changes, a community of experienced game players emerged. Members of this community played a wide variety of games, and their understanding of the conventions of game design evolved along with the complexity and ambition of the game designs. As a result, the games became increasingly difficult for novices, and the community of gamers became more culturally separated from the non-gamers or 'new' gamers.

Simultaneously, hardware companies and game designers sought to expand their scope beyond the traditional and experienced gamers (Desurvire, 2009). Currently, the ease of finding and downloading digital apps and games creates a low barrier to entry and generates an expectation these apps and games will be easy to pick up and use or play. In this environment, games must be easy to 'get into' and play in order to stay competitive. With widespread availability to buy online and download, an ever-increasing mobile market, and alternative products easy to access, the ones that are easier to use are likely to take market share and achieve commercial success. The design of a game needs to be easy enough for novices and casual players, yet challenging enough for experienced players. This balance is not always easily achieved. For example, the mechanics of these newer games often involves difficult physical skills (e.g., aiming and 'button mashing'). In addition, as games evolved, they included more complex story lines and incorporated new elements (e.g., puzzles). As a result, games became more challenging to the new or casual gamers than the earlier games had been. The visual design of games also became richer and more intricate, and as a result it was easier for new gamers to be distracted by these new environments.

Other societal elements added to this complexity and need for more game experiences to be easier to access while complex enough to satisfy the more ardent game players. Players' expectations of easy access and entry became de rigeur; as interfaces improved, player experiences improved. Even hardcore gamers expect player experiences to be easy to enter. Factors such as amount of free time and competitor games' requiring less time to learn and more time to enjoy can lead players to easy-to-learn contenders.

The combination of the trend towards richer, more complex games and the desire to appeal to a wider range of potential gamers has led game designers to focus on improving their interfaces and making them more consistent and easier to learn. In a sense, the design focus of the game industry includes not only the fun of mastering complex mechanics but also the challenge of exploring complex stories and new environments.

Casual gamers, as their name implies, lack extensive prior gameplay experience. The casual game player is often approaching a game without extensive knowledge of gaming design conventions; even those who might at one time have been experienced players usually have a briefer window of time to play (and learn). They also have a more periodic exposure to games in contrast to their current hardcore counterparts. This difference suggests that casual gamers require both an interface where difficulty is progressively staged and where careful attention has been paid to design elements that implicitly teach gaming conventions in a step-by-step manner. This progression requires a careful balance between getting the casual gamer started with gameplay and not divulging the secrets of the game itself. That is, designing the game so that casual players can feel confident as they master the game. At the same time, the game design must not alienate the experienced player who may also be part of the target audience.

Since games have not yet become an 'entertainment priority' for them, casual gamers are less likely to be willing to spend the time to learn a complex game and are less likely to see the potential rewards that accrue with experience. Thus, with the growing number of casual gamers and game developer focus on casual games, the approachability aspect of game playability is more critical than ever.

Today, game design involves a focus on traditional usability, such as using clear terminology, as well as nonintrusive, easy-to-use user interfaces. Hardcore gamers are usually more familiar with game design conventions and more willing to seek assistance in order to play games. Traditionally, these gamers have relied on strategy guides, cheat codes, online forums, and other players to master a game. In direct contrast, casual gamers are more likely to quit playing if the game seems too difficult or frustrating. They are also less likely to seek out and use any of the resources that experienced players typically use. Nevertheless, because of many factors, even hardcore gamers are likely to quit when they face time constraints.

There are several ways to address the twin problems of usability and approachability. These include usability testing, beta testing, extensive use of data logging, and the application of heuristics.

Heuristics are also known as principles. These principles serve as an aid to learning, discovery, and problem solving by experimental and especially by trial-and-error methods. A principle is 'a fundamental, primary, or general law or truth from which others are derived' (Miriam Webster). To be clear, heuristics are meant to be used as guidelines. Heuristics are a method of learning, thinking, and problem solving. The application of heuristics allows designers to avoid pitfalls, to raise the bar of the design so it does not violate known truths about player experience. Heuristic principles ensure that we are applying a general professional understanding about what will work well, using trial and error to identify potential problems with player experience.

14.1.2.1 HEURISTICS ARE KNOWN BY MANY NAMES

Heuristics are a set of tenets or principles. A heuristic evaluation is the method by which a digital product's user experience is analysed using these principles. Heuristic evaluations are also called expert audits, expert walkthroughs, and expert reviews. This method is popular in the digital product world, and now is becoming an ever-increasing method for games, as have been suggested by a number of writers (Desurvire, 2009; Desurvire et al., 2004). These heuristics can be divided into two categories: those that focus on usability for all gamers and those that focus on approachability (for new players, learning how to play a game).

14.1.2.2 USING HEURISTICS AS GUIDELINES, NOT RULES

Of course, heuristics are meant to be only guidelines and not rules. As such, they are made to be broken. As Pablo Picasso said, 'Learn the rules like a pro, so you can break them like an artist'. As long as the designer knows what is at stake in the player experience, heuristics are meant to provide insight so the designers can be knowledgeably informed about the effect of their design on the players.

14.1.3 Game player experience: PLAY heuristics

These heuristics often embody many traditional usability principles with an emphasis on the unique challenges of video games. For example, some principles cover areas such as the challenge being not too hard and not too easy, creating a sense of user control, and creating an experience where the players feel that their movement through the world has an effect. Other PLAY heuristics are similar to those of productivity applications, but applied to the unique challenges of game design; for example, players should be able to learn the tools of the game and practice without penalty. This heuristic parallels the common undo function that is a characteristic of most GUI systems. Other heuristics are unique to certain games (e.g., 'the game uses humour well'). One might argue that this would apply to productivity apps or operating systems. However, given that such applications are intended to complete tasks easily and efficiently, the use of humour is almost always ill-advised and unwelcome.

Overall, there are 54 PLAY heuristics in five categories: (1) gameplay, (2) game immersion and engagement, (3) game usability and mechanics, (4) new player experience, and (5) game story immersion (if applicable). The most recent version can be found at http://www.userbehavioristics.com/heuristics-gap-principles-new-player-experience/. The five categories each have several subcategories. See the link for a full list.

14.2 Examples of heuristics

14.2.1 Sample of Category 1: gameplay

14.2.1 D1: THE GAME GOALS ARE CLEAR

The game had clear goals and the player always knew what their goals were from moment to moment.

In Kingdom Hearts Unchained X (Figure 14.1), the player was always aware of their goals. Before starting a level, the screen would prompt player with an image and element type of the boss for the level about to begin.

1. Once the level was selected, it shows the same information and explains the boss in more detail.
2. As the level begins, it once again shows the player an image of the target.
3. During the level, there is always a signal to let the player know where the boss is located.
4. These components allow the player complete side quests without losing sight of the main goal.
5. Once the player was in range of the boss, it was clear which enemy was the target.
6. In a level there could be several enemies which resembled the boss, so it was important for the player to confirm which one was the intended target.

Figure 14.1 Kingdom of Hearts Unchained X

Figure 14.1 *Continued*

Figure 14.1 *Continued*

14.2.2 D2: THE GAME PRESENTS OVERARCHING GOALS EARLY AS WELL AS SHORT-TERM GOALS THROUGHOUT PLAY

In Mario Party 10 (Figure 14.2), the overarching goal is to collect the most stars to win the game. In order to do this, the player is presented with many different types of short-term goals, such as beating opponents in mini-games or strategically landing on parts of the board that would damage the opponent's chance of winning.

Figure 14.2 Mario Party 10

It's time for a Bowser Revolution! First off, I'll
be taking everyone's Mini Stars!

Figure 14.2 *Continued*

The beginning of the game shows the player where the end goal will be on this particular board. The goal is to get to this spot with the most number of starts in order to win the game.

The player gains stars in several ways: one of them is by playing mini-games. In mini-games, the player's goal is to outperform opponents in order to gain the greatest number of stars.

Another short-term goal is to either avoid or land on the red Bowser markers. If the player is doing well, they will avoid these markers, because they want the game to remain in their favour. If the player is doing poorly, they might aim for these spots because it may result in the game tilting in their favour by taking away points from opponents and levelling the scoring field. https://youtu.be/rmi8tzUb6tA?t=2m9s

14.2.3 D3: SKILLS NEEDED TO ATTAIN GOALS ARE TAUGHT BEFORE NEW SKILLS ARE NEEDED

In Final Fantasy XV (Figure 14.3), players are taught the basic skills needed to survive the beginning of the game. Once the player proficiently completes the skills taught, the game provides them with tutorials for more advanced gameplay. The skills they learn are pertinent to the immediate gameplay; the players are taught new skills before being asked to utilize them.

14.2.4 D4: GAME REWARDS PLAYERS, IMMERSING THEM BY INCREASING THEIR CAPABILITIES AND CAPACITY

In Kingdom Hearts Unchained (Figure 14.4), the players earn materials by completing various quests. Then they use these materials to level-up their keyblade (weapon) or to increase its capacity. Levelling up their weapon

Figure 14.3 Final Fantasy XV (https://youtu.be/LnxP3lpTJc4)

Figure 14.3 *Continued*

gives it more strength and defending capability during battles, while increasing its capacity allows the player to fuse stronger metals into the weapon (giving it new special abilities and increased stats). Rewarding the player with increased capabilities and capacity encourages further progress in the game.

Figure 14.4 Kingdom Hearts Unchained (https://youtu.be/j23beW7gSZg)

14.2.5 F2: PLAYERS HAVE THE ABILITY TO AFFECT THE WORLD AND NOTICE THEIR PASSAGE THROUGH IT

Players have an effect on the world, and when they pass through it they notice how the world is affected by their presence. This can be done through gameplay, or even, for example, by seeing a picture on the wall move when they bump into it as they pass by.

In Civilization V (Figure 14.5), the player knows they had an effect on the world by seeing the areas they explored, by knowing what parts of the map they

Figure 14.5 Civilization V (https://youtu.be/QpzT0CHwhFU?t=191)

had not been, by seeing the progress of cities they have built, and through interactions with other civilizations controlled by the AI.

14.2.2 Sample of Category 2: game immersion and engagement

14.2.2.1 A. EMOTIONAL CONNECTION

A1: the player has an emotional connection with the game world and the character
Players find the characters are believable and have an emotional range they can sympathize with.

While playing The Last of Us (Figure 14.6), players are able to identify with the father/daughter duo and find their situation to be believable. Being able to control both characters and learning about their backstories strengthens the emotional connection to Joel and Sarah.

14.2.3 Sample of Category 3: game usability and mechanics

14.2.3.1 B. STATUS AND SCORE

B1: game controls are consistent within the game and follow standard conventions, except where a novel mechanic brings increased fun
Emoji Blitz (Figure 14.7) offers both novel and conventional mechanics to a match-three type of game. The game controls are consistent with industry

Figure 14.6 The Last of Us (https://youtube/0wLljngvrpw?t=960)

Figure 14.7 Emoji Blitz (https://youtu.be/zPqH9eTkd9k?t=8m45s)

standards, which helps lower the learning curve. One of the novel mechanics is the lightning clouds. These can be dropped onto the board or created by matching four or more. This mechanic helps clear a large portion of the board in order to help a player receive a new mix of emojis. This mechanic varies the gameplay and offers a new strategy.

B2: Status and score indicators are seamless, obvious, available, and do not interfere with gameplay

In Star Wars: Commander (Figure 14.8a), the score indicators are obvious and do not interfere with the player's gameplay. While they are at their base, a variety of information is provided to the player without being intrusive. For example, in the upper right-hand corner, the player can see how much gold and metal they have in their loot as well as how many gems and robot assistants they have available. In the upper left-hand corner, they can see how many medals the players hold. Within their base, the length of training required for more units/ soldiers is also displayed (in Figure 14.8a, there are 41 seconds left before the new soldier is ready for battle).

During a battle (Figure 14.8b), the players can see how much loot their enemy has for the taking (upper left-hand corner), how many troops they have left to deploy (bottom left-hand corner), and how much damage the enemy base has suffered, along with their score (bottom right-hand corner). On the battlefield, they can see their soldiers attacking the base and watch them collect loot, as well as keep track of their health.

Figure 14.8a Stars Wars Commander

Figure 14.8b Star Wars Commander

B4: Controls follow industry standards to shorten learning curve
Subway Surfers (Figure 14.9) lowered the player's learning curve by using controls which followed industry standards. This game is similar to other games, such as the popular Temple Run, so the player was able to draw on past knowledge from other games to jump into gameplay.

Figure 14.9 Subway Surfers (https://www.youtube.com/watch?v=LN_OJlsheyk)

14.2.3.2 E. BURDEN ON THE PLAYER

E1: the game does not put any unnecessary burden on the player

In League of Legends (Figure 14.10), the player's champions' abilities are shown at the bottom of the screen. This keeps the player informed on what their potential moves are at all times. If the player forgets what a specific ability does, the player can hover their cursor over that move, and a small window will pop up that explains in detail what the ability does. This keeps the player fully engrossed and informed in the game at all times without placing the burden on the player to memorize the skill sets of all champions.

E2: Player is given controls that are basic enough to learn quickly, yet expandable for advanced options for advanced players

In Mario Kart 8 (Figure 14.11), the player can use basic controls to play the game. The basic controls are 'A' to accelerate and a joystick to turn—these allow the player to complete races. Once the player is comfortable, they are able to expand their learning of more controls to do more. Although these are not necessary for basic play, they expand the options for more fun. For example, if completed correctly, the left and right bumper will activate 'blue sparks', which helps them complete tight turns and simultaneously gives a speed boost.

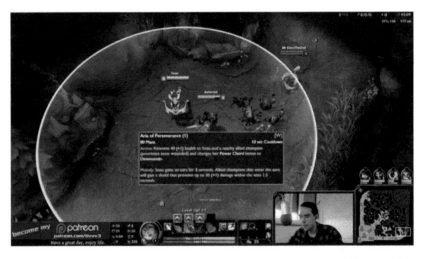

Figure 14.10 League of Legends (https://www.youtube.com/watch?v=qkF3qCJkVOQ)

Figure 14.11 Mario Kart 8 (https://www.youtube.com/watch?v=Amz4sLmrRdl)

14.2.4 Sample of Category 4: new player experience

14.2.4.1 G1: NAVIGATION IS CONSISTENT, LOGICAL, AND MINIMALIST

In Angry Birds 2 (Figure 14.12a), the navigation is simple, consistent, and easy to understand. When the player wants to go to the next level, they can click on the next available level.

Figure 14.12a Angry Birds 2

Figure 14.12b Angry Birds 2 (https://youtu.be/q7lRaKHn-iw)

For example, when in a new screen, if the player wants to return to the previous one, they can exit out by clicking the X located in the right-hand corner (Figure 14.12b).

14.2.4.2 H. ERROR PREVENTION

H1: Player error is avoided

In Dead Space 3 (Figure 14.13), player error is avoided by allowing players to view where their next objective is located by a blue guiding light. This keeps the player from roaming around the game world lost, confused, or stuck.

Figure 14.13 Dead Space 3

H3: Upon turning on the game, the player has enough information to get started to play whatever state the game was left

In Monument Valley (Figure 14.14), the game opens where the player left off with a reminder of what the player was doing.

H5: All levels of players are able to play and get into the game quickly with tutorials or adjustable difficulty levels

In Fast Finger (Figure 14.15), the game mechanics are simple and tutorials clear. An animation illustrates the movements the player needs to make in order to reach the end of the level. The levels start off very simple, and the player feels they could learn the game quickly. As the levels progress, they became more challenging and offer explanations/tutorials appropriate to the level. When the player feels the need to go back and practice previous levels, they are easily accessible on the menu screen.

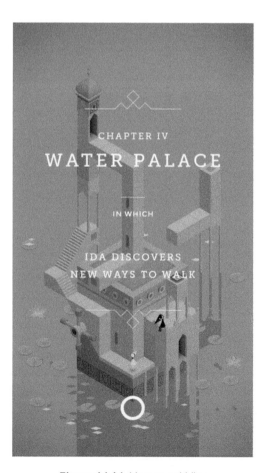

Figure 14.14 Monument Valley

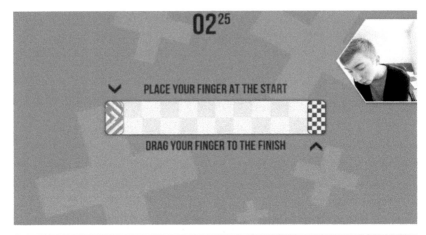

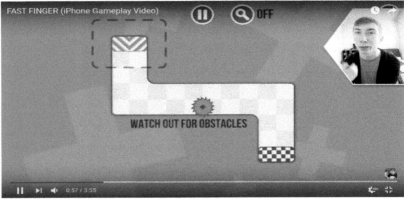

Figure 14.15 Fast Finger (https://www.youtube.com/watch?v=F2TJ0YzR23I)

14.3 Game approachability: GAP heuristics

In contrast to the PLAY heuristics, game approachability principles (GAPs) are intended for new gamers. They refer to the ease with which gamers are able to approach and avail themselves of games—for all who desire to play. In addition, they differentiate between the tools needed to play the game and the game mechanics themselves. In considering game approachability principles, three questions arise: (1) How can they be best assessed and applied? (2) What may need to be revised and redesigned in methods used to assess them? (3) How do these methods help designers include better game approachability into games? There are a total of 27 GAP heuristics. The most recent version can be found at http://www.userbehavioristics.com/heuristics-gap-principles-new-player-experience/. See the link for a full list.

14.3.1 A. Demonstration and practice

B1: THE GAME ALLOWS THE PLAYER TO PRACTICE IN DIFFERENT WAYS

In Clash Royale (Figure 14.16), in addition to the training camp, the game allows the player to watch others players' games to learn strategies and other card deck constellations (i.e., the arrangements of different characters in a card deck).

14.3.2 C. Demonstration of actions, with feedback

C1: THE PLAYER IS ABLE TO PRACTICE NEW ACTIONS WITHOUT SEVERE CONSEQUENCES

Throughout Clash Royale, the players are given opportunities to test their deck whenever they want, without negative consequences. This allows the player to have a better grasp of their abilities and gives them a greater feeling of control over their deck-building decisions.

Figure 14.16 Clash Royale

Figure 14.16 *Continued*

14.3.2.2 C2: THE PLAYER KNOWS WHAT ACTIONS THEY ARE SUPPOSED TO PERFORM AND THE CONSEQUENCES FOR COMPLETING OR FAILING THESE ACTIONS

In Fallout 4 (Figure 14.17), the player understands that the numbers next to body parts represent their percentage chance of landing their attack. The player is given a clear indication of the percentage they need in aiming.

14.3.3 E. Self-efficacy

14.3.3.1 E1: AFTER THE INITIAL TRAINING PERIOD (FIRST PLAY), THE PLAYER FEELS THAT THEY HAVE LEARNED SKILLS THAT WOULD HELP THEM SUCCEED

In Hearthstone (Figure 14.18a), after learning about card stats, the player understands how to summon minions and what the consequences of summoning the minions are, prepping the player with the mechanics necessary to play the game.

Figure 14.17 Fallout 4 (https://youtu.be/wbZtSoJtir0?t=1557)

14.3.3.2 E2: THE PLAYER IS GIVEN SUFFICIENT PRACTICE WITH NEW ACTIONS BEFORE THEY ARE PUNISHED FOR FAILING

In Hearthstone (Figure 14.18b), the player learns how to play the game through a series of six tutorials. During this time, the player is not punished for losing, but cannot proceed until they have an adequate understanding of the game. This ensures the player understands the mechanics before there are any consequences. The player would then feel that gameplay is fair.

Figure 14.18a Hearthstone (https://youtu.be/DU2h671GXkw?t=203)

Figure 14.18b Hearthstone (https://youtu.be/DU2h671GXkw?t=371)

14.3.4 I. Knowledge transfer

14.3.4.1 I1: THE GAME IS SIMILAR TO OTHER GAMES OF A SIMILAR GENRE AND PLATFORM (E.G., CONSOLE, FREEMIUM MOBILE, AND SO ON) AND GAMES IN THE SAME SERIES

In Match 3 games—such as Farm Heroes, Candy Crush, and Puzzle and Dragons (Figures 14.19 and 14.20)—the games share similar mechanics (e.g., swipe to swap spaces and match three), so that players may easily learn how to play.

Figure 14.19a Match 3 Games (https://youtu.be/OQ6Yqc6HM3Q?t=7)

Figure 14.19b Match 3 Games (https://youtu.be/g-VcqvrCS0Y?t=4)

Figure 14.20 Farm Heroes, Candy Crush, Puzzle and Dragons (https://youtube/6k1m4 1DrXpg?t=190)

14.4 How GAP and PLAY are used for evaluation

We have found that doing evaluations different ways produces different types of results, even when using the same list and the same game. The difference is attributed to two different methods of using the heuristics. The first is inductive—looking at the game and seeing if there are any violations of the heuristics. The second is deductive—playing the game as you review the prescribed list of heuristics, identifying problems holistically.

Both methods require knowing the heuristics well. The authors are quite skilled at using them, having created and worked on the lists for several years, but for people unfamiliar with them, it may be more efficient to go through the list one at a time first.

Both methods have their place, and both are useful. In a course taught on game usability, we have students use both methods in order to learn the utility of both. In this exercise, we have found students identifying different data at times, but not conflicting.

14.4.1 Inductive method

Induction is the bottom-up inference of general laws or principles from particular instances. The inductive method relies on issues happening at the time the evaluator plays through the game. This method is great for identifying issues as they arise; it focuses on the bigger problems that arise. However, because it is based on a reaction to the gameplay, some heuristics may be missed.

14.4.2 Deductive method

Deduction is top-down study, linking premise with conclusion. The deductive method is a prescribed way of doing the evaluation. It is step-by-step: issues are found based on going systematically through each heuristic in the list. This is thorough and ensures all the heuristics are addressed.

14.4.3 Adherences, violations, and enhancements

14.4.3.1 WHO EVALUATES?

Games User Researchers. Originally, PLAY and GAP were intended for game researchers who were evaluating and helping to identify and provide insight into player experience. Similar to the usability heuristics for digital products, player experience was the area researchers wanted to improve so that game designers would know what was working and where to make changes. Understanding *why* the player experienced issues at a particular point helped guide designers to how to change it. But this approach also left the creativity and design solutions to the originators of the design.

Game designers. At first, we did not think game designers would find heuristics useful. Designers' focus is not as much on the actual player experience as the planned experience. In contrast, the role of the evaluator is to be that unbiased partner in identifying and providing insight on the player experience, leaving the design decisions to the designers. However, once game designers started to use this list, they found it helpful both as a reminder of all the things 'I already knew' and, admittedly, things 'sometimes I did not think to apply.' It also helped them focus not only on the multitude of areas of the game's design, but also on the resulting player experience. Thus, using the list improves player experience.

An unexpected result is that the game designers would also use the list to help inspire designs that were already working fine. Using the principle of, say, 'player feels in control' may inspire them to find ways that players feel even more in control.

14.4.3.2 WHEN TO EVALUATE

There are several times when using the heuristic lists are useful.

- game concept innovation
  o identify player experience issues and new player experience issues
  o uncover positive player experience and inspire new design ideas
- game concept design
  o identify player experience issues and new player experience issues
  o uncover positive player experience and inspire new design ideas
- game design
  o identify player experience issues and new player experience issues
  o uncover positive player experience and inspire new design ideas

- foundational elements
  o identifying why players had a particular experience provides a foundational principle why the problem exists (such insights help prevent these issues from re-occurring)
- post-launch
  o identify player experience issues and new player experience issues

- common language and analysis of player experience in general
  o categorizes ways to look at the player experience

o provides a common language to discuss player experience between sometimes dispersed team members

14.5 Experimental findings

14.5.1 Previous work on games

In a previous study (Desurvire and Wixon, 2013), we examined the effect of role/training (evaluators vs designers) on the likelihood to generate a report of issues. That work extended previous work to identify quality of the reports, by classifying the text of inspectors' reports into four categories:

- problems identified
- fixes suggested
- effective elements
- suggested enhancements

Previous analysis showed that when compared to the informal condition, using PLAY and GAP heuristics produced more results in every category (see Figures 14.21 and 14.22).

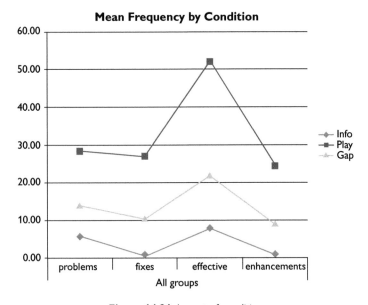

Figure 14.21 Impact of condition

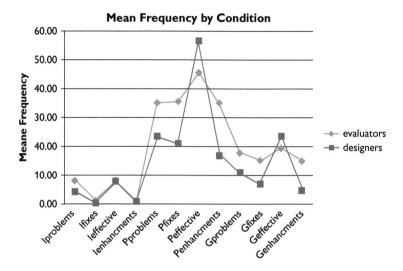

Figure 14.22 Designers vs. evaluators: impact of condition

Summarized simply, in both the PLAY and GAP conditions, the designers were more likely to report effective elements of the design while the evaluators were more likely to report findings in other categories.

We also found that in the informal condition, the pattern for both groups overlapped and the number of reports was small. This relatively low frequency of reports for the informal condition shows how effective the PLAY and GAP heuristics were in finding problems, suggesting fixes, suggesting enhancements, and identifying parts of the game that worked well. There were no effects of order or the game reviewed.

14.5.2 Study design

14.5.2.1 PARTICIPANTS

The current study analysed the reports produced in the previous study (Desurvire and Wixon, 2013). All the participants were experienced gamers. There were 13 game designers from the intermediate game design class and nine game evaluators from the game usability class at the interactive media department at the University of Southern California.

They were divided into two groups: game designers and game evaluators. Each group evaluated two games at two different times. Each group evaluated one game using no heuristics (informal condition), and the other game using the PLAY and

GAP heuristics. In the informal condition, the participants played the game and were encouraged to review that game based on their experience with that game and to draw on their experience with previous games. In the formal condition, they were encouraged to review the game using the PLAY and GAP heuristics.

14.5.2.2 EXPERIMENTAL DESIGN

Zombies, Inc. (Figure 14.23) and Elephant Quest (Figure 14.24) are both released strategic online games, similar in their complexity and challenge.

Figure 14.23 Game 1: Zombies, Inc

Figure 14.24 Game 2: Elephant Quest

As shown in Table 14.1, we counterbalanced the order of conditions: approximately half the participants in each group completed the heuristics evaluation first, and half completed the informal evaluation first. Comparing the impact of PLAY and GAP conditions to the informal condition was our focus.

14.5.3 Results

The number of reports for designers and evaluators for each of the 54 PLAY heuristics was highly correlated, $r(53) = 0.779$, $p < 0.001$. Figure 14.25 presents a scatterplot of report frequency for designers and evaluators.

The strong correlation between the frequency of reports for designers and evaluators demonstrates that the heuristic set provided an effective structure for both groups producing relatively consistent results.

Table 14.1 *Study Design*

Group	Order	Time 1	Time 2
Evaluators	1	Informal	PLAY, GAP
	2	PLAY, GAP	Informal
Designers	1	Informal	PLAY, GAP
	2	PLAY, GAP	Informal

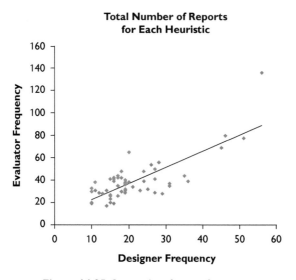

Figure 14.25 Scatterplot of report frequency

14.5.3.1 CLASSIFICATION OF REPORTS

The current study extends this work by focusing on the effect of individual heuristics and by further classifying the participants' reports. This classification examined the relationship between the text in the report and the text in the heuristic. Specifically, we classified the text from the reports into one of six categories. Three raters did this independently and disagreements were resolved by consensus. The categories were as follows:

- Direct interpretation (DI): the reviewers' observation restates the heuristic using some of the specific words from the heuristic.
- Specific observation (SO): the reviewer states a specific observation about the game (could be a suggestion or just a statement of what is happening in the game) without directly referring to the heuristic (i.e., no words were used).
- Direct elaboration (DE): the reviewer restates the heuristic and elaborates on it using specific words from the heuristic. It also refers to specific elements unique to the game (e.g., elephants).
- Rephrase (RP): the review rephrases the heuristic but does not quote it directly, and does not refer to any specific elements that are unique to the game.
- Contradictory recommendation (CR): the reviewer suggests that a violation of a given heuristic be left in the game because leaving the 'error' in the game makes the game better.
- Vague and not actionable (VN): the suggestion does not refer to any heuristic either directly or indirectly; it also does not refer to any specific element of the game nor does it provide a designer with specifics about how to take action. An example would be 'Make the game the more fun.'
- Vague but actionable (VA): the report was vague in that it did not refer to or contradict any of the heuristics. It also did not refer to specific elements of the game. However, it was specific enough that a designer could take action. An example would be 'Make the level design more consistent.'

Because the frequency of reports by designers and evaluators were highly correlated, we collapsed the two groups and analysed the data holistically. The frequencies of the above categories are depicted in Figure 14.26.

As Figure 14.26 shows, in generating reports reviewers follow heuristics closely or elaborate on them (DI + DE). They were also very likely to report details in the interface (SO). These specific observations did not directly refer

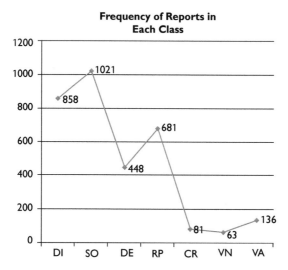

Figure 14.26 Frequency of reports for each class

to heuristics but were 'inspired' by them, as each report was linked to a specific heuristic. The rephrase category is interesting; here reviewers see a problem in the interface and relate that problem to a heuristic, but see a need to modify the heuristic slightly so that it better fits the issue with the design. Together these four categories (DI, DE, SO, RP) account for over 90% of the reports. The low-frequency categories (CR, VN, VA) are the greatest departure from heuristics and also the least useful. The vague and not actionable (category) is the best example: it contains recommendations like 'make the game more fun.' Finally, the vague but actionable comments could be seen as suggestions of areas where the heuristics could be improved or as a measure of how complete the heuristics are. This set of heuristics would seem quite complete, as the VA category accounts for only about 4% of the reports.

Table 14.2 summarizes the same data as Figure 14.26, but reports means, medians, and standard deviations for each category.

Given the low mean frequency in some categories, one might be concerned that the data are skewed. However, as can be seen in Table 14.2, in all cases the means and medians are relatively close to each other.

A one-way ANOVA reveals that differences in frequencies are statistically significant $F_{(6, 48)} = 57.061$, $p < 0.001$. Superscripts next to the category name and the means indicate which differences were significant in the ANOVA (i.e., the ones with identical superscripts are not significantly different from each other).

Table 14.2 *Frequencies of Report Categories*

Category	Mean	Median	Standard Deviation
Direct interpretation(a)	15.89cdefg	15.0	7.46
Specific observation(b)	18.91cdefg	16.5	15.32
Direct and elaboration(c)	8.30abdefg	6.0	6.52
Rephrase(d)	12.61abcefg	10.5	8.06
Contradict (e)	1.50abcdg	1.0	1.82
Vague not actionable(f)	1.17abcde	1.0	1.30
Vague actionable (g)	2.51abcde	2	2.70

14.5.3.2 SUMMARY OF EXPERIMENTAL STUDY

Like many studies, the current study shows that heuristics are effective in producing a deeper analysis of the game as measured by number of reports. The study extends these results to show that evaluators and designers produce a similar pattern of reports. The findings suggest that reviewers should be encouraged not only to report problems with an interface but to suggest fixes, report effective elements, and suggest enhancements.

A qualitative analysis which classifies reports into various types in terms of their relationship to the heuristics and the product produced a number of interesting findings. It suggested the process reviewers use when commenting on a product through the lens of an extensive set of heuristics. The process could be seen as answering a sequential set of questions, as shown in Figure 14.27.

This process describes a detailed engagement with both the product and the heuristics. In other words, the heuristics create an environment which encourages a careful and reflective review that extends beyond simply applying the heuristics in a mechanical way. This hypothesized process is supported by the both the frequency and correlational data.

These findings extend previous research which has focused on the number and quality of the problems detected, cost reduction, and overall impact. The current study clearly shows that reviewers will elaborate, extend, and even contradict heuristics. It also suggests a hypothetical process that reviewers follow when using heuristics carefully.

Taken together, previous research and the current findings suggest why heuristics are more effective than informal reviews in producing reports. Firstly, heuristics provide a checklist for reviewing the product. Next, they encourage reviewers to carefully compare the interface to the heuristic and offer reports

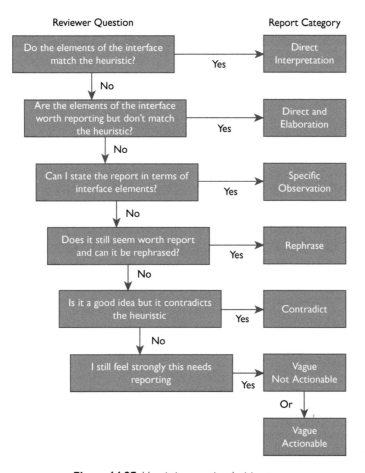

Figure 14.27 Heuristic reporting decision tree

that are derived from the heuristic and the interface. This in-depth process contrasts sharply with informal reviews where reviewers are given no structure and encouraged to review based on their experience. This experience may be disorganized, fragmentary, and idiosyncratic. As a result, few reports are produced— about a tenth as many reports as those produced with heuristics.

Interestingly, the total number of reports in the informal condition (328) is about equal to the sum of reports in the low-frequency categories (contradictory, vague not actionable, and vague actionable) when the GAP and PLAY heuristics are used (280). This result implies that in the informal condition, reviewers are simply noting what they experience, with only slightly greater frequency than those in the 'leftover' categories when a formal heuristic review is used.

Overall, these results and the proposed interpretation of the process of review suggest that researchers begin to focus on the process of reviewing designs using heuristics, even as they continue to focus on the important questions of overall quality of and effort invested in reviews.

14.6 Summary and takeaways

Heuristics are effective in helping both game designers and game research evaluators produce insights and design recommendations about a variety of aspects of player experience.

The PLAY and GAP heuristics both offer a list of good player and new player experiences. They have been used by game designers to remember concepts of good player experience, which reminds them of areas to think about. Since there are many aspects to think of when designing a game, this helps to make conscious what is most likely unconscious in many designers' minds. As an evaluation tool, when the game is in the process of design, PLAY and GAP heuristics offer designers and evaluators a reminder of what optimal player experiences can be. In that way, their use ensures that the players' perspective is more fully considered in the game design. Finally, once the game is close to being launched, or even post-launch, these lists offer a way to better understand why players may be having particular problems.

These heuristics have great utility when designing a game and evaluating the game for player experience. They do not replace the game designers' creativity or knowledge of good player experience. They simply remind them and make it convenient to ensure the player experience is optimal. They cannot replace the evaluators' inquiry into the gameplay experience, but they help evaluators focus on the areas that a player may have either a negative or positive experience.

14.7 Next steps

The current study has demonstrated the effectiveness of heuristics for games (compared to unstructured reviews) and has outlined two approaches (inductive and deductive) and a process that reviewers may employ. Future research should focus on case studies of the application of heuristics in the development of various types of games. Games differ on many dimensions: investment level, platform, intended audience, goals, and others. How these differences impact the application of heuristics is not yet well understood. Some heuristics may be more applicable than others to certain types of games, audiences, and development contexts. A curated set of case studies of the application of heuristics combined with some thoughtful reflection could be a significant advance for the understanding and application of heuristics.

Acknowledgements

We gratefully acknowledge the assistance of many of our students at the Interactive Media and Games Department, as well as the student assistants extraordinaire who helped collect the data and performed the initial analysis—Veronica Chu, Baldur Tangvald, Colleen Dimmer, Jordan Klein—and assisted in game samples: Max Kreminski, Yoshua Lo, and Laura Doumand.

We would also like to thank the participants in the study and Peter Brinson for providing a pool of game designers.

GAP Principles for Optimal New Player Experience
Latest version: http://www.userbehavioristics.com/heuristics-gap-principles-new-player-experience/
PLAY Principles for Optimal Playability
Latest version: http://www.userbehavioristics.com/heuristics-gap-principles-new-player-experience/

References and further reading

Bernhaupt, R. (ed.) (2015). Game user experience. New York: Springer.

Desurvire, H., Wiberg, C. (2009, July). Game usability heuristics (PLAY) for evaluating and designing better games: The next iteration. In International Conference on Online Communities and Social Computing (pp. 557–566). Springer, Berlin, Heidelberg.

Desurvire, H., Caplan, M., Toth., J. (2004). Using heuristics to evaluate the playability of games. In CHI '04 Extended Abstracts on Human Factors in Computing Systems (CHI EA '04) (pp. 1509–1512). New York, NY: ACM. DOI=http://dx.doi.org/10.1145/985921.986102.

Desurvire, H., Charlotte Wiberg, C. (2008). Master of the game: assessing approachability in future game design. In CHI '08 Extended Abstracts on Human Factors in Computing Systems (CHI EA '08) (pp. 3177–3182). New York, NY: ACM. DOI: https://doi.org/10.1145/1358628.1358827.

Desurvire, H., Wiberg, C. (2015). User Experience Design for Inexperienced Gamers: GAP—Game Approachability Principles. In Game User Experience Evaluation (pp. 169–186). Springer International Publishing.

Desurvire, H., Wixon, D. (2013). Game principles: choice, change & creativity: making better games. In CHI '13 Extended Abstracts on Human Factors in Computing Systems (CHI EA '13). ACM, New York, NY, USA, 1065–1070. DOI: https://doi.org/10.1145/2468356.2468547.

Nielsen, J., Molich, R. (1990). Heuristic evaluation of user interfaces. In CHI 1990 Conference Proceedings (pp. 249–256).

Rodio, F., Christian Bastien, J. M. (2013, 13–15 November). Heuristics for video games evaluation: how players rate their relevance for different game genres according to their experience. IHM'13, Bordeaux, France.

Smith, S. L., Mosier, J. N. (1986). Guidelines for designing user interface software. Retrieved from http://userlab.com/Downloads/Smith_Mosier_guideline_.pdf

Wolfshead. Bushnell's theorem: easy to learn, difficult to master. http://www.wolfsheadonline.com/bushnells-theorem-easy-to-learn-difficult-to-master/

CHAPTER 15

Heuristic evaluation of playability

*Examples from social games research
and free-to-play heuristics*

JANNE PAAVILAINEN, HANNU KORHONEN,
ELINA KOSKINEN, KATI ALHA, *University of
Tampere*

Highlights

The fierce competition in the video games market and new revenue models such as free-to-play emphasize the importance of good playability for first-time user experience and retention. Cost-effective and flexible evaluation methods such as heuristic evaluation are suitable for identifying playability problems in different phases of the game development life cycle. In this chapter, we introduce the heuristic evaluation method with updated playability heuristics, present example studies on identifying playability problems in social network games, and propose new heuristics for evaluating free-to-play games.

15.1 Introduction

The video game industry is a highly competitive entertainment domain where the rise of production values and development costs are acknowledged widely. Thousands of games are available on various computer, console, and mobile

Games User Research, Anders Drachen, Pejman Mirza-Babaei, Lennart E. Nacke (Eds).
© Oxford University Press 2018. Published 2018 by Oxford University Press

platforms. The emergence of the free-to-play (F2P) revenue model has made the competition even fiercer as games are distributed free of charge.

Improving the quality of a game is a viable approach to improving acquisition, retention, and monetization of players. Playability is a term used to describe the overall quality of a game, covering both game usability and gameplay aspects (Korhonen, 2016). Traditionally, playtesting with the target audience is utilized to improve playability by identifying design problems in the game that may result in a poor player experience. However, playtesting is time-consuming, expensive, and not necessarily a viable option in the early phases of development.

Heuristic evaluation is a usability inspection method widely used by practitioners and researchers of human-computer interaction. Known for its cost-effectiveness, heuristic evaluation is a potential method for evaluating games in different phases of the development life cycle, as it can be utilized to evaluate anything from pre-alpha prototypes to published games. By utilizing heuristic evaluation with playability heuristics, a group of expert inspectors can identify a wide range of playability problems. Identifying and fixing problems at an early stage has obvious development cost benefits.

In this chapter, we define playability and introduce the heuristic evaluation method with the updated playability heuristics for games. We present examples of our own research where heuristic evaluation has been used to study the playability of F2P social network games (i.e., social games).[1] Lastly, we provide new heuristics for evaluating F2P games. Heuristic evaluation is suited for both game development and research purposes to study playability of games.

15.2 Playability

Traditional usability principles and methods have been used successfully for evaluating productivity software for decades. The ISO 9241-11 standard defines usability as 'the extent to which a product can be used by specified users to achieve specified goals with effectiveness, efficiency and satisfaction in a specified context of use'.

However, as games and productivity software have fundamental differences in their design and philosophy of use, traditional usability practices must be

---

[1] 'Social games' is a commonly used, industry-coined term for video games played on Facebook and in other social network services.

modified to accommodate special characteristics of games. Hence, instead of 'usability', the term 'playability' is often used when discussing quality of games. Unlike usability, there is no commonly agreed definition or standard for playability. While the term is widely used in different contexts, it is often taken as granted without further scrutiny. This makes the term and its use vague and ambiguous.

Several authors have defined and discussed playability from different perspectives (Paavilainen, 2017), but none of these are considered de facto standard. However, a common element in these definitions is that playability is considered to cover more ground than usability. For the purpose of this chapter, we use the latest definition provided by Korhonen (2016) in his doctoral dissertation:

> The game has good playability when the user interface is intuitive and gaming platform is unobtrusive, so that the player can concentrate on playing the game. Fun and challenge are created through gameplay when it is understandable, suitably difficult and engaging.

This definition illustrates that playability is formed through game usability and gameplay aspects, which are both designed and programmable properties of the game. Game usability covers aspects such as clarity of audiovisual presentation, user interface layout and navigation logic, control and feedback, and help, for example. All these are related to how the game system is used by the player through the input-output feedback loop.

Gameplay focuses on aspects which make games different from productivity software. Goal structures, challenges, rewards, story components, etc. are basic building blocks for games, often regarded as 'game mechanics'. Together, these mechanics form a dynamic system which is called 'gameplay'. Gameplay is related to what the players do in the game and why.

Depending on the context, other components can be included in playability. For example, mobile and board games have their own platform-dependent factors which must be taken into consideration when discussing playability of these games. Game genres also have their own specific conventions for interaction, which should be taken into consideration as well.

It is important to emphasize that playability describes the qualities of the game, not the game play[2] situation or player experience per se. Playability is

---

[2] Gameplay (compound word) is a reference to the dynamic interaction of game mechanics; game play (non-compound word) refers to the activity of playing a game.

related to player experience only through a cause-effect relationship. Poor playability (i.e., poor quality of the game) can have a detrimental effect on player experience. Good playability does not necessarily ensure good player experience and commercial success, but poor playability can surely lead to disasters.

15.3 Heuristic evaluation of playability

Heuristic evaluation is a method by which experts inspect the target system using a set of guidelines to govern the evaluation. Heuristic evaluation is a widely known method for evaluating usability of a product, originally developed by Nielsen and Molich (1990). It belongs to the analytical inspection method category, meaning that the evaluation is conducted completely by experts instead of users from the target audience as in traditional user testing. With playability heuristics, heuristic evaluation can be used to evaluate games as well.

The advantage of the method is that the evaluations can be completed in a few hours and the results are often reported to the developers the same day. The evaluations can be repeated in fast cycles and provide feedback for the revised versions of the design. This supports the agile development process typical for game development projects. Heuristic evaluation is subjective in nature; inspectors' own evaluation expertise, previous knowledge of similar games, and gaming experience and skills play an essential role and will affect the quality of the evaluation. This bias known as the evaluator effect is compensated by using multiple inspectors.

The heuristic evaluation process can be divided into five phases. A step-by-step reference guide is presented in Table 15.1, which follows the procedure documented by Korhonen (2016).

For an analytical evaluation, there are two critical aspects in the beginning: the choice of inspectors and the choice of heuristics. Evaluations typically include three-to-five inspectors, who examine the game by playing it. Generally, it is recommended to use double experts, who are well versed with the method and understand the game genre and its conventions. If double experts are not available, a mix of method experts and domain experts is feasible. If there are no experts available, this can be mitigated by using a larger group of novice inspectors. The chosen playability heuristics (see Section 15.4) should cover both game usability and gameplay aspects at least. Depending on the game, there might be additional aspects to be inspected as well, such as mobility, multiplayer, context-aware, or F2P features.

Table 15.1 *Heuristic evaluation procedure*

Procedure step	Main tasks	Practical guidelines
#1 Preparation	Choose inspectors, select playability heuristics, reserve space for evaluation, and prepare the game (and devices).	3–5 inspectors with evaluation method expertise. Inspectors should be familiar with similar games in the genre.
#2 Individual evaluation	Evaluate game menus and different configuration and settings screens. This resembles productivity software evaluation focusing on UI evaluation.	Observe particularly issues concerning game usability heuristics.
	Play the game and get familiar with the main features and objectives of the game, focus on gameplay evaluation.	Observe gameplay heuristics and additional modules if needed for multiplayer, mobile, context-aware, or free-to-play, for example.
	Compare how well the interface elements support playing the game. Does the interface allow smooth and unobtrusive interaction with the game?	Observe both game usability and gameplay heuristics. Remember to document positive findings as well.
#3 Debrief within inspector team	Combine playability problem reports and discuss with other inspectors about the problems. Prepare a list of corrections for the playability problems. Prioritize problems.	Prioritize playability problems with severity ratings (e.g., cosmetic, minor, major, critical), assign violated heuristics to problems and remove duplicates. Include positive findings.
#4 Report findings	Present findings to the stakeholders.	Discuss with the developers about different options to correct problems. Remember to present positive findings as well.
#5 Aftermath	Analyse problems which were not covered by the heuristics and expand the existing heuristics if needed. Debrief the whole procedure with inspectors and prepare for the next evaluation cycle.	Understanding the nature of the problems is essential for preventing the creation of redundant heuristics. Documenting and sharing the findings is important so that the same mistakes are not made in future development projects.

The procedure of conducting the evaluation is straightforward and focuses on inspecting the game with the help of playability heuristics. The inspectors individually observe the design holistically and take notes on any aspects of the game that might cause playability problems by violating the heuristics. To understand the playability problems, we can apply Lavery et al. (1997) approach, which requires attention to three aspects: (1) the context in which the playability problem arises, (2) the actual immediate and eventual difficulties of the player, and (3) the assumed causes of these difficulties. While the heuristics are used to guide the inspectors to focus on different aspects of the game, inspectors should report all encountered playability problems—including those which are not covered by the heuristics. Identifying problems outside the heuristics is dependent on the inspector's expertise and experience, hence double experts are recommended.

The evaluation of the game can be further divided into three rounds. The first round is dedicated to explore the interface elements that are external to actual gameplay. Typically, these include the menu, configuration, and settings screens. The second round concentrates on gameplay. Depending on the level of completeness of the game, the inspectors might be able to evaluate only a certain portion of the game, such as the tutorial, character creation, inventory, combat system. During this round, the focus of the evaluation should be on whether the game is understandable and if the game behaves as expected. It is important to record problematic aspects in the game immediately, because the inspectors will learn and adapt quickly to bypass minor problems. In the third round, the inspectors should examine the gameplay interface with respect to goals and other game mechanics. The focus should be on whether the UI supports gameplay and whether it provides accurate and sufficient information for the player. The individual evaluation produces a list of playability problems that the inspectors have encountered during the evaluation.

In addition to identifying playability problems, it is imperative to report positive findings. There are two reasons for this. Firstly, reporting well-designed features prevents 'fixing' them accidentally, which might cause new problems. Secondly, reporting only negative aspects from the game design might have discouraging effect on developers.

The inspectors work together to consolidate a master list of playability problems based on the individual findings. It is useful to examine the game together so that problems can be easily pointed out and discussed, which increases the validity and reliability of the results. In the master list, each playability problem is presented with a description of the problem, which should identify the location of the problem in the game, why the issue was determined to be a problem, and how it could be corrected. It is also useful to annotate the problem with reference to a heuristic that the design violates. This helps game designers understand why the issue is being brought up and helps them correct it. In addition, problems should be rated on their severity. One common approach is to prioritize problems as cosmetic, minor, major, or critical. Prioritization provides information for developers to determine which problems the inspectors think are the most critical ones to fix and helps them to schedule and allocate resources accordingly.

The complete evaluation report with playability problems and positive findings is then presented to the development team. Discussing the findings and solutions is imperative, as it helps both developers and inspectors to understand the problems and the design vision. There are cases where heuristics are violated on purpose, and acknowledging false positives (non-problems) is useful for any upcoming evaluations.

The final phase is the inspectors' internal debrief focusing on the whole process. How well the evaluation covered the necessary aspects and met the objectives of the evaluation should be reviewed. Also, if there were any playability problems which were not covered by the heuristics, these problems should be studied further and the existing heuristics expanded if necessary. This helps the team find similar problems in the future and expands the knowledge of playability problems. We encourage practitioners to modify and expand whatever heuristics they start with to better accommodate their specific work environment and design space.

Lastly, it must be noted that the inspectors do not represent the target audience of the game. They might not represent the target demographic, but more importantly they are not playing the game with a mindset similar to the average player. Focusing on evaluating the game can produce false positive findings, which might not be actual playability problems for the players. Therefore, heuristic evaluation should not be considered an alternative to playtesting, but as a complementary method in situations where playtesting is not feasible. Heuristic evaluation can be used prior to playtesting to catch basic playability problems, so playtesting can focus on more important aspects in the design. Best results are achieved when heuristic evaluation is used iteratively in conjunction with playtesting during the whole development process.

15.4 Playability heuristics

A heuristic is 'a common-sense rule (or set of rules) intended to increase the probability of solving some problem' (http://www.webster-dictionary. org/definition/Heuristic). Heuristics are used in analysis methods, such as a game evaluation, as an aid to learning, discovery, and problem solving.

Playability heuristics are intended to provide a close-enough solution for problems that inspectors discover in game. Well-defined heuristics are a valuable asset for game development as well, and can be used as a reference library for common problematic areas in game design.

The history of playability heuristics goes back approximately 15 years. In 2002, Federoff conducted a case study in a game company and defined heuristics that can be considered as a first heuristic set for evaluating video games. A couple of years later, Desurvire et al. published a playability heuristic set based on Federoff's heuristics. Later, other authors published their versions of playability heuristics covering gameplay or game usability aspects as well (see Korhonen 2016 for details). In the following years, more playability heuristic sets started to emerge, focusing on different aspects of playability. Social interaction of players within the game received attention, and heuristics for multiplayer games were published by Korhonen and Koivisto (2007) and Pinelle et al. (2009). Playability heuristic sets including game usability and gameplay could be considered as a primary branch of playability heuristics in which the core aspects of playability are covered.

It became apparent that there are many video game types for both entertainment and other purposes with unique characteristics to be considered in game evaluations. Mobile games were one of the first type of games in which playability could be affected by the mobility of the players, changing conditions in the surroundings, and, of course, mobile devices as a gaming platform. Playability heuristics for mobile games were published by Karvonen (2005). Educational games were studied actively as well, and playability heuristic sets were published for these games.

Games such as pervasive and social games alter the way players play video games and bring up new aspects that need to be covered in game evaluations. For example, in pervasive games, the utilization of context information in the game design raises issues which will greatly influence playability of these games. There are few articles that cover playability of pervasive games (Korhonen, 2016), but the recent interest of augmented reality games will probably result in a validated set of playability heuristics for pervasive games in the near future.

For social games, Paavilainen (2010) has presented ten high-level heuristics to guide design and evaluation, focusing on the special characteristics of the social network integration in game design. The specific game types or genres could be considered as a second branch of playability heuristics.

Recently, the development of playability heuristics has moved to more specialized areas, and authors have published playability heuristics for specific interaction modalities or gaming platforms. Köffel et al. (2010) presented a set of playability heuristics for advanced tabletop games, while Hara and Ovaska (2014) have presented heuristics for the interaction design of motion-controller games. These kinds of heuristics could be considered as a third branch of playability heuristics, and can be used in conjunction with the core playability heuristics.

Choice of heuristics plays a critical role in an evaluation. We present playability heuristics originally developed by Korhonen and Koivisto (2007, 2006) and updated and expanded by Korhonen (2016). These heuristics have gone through a careful analysis of game design literature to make heuristics understandable and complete for game evaluations. Further, they have been validated in several game evaluations by tens of external inspectors.

The playability heuristic set contains several modules to cover different aspects of the game. Two core modules, *game usability* and *gameplay*, reflect the two most important aspects of playability. These heuristics are common to all games and can be used to evaluate any type of game. In addition, there are modules for *multiplayer*, *mobility*, and *context-aware* games, which can be used when those aspects are evaluated. Tables 15.2–15.6 list and describe the heuristics. When the heuristics are used in game evaluations, inspectors will benefit from a short summary of the heuristic, which gives more information for discovery and problem solving. More detailed descriptions of the heuristics can be found in Korhonen (2016).

Table 15.2 *Game Usability heuristics*

Code	Game Usability Heuristics
GU1a	audiovisual representation supports the game
GU1b	a view to the game world supports smooth interaction and the camera behaves correctly
GU2	screen layout is efficient and visually pleasing
GU3	device UI and game UI are used for their own purposes

continued

Table 15.2 *Continued*

Code	Game Usability Heuristics
GU4	indicators are visible
GU5	the player understands the terminology
GU6	navigation is consistent, logical, and minimalist
GU7	game controllers are consistent and follow standard conventions
GU8	game controls are convenient and flexible
GU9	the game gives feedback on the player's actions
GU10	the player cannot make irreversible errors
GU11	the player does not have to memorize things unnecessarily
GU12	the game contains help

Table 15.3 *Gameplay heuristics*

Code	Gameplay Heuristics
GP1	the game provides clear goals or supports player-created goals
GP2	the player sees the progress in the game and can compare the results
GP3	the players are rewarded and the rewards are meaningful
GP4	the player is in control
GP5	challenge, strategy, and pace are in balance
GP6	the first-time experience is encouraging
GP7	the game story, if any, supports the gameplay and is meaningful
GP8	there are no repetitive or boring tasks
GP9	the players can express themselves
GP10	the game supports different playing styles
GP11	the game does not stagnate
GP12	the game is consistent
GP13	the game uses orthogonal unit differentiation
GP14	the player does not lose any hard-won possessions

Table 15.4 *Multiplayer heuristics*

Code	Multiplayer Heuristics
MP1	the game supports communication
MP2	there are reasons to communicate
MP3	the game supports groups and communities

continued

Table 15.4 *Continued*

Code	Multiplayer Heuristics
MP4	the game helps the player to find other players and game instances
MP5	the game provides information about other players
MP6	the design overcomes the lack of players and enables soloing
MP7	the design minimizes deviant behaviour
MP8	the design hides the effects of the network
MP9	players should play with comparable players (supplements GP6)

Table 15.5 *Mobility heuristics*

Code	Mobility Heuristics
MO1	the play sessions can be started quickly
MO2	the game accommodates the surroundings
MO3	interruptions are handled reasonably
MO4	the graphical design is accommodated to current brightness (supplements GU1a)
MO5	the player should be aware of some device features while playing (supplements GU3 and GU4)
MO6	mobile devices have their own conventions for input (supplements GU7)
MO7	the tutorial should respond to immediate demand (supplements GU12)

Table 15.6 *Context-Aware heuristics*

Code	Context-Aware Heuristics
CA1	perception of the current context
CA2	players should have an equal chance to play
CA3	adjustable play sessions
CA4	communication outside the game world (supplements MP1)

15.5 Playability problems in social games

In this section, we present case studies where heuristic evaluation was used to study playability of social games (Paavilainen et al., 2015, 2014). The purpose of these studies was to gain understanding on playability problems and design of social games. Social games are interesting from the playability perspective, as they are integrated to social network services and feature the F2P revenue model. These two factors make it possible for the players to find new games easily for free due to the viral nature of the network and the lack of upfront payment. This also means that the players can easily ditch poor-quality games and find new ones, emphasizing the role of good playability in the hopes of retention. Monetization is achieved via in-app purchases selling virtual goods, in-game currency, and extra content. In-app purchase transactions are done during gameplay or on a dedicated website outside the game.

Social games started to appear in 2007 after Facebook released an application programming interface, which allowed third-party developers to create content on the social network service. Since then thousands of social games have appeared on Facebook, and some of them became extremely popular, featuring millions of daily players due to the ease of access and viral distribution. For social games, the target audience is typically very heterogeneous, and many of the players have little or no prior experience with video games. Therefore, social games are usually rather simple, casual games with a social twist—with some exceptions, of course.

We used a large number of novice inspectors to examine multiple social games with heuristic evaluation. The inspectors received training on using the original heuristics created by Korhonen and Koivisto (2007, 2006) to guide the evaluation. We analysed all reported playability problems and organized them based on frequency and the heuristic violated. Further methodological details can be found in the published studies (Paavilainen et al., 2015, 2014). In the following, we present examples of the most common and domain-specific playability problems in social games.

15.5.1 Common playability problems in social games

The common playability problems in social games (Paavilainen et al., 2014) are presented in Table 15.7. The heuristic violated and examples of individual playability problems are listed for each problem category.

Most of the top-ten playability problems in social games are related to game usability. These include problems related to UI layout, navigation design, availability of help, visual clarity of game content, feedback, and camera views. These problems make the top six of all problems found. In our studies and evaluation workshops, inspectors state that game usability problems are easier to find than gameplay problems. The probable reason for this is that players interact

Table 15.7 *Common playability problems in social games. The most common problems are related to game usability, but there are also important gameplay problems which need to be addressed*

	Problem category	Violated heuristic	Examples of common playability problems
1	User interface layout	GU2	• Screen is crowded with too many UI elements • UI elements hide important gameplay elements • UI does not scale with windowed and full-screen modes
2	Navigation	GU6	• Players are unable to find the correct action from UI • Confirmation is not asked for in-app purchases • Minimap cannot be used for game world navigation
3	Help	GU12	• Help is not readily available for the player • Player is missing information how to complete actions • Soft and hard currencies[3] are not explained for the player
4	Visual clarity	GU1a	• Avatar's movement animation is not consistent • Small texts are difficult to read • Difficulties to distinguish game units from each other
5	Feedback	GU9	• Feedback from the game is sluggish • Certain actions have no feedback loop at all • There are no visual indicators for upgraded units
6	Camera	GU1b	• Manipulation of the camera is not possible (zoom/angle) • Moving around the camera in the game world is awkward • Some gameplay elements are off-camera
7	Challenge	GP5	• Difficulty ramps up too quickly • Game items wear out too fast • Random element plays too much of a part in the game
8	Browser/Flash	N/A	• Right click cannot be used in a game • Keyboard shortcuts do not work in full-screen mode • Chat functions are removed in full-screen mode
9	Goals	GP1	• Player is given too many tasks at a time • End condition for the level is not presented clearly • Game lacks long-term goal
10	Rewards	GP3	• Rewards are too small when compared to effort • Player gains ranks which have no meaning in the game • Resource-consuming actions do not provide rewards

[3] Free-to-play games commonly feature resources which are often referred as 'soft' and 'hard' currencies. Soft currency is earnable resource which can be collected by doing gameplay tasks. Hard currency is premium resource which can be purchased with real money.

with user interface elements constantly, and therefore they are easier to discover. Gameplay-related problems are hidden deeper in the game system; their discovery demands more effort from the inspectors.

As an example, we present a UI layout problem (Figure 15.1). The game's UI is taking up a lot of space on the screen, with numerous interface elements making the screen crowded. This often leads to navigation problems, as the player is unsure where to find correct information or action. In addition, the crowded UI design obscures gameplay elements. This can be overwhelming and confusing for the player.

In addition to game usability problems, there are gameplay problems. These are commonly related to challenge, goals, and rewards. Problems related to challenge come in many forms. Either the game features no challenge, as in many world-building games, or the challenge is too high, as in puzzle games that ramp up the difficulty deliberately to steer the player towards in-app purchases. There might also be too many random elements present, which diminish the element of skill in the game. Usually there is no definite end goal in social games, but the player is swarmed with parallel tasks that require a lot of time and clicking—which can be often bypassed with in-app purchases (see Section 15.5.2 for domain-specific problems). Meaningless tasks with a lack of challenge and motivating goals tend to result in meaningless rewards.

Figure 15.1 Screenshot from League of Angels (Youzu, 2013) presenting a heavy user interface layout. There are over 30 clickable UI icons on the screen

Some of the problems are related to platform technology, such as Flash, which is commonly used in social games running on a browser. Typically, Flash prohibits the use of a right-mouse click (as it opens the Flash menu), and often some features such as in-game chat or keyboard shortcuts are disabled when Flash games are played in a full-screen mode. There is no specific heuristic to cover such a platform-dependent problem, but it is an example on how the platform can have an effect on playability.

15.5.2 Domain-specific playability problems in social games

In addition to common playability problems in social games, there are several domain-specific playability problems which should be considered in a more detailed analysis, as they can influence the common acceptance of the social games. These problems are caused by the social network integration features or the F2P revenue model. Through our studies, we have identified six domain-specific playability problems (Paavilainen et al., 2015). These problems are presented with the heuristic violated and examples in Table 15.8.

Repetitive gameplay is one of the most common domain-specific problems in social games. As social games are typically aimed at a large heterogeneous

Table 15.8 *Domain-specific playability problems in social games*

#	Problem category	Violated heuristic	Examples of domain-specific playability problems
1	Repetitive gameplay	GP8	• Core mechanic becomes boring quickly • Tasks are repetitive and meaningless • Gameplay is lacking depth
2	Aggressive monetization	FP1	• Player must pay to advance in the game • Sending gifts to friends require in-app purchases • Quest rewards must be unlocked with in-app purchases
3	Interrupting pop-ups	GU6	• Too many pop-ups when starting the game • Ad pop-ups appear randomly during gameplay
4	Friend requirements	MP6	• Player must invite friends to advance in the game
5	Click fatigue	GP8	• Major tasks require too much mindless clicking • Clicking individual rewards takes too much time • Game world requires too much micromanagement
6	Spammy messages	CA4	• Too many posts and notifications from the game (spam)

audience who often play these games with little or no experience, the gameplay is often designed to be simple and casual, thus lacking depth. Such games are easy to pick up and learn, but ultimately they start to feel repetitive and boring. This is a design trade-off, where versatility and depth of gameplay are sacrificed for easy acquisition and casual feel. A related domain-specific problem is click fatigue, which is apparent especially in world-building games where the player must tend their city, castle, farm, home, etc. As the player progresses in the game, these environments expand and require more tending (Figure 15.2). Tending the game world usually boils down to clicking characters and items between timed intervals, which eventually becomes time-consuming and tedious as the game requires more and more tending (clicking), making the game feel frustrating and boring.

Aggressive monetization is a domain-specific problem to make a quick profit from the players. As in F2P games, players are monetized through game mechanics; therefore, the gameplay must be designed in such a way that it drives players towards in-app purchases. Hard paywalls or gameplay rewards which can be only unlocked with in-app purchases are examples of aggressive monetization strategies. Players get frustrated as progression in the game requires in-app purchases, but the player might not know or understand this before investing considerable amount of time and energy in the game.

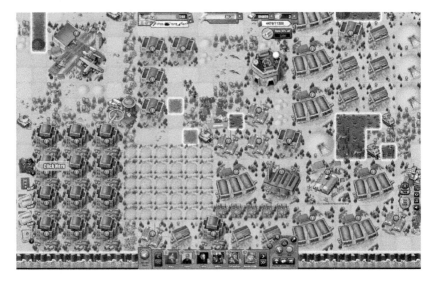

Figure 15.2 Example of click fatigue in a strategy game. Buildings in Army Attack (Digital Chocolate, 2011; RockYou!, 2014) produce resources that must be separately collected by clicking

Interrupting pop-up windows have been considered problematic for a long time in productivity software and websites. Our studies reveal that some social games feature interrupting pop-ups in conjunction with aggressive monetization. During gameplay, a sudden pop-up dialogue might be advertising in-app purchase sales. This is irritating for the player as it interrupts the task at hand unexpectedly. When getting back to the game after some time, there might be several pop-up dialogues promoting sales, updates, and other content after the game loads. These dialogues create additional and unwanted navigation paths, as they must be closed manually.

Pop-ups are also used to ask players to invite their friends into the game. Similar to hard paywalls, some games require the player to invite friends to progress in the game. This is another domain-specific problem based on social network integration, and irritating for those players who think it is awkward to invite friends to play—or simply do not have enough playing friends. Sending out numerous invitations relates to the final domain-specific problem, spammy messages. Constant notifications, which are often encountered outside the game, become irritating and result in blocking and ignoring the game altogether. Notifications and reminders sent by the players and the game is a retention strategy to get players back into the game, but, like aggressive monetization, it can backfire and turn against itself.

These are examples of playability problems we have discovered with heuristic evaluation experiments. For us, heuristic evaluation has been a valuable tool to gain understanding of playability and the design of social games. These findings have also been confirmed by player and developer interviews focusing on social and other F2P games (Alha et al., 2014; Paavilainen et al., 2013).

Understanding these playability problems is useful for both researchers and developers. For researchers, it opens up new and more nuanced research questions while providing information on challenges of social games design related to monetization and player experience. For developers, these findings can be used to improve the quality of games by paying attention to the problem areas in game design that have been identified.

15.6 Heuristics for F2P games

Based on our research on social games and F2P games in general, we introduce a new module including six heuristics which should be taken into account when evaluating F2P games (Table 15.9). These heuristics are based on game

Table 15.9 *Free-to-Play heuristics*

Code	Free-to-Play Heuristics
FP1	Progression is possible without in-app purchases (supplement to GP11)
FP2	In-app purchases and transactions are clearly informed
FP3	In-app purchases provide meaningful value
FP4	In-app purchases can be made inaccessible for minors
FP5	Hard currency can be earned through gameplay
FP6	Gameplay is fair for both paying and non-paying players (supplement to GP5)

developer and player interviews, evaluation experiments, and game analyses done in the SoPlay, Triangle, and Free2Play research projects (2008–2015) in Game Research Lab, University of Tampere, Finland (http://gameresearchlab. uta.fi).

In F2P games, the revenue model and monetization strategy is an integral part of game design, and therefore affect the player experience, as in-app purchase transactions are done usually during game play. For this reason, there is a need for heuristics covering the monetization aspects in relation to game design. These new heuristics cover important playability issues related to monetization in F2P games, focusing on fair play, transparency, and ethics.

We present the heuristics here as an initial list, which has not yet been validated thoroughly. When evaluating F2P games, inspectors should pay close attention to these heuristics, as violating them might result not only in poor player experience, but in bad media representation in some cases.

15.6.1 Progression is possible without in-app purchases (FP1)

Progression in the game should be possible without resorting to in-app purchases. Based on interviews and game evaluations, forcing the player to make in-app purchases to progress causes frustration. In a commercially viable F2P game, the content must be throttled for the non-paying player to make in-app purchases appealing. However, denying progression without in-app purchases, known as a 'hard paywall', is deemed detrimental by players and developers alike. All game content should be accessible for non-paying players at least in theory, while progression can be made faster for paying players. This heuristic is a supplement to GP11 heuristic (stagnation) and it is also related to GP2 heuristic (progression).

15.6.2 In-app purchases and transactions are clearly informed (FP2)

This heuristic focuses on how purchases with real money or hard currency are presented to the player. The prices for such purchases must be clearly visible and all transactions should be confirmed separately. Neglecting this heuristic might cause players to make unintentional purchases, which can lead to complaints and demands for refunds. In addition, the benefits of such purchases must be made clear to the player.

15.6.3 In-app purchases provide meaningful value (FP3)

In-app purchases must be meaningful, thus provide value for the paying player. If the purchases do not provide meaningful value, the player has wasted real money or hard currency for nothing. For example, the player should not be lured to purchase inferior items in the game or otherwise tricked into purchasing obsolete content.

15.6.4 In-app purchases can be made inaccessible for minors (FP4)

It should be possible to make in-app purchases inaccessible for minors so that they cannot make unwanted purchases. This is an ethical issue brought up by both players and developers in our interviews. There have been many stories in mass media how children have caused massive credit card debt for their parents by making in-app purchases either on purpose or by accident. Such news is bad press for game companies and therefore these situations should be avoided when possible.

15.6.5 Hard currency can be earned through gameplay (FP5)

Games with hard currency should give it out in a limited amount for non-paying players for progression. The rationale is that non-paying players can then get an idea of the benefits of in-app purchases, which further motivates them to make actual in-app purchases with real money. In many F2P games, there might be a small amount of hard currency available for the player right from the start, which is one way to support this heuristic. If the non-paying players never experience the benefits of in-app purchases, they are less likely to convert to paying players.

15.6.6 Gameplay is fair for both paying and non-paying players (FP6)

The sixth heuristic is related to game balance and is a supplement to the GP5 heuristic. In F2P multiplayer games, especially those with competition between players, the paying players should not have a decisive advantage over non-paying players. Such pay-to-win scenarios are frowned upon by players and developers alike. Hence the gameplay should be fair for non-paying players while still providing value for paying players. The extra value for paying players can be offered in many ways without unbalancing the gameplay. Non-functional cosmetic items (e.g., exclusive character outfits or weapon textures) are popular in many successful F2P games, while functional benefits can include, for instance, faster progression and the possibility to modify the gameplay towards one's own playing style.

15.7 Conclusions

In this chapter we have presented heuristic evaluation with updated playability heuristics. We have also given examples of studies where heuristic evaluation was used to identify common and domain-specific problems in social games. Lastly, we have introduced a new heuristic module with six heuristics for evaluating F2P games.

Heuristic evaluation is a viable method for identifying playability problems; it is cost-effective and more flexible than playtesting with the target audience. As development costs and production values are getting higher, it is important to identify playability problems early in the development phase when playable prototypes become available. Identifying and fixing problems early allows playtesting to focus on more important issues than catching basic playability problems, which can be found easily with heuristic evaluation. It is important to note that heuristic evaluation does not replace playtesting, but it is a flexible, complementary method that can be utilized quickly when needed.

Heuristic evaluation is also a formidable research tool to study and understand playability. We have used heuristic evaluation in number of experiments to study playability and game design of social games. Through these experiments, we have identified the most common playability problems for social games, and also domain-specific problems that stem from the social network integration and F2P revenue model. These findings are beneficial for both researchers and developers alike.

The updated playability heuristics presented in this chapter can be used in a flexible manner to evaluate games. The game usability and gameplay modules can be used to evaluate all kinds of games, while the additional modules cover the specific characteristics of multiplayer, mobile, and context-aware games. As games evolve to new domains, new heuristics are needed as well. Our research has indicated the need to include heuristics covering monetization aspects in F2P games. The newly proposed six heuristics for evaluating F2P games focus on fair play between paying and non-paying players, transparency of transactions, and ethics for protecting minors. This is an initial list for researchers and practitioners to take on as a basis for evaluating F2P games. We encourage practitioners and researchers to explore these heuristics further and possibly amend the heuristics.

A good set of heuristics is a valuable asset for the development team. Not only does it help to understand playability holistically in a practical manner, it is a communication tool, ensuring everyone is on the same page. The playability heuristics presented in this chapter work as a basis which can be extended further when new types of problems are identified or when new technologies are used for playing games. For example, new emerging domains such as augmented and VR games will need their own heuristic modules to cover the domain-specific issues relevant to them.

Heuristics are not set in stone, nor are they be-all-and-end-all solution to improve playability. When designing a game, they can and should be violated when there is good reason to do so. The emphasis is in good judgement and making a just call for violating a heuristic. This concerns especially gameplay heuristics, which are more subjective in nature than game usability heuristics. Game design is often a matter of trade-offs, where one tries to achieve the best trade-off possible. This requires good communication between inspectors and developers, and a thorough understanding of the causes of playability problems. The heuristic evaluation method together with the playability heuristics presented here is a ready-to-use tool for developers to improve the quality of their games and for researchers to study playability of games.

15.8 Takeaways

- Heuristic evaluation is a cost-effective and flexible tool for identifying playability problems, making it suitable for the agile and iterative game development process.

- Three-to-five double expert inspectors are recommended, but novice inspectors can be also used in greater numbers.
- The game usability and gameplay heuristics presented in this chapter can be used to evaluate the most important aspects of any type of game.
- The additional heuristic modules focusing on multiplayer, mobile, context-aware, and F2P games can be flexibly used when needed.
- Iterative use of heuristic evaluation helps to improve the design so that actual playtesting can focus on more important aspects than basic playability problems.

References

Alha, K, Koskinen, E, Paavilainen, J, Hamari, J & Kinnunen, J. (2014). Free-to-Play Games: Professionals' Perspectives. In Proceedings of the 2014 International DiGRA Nordic Conference. Retrieved 31 July 2016 from DiGRA Digital Library.

Hara, M., Ovaska, S. (2014). Heuristics for motion-based control in games. In Proceedings of the Proceedings of the 8th Nordic Conference on Human-Computer Interaction: Fun, Fast, Foundational (NordiCHI'14). Retrieved 31 July 2016 from ACM Digital Library.

Karvonen, J. (2005). Mobiilipelin pelattavuuden arviointi [master's thesis]. University of Jyväskylä.

Korhonen, H. (2016). Evaluating Playability of Mobile Games with the Expert Review Method. PhD thesis, University of Tampere.

Korhonen, H., Koivisto, E. (2006). Playability Heuristics for Mobile Games. In Proceedings of the 8th Conference on Human-Computer Interaction with Mobile Devices and Services. Retrieved 28 July 2016 from ACM Digital Library.

Korhonen, H., Koivisto, E. (2007). Playability Heuristics for Mobile Multi-Player Games. In Proceedings of the 2nd International Conference on Digital Interactive Media in Entertainment and Arts. Retrieved 28 July 2016 from ACM Digital Library.

Köffel, C., Hochleitner, W., Leitner, J., Haller, M., Geven, A., Tscheligi, M. (2010). Using heuristics to evaluate the overall user experience of video games and advanced interaction games. In R. Bernhaupt (ed.), Evaluating user experience in games: concepts and methods. London, UK: Springer-Verlag.

Lavery, D., Cockton, G., Atkinson, M. P. (1997). Comparison of Evaluation Methods Using Structured Usability Problem Reports. Behaviour & Information Technology, (16)4, 246-266.

Nielsen, J., Molich, R. (1990) Heuristic Evaluation of User Interfaces. In Proceedings of the SIGCHI Conference on Human Factors in Computing Systems. Retrieved 28 July 2016 from ACM Digital Library.

Paavilainen, J. (2010). Critical review on video game evaluation heuristics: social games perspective. In Proceedings of the International Academic Conference on the Future of Game Design and Technology (Future Play '10). Retrieved 28 July 2016 from ACM Digital Library.

Paavilainen, J. (2017). Playability - A Game-Centric Definition. CHI PLAY'17 Extended Abstracts on Computer-Human Interaction in Play. Retrieved 15 October 2017 from ACM Digital Library.

Paavilainen, J., Hamari, J., Stenros, J., Kinnunen, J. (2013) Social Network Games: Players' Perspectives. Simulation & Gaming, (44)6, 794-820.

Paavilainen, J., Korhonen, H., Alha, K. (2014). Common playability problems in social network games. CHI'14 Extended Abstracts on Humans Factors in Computing Systems. Retrieved 28 July 2016 from ACM Digital Library.

Paavilainen, J., Alha, K., Korhonen, H. (2015). Domain-Specific Playability Problems in Social Network Games. International Journal of Arts and Technology, (8)4.

Pinelle, D., Wong, N., Stach, T., Gutwin, C. (2009). Usability Heuristics for Networked Multiplayer Games. In Proceedings of the ACM 2009 International Conference on Supporting Group Work. Retrieved 28 July from ACM Digital Library.

CHAPTER 16

Introduction to Biometric Measures for Games User Research

LENNART E. NACKE, *University of Waterloo*

Highlights

Biometrics provide real-time measures of human responses essential to player experience in Games User Research (GUR) projects. This chapter presents the physiological metrics used in GUR. Aimed at GUR professionals in the games industry, it explains what methods are available to researchers to measure biometric data while subjects are engaged in play. It sets out when it is appropriate to use biometric measures in GUR projects, the kind of data generated, and the differing ways it can be analysed. The chapter also discusses the trade-offs required when interpreting physiological data, and will help Games User Researchers to make informed decisions about which research questions can benefit from biometric methodologies.

16.1 Introduction

Physiological or biometric measures use signal-recording technologies for doing real-time assessment of players when engaging in gameplay. As the equipment needed to collect biometric data becomes more sophisticated and cheaper, physiological testing of players during a game's development will become more common. At the same time, Games User Researchers will become more discriminating in its use (physiological data cannot crack every nut; they have value

Games User Research, Anders Drachen, Pejman Mirza-Babaei, Lennart E. Nacke (Eds).
© Oxford University Press 2018. Published 2018 by Oxford University Press

for game designers in considering a delimited range of specific issues in game design). Where in the past professionals in the games industry have used biometric testing to generate quick, actionable feedback about player responses to elements of a game, and have been less concerned with the scientific robustness of their methodology, GUR has now spawned a new breed of games industry professionals who are attempting to deploy scientific practice in their research. Work by Pierre Chalfoun and Jonathan Dankoff, to be found in Chapter 17 in this book, will provide useful context.

The enormous size of the games industry, which outsold movies and music combined at USD \$92 billion in 2015 and rising, means that game developers and technicians have the means to pursue every avenue they like in their work. Biometrics, which collects data on brain and body changes, is an obvious port of call. Levels of excitement, for example, can be assessed through skin conductance (or electrodermal activity or galvanic skin response); excitement or physiological arousal being a useful metric for game developers.

Of course, GUR deploys a range of methodologies in assessing the experiences players have during gameplay. The least expensive and probably most common of these is direct observation, and possibly post-play questionnaires and interviews. However, physiological metrics can supply data *during* rather than *after* gameplay, without stopping the play or distracting the player. Games are a dynamic form of interaction which can generate a variety of sensations in a short period of time. The goal of GUR, then, is to develop ways of assessing player experience, over time, and with as much precision as possible. Researchers want as few processes as possible standing between players and games, and favour any effective reduction in the obtrusiveness of their methods. This means that physiological metrics will in the end be leveraged to the maximum possible extent.

16.1.1 Games User Research

The field of GUR combines knowledge and techniques from human-computer interaction (HCI), game design, and experimental psychology. Its objective is practical rather than theoretical: to improve player experience in games, which I summarize as follows: 'GUR aims to create methods, techniques, and tools to collect data and evaluate player experience, informing the design process to improve the resulting experience.' In the games industry, GUR aims to optimize user experience (UX) of games and virtual entertainment products (Figure 16.1), while the domains of quality assurance (QA) and game testing focus on finding and eliminating technical errors (bugs) in the game code.

Figure 16.1 University students playing a game

Assessing player experience by means of direct observation, post-play surveys, interviews, and focus groups is the easiest and least expensive approach to GUR. However, because these methods generally rely on the player's memory, the obtained information cannot be deemed wholly reliable. Impressions and thoughts will inevitably be lost in the delay between action (gameplay) and recall (interview, questionnaire, or focus group). A further demerit for this type of GUR is that it gathers material only on the *conscious* reactions of players to the games under consideration. These interlocutory methods are an explicit approach involving direct interaction with the player. Surveys are good for this explicit eliciting of players' attitudes, but cannot tell us much about what is happening to players in real time and 'under the hood' (at a level below human consciousness).

Using physiological or biometric methods capable of measuring players' emotions and biological processes in real time affords Games User Researchers access to a more granular data set. These methods do, however, require extra work and expertise and the recording technologies are typically, more expensive (though they are becoming cheaper). For this reason, GUR tends to deploy mixed methods, combining physiological data with those derived from surveys and interviews, and from in-game metrics. Biometric measures are the most recent innovation in GUR (they have been on the scene for little more than a decade); observations, surveys, and in-game metrics have a longer pedigree.

While GUR draws significantly on HCI, many of the measures and tools used in traditional HCI are intended to assess productivity applications and maximize user performance. This means that many HCI techniques do not fit well with GUR, because the entertainment value or positive experience derived from a game is not merely a matter of user efficiency or an objective measure of ease of interaction. An error of any kind in the realm of productivity is deemed negative, but repeated failures are common and accepted in games, where tough challenges can require dozens of attempts. Indeed, failure and the will to overcome a game's obstacles are a central component of player motivation.

16.1.2 Emotions and arousal

While in-game metrics (e.g., tasks accomplished, enemies killed) provide much useful data for gauging player behaviour within the world of the game, they do not say much about the emotions experienced by a player during gameplay.

Figure 16.2 University researchers preparing a playtester for EEG measurements

Emotional signals equate to observable changes in the state of the human player, and are indicated by facial expressions, body posture, and physiological changes in the player's body. Facial expressions and posture can be recorded with video equipment, while many biometrics require recording via gadgetry other than the human eye. Physiological metrics consist of data representing the signals our body produces when it is in varying states of arousal or excitement, or when we experience emotions or mental activity. We measure (physical) phenomena such as skin conductance to deduce what is happening in players' minds (their psychology) during gameplay. Methods include among others electroencephalography (EEG), electromyography (EMG), and galvanic skin response (GSR) recording systems.

16.1.3 What are physiological signals?

Physiological signals are small energy measures gathered from the surface of the body (though they may be measures of more internal bodily processes such as heart rate or brain activity). We need an understanding of bodily neurobiological processes to interpret these signals. At a macro level, the body's operations are controlled by the human nervous system, itself a combination of two elements, the central nervous system (CNS) and the peripheral nervous system (PNS).

The CNS manages all the body's sensory data, coordinating activity accordingly. Comprising the brain and the bundle of spinal nerves, this extremely delicate system is protected by the skull and the bones of the spine, which also happen to prevent easy access to this system. The PNS, meanwhile, includes all the nerves outside the CNS, and has the job of collecting sensory information and transmitting it to the brain via the CNS. The nerve endings comprising the PNS are largely found on the body's skin, which thus expose PNS signals to relatively easy measurement. The PNS itself is further subdivided into the somatic and autonomic nervous systems. The former regulates bodily activity that is under conscious control, such as deliberate muscle activity, while the latter (ANS) controls unconscious or visceral responses (including reflexes). The ANS has two separate players: the sympathetic nervous system, which triggers so-called fight-or-flight reactions in emergency situations, and the parasympathetic nervous system, which regulates relaxation, resting, and digestion.

Physiological and mental processes contribute equally to the formation of emotions, which we may associate with feelings, behaviours, and thoughts. Research suggests strong connections between affective and cognitive processes as a precursor of emotions. Russell's circumplex model is much-used in psycho-physiological research; it posits two emotional dimensions, valence (pleasant/unpleasant emotions) and arousal/excitement (high or low levels of stimulation).

The PNS is more reliable when we are trying to measure stimulation or arousal than when we are attempting to measure emotional valence. However, techniques that detect muscular activity in the face (movement in the cheek or brow musculature) allow us to infer emotion via the medium of facial expressions. Negative emotions are associated with a frowning expression, and positive emotions make us smile.

16.2 Physiological data collection: methodologies

The range of biometrics available to Games User Researchers has grown, its accuracy has increased, and biometric apparatus has fallen in price and continues to get cheaper. This is bound to increase the prevalence of biometrics in GUR, but it should be noted that physiological data, for all its real-time advantages, also have drawbacks, which we will discuss later. The game evaluation community dream is of a plug-and-record system that attaches easily to players and tells them within minutes whether the game is good or not, or indeed which sections need improving in terms of user experience. However, in reality, using physiological signals is not as straightforward as this; there is analysis to be done before the data can be deemed useful to researchers. It should be noted, however, that technological advances mean that a plug-and-record type system is not all that far off.

Because physiological data can reveal a person's psychological state (both cognitive and emotional), it has clear applications in assessing experience. Physiological signals yield immense amounts of data and, as we have seen, provide Games User Researchers with an objective indicator of user experience without the need to interrupt the gameplay experience.

A range of methodologies exist for collecting physiological user experience data. We do not have the space to cover every detail of these here. However, I distinguish between two separate contributions of biometrics to GUR: biometrics for innovating game interaction, and biometrics for evaluation (understanding players and their experiences). This chapter focuses on the latter.

The following methodologies, which can be broadly split into brain-based (collecting metrics on brain neural activity) and body-based sensing (collecting data from the surface of the body such as the skin), are commonly used to gather physiological data in GUR:

- Electromyography (EMG), predicated on the fact that electrical signals govern muscle activity, is the measurement of the electrical activation of muscle tissue. This body-based technique is most often used in game evaluation to record stimuli to the facial muscles.
- Electrodermal activity (EDA)—also known as skin conductance level and galvanic skin response when referring to specified points in time— is a common psychophysiological measurement whose application is relatively easy. EDA is regulated by sweat production in the eccrine glands, which in turn is associated with psychological arousal.
- Cardiovascular metrics, including electrocardiography (EKG), which is the use of physiological sensors on the body to monitor heart activity, and is based on the fact that each pump of the heart is governed by an electrical impulse. The EKG signal can be used to measure heart rate variability (HRV). Heart rate (HR) monitoring is now much cheaper and more accessible through the plethora of HR apps, smartwatches, and exercise monitoring equipment.
- Electroencephalography (EEG) is the sensing of brain activity through sensors placed on the scalp. Brain activity is usually distinguished by the amplitude and frequency of the signal in comparison to a reference location. This measurement and analysis of brain activity allows us retroactively to infer details of emotional or neurological state. In evaluating video games in GUR, EEG can provide extremely valuable input, because it allows us to infer a player's cognitive state in real time.

16.2.1 Electromyography

Because EMG measures muscle activity, an EMG electrode attached to the surface above a muscle is capable of sensing even the slightest activation of the relevant muscle. For longer-term evaluation (say over a few minutes of gameplay), the eye muscle (orbicularis oculi) has also proven helpful in registering high-arousal, pleasant emotions. EMG electrodes (usually silver-silver chloride) register data whenever we flex the relevant muscle, because doing so produces a change in electrical activity or isometric tension that is measurable by EMG. EMG measures PNS activation, in contrast to EEG, which generally measures activity in the CNS.

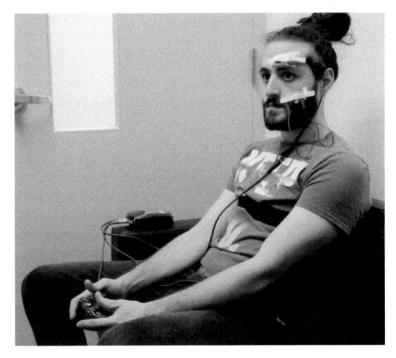

Figure 16.3 Locations of facial EMG electrodes

Because much of the body's musculature is under direct control, EMG is of high-level interest to researchers seeking to make human-computer interaction more easeful and natural. Facial EMG is most prevalent in games research, especially when using the brow muscles (corrugator supercilii) to indicate negative emotion, and cheek muscles (zygomaticus major) to indicate positive emotion or even fun and flow in a game (Figure 16.3). EMG's drawbacks include, in particular, the danger of introducing large-scale artefacts into the data derived from major muscle movements associated with, say, laughing, talking, or chewing gum (which must be strenuously avoided during a research session). Careful signal processing is required to ready the data for interpretation (such as a log normalization or a Butterworth low-pass filter).

16.2.2 Electrodermal activity

EDA relates to the electrical properties of the skin itself and is a commonly used biometric signal in GUR. EDA leverages the fact that while the skin has a baseline conductivity (known as the 'tonic baseline', or the EDA of the skin),

skin conductivity changes in response to stimuli. These short-term changes are known as phasic responses or GSR. The eccrine sweat glands in the palms and on the soles of the feet are used for measuring EDA. These glands are used because they respond to psychological stimulation as well as to temperature changes (e.g., when we are nervous, we may have cold, 'clammy' hands). Subjects need not be actually sweating for changes in EDA to be measured: rising sweat in a gland will affect GSR through the gland's resultant higher electrical resistance. EDA is correlated with arousal and reflects both emotional and cognitive activity. An indicator of both stress and mental workload, EDA is also the principle at work in the lie-detector technology favoured by American law enforcement agencies.

A salient factor in EDA is that a large number of factors can influence the data: age, sex, race, ambient air temperature, humidity, subject's stage in the menstrual cycle, time of day, season, recent exercise, and deep breathing. It is reckoned that even less tangible factors such as personality traits (e.g., whether one is an extrovert) affect EDA. While these interpolations do not eliminate the possibility of getting a worthwhile baseline reading from which to work, it does mean that GSR is less amenable to comparison between differing participants in a study, or even different sessions conducted by the same player.

Dry electrodes attached to the fingers, the palms of the hand, or the soles of the feet are used in EDA (Figure 16.4). Elsewhere, we summarized the efficacy of this method:

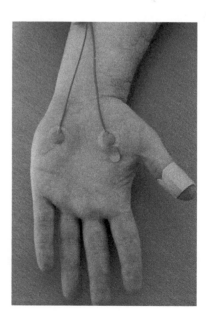

Figure 16.4 EDA electrodes on the hand

> Although operating a mouse or game controller can affect the measurement
> of EDA on the hands by affecting the connection between the electrode and
> skin …, our experience has been that using surface electrodes sewn in Velcro
> straps that were placed around two fingers on the same hand was robust
> enough for EDA measurement. (Mandryk and Nacke, 2016)

We also found that finger clips were as responsive as pre-gelled electrodes on the
feet, whereas palm-fixed electrodes suffered from movement artefacts.

16.2.3 Cardiovascular metrics, including electrocardiography

A number of cardiovascular metrics are suitable for application to GUR. HR is the
most obvious, and while this can be measured using electrocardiography (EKG),
even a standard modern exercise HR monitor can suffice in evaluating player
experience. HR can be influenced by age, posture, level of physical conditioning,
breathing frequency, and circadian cycle. EKG electrodes are placed on the skin
surface. HR can allow Games User Researchers to differentiate between positive
and negative emotions (with finer-grained differentiation afforded by the use of
finger temperature monitors). It can allow us to tell anger from fear, for example.

In a GUR context, HR is responsive to competition with human (as opposed to
AI) players, and can thus be used in research related to multiplayer game modes,
an ever-growing feature of gaming set to develop further as player connectivity
becomes faster and more data-rich. HR has also been used to model emotional
responses to games. However, other metrics can be culled from the cardiovascular signal. Where quality sensors are deployed, the oscillation between consecu-
tive heartbeats can allow a calculation of HRV. HRV is an intriguing biometric
in UX evaluation, because where an individual's HR is normatively irregular,
this irregularity can be suppressed by factors such as mental effort and cognitive
workload. Already used extensively in HCI, HRV has great untapped potential
as a GUR metric.

16.2.4 Electroencephalography

EEG data consist of the electrical impulses generated by neurons firing in the
brain. A chemical reaction occurs when a neuron is stimulated, which in turn
triggers an electrical impulse, measured with a passive electrode placed on a subject's scalp. These data are collected over time and provide a continuous reading

(Box 16.1). In GUR more generally, practitioners have found EEG to be rather prone to artefacts caused by head movement and slippage of electrodes. This means that today's active games such as Guitar Hero, Kinect, or the games played on the Wii console are less suited to EEG monitoring. Movement artefacts are an issue with all physiological measures but are particularly problematic where EEG is concerned, as the technique measures low-level electromagnetic activity. Researchers often 'clean' data by visual inspection, removing artefacts and inspecting for irregular signals, peaks, or rectangular patterns associated with lateral eye movement. As with all physiological measures, a baseline reading is taken before a subject begins the activity to be monitored. With EEG, a subject may be asked, for example, to do nothing but stare at a cross on a grey background to provide a (relatively) neutral reading. The purpose of this is to enable later algorithmic filtering out of the signals related to this resting state. The filtering is important because each person's resting EEG signature is different, and corrections must be made for these individual differences, allowing researchers to focus on deviations from the norm when the subject is undergoing testing proper.

Box 16.1 Experimental protocol for physiological examination

Here is a ready-to-roll sample protocol for GUR professionals interested in using biometrics in their research.

1. Check inventory. Physiological metrics require apparatus that needs maintaining and checking. Experiments may require pre-gelled electrodes, surgical tape, electrode paste, and other items. If you are a GUR professional planning an experiment, make sure your inventory is up-to-date (and check it a week before any experiment so you have time to order any replacement stock). Check any relevant batteries, too, to ensure you will not run out of juice.

2. Prepare informed consent forms. These are required for any experimental work and are certainly needed in physiological experimentation. Subjects should be informed that the procedures will not harm them and that they can at any point opt out. Forms can be used to familiarize subjects with the protocol and should also remind participants not to consume anything which may have a physiological effect (such as coffee, energy drinks, or candy) prior to the session.

continued

Box 16.1 Continued

3. Prepare and attach the electrodes. Different recording systems require different preparations. Remember that pre-gelled and dry electrodes are easier to handle and will save time, so are preferable to electrodes requiring paste. If EEG is being used, a cap will be needed to align the electrodes properly. When using multichannel systems, make sure you label or number the channels so that you can identify them (e.g., mark which EMG electrodes are measuring which muscle).

4. Check noise; start recording. Make sure you have a measurement of a subject's resting state where required as a baseline. Check instrumentation for noise in the form of spikes or unusual readings. These anomalies can result from a variety of factors, including broken or bent cables, excess of gel, or insufficient gel. It is good practice to repeat the attachment procedure until any error disappears. Baseline recording requires participants to sit calmly and with eyes open while the relevant measurements are taken. Ensure you have a workable system for numbering files containing data, to avoid mismatches of data files and subjects.

5. Run the experiment; note and follow up on any additional measures required. Participant behaviour should be observed and the data stream marked where excessive movement is observed (a reference point for potential movement artefacts).

6. Have surveys prepared for participants to complete after an experimental session. These are a valuable addition to the physiological data; survey content should be carefully calibrated to support the experimental goals.

7. Debrief and data back-up. Thank participants and debrief them about the study. Ensure that you back up any files of data collected.

16.2.4.1 EEG DATA COLLECTION

EEG data are recorded via a number of electrodes aligned according to the normative '10–20' map of electrode placement (alternatives are the '10–10' and '10–5' systems). The locations on this map correspond to those of brain lobes. The electrical activity recorded by all these electrodes thus corresponds to neural activity, which is rated in comparison with one or two reference points (e.g., at the centre of the scalp). This referencing may also be accomplished by calculating the average as a global reference, or using driven right-leg and common-mode sense (i.e., this is an electric circuit that is often added to biological signal amplifiers to reduce signal interference). The electrical charge measured at each electrode is subtracted from the reference figure to provide information about the subject's brain activity. EEG data can be analysed using frequency analysis, hemispheric asymmetry, event-related potential (ERP), or connectivity. Recordings can be undertaken with as many as 512 electrodes or as few as one (most commercially available EEG head caps are equipped with 32, 64, 128, or 256 electrodes). The more electrodes introduced, the higher the spatial resolution, but there is a concomitant increase in system cost risk of artifacts, increase in prep time, and likelihood of electrolyte gel spreading (so called "salt bridges" can lead to short circuits for some electrodes). Extra electrodes also make analysis more complex, though this depends on the particular technique deployed. Some electrode arrangements preclude certain methods of analysis (e.g., hemispheric asymmetry cannot be used with a single-electrode system).

Research-grade EEG devices compute brain waves in differing frequency bands. These are alpha (8–13 Hz), beta (13–30 Hz), theta (4–8 Hz), delta (1–4 Hz), and gamma (30–50 Hz). Alpha activity indicates a drowsy or relaxed state, and fewer active cognitive processes. It has also been tied to information and visual processing. Beta activity replaces alpha rhythms when the mind engages in cognitive activity. It is related to 'alertness, attention, vigilance, and excitatory problem-solving activities' (Mandryk and Nacke, 2016). Theta activity is associated with decreased alertness and lower levels of information processing. However, frontal midline theta activity in the anterior cingulate cortex scalp area has been linked to 'mental effort, attention, and stimulus processing'. We thus have two types of theta activity: low alertness, which normatively leads to sleep; and selective cognitive inactivity resulting from automated processing. Delta waves, which diminish with advancing age, come to the fore during sleep, relaxation, and fatigue. Gamma activity remains underexplored, though recent studies have related it to the process of parsing meaning from heterogeneous information.

While much of what we know about these waves comes from research in medicine and psychology, it is to be hoped that these summarized interpretations facilitate the task of GUR practitioners in evaluating a game based on brainwave activity readings via EEG. In Mandryk and Nacke (2016), we concluded that if increased beta activity is prevalent during gaming, it could be linked to player attention and increased arousal during a focused task. More studies are needed, and will surely come, to increase our ability to interpret EEG metrics.

16.2.4.2 A QUICK NOTE ON EEG ANALYSIS

With EEG being the toughest metric from which to draw inferences, it is worth a short paragraph on analysis methodologies. Analyses depending on power of a frequency band or on decomposition of the EEG signal include frequency analysis, neurofeedback, hemispheric asymmetry, and synchrony techniques. ERP techniques are used to identify changes in brain activity after a particular event or stimulus. Synchrony and power change are of interest during connectivity studies or studies that explore deeper connections within the brain. The type of analysis will specify what equipment to use and how to set it up, and it will affect the study design and the choice of statistical analysis procedures (Manryk and Nacke, 2016).

In frequency analysis, the signal is separated into its constituent waves, which are divided according to frequency bands. Researchers commonly deploy a fast Fourier transform to translate these data. The area of collection will govern the nature of the information obtained. We outline the differing bands elsewhere in this chapter, but it should be noted as an example that Salminen and Ravaja (2008) found an increase in oscillatory theta activity in response to violent events in games.

Pre-calculated frequency measures for entertainment and relaxation are commercially available. Other researchers have investigated player experience by comparing these off-the-shelf formulas to questionnaire data after gameplay. The EEG data they examined, however, contrasted with that in the questionnaires. These approaches commonly seek to analyse a more generalized brain frequency, but different research questions will demand differing approaches from GUR practitioners, who may wish to look at data from a limited area of a subject's skull.

The mu rhythm metric is also worth mentioning, offering a further approach. This is collected over the motor cortex in the alpha frequency range (8–13 Hz). Electrodes are placed on a horizontal from ear to ear, near the motor cortex. The mu rhythm is generated when subjects observe an action performed using either the hand or the mouth, and is suppressed when the subjects themselves mimic or mirror that action. One advantage of mu rhythm analysis is that topography can be incorporated into the analysis, with the disaggregated signal frequencies mapped on a depiction of the skull. An exemplar application of this technique would be the use of mu rhythms to interrogate the process of learning in video games.

Another commonly used technique is hemispheric frontal alpha asymmetry (HFAA). HFAA uses frequency analysis to process hemispheric activity in opposing lobes of the brain. Analysis may require comparing the relative statistical power derived from frequency analysis of waves originating in the right and left hemispheres of the brain. The data can also be subjected to further statistical analysis to identify significant differences in activation levels in each lobe. One useful protocol that can be followed in this type of analysis is presented by Coan and Allen (2004).

16.3 Biometrics analysis more generally

There is no space here to provide a detailed treatment of biometrics analysis (for that, one can turn to the literature listed at the end of the chapter). However, it is worth rehearsing some of the basic issues.

Firstly, correction must be made for the high levels of individual variability found in biometrics, which make comparisons between participants difficult without normalization. The most common method of normalization is to represent the biometric value as a percentage of the total span for that participant. Normalization does require GUR practitioners to know the minimum and maximum values for any given test subject, which in turn means that any analysis must be conducted after all of the data are in, rather than in real time. Researchers should also remember that sensor readings can be affected by factors wholly unrelated to the participant's experience, and that although some of these factors can be controlled, not all can be avoided. It is impossible, for example, to prevent a study subject sneezing during a session, because sneezing can have a major effect on the data at that particular point as well as having the potential to move or dislodge sensors. A sneeze would, for example, lead to highly variant EMG readings for facial musculature.

When it comes to GSR, it is important to ensure that electrode placements obviate the potential for variations in conductivity. Attaching electrodes to skin that is less prone to movement (e.g., clipped to toes or fingers rather than stuck onto the palm of a subject's hand) should be considered good practice.

You can deal with sensor error in various ways. Knowing when the errors occurred can allow researchers to simply remove these data from subsequent analyses. 'Noisy' data can be cleaned using a moving average window or a low-pass filter. Both techniques result in a smoother signal, and simple spreadsheet software can generate a moving average window (a low-pass filter takes more sophisticated tools to create but affords greater capability to keep or discard frequencies).

16.4 Methodological issues

Players' physiological signals are sensitive to a wide range of stimuli, so it is important to control as many factors affecting physiology as possible (these might include changing light, physical activity, moving, and talking). Researchers should do everything they can to put subjects at ease, remembering that merely applying electrodes to a subject can in itself be a stressful experience.

Recording baseline data can be harder than it might seem, too: subjects may already be nervous or apprehensive before a user study, and their resting baselines may thus be artificially high. This makes it harder to use resting rates to normalize biometric data. One way around this is to record several baselines during an experimental session, and use an average figure as a comparator. Another way of getting cleaner signals is to use participants who are familiar with the processes involved in acquiring biometric data, such as applying electrodes and hooking up to recorders.

Ensuring that participants are as natural as possible during data collection can also be achieved by running a training or practice session prior to collecting resting values. In any case, it is worth remembering that a regular participant in your experiments will also relax over time, gradually becoming used to the environment and paraphernalia.

16.5 Theoretical issues, an example: many-to-one

Over and above the issue of 'noise', EEG's key problematic is the difficulty of interpreting the data. This is something the technique shares with other biometric data, known as the 'many-to-one relationship' between physiologically visible signals and the underlying psychological causes. One visible, or recordable, signal may be a marker for a number of psychological causes. We have offered the following example in the past: When delta activity is higher during a playing session, do we argue that the game is relaxing, or that it is boring and fatigue-inducing? (Mandryk and Nacke, 2016). We argued that for GUR professionals, it is important to keep in mind the design goals when analysing EEG or any other physiological data.

The counterpart to the many-to-one problem is its precise opposite, the 'one-to-many' issue: a single emotion or thought can have a number of recordable manifestations. Anger, for example, can have differing physical manifestations, from a raised heart rate to a tensing of musculature. GUR practitioners should remain aware of these issues and try to construct evaluation protocols that minimize these problems as far as possible.

It is also vital to make inferences with great care and clarity. The goal of using biometrics in GUR should be to identify correlations between physiological data, events related to the game being played, and psychological events. The final goal of a mathematical model should be to recognize psychological events directly from sensor readings. We believe this is possible, though with the following caveat about drawing inferences:

> Let us take a very simple example of a neurofeedback game to train focus, in which a player's EEG activity reflects a loss of concentration after each level is completed. Basic logic prevents us from assuming that every time the player loses focus, they have just completed a level. Although this example is obvious, it demonstrates the care that must be taken when making inferences. (Mandryk and Nacke, 2016, page 221)

16.6 Why use physiological evaluation in GUR?

In the following chapter in this book, Chalfoun and Dankoff (GUR professionals working at Ubisoft's Montreal campus) detail case studies where they used biometrics in game development, and describe how they developed biometrics methodologies in their work. For example, they show how mixed-methods research alongside biometrics has enabled them to successfully provide concrete answers for the stealth issues encountered when making Assassin's Creed Unity. This study, typical of the kind of work they do at Ubisoft, sought an answer to a specific question: 'Why are players having a hard time making efficient use of stealth mechanics in the game?' A reason I have chosen not to talk about eye tracking in this chapter is that they discuss in detail eye tracking as a biometric for their analysis. Indeed, along with post-play interviews, eye tracking afforded a key insight: players were unaware of a line-of-sight feature on the screen that aided the character's ability to stay stealthy. The researchers recommended that designers change the location of this feature to make it more central to players' normative line of sight.

Over and above its drawbacks, noted earlier, physiological evaluation has enormous value for the games industry. It allows for continuous recording of metrics without interrupting gameplay, and is thus less obtrusive than other methods of gathering player feedback. Against this must be set the fact that, while less obtrusive, physiological evaluation does require preparation and, to a certain extent, controlled surroundings. However, when properly planned and executed, biometrics can provide answers to specific questions related to GUR.

16.7 Conclusion

There can be no question that the science and application of physiological metrics are evolving, and rapidly at that. Their use is growing, and they are important tools for people getting into GUR. Video games may have been a form of entertainment for some time, decades even, but their dominance of the entertainment industry is a relatively recent phenomenon. More resources, not less, will flow into game development, and physiological metrics can only become a more central part of the development process. This is especially true given that the era of virtual reality (VR) is in its infancy, and that several leading industry players are already in the marketplace with VR sets (from Zeiss's VR One Plus, to Sony's PlayStation VR, to Oculus Rift, to Google's Daydream View). Advances in both hardware and software have led to innovations such as natural interaction, gestural control, and voice activation. The potential for biometrics not just in gaming, but in the twenty-first century's wider world of big data and the Internet of things, could be viewed as without any foreseeable limit. That said, we should always bear in mind that biometrics are a combinatory methodology, to be used alongside observations, questionnaires, focus groups, and all the other ways in which GUR practitioners gather information during user research sessions.

Acknowledgements

My heartfelt thanks go out to all my students that are supporting me in my research endeavours over the years. For this book chapter, I am specifically thankful for the help of Giovanni Ribeiro, Colin Whaley, Pejman Mirza-Babaei, and Karina Arrambide. In addition, I thank my editor John Clamp for his strong support in writing this article. Academic references were mostly omitted from this article to improve readability, but the following list provides some pointers towards the research that this work is based on. Thank you to the Natural Sciences and Engineering Research Council, Canada Foundation for Innovation, and the Social Sciences and Humanities Research Council for funding my research.

References and further reading

Cacioppo, J. T., Tassinary, L. G., Berntson, G. (eds.). (2007). Handbook of psychophysiology. Cambridge: Cambridge University Press.

Mandryk, R. L., Nacke, L. E. (2016). Biometrics in gaming and entertainment technologies. In Biometrics in a data driven world: trends, technologies, and challenges (pp. 191–224). Boca Raton, FL: CRC Press.

Mirza-Babaei, P., Nacke, L. E., Gregory, J., Collins, N., and Fitzpatrick, G. (2013). How does it play better? Exploring user testing and biometric storyboards in games user research. In CHI '13(pp. 1499–1508). New York: ACM. doi:10.1145/2470654.2466200

Nacke, L. E. (2011). Directions in physiological game evaluation and interaction. In CHI 2011 BBI Workshop Proceedings.

Nacke, L. E. (2013). An introduction to physiological player metrics for evaluating games. In Game analytics: maximizing the value of player data (pp. 585–619). London: Springer.

Nacke, L. E. (2015). Games user research and physiological game evaluation. In Game user experience evaluation (pp. 63–86). New York: Springer International Publishing.

Russell, J. A. (1980). A circumplex model of affect. Journal of Personality and Social Psychology 39(6), 1161–1178. doi:10.1037/h0077714

Salminen, M., Ravaja, N. (2008). Increased oscillatory theta activation evoked by violent digital game events. Neuroscience Letters, 435(1), 69–72.

Wehbe, R. R., Nacke, L. E. (2013). An introduction to EEG analysis techniques and brain-computer interfaces for Games User Researchers. In Proceedings of DiGRA 2013 (pp. 1–16). Atlanta, GA: DiGRA.

CHAPTER 17

Developing actionable biometric insights for production teams

Case studies and key learnings

PIERRE CHALFOUN, *Ubisoft Montreal*

JONATHAN DANKOFF, *Warner Brothers Interactive Entertainment*

Highlights

In this chapter we describe the challenges and learnings in establishing processes for developing actionable biometric procedures for production teams. The chapter, divided into four main sections, will describe the ongoing efforts of recent years to facilitate the incorporation of the science of biometrics into the culture of video game production, as illustrated through several case studies. The end goal is making biometric data an accessible option in the tool chest of user researchers and an ally in the team's decision-making processes. Throughout the chapter, references to related work in Games User Research (GUR) and academia will be presented.

Games User Research, Anders Drachen, Pejman Mirza-Babaei, Lennart E. Nacke (Eds).
© Oxford University Press 2018. Published 2018 by Oxford University Press

17.1 Introduction: humble beginnings

Physiological evaluation of players' experience through biometrics has been an active field in Games User Research (GUR) for more than a decade now. Biometrics, in a nutshell, is the art of recording subjective experiences through objective measures. Numerous pioneers in that field of research have used various methods ranging from eye tracking to electrodermal activity (sweat for emotional arousal), heart rate to electroencephalography (brain sensors for cognitive tasks), and electromyography (muscle movements on the face for emotional valence) (Ambinder, 2011; Mandryk et al., 2006; Mirza-Babaei et al., 2012; Nacke and Lindley, 2008; Yannakakis et al., 2008; Zammitto et al., 2010. Ubisoft Montreal's first forays into biometric research began in 2012 with the hiring of Pierre Chalfoun, a PhD graduate in human-computer interaction and emotional intelligence. Brought on as the project manager for all biometric initiatives at the Montreal User Research Lab, his role was to evangelize the value of biometric testing both within the lab to the brand project managers and to the production teams themselves. He immediately set out to find a viable research partner to conduct a first study. Jonathan Dankoff saw an opportunity to explore a game development problem he had long struggled with back when he was working at Ubisoft: the efficiency of tutorials for new players in the Assassin's Creed series. Traditional research practices at Ubisoft Montreal at the time had pointed towards some issues with the way the series onboarded new players, but Jonathan was curious to gain a deeper understanding of how it could be improved. Both of us, as researchers, saw an occasion to learn more about how players interacted with these tutorials above and beyond the usual scope of user tests, which were limited in their ability to understand players' comprehension and attention to the text boxes which appear in the first moments of the game and objectively evaluate players' emotional states during failures.

This would be Jonathan's first test with biometric tools, and Pierre's first study for a game development team. It would prove to be a valuable learning process for us. Pierre wanted to approach the problem with the same scientific rigour and academic thoroughness that he had maintained throughout his education, whereas Jonathan wanted to 'vulgarize' the results and deliver simple, highly actionable findings in the manner he had learned in his user research career.

The test goal for this first exploratory study was fairly loosely defined: 'Determine if our tutorials work effectively.' From there we developed a broad initial test plan to conduct a study examining three tutorial scenarios of increasing complexity using a combination of user test protocols such as think-aloud and questionnaires, as well as two biometric sensors: an eye-tracker (Holmqvist et al., 2011) and a sensor to track electrodermal activity, or EDA (Boucsein, 2012). We recruited 28 participants with no experience with the Assassin's Creed franchise, and had them play selected portions of the tutorials of the recently released Assassin's Creed 3. Their successes and failures to complete the tutorial tasks were recorded by a researcher. Between each section, players filled an in-house adapted version of the NASA-RTLX questionnaire (Hart et al., 1988) to games in order to assess their subjective workload. Barring a few issues with eye-tracker calibration, the test ran fairly smoothly.

The compilation, analysis, and presentation of the data to the development team took nearly three months. For one, the test was over-scoped. The incredible quantity of data collected in service of the loosely defined goal of the study made it difficult to focus the analysis and reporting. This was the most important internal learning. Eye tracking and EDA data take significantly longer to interpret, and a purely exploratory investigation of the data proved to be quite time-consuming.

Another issue which led to the extended analysis time was the lack of existing tools and technology to automate data compilation and synchronize biometric data with Ubisoft's in-house game and face recording tools. Pierre needed to simultaneously code his own tools to be able to work with the collected data. This investment is extremely important but impacted the delivery date of the results. Future testing would need to include tool development within the scope if necessary.

In spite all this, the results were eye-opening for the developers, and brought a lot of interesting insights on the importance of crafting better tutorial segments. The findings were presented throughout the studio and had a significant impact on our development process, namely, facilitating the creation of a tutorial task force composed of the main stakeholders of the game—such as the game, level, mission, and presentation directors—as well as best practices that have been applied on AAA games in production at that time. Additionally, we learned a lot about conducting biometrics studies for game development. Balancing scientific rigour against timeliness, cost-effectiveness, and simplicity is not a trivial task.

Overall, the test was a success and gave us interesting insights for our in-game tutoring techniques, and also informed the future of biometric testing within Ubisoft. Future tests would have much more clearly focused objectives, with tighter control of the overall scope of the objectives. We would need to refocus on studies that provided higher return on investment.

17.2 Case studies

Following the first exploratory study, we continued to apply its learnings to upcoming biometric tests. We also started building our own in-house synchronization tool for contextualizing biometric data alongside gameplay videos, player facial reactions, controller inputs, in-game telemetry, and others. We mainly concentrated on answering user research questions and objectives where biometrics would have an added value and be actionable—we were aiming for quick wins to begin with. We will highlight four such wins while using eye tracking and EDA for our AAA games. This section will present four different kind of studies centred around the actionability of biometrics for our production teams for the games Far Cry, Assassin's Creed, and Rainbow Six.

17.2.1 Trailer studies on Far Cry 4

The first type of study was done on trailer assets for E3 2014. Typically, such trailers can be of two sorts: computer graphics (CG) and in-game. The first refers to footage pre-rendered outside of the game engine, resulting in very high-resolution images that are more like an animated movie than actual gameplay. The second, as the name implies, refers to footage rendered directly by the game engine and edited into something more cinematic, but much more representative of the final product. Using biometrics to analyse CG footage is interesting and relevant, but cannot be done too early because the lack of textures, absence of special effects sound, and heavy presence of stick figures while a CG is in development drowns the EDA signal in noise. In order for the biometric service at the Montreal User Research Lab to be actionable, we focused on in-game trailers early on, enabling us to iterate and have an impact on the creative process of the team, since these trailers use assets that are more easily modified and controlled throughout the process. We will describe this process with the E3 2014 Sony Stage trailer from FC4.

17.2.1.1 OBJECTIVES

The main objectives of the FC team were three-fold: (1) identify the most physiologically salient moments in the stage demo, (2) evaluate the level of understanding of the various features introduced, and (3) assess the trailer's appreciation. An iterative process was implemented in which the feedback of each iteration was quickly communicated to the team's stakeholders to learn from and modify the trailer before the next test.

17.2.1.2 METHODOLOGY

We recruited eight players for each iteration and chose to use EDA to record players' physiological reactions. The number of players corresponds to the number of seats in a playtest room. After the nature of the study was explained to the players, they were individually asked to gently hold an EDA bracelet (QSensor) at their fingertips. For baseline purposes, each was then given a long platonic text about an arbitrary history subject not related to the task at hand for about two minutes to read. All players were then presented with the Far Cry 4 Sony E3 Stage demo to watch. Following the initial viewing, a retrospective think-aloud protocol was used to evaluate appreciation and understanding of the trailer's features. A second viewing of the trailer was then presented individually to players in which they were asked to freely express their thoughts. They were free to stop the video anytime during playback and provide feedback and impressions as much as they felt necessary.

17.2.1.3 RESULTS

We chose to isolate the phasic component of EDA following the recommendations of Boucsein (2012) and used a series of skin conductance response (SCR) metrics as physiological indicators of arousal. Significant SCR levels above baseline were considered salient and referred to as 'upswing'. In contrast, significant downward slopes in the EDA signal with respect to baseline values were identified as a 'downswing'. Downswings are not necessarily negative or bad—they are simply indicators of a significant drop in arousal for a specific segment of the trailer. The trailers were broken down into beats, smaller segments of a few seconds, to better focus the analysis. These segments were provided to our moderators as guidelines when coding players' comments in the think-after protocol as positive or negative.

Figure 17.1 shows one of the ways we simplified EDA data. Significant SCR reactions are displayed in an area of the graph behind the think-after bars for each game segment. For example, Segment 23 shows four positive comments from the think-after and three distinct SCR upswings from three different players. The downswing does not express valence, but simply a downswing in the physiological reactions of one player. This visualization is interesting to inform the teams of potential drops in interest throughout the video rather than point at very specific elements in the video to work on. Figures 17.2a and 17.2b illustrate the impact of such actionability after numerous iterations.

As shown in Figures 17.2a and 17.2b, the first iteration showed some promising positive comments but very few positive upswings. By combining player

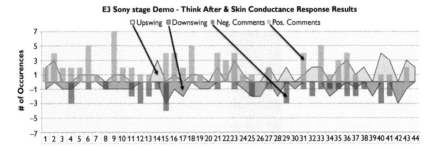

Figure 17.1 Think-after and skin conductance responses from one iteration of FC4

Figure 17.2 Results after numerous iterations combining biometrics and user research

comments with biometrics to identify areas to improve upon, the team was able to make a more engaging trailer with (1) better co-op showcase and introduction, (2) optimized outpost approach, and (3) highly salient, packed sequences. Combined with the results of the think-after protocol, biometric data are an efficient tool to pinpoint areas of improvement for our teams.

17.2.2 Assassin's Creed Unity stealth HUD

In this second study type, we will detail how mixed-methods research alongside biometrics has enabled us to successfully provide concrete answers for the stealth issues encountered when making Assassin's Creed Unity (ACU). This type of study is typical at the Montreal User Research Lab.

17.2.2.1 OBJECTIVES

The ACU team wanted to better understand why players were having a hard time making efficient use of stealth mechanics in the game, that is, the use of the environment and controls in a way that enables the player keep their character hidden or out of sight from other characters controlled by the computer, or NPC (non-player character). The objectives were thus to assess the player's comprehension of a stealth loop which begins when a character is detected by enemies and ends after a successful stealth attempt. This loop revolves around three components, each represented by distinctive icons in separate areas of the screen: (1) line of sight for the character's visibility in the world; (2) conflict state, where enemies seek to hunt you down; and (3) escape state, where the hero safely breaks away from pursuers (at least those who are still alive). The end goal was to answer two main questions. (1) Do players understand the link between the three components? (2) Do players understand when the loop ends?

17.2.2.2 METHODOLOGY

We chose to run a balanced task analysis with eye tracking where players were asked to execute three different stealth tasks in a predetermined mission. Each task revolved around starting a conflict with guards and then escaping in three different ways without killing the guards. The first way to escape was 'freestyle', where players could use any means they wished; the second was using a haystack to hide in; and the third was blending in with a crowd. We decided to recruit seven players from an ongoing playtest after a full day of play in order to give them a chance to play with the stealth mechanics and get comfortable with the controls. Following the stealth tasks, an in-depth, one-on-one interview was conducted in which players were presented with a set of ten in-game screenshots. The first six represented various states during a stealth loop and the rest various map and line-of-sight states. Besides eye tracking, we also recorded game and player audio as well as mouse clicks embedded with the eye tracking data during the one-on-one interview.

17.2.2.3 RESULTS

The gaze heat map (Figure 17.3) displays the aggregated results for all seven players during stealth tasks. The main findings of this study were three-fold. Firstly, for all tasks, the line-of-sight icon, located in the top-left part of Figure 17.3, was not looked at by players.

As to be expected, the map was looked at about 10% of the time because players were trying to actively search for a haystack to hide in. However, once they were hidden, their scanning pattern did not go near the line-of-sight icon. Players behaved exactly the same across all tasks, and yet they were still able to complete the tasks. The one-on-one interview gave us more insight as to why: players were unaware of the existence of the line-of-sight feature, but were able to elude the guards by making their own assumptions of line of sight based on

Figure 17.3 Gaze heat map for all players trying to hide from the guards using a haystack

Figure 17.4 Excerpts from the one-on-one interview with players

the 3D elements and their disposition in the world. Players would also use the colour transition of the map as an indicator of a conflict state. Figure 17.4 illustrates these findings.

As shown in Figure 17.4, players click on visual cues used to identify the location of enemies in relation to the avatar. Notice how they click on the roof ledge as a proof of visibility because their avatar is 'in the open' and thus 'visible'—they do not look at the top-left line-of-sight indicator as shown by eye tracking. Furthermore, players tended to report the map's border colour change as a strong visual cue for ending the stealth loop. The interview results and the eye tracking data led us to compute 'fixation corridors' to better understand where players' visual attention was concentrated during stealth-focused missions. Figure 17.5 illustrates such a corridor during a stealth task where a player is asked to escape using a haystack.

We can see that almost half of the player's attention was located in that corridor. This finding was consistent across players. Not a single fixation was located on the line-of-sight indicator. The results led us to suggest to the teams to move the line-of-sight indicator either on the avatar or within the fixation corridor. The latter was chosen and Figure 17.6 shows the change.

Figure 17.5 Representative visualization of all fixations in stealth tasks for one player

Figure 17.6 Line-of-sight indicator moved within a fixation corridor

This change might seem minor, but it was a major win considering the UI was going to be locked down very soon, and any further changes would be impossible. The teams decided to move the line-of-sight indicator to a visible position on the map, both within the fixation corridor and within the peripheral vision of the player. We could not retest the changes due to time constraints, but we noticed a decrease of self-reported miscomprehension issues related to stealth in subsequent playtests.

17.2.3 Rainbow 6 gaze behaviour on assets

The third study type is more exploratory in nature and uses eye tracking in an attempt to determine the natural gaze pattern of players in a specific scenario. These types of studies are tricky because of the bias involved since we obviously cannot ask the player where they looked or what layout they preferred. To pick up a line from the previous ACU study, we need to be stealthy about how we proceed in order to achieve the desired result.

17.2.3.1 OBJECTIVES

The objectives of this study for the Rainbow 6 team were twofold. Firstly, the team wanted to identify players' natural scanning patterns for three distinctive in-game layouts (Figure 17.7). Secondly, the team wanted to investigate the possibility of a link between scanning patterns and box priority.

Investigating a potential link between how players instinctively scan such layouts and the order of the scan will inform the team on how to properly display icons on the screen. The initial hypothesis of the team was that a typical scanning pattern is done in a clockwise fashion starting from the top-left and ending in the bottom-left part of the screen. As an example, in the first layout of Figure 17.7, scanning would begin with the heart icon and end with the clockwise arrow. Results from his study will help them test this hypothesis with objective and qualitative data instead of only relying on design intuition.

Figure 17.7 Three layouts tested in the study

17.2.3.2 METHODOLOGY

A total of nine players (all men) took part of this study. The order of the layouts was counterbalanced using a Latin square design, and the eye-tracker calibrated to each player. A blank screen with a grey background was presented instructing the player to look at the next presented image and answer a question related to it. The layout was then presented for five seconds, followed by a question. The questions were carefully chosen to introduce the least possible amount of bias and reduce the need for the player to mentally prepare for the next image. Examples of questions are 'Please tell us what your favourite icon is' and 'Please tell us how many boxes of grey icons you see'. Answers were then noted, and the procedure repeated for all three layouts, each time asking a different question. This was a win-win situation because players have the impression of contributing to the study while the true value is within those first five seconds of exploration.

17.2.3.3 RESULTS

The scanning patterns found within the first five seconds of layout exposure were classified in four categories, namely, zig-zag, clockwise, anticlockwise, and other. The 'other' category refers to chaotic-like eye movements where players were scanning the entire screen without any specific pattern. The zig-zag category represents a typical reading pattern where eye movements shift from left to right or in a slightly diagonal manner. The right-hand panel of Figure 17.8 illustrates two examples of scanning patterns found.

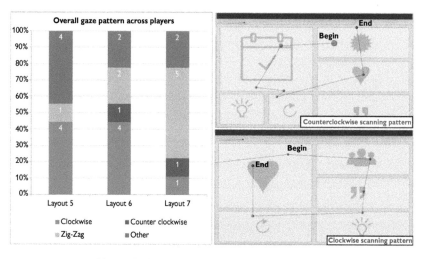

Figure 17.8 Natural scanning pattern across players

Figure 17.9 In-game layout based on wireframes

These results seem to suggest that square holistic shaped designs with a granularity of 6 or less seems to naturally get scanned 45% of the time in a clockwise fashion. Clockwise and anticlockwise initial patterns seem to fade for the layout with seven boxes. We observe a strong tendency for 'reading patterns' for boxes with more than seven boxes, as if the players perceived the holistic shape closer to a text-based shape than layouts of five or six boxes. Although the number of participants was low, the tendencies observed were enough to help the team have a better understanding of the number of boxes to use for their design. Furthermore, the initial hypothesis was confirmed by the data. Figure 17.9 gives an example of how the Rainbow 6 team used the data to establish a first working version of their menus.

Although the final version of the menus will quite possibly not look like those presented in this study, the return on investment of such a study was quite high. It was very fast to do, quite cheap, and results delivered within three working days.

17.2.4 Iterative eye tracking on wireframes in FC4

The last study we will present involves eye tracking and WirePoint, a new in-house tool to do fast prototyping. The three tests done early on FC4 have helped deliver valuable insights for the team throughout their iterative process of menu design and testing.

17.2.4.1 OBJECTIVES

The main objective of all three studies was to test players' efficiency at executing simple tasks in the early HUD prototypes. The team started testing mock-ups and wireframes quite early in the production cycle, and biometrics was lucky enough to have been part of that process. Every study focused on menu structure and understanding, namely, navigation, flow, and general usability. The first study focused on purchasing and customizing items through the FC4 shop; the second focused on navigation, flow, and general understanding of presented information; and the third tested the usability issues involved in menus regarding the multiplayer facet of FC4, namely, map creation, in-game editor, and match joining.

17.2.4.2 METHODOLOGY

The typical set-up for this type of study is quite similar. Participants are borrowed from an existing test, usually on a different game than FC4. The researcher explains to the player the purpose of what they will be doing and a few details about what will be required. Eye tracking will also be presented and calibrated. All tasks are balanced using a Latin square design. For example, players were asked in the first study to execute three tasks: (1) purchase a machine gun, (2) customize a sniper gun with a scope, and (3) purchase a healing syringe. After result delivery and iteration, the tasks evolved in the second study around exploring and finding items in the menu and testing the flow and general navigability. Each session was followed with a one-on-one interview involving comprehension questions.

Throughout this iterative process, the team wanted to find a very quick way to realistically test static menus without the use of extra resources such as a flash programmer, or a complex and expensive tool like Axxure mixed with third-party applications such as Joy2Key for mapping controller inputs to buttons. To answer this need, the Montreal User Research Lab tools team built WirePoint. This tool quickly loads static images from PowerPoint and greatly simplifies the transition logic between slides, and logs every input into a text file. Designers can then animate slides using a controller, and have a quite complex menu working in under a day without external help. All three studies described here were done using WirePoint and eye tracking.

17.2.4.3 RESULTS

The results from the first study using eye tracking and one-on-one interviews study led to important findings. Firstly, as illustrated by the dotted rectangles in Figure 17.10, players were unable to recognize the tabs in the top-left as navigation indicators. Secondly, as highlighted by the ellipse, eye tracking data combined with key presses showed that participants failed to correctly identify that the customization region was actually a store interaction.

Following those initial results, the FC4 team continued to work on the menus. A second study run with eye tracking and WirePoint uncovered two main issues.

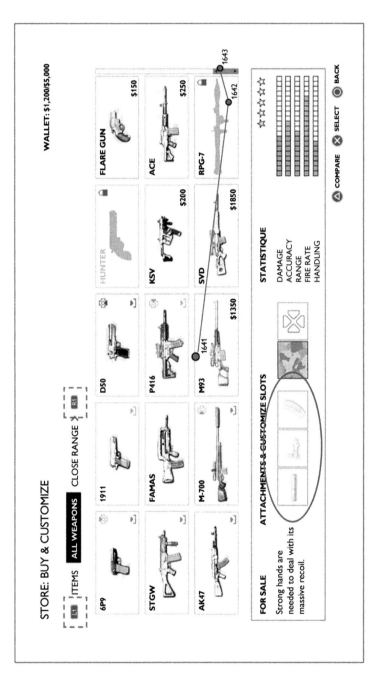

Figure 17.10 Second draft of the weapon store

The first related to menu flow: players have difficulty navigating the multilayered menu structure. The second related to task execution: players had difficulty locating a treasure map. Indeed, players were constantly looking over the 'loot' section in the root menu instead of navigating to the 'other -> treasures' section where the map was to be found. The majority of players associated the object 'treasure' with the concept of 'loot' and therefore felt that it was logical to find the item within that menu.

Once those changes were incorporated into the design process, the teams were able to produce a draft version of their menus which they felt confident about, and delivered it before their important first playable gate in front of editorial. This version, illustrated in Figure 17.11, was implemented in the game as-is, saving time and money in the long run.

Further enhancements to the FC4 HUD were taken from previous eye tracking and EDA findings on the Assassin's Creed 3 brand. According to these findings, (1) players have a very limited fixation time for long text messages, (2) players do not read long objective text but scan quickly icons and keywords, and (3) players' gaze tends to rest in the center of the screen. All these changes contributed to reducing UI bugs by 46% compared to FC3, while increasing the number of developers by 33% and the total number of menus by 24%. The close collaboration with the FC team and the iterative nature of this process are two important reasons that leveraged biometrics and its relevant actionable findings.

Figure 17.11 Three draft stages of the weapon store

17.3 Message delivery

Throughout the process of running the aforementioned studies and delivering the results to our partner development teams, some best practices in delivering biometric-based feedback have emerged. In order to be maximally effective at driving the insights created, we recommend the following six guidelines: high-level abstraction, easy-to-use terminology, mixed methods, visual reporting, properly shared results, and iteration to ensure impact.

17.3.1 High-level abstraction

When presenting the results of a biometric study to a development team, it is vital that the researcher focuses on the insights and key learnings rather than the protocols behind it. The insights should drive the presentation, supported by the collected data. The methods used to collect these data can be abstracted so that the audience has a high-level comprehension of how the study was conducted, but it is not necessary to educate everyone on the specifics of biometric signal interpretation. Additionally, the science that lies behind the methods can be made available to those who are curious to learn more, but it is unnecessary while presenting results to a team.

The team is primarily concerned with creating better games, and while supporting evidence helps support the insights and build a strong case, it is not necessary to overload them with data, nor provide an overly long explanation of how the tools work. It is important to understand the distinction between academia and practice.

17.3.2 Easy-to-understand terminology

Avoid jargon at all costs. Game developers will generally be unfamiliar with most of the more complex terminology used in biometric testing. Additionally, even some simple words will require a small amount of explanation to ensure improper conclusions are not layered over the research. Terms as simple as 'look' vs 'read' or 'reaction' vs 'emotion' will require a small amount of clarification to prevent misinterpretation by the audience. Be clear with your definitions and consistent with your usage as much as possible in all communications related to biometric results.

17.3.3 Mixed-methods research

The use of varied mixed methods is invaluable both for the presentation and the analysis of the data collected. Being able to pair physiological responses with observational data and attitudinal data from questionnaires enriches comprehension of the player experience by adding context to frame it. Most game developers have experience receiving traditional user test feedback, and combining this type of data with a biometric test helps them frame the results within a model they already comprehend.

17.3.4 Visual reporting

While the reporting should focus on insights, the supporting data used to drive the point home should be visual as often as possible. Even though biometrics signals are very complex, they generally tend to lend themselves to simple visualizations quite well. The heat maps of an eye-tracker and the peaks and valleys of an EDA signal are excellent at communicating simply and visually to a game developer without requiring a ton of explanation. Given their ability to quickly communicate to the untrained eye, these images are vastly superior to a long sequence of slides of figures and tables or explanatory text. As noted earlier, ensure that you give enough context so that the visual aids are not poorly interpreted, nor that you spend a lifetime explaining them. Their mere presence will lend credibility to and adoption by your audience.

17.3.5 Sharing

It is important that all report material be complete enough its own that it can travel around an organization without an accompanying presenter and still be properly interpreted. This requires keeping your insights crystal clear and understandable, but, just as importantly, making sure that they do not allow haphazard reinterpretation or erroneous extrapolation.

17.3.6 Impact

The final piece of advice is to always include a call to action for further iterative testing in the report. Continuously pushing the value of continued investigation and confirmation of changes based on the results is vitally important. This ensures that the team is aware that they must continue to follow up on the outcomes of a test. It also gives the researcher the opportunity to understand the outcome and the value of the conducted research.

17.3.7 Example

Typically, Pierre's latest academic talk plan looked like this: introduction, state of the art, methodology, study, results, and conclusion/takeaways, whereas his latest industrial report plan looked more like this: brief intro, study goals, takeaways, limitations, brief description of methodology, study, top findings, recommendations. This shift in presentation order reflects the change in importance from methodology to results-oriented reporting.

For example, when presenting EDA to our stakeholders, we would much rather use figures and familiar references to present our data. Instead of presenting the EDA data as a time-based series with curves going up and down, we prefer to present averages or numbers of relevant EDA spikes normalized on a bell-shaped curve, where the middle is 'average' and both extremes can be seen as 'low/high' arousal states, such as displayed in Figure 17.12.

Figure 17.12 is also another high-level abstraction of skin conductance response from EDA data presented in a meaningful and easily understandable manner for stakeholders with very little time to spare for analysing and deeply understanding biometrics as a whole.

We explain enough so that the audience understands that high EDA responses correspond to large fluctuations of arousal, but do not attempt to measure emotional reactions without more context. The context is obtained thanks to the mixed methods, and allows us to colour between the lines and make a best guess at experience. If the player was frowning and gave a poor rating, the interpretation of an EDA spike is vastly different from a participant who was gleeful and

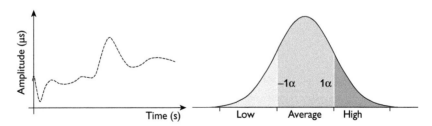

Figure 17.12 Visually abstracting normalized EDA variations for a group of individuals

gave a high user score. Properly delivered, this level of detail is difficult to misinterpret and easily actionable for a designer.

17.4 Challenges

Throughout this chapter, we have described how biometrics at Ubisoft Montreal grew from a proof-of-concept to an actionable force for our teams by providing valuable insights at various stages of production. However, many challenges still await and this section will briefly address four of them.

17.4.1 Art

This area in video game production has not yet benefited from biometrics, mainly due to the lack of immediate feedback and return on investment that one may perceive. Eye tracking different drawings of a character in order to identify the difficulties of a player to identify the class, and understand the parts that stand out from gaze pattern while trying to identify its class is an interesting application. Art is generally developed very early on and iterative testing with biometrics can provide valuable information for designers and artists.

17.4.2 Narrative evaluation

Narrative in games is not only important, but plays a vital role in player immersion. A combined use of EDA and heart rate variability with mixed-methods research would be more than interesting to assess player's affective variations throughout missions. Biometrics can also be useful to assess affective variations in areas where narrative is non-existent versus heavily scripted ones. However, this venture is very time consuming and quite possibly game-specific which might make the findings difficult to apply across genres. Additionally, narrative evaluation is currently an area of development for user research of increasing importance.

17.4.3 New tools

With the never ending advancements in miniaturization, low-cost biometrics and wearable devices, getting access to biometrics is more affordable now. Fitness equipment delivering real-time heart rate, small USB3 portable eye trackers display real-time gaze within games and for games, and even affordable wireless sensors to record encephalographic data (that is data from the brain surface). Although these tools are all exciting from a biometrics point of view, we would advise extreme caution regarding the reliability and claims in GUR. From our experience, we generally found that price does go with quality and that most of the claims from those gadgets have not been backed by the same data robustness as their classical counterparts. It may be inexpensive, but it is at a price that video game production may not yet be ready to pay.

17.4.4 Timing

If there is one main takeaway from this book chapter, it is to test at the right time. Not too early, not too late, just at the right time. Producing a AAA game is a complex endeavour with ever changing timelines and continuous planning adjustments. The main challenge we are constantly facing is finding the proper opportunity to intervene and help biometrics make better games.

17.4.5 Limitations

Generally speaking, our key to success has been smart scoping and honest delivery. Biometrics, to the untrained eye, can seem overwhelming to interpret. Make it small, clear, focused, and, above all, honest. If a team is desperately looking at knowing 'the players' emotions throughout the game', do not hesitate to say refuse (or suggest a smarter alternative). Science is not there yet. Biometrics and mixed-methods research is slowly making its way there. Keeping it honest is definitely the way to go for developing actionable biometric insights for your production teams.

17.5 Conclusions

As can be seen, the advantages of using biometrics to support decision making for development teams are numerous, and, in our experience, have allowed us to provide informed, robust recommendations that have been put into practice. It has been our experience that presenting the information in a package amenable to rapid information extraction and use for the development team has been particularly instrumental to the success of the biometric testing that we have done at the Ubisoft Montreal Research Lab.

Acknowledgements

We would like to thank all our colleagues at the Montreal User Research Lab who helped in compiling complex biometric data, and especially our fellow project managers on the Far Cry (Ian Livingston) and Rainbow 6 (Jean-Baptiste Halle) brand, without whom these biometric projects would simply not be possible. As a final note, this chapter was written while Jonathan Dankoff was working at Ubisoft. This chapter was edited and published while he was working for WBIE, which is used as his workplace/title for the purpose of the chapter.

References

Ambinder, M. (2011). Biofeedback in gameplay: how Valve measures physiology to enhance gaming experience. Presented at the Game Developers Conference, UBM, San Francisco, CA.

Boucsein, W. (2012). Electrodermal activity. New York: Springer.

Hart, S. G., Staveland, L. E. (1988). Development of NASA-TLX (Task Load Index): results of empirical and theoretical research. In P. A. Hancock and N. Meshkati (eds.), Human mental workload [PDF]. Advances in Psychology, 52, 139–183. Amsterdam: North Holland. doi:10.1016/S0166-4115(08)62386–62389

Holmqvist, K., Nyström, M., Andersson, R., Dewhurst, R. Jarodzka, H., Van De Weijer, J. (2011). Eye tracking: a comprehensive guide to methods and measures. Oxford, UK: Oxford University Press.

Mandryk, R., Inkpen, K., Calvert, T. (2006). Using psychophysiological techniques to measure user experience with entertainment technologies. Behaviour and Information Technology [Special Issue on User Experience], 25(2), 141–158. doi:10.1080/01449290500331156

Mirza-Babaei, P., Nacke, L., Fitzpatrick, G., White, G., McAllister, G., Collins, N. (2012). Biometric storyboards : visualising games user research data (pp. 2315–2320). In Proceedings of CHI Extended Abstracts on Human Factors in Computing Systems. New York: ACM. doi:10.1145/2212776.2223795

Nacke, L. E., Lindley, C. A (2008). Flow and immersion in first-person shooters: measuring the player's gameplay experience. In Proceedings of Future Play. New York: ACM. http://dx.doi.org/10.1145/1496984.1496998

Yannakakis, G. N., Hallam, J. Lund, H. H. (2008). Entertainment capture through heart rate activity in physical interactive playground. User Modeling and User Adapted Interaction, 18(1), 207–243.

Zammitto, V., Seif El-Nasr, M., Newton, P. (2010). Exploring quantitative methods for evaluating sports games. CHI 2010, Workshop on Brain, Body and Bytes: Psychophysiological User Interaction.

CHAPTER 18

Reporting user research findings to the development team

PEJMAN MIRZA-BABAEI, *UXR Lab, University of Ontario Institute of Technology*

Highlights

As part of conducting research, reporting must occur. In addition to communicating the research result accurately, a report must motivate the team to act on the result, which often means modifying their build to increase the quality of their product. Approaches used to report user research findings back to the development team are just as important as the findings themselves. If the findings are not communicated to the development team effectively, the developers may not take actions and miss potentially critical changes that could have made a difference in their development cycle and overall success of the project. If user researchers conduct the best possible study and identify the most critical issues but fail to communicate or explain the findings in a way that motivates the development team, then changes may not occur (Mirza-Babaei and Nacke, 2013). Many chapters in this book discuss methodologies for conducting user research; this chapter focuses on approaches to communicate the findings to the development team.

Games User Research, Anders Drachen, Pejman Mirza-Babaei, Lennart E. Nacke (Eds).
© Oxford University Press 2018. Published 2018 by Oxford University Press

18.1 Why is reporting important?

Research and reporting go hand in hand. User research must be reported for changes to occur to the current project. A report is a summary of what the findings were during a research session. The research in its own is useful (perhaps only to the researchers); however, without an effective approach to communicate the findings to a development team, the findings would be harder to understand and will appear to be just data. This opens up the findings to misinterpretation and risks changes occurring that were unnecessary or detrimental to the project. A report, above all, must show where improvements could be made, and must motivate the development team into making changes for the better of the project. A report must do this in a clear and concise manner to reduce the chances of misinterpretation and to be useable by the development team.

18.2 Common sections in a user research report

Although there are various ways to prepare a report (I will discuss them later in this chapter), there are some key sections that are common in user research reports. This includes sections that highlight the *aim/goal* of the user test, the *methods* used in the research session, descriptions of what was *found*, and the *next steps* to take with the development and evaluation.

18.2.1 Aim

The aim of a user research session is varied, but always leads back to the questions the development team wanted to answer by conducing user test sessions, and what the session was trying to achieve. The aim of a user research session can be summarized as *why* the session took place. Obviously this could be varied; for example, to evaluate a specific game mechanic, user satisfaction in different levels, or the effectiveness of a game's onboarding phase. The aim makes it clear to the readers that a specific focus was put on the research session.

18.2.2 Study design and methods

A user test session can use different methods and take many different forms of study design. It is important to summarize the study design and justify why certain methods were used before discussing the findings. This will help the readers to better understand the process and adds credibility to the findings, both of which are critical for motivating developers to take actions based on the findings. In addition to study design and method justification, this section may include participant profiles, what build or game version was being tested, and the analysis used in generating the research results.

18.2.3 Executive summary and severity

It is common for a user research report to include an executive summary and a list of findings before it discusses results in detail. It is recommended to have the findings listed under different levels of severity. These would help the development team to have a quick overview of the user test result and priorities on how to act on the findings. There are various factors that could determine a severity of each issue. These may include location of the issue, frequency of occurrence during gameplay, and the impact it may have on the gameplay (Mirza-Babaei et al., 2012).

18.2.4 Description of findings

The report should contain a list of identified issues, where in the game they are located, and short descriptions. It would be beneficial if the report could provide reasoning as to why the issue may have occurred (e.g., 'The game did not teach players how to perform this mechanic'). It is recommended that the report provide some forms of support to better highlight the identified issues. These could include gameplay video clips showing a participant experiencing said issue, quotes from participants describing the issue in post-gameplay interview, or information generated from a questionnaire.

Some reports also propose potential solutions to fix each issue, although it could be argued that user research reports should only focus on discussing issues, and leave it for developers/designers to come up with the solutions that bring the game closer to their intended vision. These issues and their descriptions will aid and provide motivation for the development team to make meaningful changes to their product (Mirza-Babaei et al., 2013).

18.2.5 Next steps

User research reports often conclude by providing recommendations regarding future evaluation sessions for the product. These recommendations may include proposals regarding (a) the evaluation of the effectiveness of fixes (e.g., to re-evaluate tutorial after changes have been made), (b) inclusion of new metrics (e.g., to collect metrics regarding players' movement and death location in the game that can help answer certain questions), and (c) the focus of future tests (e.g., to conduct a diary study to evaluate the effectiveness of the onboarding session after all major usability issues are removed).

18.3 Approaches in reporting Games User Research findings

How information is reported to the development team is as important as the information itself. However, approaches used in reporting are not equal in all situations. Whether they are quick notes emailed after a session or a visual report shown to the team, each approach has its own advantages and drawbacks in communicating with the development team. This section looks at different approaches of reporting user research findings.

18.3.1 Short-form note

The basic and possibly most frequently used form of communication for user research findings is a short-form note. Depending on the relationship of the research team to the development team (e.g., third-party team, internal team), these short-form notes are often delivered as the first communication after a research session and send most commonly through email to the development team. These notes would entail basic information about what occurred during the testing session and often contain a high-level report of what went well and what went poorly during the research session. These basic reports often would not include the aim of the research session or comprehensive results. They are often followed up by a more in-depth report. On their own, they are a good starting point; however, they only show a glimpse of the information gathered during a user research session. This style of report can leave room for misinterpretation, as they are often not accompanied by visuals (such as screenshots or videos). However, they may inform the team of major issues that could impact future test sessions (e.g., researcher may request a new build) or answer time-sensitive questions that were requested by the development team (e.g., feedback on a specific feature that is being finalized).

18.3.2 Comprehensive report

This would be a more structured approach to report user research findings, and researchers (either internal or external consultants) often have a template for preparing the report. These detail-oriented reports show an in-depth explanation and analysis of the user test session. These reports often include the common sections that we discussed earlier (Section 18.2). They may contain a large density of information, which can be a huge aid to the development team; however, this also means that developers may scan over these reports rather than fully read them. The challenge is to produce concise reports that communicate the findings clearly and remove any possibilities for misinterpretation. Hence, these reports are often used in conjunction with additional communication methods. For example, they could be used in a workshop-like meeting supported by slides and gameplay video. In the following sections, I discuss some additional report types that often support the comprehensive report.

18.3.3 Spreadsheet-based report

For linear games or even linear sections of games, a spreadsheet-based report may be used. This reporting approach is fast and easy to read but misses the details and the interactivity of some other forms of reports (see Figure 18.1).

Spreadsheet-based reports could be colour-coded to make them easy to read, and easy to use for both the development team and the user research team. They can clearly display areas of the game being tested (e.g., Column A in Figure 18.1), aligned with data gathered from different users. This can show a development team quickly what areas the users have an issue with (e.g., Row 25 in Figure 18.1 shows that all users experienced issues in that area), as well as highlight areas that the players performed as intended (these could be marked green, for instance). This creates focal points on what was good and where users experienced issues, which clearly show the developers what may need changes and what should be left as is. Notably, this report type is missing in-depth details on different issues; hence, this type of report is often used in conjunction with other communication methods as discussed earlier.

18.3.4 Experience graph report

The experience graph is a visual reporting style that shows how a player experienced the game or levels tested. This reporting style may ask the user to draw a

	A	B (player 1)	C (player 2)	D (player 3)	E (player 4)	F (player 5)	G (player 6)
1		player 1	player 2	player 3	player 4	player 5	player 6
2	hrs per week	15 hrs	6 hours	10 hrs	5 hours	10	10
3							
4	act 1 - chapter 1						
5	door 1 (tutorial)	ok	ok	should prompte	ok	look tutorial icon	ok
6	door 2	ok	Struggles with getting in final	ok	ok	ok	ok
7	door 3 (key)	ok	how the final	ok	ok	ok	ok
8	act 1 - chapter 2	07:00	10:30	06:55	08:00	13:35	08:50
9	door 1	ladders are difficult for the user (18:45)	ok	ok	ok	ok	
10	door 2	ok	frustrated (25:00) eventually figures out how to solve	ok	ok	31:34 ladders problem with big jumps (L1+ Jump)	
11	door 3	ok	ok	ok	ok	ok	
12	act 1 - chapter 4	22:10	31:00:00	22:00	27:50:00	41:45:00	36:45:00
13	door 1	ok	ok	ok	ok	ok	ok
14	door 2	frustration shown. (25:10) user	ok	ok	ok	ok	ok
15	door 3	ok	ok	ok	user dies at the end of the level	ok	ok
16	act 1 - chapter 5	29:00:00	43:00:00	29:30:00	42:00:00	58:30:00	50:54:00
17	door 1	ok	ok	ok	ok	ok	
18	door 2	ok	user becomes very focused. (48:00)	ok	ok	ok	
19	door 3 (key)	ok	ok	ok	ok	ok	
20	act 1 - chapter 6	38:00:00	51:30:00	36:35:00	54:00:00	01:08:18	59:45:00
21	door 1	ok	ok	ok	ok	ok	
22	door 3	ok	ok	ok	ok	help with ladders 1:29:00 bug - re watch	
23	door 4	ok	ok	ok	ok		
24	act 1 - chapter 7 (boss)	50:40:00	1:06:00:00	48:50:00	1:20:00:00	1:33:30 - 1:50:00 bug to finish	01:33:00
25	door 1	when the floor fails out under him	as the there are no checkpoints during	in the user (1:02:00) user died	what to do for the beginning of the	1:54:50 K1 up Jump	1:41:40 bug
26	act 2 - chapter 1	55:40:00	1:18:00:00	1:15:00:00	recording	with the moving	01:42:00
27	door 1	ok	user is far more focused with 2 characters to control. (1:19:30)		07:00 bugy hack machine (visual)	n/a	
28	door 2	had difficulty with cannon tutorial (1:00:00) eventually got it on his own. User has become much	ok	cannon mecnanic should show a dotted line of the projectile to help users properly aim and help solve	ok	n/a	
29	door 3	frustration shown because if one	user is unaware of the level being a	user has difficulty using touch pad on	user found the game too difficult	n/a	

Figure 18.1 A segment of a spreadsheet-based report

graph of how they recall their experience through the session (Thomsen et al., 2016). Alternatively, the graph could be generated based on gathered metrics (e.g., biometric storyboard approach; see Figure 18.2).

These graphs could show how players experienced the game and highlight the areas they felt most engaged or frustrated. They could assist researchers to emphasize the impact of identified issues to the development team, therefore

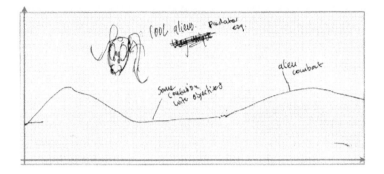

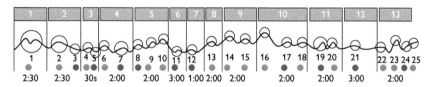

Figure 18.2 (top) Player's self-drawn experience graph (from Thomsen et al., 2016). (bottom) Biometric storyboards (from Mirza-Babaei, 2013)

motivate them to act on the issues. These graphs are often used in conjunction with another report.

18.3.5 Presentation-based report

Possibly the most common and versatile reporting type would be a presentation-based report, often to be delivered in a meeting or workshop. These reports have both visual and text elements that can be presented in various forms, as well as the interaction with a presenter (often user research lead or project manager), allowing the developers to discuss directly with the researcher about the user testing findings. As findings alone can be misinterpreted, having a presentation, with both visual elements and text descriptions supported by data collected during the test session, can be more effective. A presentation-style report can use different communications methods (as mentioned earlier) to explain the data gathered. These reports can show videos of a specific event alongside quotes from participants' interviews or ratings from questionnaires. These would make the presentation stronger, as the presentation can include multiple types of analysis as well as direct examples from the user test sessions. Presentation-based report can take many different forms to convey the user research findings in a more demonstrative manner. As a member of the research team would often present this report, findings can be explained, so there is less room for misinterpretation. It also gives a chance for the development team to pose questions to discuss with both the development team and a member of the user research team.

18.3.6 Interactive customizable report

Some user research teams have developed interactive, customizable tools to facilitate reporting user research results. These customizable reports aim to be more accessible and effective for developers by using embedded plugins or tools. For example, these tools can visualise where the players spent time, what they have missed or skipped, or if the players had issues in certain locations. Although various techniques have already been used to facilitate the analysis of game metrics collected during play (such as players' movements in a level or death locations), most of these techniques focus on static visualizations of the data without integrating qualitative or contextual data on players' experience. However, customizable reporting tools could represent the data based on the developer's need (e.g., game producers may use the data differently from game programmers). Hence, customizable reporting can adjust data representation based on the level of detail required from different members of a development team. An example of this type of report would be Vixen (Drenikow and Mirza-Babaei, 2017) (see Figure 18.3).

Vixen is a customizable reporting tool that can be used with Unity to collect and present common data collected in a user test (such as players' in-game movement and think-aloud comments). Game developers can use the tool to selectively view data (e.g., from a specific group of players, or toggle players'

Figure 18.3 Vixen

movement data or death locations in the representation) and move around within the game environment they created to see how the players experienced their world. This customizability and interactivity creates a compelling report that shows the developers what they could adjust or change in the game to optimise player experience. As it can visually show where players went, what slowed them down, and how long they spent in an area, the developers can quickly see where they need to change or adjust in their game.

This form of report could be used to complement other reporting styles to provide the game developer with a possibility of exploring and interacting with the collected user test data from various perspectives.

18.4 Conclusion

Conducting user test sessions (either internally or through contractors) and applying correct methods and thorough data analysis would not improve the game if the final results are not communicated well, not convincing, or not actionable for the development team. This chapter has discussed user research reporting, a critical step in the user research process.

References and useful reads

Mirza-Babaei, P., Nacke, L. (2013). Storyboarding for games user research. http://www.gamasutra.com/view/feature/186514/storyboarding_for_games_user_.php

Mirza-Babaei, P., et al. (2012). Biometric Storyboards: Visualising Games User Research Data. In CHI EA '12 (pp. 2315–2320). New York: ACM. doi:10.1145/2212776.2223795

Mirza-Babaei, P., et al. (2013). How does it play better? Exploring user testing and biometric storyboards in games user research. In CHI '13 (pp. 1499–1508). New York: ACM. doi:10.1145/2470654.2466200

Thomsen, L., Petersen, F., Drachen, A., Mirza-Babaei, P. (2016). Identifying onboarding heuristics for free-to-play mobile games: a mixed methods approach. In Entertainment Computing–ICEC 2016. Lecture Notes in Computer Science, vol. 9926. New York: Springer.

Mirza-Babaei, P. (2013). Biometric storyboards: a games user research approach for improving qualitative evaluations of player experience [PhD thesis]. Sussex, UK: University of Sussex.

Drenikow, B., Mirza-Babaei, P. (2017). Vixen: interactive visualization of gameplay experiences. In FDG 2017. ACM. doi:10.1145/3102071.3102089

Game Analytics for Games User Research

ANDERS DRACHEN, *Digital Creativity Labs, University of York*

SHAWN CONNOR, *Data Insights*

Highlights

Game analytics (GA) provides new ways to conduct user research, counteracting some of the weaknesses of traditional approaches while retaining essential compatibility with the methodologies of Games User Research (GUR). This chapter provides an overview of what GA is and how it fits within the daily operations of game development across studio sizes, with an emphasis on the intersection with GUR and the synergies that can be leveraged across analytics and user research.

19.1 Introduction

Game development is a wonderful combination of art, craft, and science. GA, like GUR, falls under science. It is a professional discipline focused on collecting and analysing data to support decisions about designing and producing games, improving user experiences, prioritizing features, and much more, across all parts of an organization (design, marketing, user research, management, etc.), in operational, tactical, and strategic contexts. It sounds like quite a mouthful because GA is so broad in scope, but as a discipline it shares DNA with

Games User Research, Anders Drachen, Pejman Mirza-Babaei, Lennart E. Nacke (Eds).
© Oxford University Press 2018. Published 2018 by Oxford University Press

GUR in that each supplements the personal experience and intuition that is key to game development with empirical methods and evidence.

Both GA and GUR have a heavy focus on how users (i.e. players) interact with the game. It can be hard to draw a clear boundary between the two fields, and it makes more sense to think of them as two sets of activities that overlap in their focus and the problems they are trying to solve, but have fundamentally different toolkits for trying to address those problems. In this way, game analysts and Games User Researchers are like fire mages and ice mages: similar in their approach and methods, but with divergent strengths and weaknesses owing to their choice of specialty.

Each domain is subject to requirements and challenges that the other is not. GA deals with technical infrastructure in ways GUR can typically avoid. GUR most often relies on subjective assessments of players' experiences and attitude, whereas GA is by nature quantitative. In behaviour-focused GA, the data of interest are often ultra-detailed event streams from *each and every player*, a scale traditional GUR typically cannot tackle. However, with only a few dozen subjects, GUR can achieve an understanding of player motivations and opinions that GA can only guess at.

Broadly, GA is best suited to answering *what*-type questions (e.g., What are the players doing? What indicates a player will keep playing?), whereas GUR is very good at answering *why*-type questions (Why are players making particular choices? Why do they keep playing?). This makes the two fantastic supplements to one another, enabling links between the quantified behaviours of an entire population of players and the more holistic, qualitative observations of lab-based GUR (Figure 19.1).

The value proposition of GA to GUR is simple: GA provides new ways to conduct research, counteracting some of the weaknesses of traditional approaches while retaining essential compatibility with the methodologies of GUR. In *Doom* terminology, we are going from a single-barrelled shotgun to a double-barrelled one—with a grenade launcher slung underneath. In this chapter, we will focus on how the GA toolkit fits into the daily operations of game development, whether you are in a small or big studio, and how it intersects GUR in particular. We will be doing essentially three things:

1. What GA is: the theory of GA and what questions it can answer.
2. How GA is performed: close cousin to GUR, but with lots of data points.
3. GA as a GUR asset: what GA can offer to GUR practitioners.

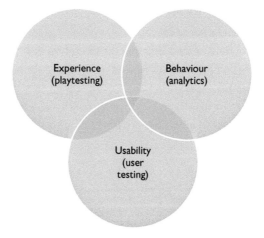

Figure 19.1 The triumvirate of user-focused evaluation in game development: experience, usability, and behaviour. The first two traditionally rest with GUR and the third with GA, but in recent years the boundaries have blurred, giving way to substantial collaboration between the two.

On a final note, this chapter is based on a significant amount of published research and experience across industry and academia, as well as the authors' personal hard-won experiences from the trenches. The narrow focus of this chapter means that many complex concepts can only be superficially touched upon, but we will provide references to further materials for those who may be interested.

19.2 Introducing game analytics

GA has become a cornerstone of game development within a short decade. This rapid introduction stems from a confluence of factors, notably:

1. A general requirement for business intelligence and analytics in the game sector, as detailed data from platforms, players, advertisers, and payment processors became available.
2. Within the AAA context, the need to enrich traditional kinds of live user testing data such as screen capture and surveys with details about player choices and actions.

3. The emergence of online social games embedded in pre-existing, data-rich networks such as Facebook.
4. The rise of the mobile phone and the freemium business model which, like an online storefront, relies on analysis of user behaviour to optimize revenue.
5. The advent of new, better, and more readily accessible tools for collecting and searching large volumes of information (i.e. 'big data' technologies).

The games industry today serves over 2 billion customers and comprises a US $100 billion market, with high rates of innovation across design, technology, and business models. With exponential increases in data processing added to the mix, it is no wonder that data-driven analytics have seen as rapid growth in the games industry as in many others in recent years.

19.2.1 So what does game analytics do? Two practical examples

Let us say we have a live match-3 mobile game, à la Candy Crush Saga or Bejeweled. We will call it SpaceSlam, on account of its outer-space theme, with asteroid tiles that make neat explosions when matched. When players finish a level, the game client transmits a record of this action to an online server, where it is collected. Later, by counting these events we can generate a simple graph showing the number of players who have reached each level (Figure 19.2). The difference between sequential levels thus represents the users who have either given up and stopped playing while at that level, or who are still active but have not finished their current level yet. This is not especially mathematically sophisticated, but these kinds of simple descriptive analyses can be still be invaluable for spotting problems in a game.

The graph shows us that we lose a large proportion of players who reach Level 4 before they reach Level 5—from 140,000 down to just 50,200. Perhaps Level 4 is difficult or time-consuming and players give up, perhaps a bug is preventing people from reaching Level 5, and so on. Perhaps this is not a problem at all, and just evidence of a natural break point for new players, such as the end of the first play session. To find out, we will need to look at other types of events to determine what people do while at Level 4, *drilling-down* through the problem until we find out where this pattern comes from. Drill-down analysis means moving from summary/aggregate information to detailed data, following leads as they present themselves.

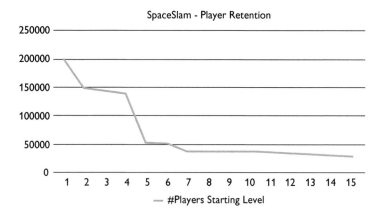

Figure 19.2 SpaceSlam level-completion graph: an example of a basic retention analysis

For a more sophisticated example, let us consider Dota 2, currently the second-most heavily played MOBA after League of Legends, and one of the major eSports titles globally. For those unfamiliar with the game, a Dota 2 match is played by two teams of five players. Each player controls a character selected from a roster of over 100, with different abilities suited to different tactical roles. The two teams compete in a square, geographically balanced virtual arena, and the same arena is used in every match. As a match progresses, individual players advance their character's abilities by killing opposing characters and non-player units to collect experience points and gold. The overall objective of a match is to reach and enter the opposing base and destroy a structure there called the Ancient.

Telemetry from Dota 2 is very detailed, including the second-by-second position of the players on each team and every single power used, purchase made, kill, etc. We can perform a lot of different types of analyses to help us figure out if there are imbalances in the map layout that favour a particular team, if certain heroes are more powerful than others, and so on, which are all important considerations in a competitive title. Two examples are given in Figure 19.3 and Figure 19.4.

19.2.2 What is game analytics?

GA is formally the process of discovering and communicating patterns in data as applied to game development and research. GA is a source of business intelligence in game development, not only about games and the people who play

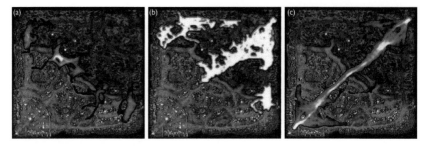

Figure 19.3 Dota 2 heat maps. Teams begin in the bases in the upper-right and lower-left corners. (a) Early-game encounter heat map across 412 matches over the first 10 minutes of gameplay. Encounters generally occur along the border between the two teams' areas. (b) Encounter heat map for one full Dota 2 match. The encounters have happened predominantly in the upper-right half of the map, indicating that the lower-left team has probably dominated the entire match. (c) Late-game encounter heat map across 412 matches (40 min. of playtime or more), showing that encounters near the end of these long-running matches generally occur in the middle lane, the shortest and most direct route to the opposing base. At this point, the teams are pressing the attack on the opposing base (or trying to defend against the same!). (Original illustrations by Matthias Schubert, Anders Drachen, and Tobias Mahlmann, 2016, used with permission.)

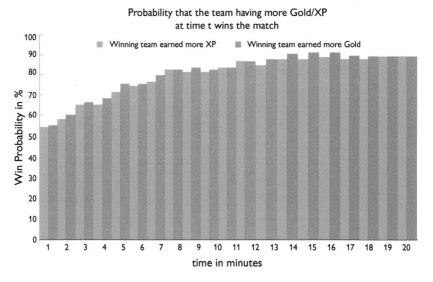

Figure 19.4 Example of a simple win probability model for Dota 2. The chart shows the probability that the team which is ahead in total gold or XP t minutes into the game (for the first 20 minutes) will end up winning the match, based on aggregating our observations of many matches. The further we get into a Dota 2 match, the more predictive the gold and/or XP leads become. Though this conclusion (stated broadly, 'the team who is doing better tends to eventually win') may not be very interesting to someone who knows the game well, the specifics of how quickly matches are decided and how deterministic these indicators appear to be are certainly are. (Source: Schubert et al., 2016)

them, but also the process of developing games, and the process of running a game company. Despite some trepidation to the contrary, GA emphatically does *not* mean eliminating personal experience or common sense in game design, but rather empowering these perspectives through empirical insights.

Analytics combines statistics, data mining, machine learning, engineering, programming, and operations research, as well as data visualization, communication, and systems thinking. It is a broad field covering virtually all aspects of collecting, storing, analysing, and communicating data and information. Despite being a relatively new element in game development, GA has grown to be virtually ubiquitous in the industry because it improves our understanding of the players—just like GUR.

GA's focus on user behaviour often considers users from two perspectives: as customers and as players. In the former case, we focus on the value the user provides to the business, and typically investigate patterns in purchasing/spending behaviour, churn prediction, finding average revenue per user, etc. In the latter, the focus is the value we are providing to the user, as reflected by their behaviour and the user experience. These can be hard to separate, especially in free-to-play games, but remembering this distinction is important because it can also be a source of friction between GUR and GA. While the former almost always emphasizes the player's perspective, GA by contrast is sometimes seen as focusing on business value.

In analytics we often talk about 'actionable insights' or 'improving performance', and while these terms are definitely based in business jargon, GA is not all about business any more or less than is game development as a whole. This common misunderstanding is in large part our own fault, as analytics practitioners. Until very recently there has been a relative dearth of knowledge sharing in GA as compared to GUR. The reluctance to share knowledge across the industry is rooted in the perception that because the insights produced have business value, knowledge related to the *practice* of analytics should be treated as a trade secret. This is a nuanced issue, but suffice to say that perceptions are rapidly changing to favour more open collaboration.

19.2.3 What is game analytics *for?*

Analytical methods can generate answers to a wide variety of questions. The most complex of these benefit from or even require direct collaboration with other disciplines (design, marketing, GUR, etc.) to get past the raw behaviours of the players to an understanding of player motivation, personality, and the context of play, in order to provide actionable insight.

Requirements on the data science expertise of the analyst vary. Basic questions, such as finding out the number of daily active users, tend to be close to or entirely automated these days, and require minimal in-house data science resources. Problems like predicting player churn, on the other hand, require more advanced expertise and resources, and thus are commonly outside the capacity of a small developer (Figure 19.5). Middleware companies and

What is happening?	How the game is being played right now, or in the current build. Example: measuring the number of daily active players or the average session length of players.
What has happened?	Historical patterns: How has behavior evolved over time. Cohort comparisons, evaluating the result of marketing campaigns, and so on. Example: How has class balance in an RPG developed along with game updates? How has the number of retained players per month changed? Did people who signed up in November play more than those who signed up in December?
What is likely to happen?	How current players will act in the future. Predicting the future impact of design changes. Informing strategic business planning. Example: Churn prediction, predicting purchase patterns, Lifetime Value prediction, forecasting player behavior
What will happen if I do X?	How a specific design change will impact player behavior at the operational level. Judging the likely impact of a design change on immediate behavior is often done in coordination with GUR or via A/B testing. Example: Impact on user experience, engagement, monetization, completion rates of adding or modifying a feature or mechanic, such as adding a new social game mode and running experiments on potential resulting changes in player retention.
How do I make X happen?	What changes need to be made to a game in order to encourage specific types of player behavior or performance. Example: Operating from knowledge about current behavior, and the causes of the behavior, engineering the required design changes to foster a specific behavioral change.
Why did X happen?	Investigating specific phenomena in player behaviors and their causes. This commonly requires integration with GUR and experimental testing; causal relationships are difficult to determine from evidence alone. Example: Determining if a group of players earning in-game currency very fast are cheating. Invistigating drop-offs in the new user funnel.
How do I optimize X?	Optimizing an already-known analytical process from any of the above categories. The ultimate goal with optimization is automating the analytics, insights, and responses. Example: A game client making changes to the parameters of a game based on a heuristics model at the level of the individual player. Reacting to player state with just-in-time offers or incentives.

Figure 19.5 The kinds of questions user-focused game analytics can answer, in ascending order of complexity and difficulty. The further down on the scale, the harder it is for analytics to answer the question in general, and the more substantial the benefits of integrating Games User Research.

consultants are readily available to fill this gap, but small organizations especially need to be careful that the optimizations these groups can provide are worth the fees.

In essence, the more complex the kinds of analytics you want to run, the higher the organizational maturity in GA needs to be. A full-blown discussion of maturity and capacity-building is outside the scope of this chapter, but there are four key dimensions to consider:

1. **Volume:** How much data do you have? This is mostly a function of the scale of your game (e.g., the number of players) and the level of detail you log. Equally important is how much data you can effectively *use* based on your infrastructure.
2. **Variety:** How many different types of data do you have? Which different behaviours are recorded from the game itself, and what additional data sources (advertising, revenue, operational logs, etc.) do you have access to?
3. **Capability:** What types of skills and tools can your analysts bring to bear to answer your questions and solve your problems? Data wrangling, data visualization, data science, and technical communication skills are all important here.
4. **Acceptance:** How is your organization *acting* on the insights analytics provides? You can expect product owners to consider key performance indicators (KPIs) when making business decisions, but acceptance can range from there through to informing the design process with detailed behavioural analysis to incorporating machine learning tools (or the outputs thereof) directly into the user experience.

These dimensions push and pull on one another to determine what an organization can *really* do with GA.

19.2.4 The process of game analytics

Like GUR, GA is a scientific approach to building evidence. The analytical process is cyclical and iterative, with analysis leading to new knowledge, which leads to new analysis, and so on. The knowledge discovery process includes the following phases (see also Figure 19.6):

1. **Set goals:** Define the objective and requirements of the analysis. During this phase it is also determined, provisionally, which data are relevant. Another important step in this phase is thinking about

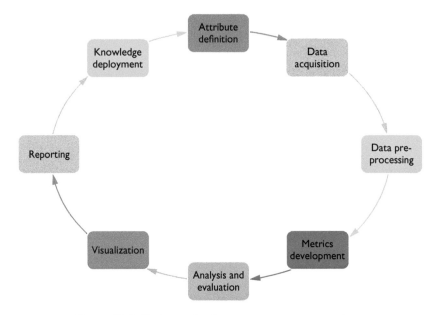

Figure 19.6 The knowledge discovery process in game analytics

acceptable/expected values (e.g., how long should a game take to finish, how fast is too fast, etc.).

2. Acquire data: Collect behavioural telemetry data and evaluate its
   quality. Typically, this happens continuously once the game is instrumented, since we cannot go back in time and collect more data about
   past events.

3. Prepare data: Choose cases and features to analyse, and perform any
   necessary pre-processing and/or aggregation to prepare the data for
   modelling.

4. Generate model: Select and apply one or more statistical techniques
   or machine learning models, or otherwise generate results. This is the
   step most commonly thought of when we say 'analytics', but as we can
   clearly see it is actually only a small fraction of the analysis process.

5. Evaluate result: Examine the results and confirm that they reach the
   initial objectives. This does *not* mean confirming your expectations
   were right, but rather that you ended up learning something.

6. Visualize: Almost all analysis benefits from thoughtfully visualizing
   the results, a key bridge between evaluation and communication. Visualization helps humans like us understand the patterns we use algorithms to detect.

7. Communicate insights: Take the results to whomever is likely to find them actionable. That may be a level designer, a marketer, an executive, or anyone else in the development process—maybe many someones!

8. Deploy knowledge: Given the goals of the game and the business, adjust the game based on the information gained. Except in small organizations, this is probably not the role of the analysts, but rather the stakeholders they communicate the results to. Traditionally, these changes are implemented 'by hand', but depending on context, semi- or full automation of this process is seeing increased use, especially with middleware providers for whom the promise of turnkey optimization is particularly valuable.

19.3 Gathering and analysing behaviour data

In this section we will briefly introduce the basic concepts behind user behaviour telemetry—the player behaviour data we work with. We will outline how raw data becomes metrics, and how these form the basis for analysis.

19.3.1 Events and metrics: the building blocks of analytics

Every action performed in a game means executing code, and that execution can be tracked and logged: every virtual step taken, weapon fired, or interaction with an Non-Player Character (NPC). The same goes for external information such as navigating to the game's download site, geographical information, associated data from social networks, etc. There are many sources of data about player behaviour, and about players themselves, but collectively we refer to information captured directly from user behaviour as 'telemetry'. It is a term used for any technology that allows measurements to be made over a distance; telemetry just means remotely captured data.

Telemetry data makes up the most important source of data in user-focused GA. Most commonly, the game client (or the game server, in the case of a hosted online game) transmits data to a collection server. Once received, data can be stored in various formats. As mentioned in the Introduction, we will not here deal with the relative merits of Spark, Hadoop, Hive, or other big data tools, but suffice to say that such back-end data storage and retrieval systems need to be flexible and scaleable to cope with the stream of incoming data. Analytics pipelines are often proprietary, but today there are also a number of third-party providers who sell various segments of this process as a service.

Individual records of actions, either by a user or by the game system responding to a user, are referred to in GA as 'events': for example, when we track a player firing a weapon at an opposing player. Around each event we can usually capture sets of related data, such as the type of weapon being fired, the projectile used, the position of the player at the time of firing, how long into the match the shot happened, the camera angle, whether the shot hit or not, the damage dealt, and so forth. When designing events, it is important to think about the relationships between disparate events. An event represents a code-path being triggered, but the various behaviours we want to study may be described by several events happening in a particular sequence or context, so it is useful to be able to tie events together through common identifiers.

The raw telemetry data can be transformed into various interpretable measures (e.g., average completion time as a function of individual game levels) either immediately upon entering the collection system or later with prepared queries. In the context of user behaviour, these resulting measures are called 'gameplay metrics', telemetry data that have been summarized somehow. Any measure of player behaviour inside the game environment (e.g., object interaction, trading, navigation, player-player interaction) is a gameplay metric (Figures 19.7–19.9). Gameplay metrics are the most straightforward way to evaluate user experience and game design, but can also seem far removed from the revenue chain, and hence are sometimes under-prioritized compared to revenue-related metrics.

19.3.2 From metrics to analytics

Working with metrics and the raw events that compose them, we can find patterns in the behaviours of players, and sometimes even uncover their root causes. For example, we may find that a specific level segment where players tend to quit the game is exceedingly lethal, that a specific item is not being found or used, that the omega gun is overpowered in the hands of a particular class in a shooter game, or that players who visit an important quest hub in a role-playing game are ignoring the quest providers there.

There are a lot of ways to work with metrics. Generally speaking, we need to make two choices when we start an analytics process: our overall methodological approach, and which statistical models or machine learning algorithms we employ to derive insight from the data. Recognizing that these two fundamental decisions underlie all analytics work is crucial; it is worth noting that equivalent considerations exist in GUR as well.

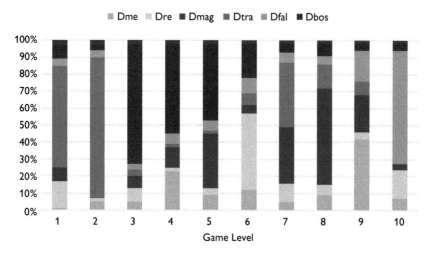

Figure 19.7 A progress-frequency chart—very commonly used in analytics—showing the relative frequency of four major causes of death in a fictive game, summed to 100% (Dme = melee enemies, Dre = ranged enemies, Dmag = magic enemies, Dtra = traps, Dfal = falling, Dbos = boss fight) by game level. Note that the 'level' can be replaced with any other breakdown of a game or section of a game—e.g. parts of a single mission, different parts of a room, or even sequential encounters. Basic visualizations of player behaviour are often useful as a high-level 'sanity check' when looking for potential problems, debugging the player experience, exploring if the design leads to the desired player behaviours, etc. Lots of falling deaths may be expected around platforming puzzles, but surprising in a 'boss fight' room

19.3.3 Methodological approach

When it comes to the overall approach, behavioural analysis in games is typi-fied by either *explorative* or *hypothesis-driven* research. Either we are looking for leads and patterns that may be enlightening (explorative analysis) or we are looking to confirm or refute some specific idea we have (hypothesis-driven).

Explorative work is most valuable when the answers are difficult or impos-sible to predict from looking at the game design in the abstract, such as finding which of a set of 2000 virtual catalogue items are the most important drivers for converting non-paying users to paying users in a social online game, or the most effective build order in an Real-Time Strategy (RTS) game like StarCraft. Drill-down analysis, mentioned earlier, is a common data-driven method for explorative research, using more and more detailed levels of data and differ-ent combinations of filters until a useful insight is found. Hypothesis-driven metrics, on the other hand, require us to have a preconceived notion of where to find an answer and what it will look like. For example, we may think that

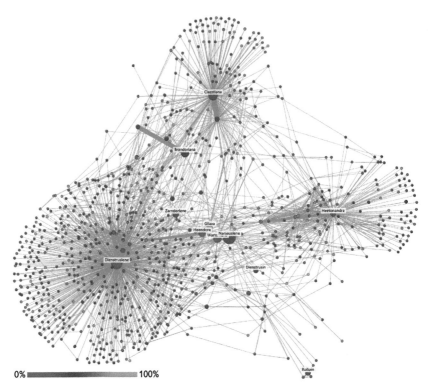

Figure 19.8 Example of a visualization of social networks in games, used to drive social network analysis (SNA). SNA is highly useful for investigating the connections in a game community, for example, towards finding strongly connected players who are important to keeping the community active, and supporting them. Here an example of a mini-network from Bungie's hybrid MMORPG-shooter Destiny, focusing on a few players and their connections. All connections formed via PVP matches between the named players are included (names are anonymized). The nodes (dots) are players, and their win/loss rate is given as a color ramp, with green meaning higher win rates (from 0–100% wins). The size of the node scales with the number of Crucible matches played. The thickness of the lines connecting players scales with the number of matches the players played together as teammates. (Source: Drachen et al., 2016, used with permission)

the zombies on Level 10 are too powerful, and subsequently perform metrics analysis in order to confirm or refute this suspicion, say by summarizing causes of player death at that level to see if zombies are over-represented.

Explorative questions tend to be more time-consuming to answer than specific, hypothesis-driven questions. It is necessary to put some structure around an investigation, even given open-ended questions. Purely explorative research is rare in industry settings—a game developer usually does not have the luxury of throwing a data set at an analyst and tasking them to see what interesting stuff

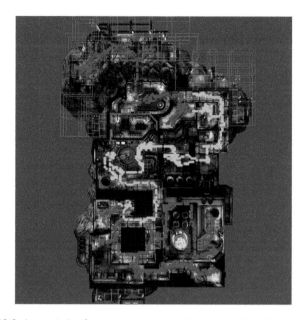

Figure 19.9 An example of an aggregate progression analysis, also using a map overlay. Each dot indicates the position of a player, with the shades delineating 30-second intervals (darker shades indicate longer intervals), summarizing the behaviour of many players so we can look for patterns

they can find. Where it does exist, it tends to be part of a collaboration between analysts and designers, essentially structuring the analysis through continual feedback rather than predefined requirements.

In practice, as soon as you move outside of the kinds of questions that can be answered with simple queries of the available data (e.g. 'What is the number of active users today?', 'What is the average playtime for Level 22?'), you often end up mixing hypothesis-driven and explorative approaches, alternating between them as evidence begets insights which beget more evidence. This is the case in GUR as well as in GA, because both are fundamentally empirical, scientific endeavours. This typically helps make communication across GUR and GA teams more seamless than between either discipline and most other groups.

19.3.4 Models and algorithms: GA as a toolbox

Just as GUR has tools like think-aloud protocols to help understand player behaviour and experience, GA has a collection of tools that can be employed to expand the scope and reach of GUR. There are hundreds of different models, algorithms, and concepts available for solving a variety of different problems.

We borrow these tools from statistics, data science, and related disciplines, and apply them to answering questions more akin to those found in the behavioural and social sciences—the same types of questions GUR is interested in.

When talking about tools, it is important to recognize that GA can operate on all levels from analysing a single user to millions. Especially when dealing with small samples, we use statistics to help quantify our findings. When dealing with very large data sets, we move into the domain of 'data mining'. In practice, we use the term data mining when data sets are so big, diverse, or unstructured that traditional statistical models break down. It is good to keep in mind that the terminology when applying these techniques can be fuzzy, with 'statistics' often used in the colloquial sense to describe the measurements that are the output of data mining.

With data mining we sometimes need specific algorithms to deal with diverse or large data sets, even if the purpose is just to describe the data, draw graphs, etc. (Figure 19.10). Wrangling these data sets, however, also opens up the potential for applying machine learning. Machine learning forms a branch of artificial intelligence (AI) and is a term describing diverse techniques for training a computer to spot patterns in data, especially those that would be hard to spot

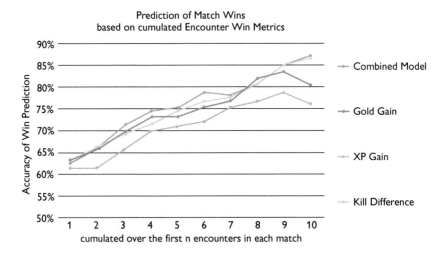

Figure 19.10 Example of a simple prediction analysis for Dota 2, extending the example in Figure 19.4. In this example, a logistic regression model was trained on a number of Dota 2 matches, for four different sets of features (kill difference, XP gain, gold gain, and a combined model including all three). We can use the model to make predictions about the result of an in-progress match, but it can be informative to find and examine matches which do not conform to the patterns found by the model as well. (Source: Schubert et al., 2016)

ourselves. It is a broad and exciting field which we can only touch the surface of. One of the core divisions in machine learning techniques worth discussing is between supervised and unsupervised learning.

In supervised learning, we start with some observations for which a particular label (such as an outcome) is known, and use them to learn what that label will *probably* be in cases where it is unknown. The patterns that we learn are the 'model', and the process of producing the model is 'training'. Fed the same type of data (without the label), the model will output its guess(es) about what the label should be. The output from the algorithm can be a continuous value, as in the case of regression analysis, or a nominal category, as in classification analysis. A supervised learning algorithm generalizes the training data to unknown situations in a way that is reasonable; part of the algorithm determines what 'reasonable' is, usually by penalizing wrong guesses. In games, supervised learning can be used when we can observe a behaviour for some users (they stop playing, convert from a non-paying to a paying user, purchase different types of items, etc.), and we want to determine how likely it is that other players will exhibit the same behaviour. Churn- and purchase-prediction analyses in free-to-play games are heavy users of supervised learning techniques.

Unsupervised learning also fits a model to observations, but unlike supervised learning, there is no predetermined label to learn. Instead, the input variables are treated as random, and a density model is built for the data set. The algorithm looks for 'natural' patterns: collections of observations that are similar to one another but meaningfully distinct from others. In GA, unsupervised learning can be particularly useful when looking for general associations rather than direct behavioural links. For example, in a massively multiplayer shooter like Destiny, we might look for distinct (or somewhat distinct) player types in the activities users choose to engage with using a clustering algorithm, and then plan our next content release so that each of these types has something new to suit their play style. We might also examine how these types overlap other player classifications we are interested in: do our Downloadable Content (DLC)-purchasing players come predominantly from one or two types, perhaps?

19.4 Game analytics for Games User Research

Now that we have covered the basics of GA's methodologies and tools, in this section it is time to look at how we can apply analytics to boost GUR. User-focused GA has much to offer GUR, and vice versa, but in order to obtain this synergy you have to specifically tailor the two processes to work together. If, in your organization, one discipline is well-developed but the other is absent, do not despair! It's definitely possible for one team to extend their skills a bit (usually learning some SQL for querying databases or other coding in the case of dedicated GUR, or some GUR techniques in the case of dedicated analysts) and gain some entry-level benefits of this synergy without building an entirely new discipline.

19.4.1 Precise behavioural recording

Possibly the most powerful single application of analytics to GUR is triangulating data sources obtained via 'normal' user testing with in-game behavioural metrics. This is so valuable that it is close to being common practice to collect at least some basic metrics during user testing sessions—at least within medium-to-large companies and publishers. We only have to look at some of the pioneering work done at Microsoft Studios Research from the mid- to late-2000s on to see why. Back then Microsoft developed a set-up referred to as TRUE, which essentially combined several different data channels employed in user testing with in-game behavioural metrics. For example, in Halo 3, as game testers played the missions and their screens were captured, interviews performed, and so on, the locations where they died, eliminated enemies, found items, etc. were also recorded and displayed on maps of the game environment. This allowed the user researchers to provide incredibly detailed analyses of, for instance, progression problems. When compiling the findings from a testing session, we have a record of the user's behaviours that is much more searchable than hours of video footage. This makes chasing down hypotheses much more efficient; if you suspect that a player became confused because they encountered X before seeing Y, it is an easy matter to find other test subjects who had the same experience and see if they were also confused (and if players without that experience were not confused).

19.4.2 Triangulation

GUR analyses the behaviour of relatively small numbers of players but tends to understand their motivations very well. GA analyses the behaviour of a virtually unlimited number of players, but can only guess at their motivations. By locating players in the GA analysis who have similar behavioural traces to the ones observed in the GUR analysis, we can begin to infer, with some margin of error, the motivations of the much larger population. We can also go some way towards determining whether the users we observe in the GUR lab are typical of users in the larger population, or if they are exceptional in some way. Demonstrating that GUR subjects are representative of players in general can do a great deal to improve confidence in GUR results among other teams. Finally, if GUR can identify behaviours that indicate a player is having a problem or conversely a good user experience, analysts can go look for players with the same behaviors within the larger population.

19.4.3 Extended reach

GA extends the ways in which we can investigate how people interact with games. Traditional user testing is done in labs or possibly in the field (i.e. the natural environment of the players). GA extends our capacity for recording player behaviour when they are playing in their natural environment. There is no need to enforce a lab-based setting, and no bias is imposed by the tracking itself, as it is mostly invisible to the user. We can track everything players do, to the limits of our instrumentation, not only inside the game environment but sometimes on their pathway to the game environment, via third-party data.

19.4.4 Large-scale analysis

GA further extends GUR by enabling the tracking of behaviours from the entire population of players, as well as to some degree the ecosystem around a specific game. For example, we can obtain additional data from a game on Steam, or associated information for Facebook-hosted games. Large-scale analysis brings with it its own challenges, but the value of being able to verify small-scale findings at the population level should not be underestimated.

19.4.5 New data sources, more knowledge

Behavioural telemetry from game clients is just one of the new sources of data offered by analytics. We can merge data streams to obtain insights, and this goes for connecting GUR not only with behavioural telemetry but also marketing data, benchmarks, demographic information, attribution models, social media data, etc. While a deep integration of data sources is, at the time of writing, still somewhat limited in the game industry, the potential for using these varied sources of data to drive better user experiences and extending market reach is definitely present.

19.4.6 Live hypothesis testing

One of the key methods in user-focused analytics is A/B (or 'split-level') testing. This refers to the practice of delivering a specific change, update, or feature tweak to a specific sample of players, and comparing the behaviour of this experimental group to a similar sample which has not been subjected to the change. Multiple different versions of features, mechanics, etc. can be tested at the same time. This complicates the statistical evaluation somewhat, but provides us with the ability to run empirical hypothesis-testing experiments across large sections of the player population, towards optimizing various KPIs, from user experience to monetization.

19.4.7 Incorporating business metrics

This is a subtle advantage, but powerful in practice. Commonly, it is the role of analytics is to deliver data to drive high-level business decisions, but often such insights are disassociated from GUR work. However, these insights become much more powerful when combined with user testing, not the least because this allows us to start generating ideas about why specific behaviours occur: 'Why does Feature X test well, and how can we use that to drive retention in the future?'. Essentially, GA provides a bridge for GUR (and more specific UX) work to reach the higher managerial levels of decision making.

19.4.8 Numbers

It may be obvious at this point, but numbers lend themselves well to communicating with various stakeholders from design to management, because they are eminently explainable. A well-developed analysis with clear, concise numbers backing it up is inherently convincing, and in much less space than a detailed playtesting report with dozens of quotes from players. On the other hand, we have to be careful not to be blinded by numbers, and always be aware of the limitations attached to the explanatory value of a number. A common problem in analytics, for example, is to consider KPIs such as 'daily active users' (DAU) and interpret them based on preconceptions of their meaning without full understanding of what factors impact them. For example, if we observe our DAU increasing 10% this week, but our user retention has halved, then on the whole we are probably doing worse, not better. We are bringing more users through the door, but they are not sticking around. KPIs and other numbers always have to be dealt with in the context they are generated.

19.5 Summary

In this chapter we have attempted to provide a very condensed introduction to game analytics for the aspiring or professional Games User Researcher. We hope we succeeded in providing a succinct overview of how analysts work and think, and how this ties in with, and adds value to, GUR. In practice, it is not always the case that GUR and GA are intrinsically linked in organizations, but they very much should be, as in games they operate under very similar principles and with a large degree of overlap in purpose. Analytics is highly important in game development, and a fantastic source for information to drive and reinforce user research.

Useful reads and image sources

Drachen, A., Rattinger, A., Sifa, R., Wallner, G., Pirker, J. (2016). Playing with friends in Destiny. https://andersdrachen.com/publications-2/

El-Nasr, M. S., Drachen, A., Canossa, A. (2013). Game analytics: maximizing the value of player data. New York: Springer Publishers.

Fields, T., Cotton, C. (2011). Social game design: monetization methods and mechanics. Baton Rouge, FL: Morgan Kaufmann Publishers.

Han, J., Kamber, M., Pei, J. P. (2011). Data mining: concepts and techniques. Baton Rouge, FL: Morgan Kaufmann Publishers.

James, G., Witten, D., Hastie, T., Tibshirani, R. (2013). An introduction to statistical learning. New York: Springer.

Seufert, E. B. (2014). Freemium economics: leveraging analytics and user segmentation to drive revenue. Boca Raton, FL: Morgan Kaufmann Publishers.

Schubert, M., Drachen, A., Mahlmann, T. (2016). Esports analytics through encounter detection. In Proceedings of the 10th MIT Sloan Sports Analytics Conference. http://www.sloansportsconference.com/wp-content/uploads/2016/02/1458.pdf

PART III

Case Studies and Focus Topics

Punching above your weight: how small studios can leverage data for an unfair advantage

LYSIANE CHAREST, *Outerminds*

Highlights

This chapter is aimed at small-to-medium-sized studios wanting to introduce analytics into their development process. It focuses on concepts and techniques that are most useful for smaller studios, and that require minimal skills. While money is always an issue, plenty of free analytics tools exist, whether they are third-party tools or simple in-house solutions. The chapter details how the most important factor is the availability of human resources and gives specific application examples.

20.1 Introduction

A common misconception about analytics is that they are mostly useful when working on a mobile free-to-play (F2P) title. However, it has been years since larger AAA studios have been using data to inform their design decisions and build stronger IPs, and there are no reasons why smaller studios could not harness the power of data to improve their games, too. This chapter is aimed

Games User Research, Anders Drachen, Pejman Mirza-Babaei, Lennart E. Nacke (Eds).
© Oxford University Press 2018. Published 2018 by Oxford University Press

primarily at small-to-medium-sized game studios and micro-studios wanting to integrate analytics into their development process.

There is a plethora of articles, blogs, forums, and books discussing game analytics. However, only a few of them are written with the needs and resources of smaller studios in mind. In this chapter, we will focus solely on concepts and techniques that tend to be the most useful for smaller studios and that require minimal skills.

Small-to-medium-sized studios are often limited by the money they can invest in a particular project. In many cases, the budget they can allocate to analytics is nearing $0. Luckily, this reality does not prevent them from implementing and using game analytics. Plenty of free analytics tools exist, whether they are third-party tools or simple in-house solutions. In fact, while money needs to be considered, it is not the most important factor; the availability of human resources is.

Over the last few years, I've partnered with nearly two dozen studios working on games for various platforms and business models, advising them on how to use analytics at their advantage. In a small studio of three-to-six developers, development time is precious, and every minute spent on the analytics needs to be well thought out. We have seen great success implementing analytics with multiple studios of this size, and this chapter presents the approach that they used to start implementing and using analytics for gameplay fine tuning and more economics-related data.

20.2 Getting started with game analytics

20.2.1 Development stages

It is never too soon to start thinking about analytics and how to use them to improve a game and guide design decisions.

During the concept and design phases, the focus should be on identifying the high-level metrics and key performance indicators (KPIs) that matter for this particular title, the market benchmarks for these metrics, and the studio's targets. Knowing these is especially useful when seeking investment or publishing support.

Once the pre-production and production start, analytics should become a lot more tangible; it is time to define the data needs, implement the tracking accordingly, and start collecting data. In pre-production, the game starts small and grows with every iteration, and so should the analytics. If it is never too soon to start thinking about analytics, it is also never too late to start it, and it is possible to start thinking about and implementing analytics at a later stage of development—even after its launch (Figure 20.1).

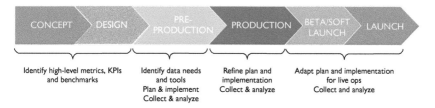

Figure 20.1 Example of development stages and their corresponding analytics efforts.

During the soft launch or during beta tests, analytics are a huge part of the iteration process with real players' data being collected and analysed on each iteration. During the pre-production and the production phases, collecting data is more challenging because the game is not entirely ready. Small- and medium-scale playtests and closed alpha tests are a good source of data during these phases (See Chapter 21 for more details about this).

20.2.2 Asking the right questions

The first step to start implementing and using analytics is to think about which questions need to be answered. In general, game and level designers can easily come up with some assumptions they would like to test. Section 20.4 gives multiple real-life examples of common areas of interests that can be looked at with analytics.

For each element to test, it is important to understand the underlying design intent. For instance, when building a new level, the question could be 'Is the level's difficulty well-balanced?' and the design intent could be 'Almost every player should eventually succeed the level in five tries or less but not on the first try.'

Once the questions and the design intents are defined, it is time to determine if and how game analytics can be useful to address them. It can be done in two steps: First, determine which measures can help answer the questions by validating, invalidating, or quantifying the phenomenon. Second, determine which events the programmers will have to track in the game to be able to calculate these measures (Figure 20.2).

Figure 20.2 Example of the process to go from questions to events definition.

It can be hard to distinguish measures from events, but this step is indispensable to generate simple yet useful events that can be used in many contexts (Table 20.1). A measure ascertains the size, amount, or degree of 'something' while an event is a discrete record of an activity or an action. It includes active interactions of the player with the game, such as when the player clicks on the start mission button, and passive interactions, such as when the 'rate us' window pops up to the player.

Each tracked event can hold additional information in parameters. These parameters give further information on the context in which the event happened. For example, if an analytic call is triggered when a player starts a mission, it should have a parameter indicating the name of the mission.

Table 20.1 *Examples of measures and events*

Examples of measures
the frequency of an event (in total, per player, per session or per day)
the number of players performing an action or a set of actions (in total or per day)
the proportion of players performing an action or a set of actions
the frequency of an event with a breakdown by one of its parameters

Examples of events
starting/finishing a session
upgrading an inventory item
getting a reward
entering/leaving a particular game area

Examples of what is not an event
a battle is not an event
the start and the end of a battle are events that describe a battle
the things that happen during a battle can also be events
being a level 7 character is not an event
levelling up from level 6 to level 7 is an event
starting a session while being a level 7 character is an event

Tips:

- Keep the measures and events simple. Complex measures or events often indicate that the question you have should not be answered with analytics. Many other GUR methods can be used to address your questions.
- The players' progression or their degree of experience with the game is a useful parameter to include in each of your events. It allows you to look at rookie and expert players separately, for example.

20.3 Implementation

This section gives a short overview of what an analytics system can look like and how to choose it.

20.3.1 In-game event tracking and documentation

Regardless of the tools used to implement the analytics, in-game events have a very similar structure (Table 20.2).

Table 20.2 *Example of a standard event structure*

Information	Additional Comments
Event name	Indicate which action happened. Should use verbs and action words.
User ID	Identify who performed the action or to whom it happened. If the game has a back-end, it should use the same user ID.
Timestamp	Indicate when the action was performed. The time zones need to be handled -> UTC or local?
Session ID	Uniquely identify the play session for this user. Most of the time, it is created automatically in third-party tracking tools. This ID can be unique across all users or unique for this user specifically. For instance, the session count is a unique session ID for a user.
Build version	Indicate the current build version. It can easily be automated, and it saves a lot of time when analysing specific versions of the game.
Platform	Ex. iOS, Android, Windows, Amazon, web, browser name, etc.
Device/OS/ hardware	Indicate any technical details that are important to the game. For example, controller vs. keyboard.
Event parameters	Indicate any additional parameter specific to the event.

Tip:

- Third-party solutions that do not support the custom events' parameters should not be considered as they significantly limit the flexibility of the analysis that can be done.

The tracking plan should document all the events that need to be tracked. Table 20.3 illustrates what such a document can look like.

Table 20.3 *Example of a tracking plan*

Event Name	Event Description	Trigger(s)	Parameters Name	Parameters Description	Parameters Values
StartMission	the player starts a mission	the mission fully loaded	UserID	Unique ID of the user	string
			TimeStamp	UTC timestamp	datetime
			SessionID	Unique ID of the session	int
			Platform	Platform of the player	PC or PS4
			BuildVersion	Version number	Ex. 1.12.74
			PlayerLevel	Level of the player	int
			MissionName	Unique mission name	string
SucceedMission	the player succeeded a mission	the success pop-up appeared	UserID	Unique ID of the user	string
			TimeStamp	UTC timestamp	datetime
			SessionID	Unique ID of the session	int
			Platform	Platform of the player	PC or PS4
			BuildVersion	Version number	Ex. 1.12.74
			PlayerLevel	Level of the player	int
			MissionName	Unique mission name	string
			Number Of Stars	Number of stars from 1 to 3 received by the player for this mission	int

...

20.3.2 Game analytics tools

The choice of an analytics solution depends on many factors. Costs, supported platforms, robustness, and availability of specific visualizations/analysis are all important things to look at. The game's monetization strategy (F2P, premium, DLC), the targeted platforms, and whether or not the game will be soft launched are even more important criteria to consider. Moreover, the more data-driven a studio wants to be, the more flexible their tools need to be.

An analytics solution can be as simple as adding an event-logging system that collects player actions in the game and saves them locally. It can also send the data to a server that validates the HTTP requests and writes the results to a flat file. The Figure 20.3 shows a more complex system that receives and pulls data from many sources. This data can then be analysed in any spreadsheet software.

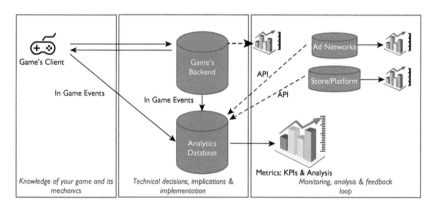

Figure 20.3 Example of a complete analytics infrastructure.

The entire team needs to be involved, whether it is in the planning, the implementation, the analysis, or the interpretation of the output. There also needs to be someone in charge. This person will make sure analytics are happening! A single person can hold all of these roles or the responsibilities can be shared across many people. In general, game designers and producers are good candidates to be in charge of analytics and take care of the interpretation of the data, as well as making sure it has an impact during the game development. Programmers tend to be better at planning and implementing the tracking, based on the questions asked by the team, and preparing the data for interpretation.

20.4 Real-life examples

Even though every game is a snowflake, there are some commonalities, and for most games, a lot of the questions and assumptions revolve around the same themes.

This section includes multiple examples from real-life situations where analytics were used to answer development needs.

20.4.1 First-time user experience and training

Providing a good first-time user experience to new players, whether it is with a scripted tutorial or not, is one of the most important factors of a game's success. Analytics can provide a lot of pertinent information to help optimize this aspect.

20.4.1.1 SCRIPTED TUTORIAL

When a game has a tutorial, the tutorial completion rate needs to be tracked to know the proportion of players who start and complete it. It is also important to include in-game events to identify where people get stuck and drop off from the tutorial. Every mandatory step of the tutorial should be tracked in a way that they can easily be used to build funnels to identify where players are having more difficulties.

In the example shown in Table 20.4, the developers sliced their tutorial into nine steps and collected data during their soft launch. For ease of reading, the most important information in the table is in bold.

Figure 20.4 shows the proportion of new players retained for each step of the tutorial. It is calculated by dividing the number of players reaching a particular step by the number of players who started the game at least once. The higher the percentage, the better it is. This way of presenting a funnel is very common, but it can be hard to identify which step should get closer attention.

Figure 20.5 uses the same data, but it shows the proportion of players who dropped off from the previous step. For instance, in Step 7, the percentage is obtained by subtracting the number of players who reached this step from the number of players who reached Step 6 and dividing the result by the number of players from Step 6. The lower the proportion is, the better it is. In this example, it is easy to notice the bigger drops after Step 3 and Step 7. These steps require some attention from the team.

Table 20.4 *Extract of the tracking plan for the tutorial steps events*

Event Name	Event Description	Trigger(s)	Parameters Name	Parameters Description	Parameters Values
Tutorial - Step1 (name)	*the player performs the action _____ as part of the tutorial.*	*Step 1 is completed*	*UserID*	*Unique ID of the user*	*string*
			TimeStamp	*UTC timestamp*	*datetime*
			SessionID	*Unique ID of the session*	*int*
			Platform	*Platform of the player*	*PC or PS4*
			BuildVersion	*Version number*	*Ex. 1.12.74*
			StepNumber	*Index of this tutorial step*	*int*
...					
Tutorial - StepX (name)	*the player performs the action _____ as part of the tutorial.*	*Step X is completed*	*UserID*	*Unique ID of the user*	*string*
			TimeStamp	*UTC timestamp*	*datetime*
			SessionID	*Unique ID of the session*	*int*
			Platform	*Platform of the player*	*PC or PS4*
			BuildVersion	*Version number*	*Ex. 1.12.74*
			StepNumber	*Index of this tutorial step*	*int*

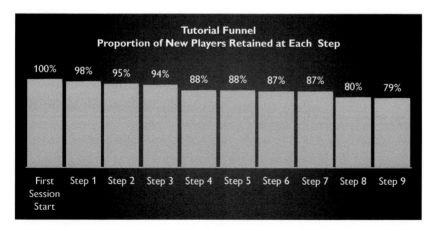

Figure 20.4 Proportion of the new players retained from the first application launch to each step of the tutorial.

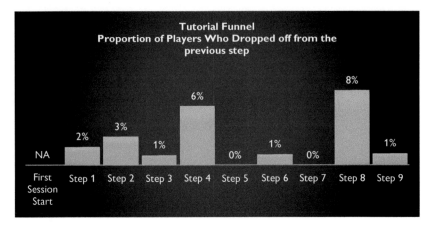

Figure 20.5 Proportion of the players who dropped off from the previous step during the tutorial.

Tip:

- Sometimes, improving the current funnel is not the best option. A complete redesign can lead to better results. For example, the current tutorial may not use the correct approach for the type of users who are playing your game.

20.4.1.2 TRAINING

In the case discussed next, the studio was working on a mobile application with innovative touch controls. In the first four levels of the game, the players learn how to move, punch, and perform uppercuts. In the fifth level, they learn how to throw things and enemies.

An event is triggered each time a player performs the touch movement to throw something (Table 20.5). One of the parameters indicates if the throw was successful (i.e. the character was able to grab something and throw it as opposed to doing the movement while not in a range of an object that can be thrown).

Figure 20.6 shows that once the players are taught how to throw, in the fifth level, the proportion of failed throw attempts drops significantly, indicating that the training is adequate. These numbers are obtained by dividing the number of successful throw attempts by the total number of throw attempts for each level.

Table 20.5 *Extract of the tracking plan for the throw attempts event*

Event Name	Event Description	Trigger(s)	Parameters Name	Parameters Description	Parameters Values
AttemptThrow	*the player attempts to throw something.*	*the touch movement to perform a throw was detected (circle)*	*UserID*	*Unique ID of the user*	*string*
			TimeStamp	*UTC timestamp*	*datetime*
			SessionID	*Unique ID of the session*	*int*
			Platform	*Platform of the player*	*PC or PS4*
			BuildVersion	*Version number*	*Ex. 1.12.74*
			LevelName	*Name of the level*	*string*
			Success	*Indicates if the player successfully grabbed something and threw it*	*boolean*

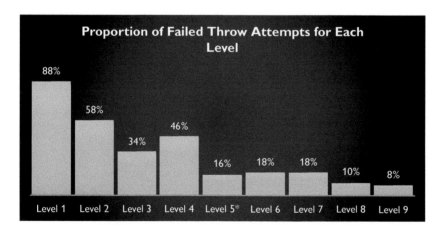

Figure 20.6 Proportion of the failed throw attempts for each level.

20.4.2 Players progression

20.4.2.1 DIFFICULTY AND BALANCING

In the following example, the development team wanted to get a better understanding of the difficulty of their levels. To achieve that, they implemented tracking at the beginning and the end of each level (Table 20.6).

Table 20.6 *Extract of the tracking plan for the level starts and level successes events*

Event Name	Event Description	Trigger(s)	Parameters Name	Parameters Description	Parameters Values
StartLevel	*the player starts a level*	*the level fully loaded*	*UserID*	*Unique ID of the user*	*string*
			TimeStamp	*UTC timestamp*	*datetime*
			SessionID	*Unique ID of the session*	*int*
			Platform	*Platform of the player*	*PC or PS4*
			BuildVersion	*Version number*	*Ex. 1.12.74*
			LevelName	*Name of the level*	*string*
			TryNumber	*Number of times the player started this level*	*int*
SucceedLevel	*the player succeeded a level*	*the success pop-up appeared*	*UserID*	*Unique ID of the user*	*string*
			TimeStamp	*UTC timestamp*	*datetime*
			SessionID	*Unique ID of the session*	*int*
			Platform	*Platform of the player*	*PC or PS4*
			BuildVersion	*Version number*	*Ex. 1.12.74*
			LevelName	*Name of the level*	*string*
			TryNumber	*Number of times the player started this level*	*int*

In Figure 20.7, the unique success rate for each level is obtained by dividing the number of players who start each level by the number of players who succeed that level. This chart seems to show that every level is equally easy, with almost all the players succeeding them. However, one playthrough of the game is enough to know that this is far from being the case! Some levels feel like they are almost impossible to complete. In fact, this chart simply tells us that the levels are not impossible to succeed, but it does not tell us how hard it is to succeed them.

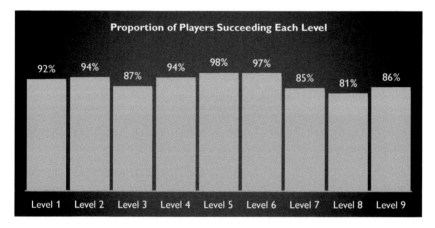

Figure 20.7 Proportion of the players succeeding each level.

In Figure 20.8, the same metric is broken down by the number of tries to succeed the level. It becomes apparent that the levels are not all of the same difficulty, with some levels often succeeded on the first try and some of them almost

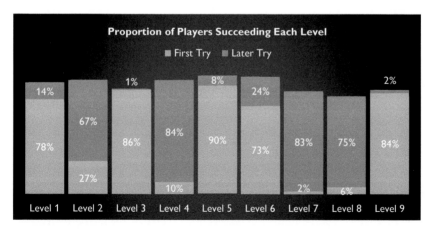

Figure 20.8 Proportion of the players succeeding each level on the first try or on a later attempt.

never succeeded on the first attempt. With this information, the level designers can take a closer look at the levels with a very small percentage of success on the first try to make sure these levels are not too frustrating and that the players enjoy the challenge. They can also use this information to reorder some levels to keep the players motivated and challenged at all times.

20.4.2.2 PROGRESSION AND ENGAGEMENT

In the next example, the development team knew that their retention figures were too low, and they wanted to understand at which point players were disengaging with the game. During the first session, the players start an introductory level that teaches them the basics of the game. After this introduction, the players are expected to keep going for other expeditions until they have had enough. The initial thought was that players who like their experience would do between three and four expeditions on their first day.

In addition to the number of new users (first app launch), the team implemented tracking at the beginning of each expedition (Table 20.7).

Table 20.7 *Extract of the tracking plan for the expedition starts event*

Event Name	Event Description	Trigger(s)	Parameters Name	Parameters Description	Parameters Values
StartExpedition	*the player leaves for an expedition*	*the player clicks on 'Start Expedition'*	*UserID*	*Unique ID of the user*	*string*
			TimeStamp	*UTC timestamp*	*datetime*
			SessionID	*Unique ID of the session*	*int*
			Platform	*Platform of the player*	*PC or PS4*
			BuildVersion	*Version number*	*Ex. 1.12.74*
			Expedition Number	*Number of times the player left for an expedition*	*int*

Figure 20.9 shows the funnel from the first time the players launch the application up to their third expedition. The low proportion of players reaching the introductory expedition suggests that the problem comes from very early on in the game since a good number of players don't even play the introductory level.

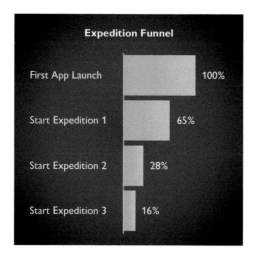

Figure 20.9 Proportion of the players retained from the first application launch to the next expedition.

20.4.3 Level design: maps and scenes

For games heavily relying on maps/scenes, using geospatial data can be a good way to answer complex questions. Geospatial data can be used to build heat maps when precise coordinates are recorded with the events. It can also be analysed in a more macro way using zones and regions (with tables or charts) as shown in the following example.

The development team wanted to add checkpoints where players spawn each time they die in a level. To help them identify adequate locations to place these points, they sliced each level into ten zones of equal size and tracked deaths in each of these one-dimensional regions (Table 20.8).

Figure 20.10 shows the number of deaths per zone in four different levels. For an external observer, these histograms are very generic but for the development team, they are very informative since they perfectly know the layout of each of the levels in the game, and they know where Zone 2 and Zone 3 are located. With these charts, they can better decide where to place the spawn points.

With precise two-dimensional coordinates (horizontal and vertical), they were also able to draw two-dimensional heat maps. Figured 20.11 shows the deaths' heat map for Level 1. This level takes place in a three-storey house, and the two-dimensional heat map gives more details on where the deaths are concentrated.

Table 20.8 *Extract of the tracking plan for the players' deaths event*

Event Name	Event Description	Trigger(s)	Parameters Name	Parameters Description	Parameters Values
PlayerDeath	*the player dies*	*the player reaches 0 health*	*UserID*	*Unique ID of the user*	*string*
			TimeStamp	*UTC timestamp*	*datetime*
			SessionID	*Unique ID of the session*	*int*
			Platform	*Platform of the player*	*PC or PS4*
			BuildVersion	*Version number*	*Ex. 1.12.74*
			LevelName	*Name of the level*	*string*
			Zone	*Region where the player died (1 to 10)*	*int*

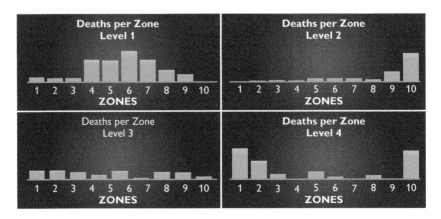

Figure 20.10 Repartition of the players' deaths per zone in four different levels.

Figure 20.11 Heat map of the players' deaths in Level 1.

When maps are too complicated to easily read their corresponding heat maps without seeing them at the same time, it is always possible to overlay the heat maps with the levels, as in Figure 20.12. In this example from another game, three areas, one with spikes and two with spinning saws, are easily identified as the deadliest zones in the level.

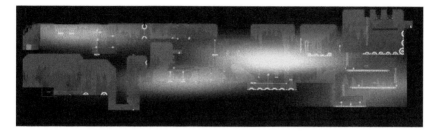

Figure 20.12 Heat map of the players' deaths with an overlay of the level.

20.4.4 Monetization

Most people usually assume that for F2P games, monetization is the focus. While it is true that it is important, it should not be the primary focus when implementing analytics. In general, very few events are required to capture enough information to get a rough idea of the way people monetize in the game and identify major issues with the in-app purchase (IAP) funnel (Table 20.9).

In the following example, the development team wanted to simplify some interface elements in their menus and wanted to know if they could remove some points of entry to the store. By tracking the first three events from Table 20.9, they were able to prepare the following table (Table 20.10) showing the transaction funnel for each point of entry in the store. The player versus environment (PVE) combat menu, the navigation menu, the crafting menu, and the player versus player (PVP) combat menu all have a very small percentage of successful purchases compared to visits. The PVE combat menu, however, still represents almost a quarter of all IAPs. It was decided to keep this point of entry but to modify the store to include more IAPs that fit the needs of someone coming from this menu. The management and collection menus have a relatively high proportion of successful purchases, and they represent a significant portion of the total transactions. These two menus were kept as entry points to the store. The three other points of entry were removed because they did not bring much value to the players or the game.

Table 20.9 *Extract of the tracking plan for the IAP-related events*

Event Name	Event Description	Trigger(s)	Parameters Name	Parameters Description	Parameters Values
IAP_ EnterStore	*the player enters the IAP store*	*the IAP store has loaded*	*UserID*	*Unique ID of the user*	*string*
			TimeStamp	*UTC timestamp*	*datetime*
			SessionID	*Unique ID of the session*	*int*
			Platform	*Platform of the player*	*PC or PS4*
			BuildVersion	*Version number*	*Ex. 1.12.74*
			PlayerLevel	*Level of the player*	*int*
			EnterFrom	*From where the player opened the store*	*string*
			HardCurrency Balance	*the amount of hard currency the player owns*	*int*
			SoftCurrency Balance	*the amount of soft currency the player owns*	*int*
IAP_Start	*the player initiates a transaction*	*the player pressed buy and is sent to the payment system*	*All parameters from IAP_EnterStore*		
			ItemId or ItemName	*Unique ID of the item Name works*	*string*
			ItemPrice	*the price in a fixed currency; do not use the player's currency*	*int*
IAP_ Succeed	*the transaction was successful*	*the payment system came back with the confirmation that the transaction was accepted*	*All parameters from IAP_EnterStore*		
			ItemId or ItemName	*Unique ID of the item*	*string*
			ItemPrice	*Item price*	*int*

continued

Table 20.9 *Continued*

Event Name	Event Description	Trigger(s)	Parameters Name	Parameters Description	Parameters Values
IAP_Failed	*the transaction was not successful*	*the payment system came back with the confirmation that the transaction was not accepted*	*All parameters from IAP_EnterStore*		
			ItemId or ItemName	*Unique ID of the item*	*string*
			ItemPrice	*Item price*	*int*
			FailReason	*Why the transaction was rejected: timedOut, notVerified, etc.*	*string*

Table 20.10 *Various figures describing the six entry points to the IAP store and the resulting transactions*

Menu	Enter Store	Start Purchase	Succeed Purchase	Proportion of All Purchases
Management	100 %	55 %	42 %	38 %
Collection	100 %	38 %	32 %	36 %
Combat – PVE	100 %	11 %	9 %	22 %
Navigation	100 %	10 %	9 %	2 %
Crafting	100 %	9 %	8 %	2 %
Combat – PVP	100 %	8 %	7 %	< 1 %

In another example, the development team was not interested in the monetization funnel but in knowing if the design encourages players to spend money at certain points in the game. For instance, it is expected that players will be able to go through the first three levels relatively easily. When the player reaches Level 4, the PVP combats are unlocked, which is expected to encourage some players to make their first transaction (Table 20.11). The highest level a player can reach is 7; at this point the competition level is pretty high: it should become almost necessary to make a transaction to be able to stay in the game.

Table 20.11 *Proportion of paying users and new paying users based on the player's level*

Player Level	Proportion of Paying Users	Proportion of New Paying Users
1	0.2 %	0.2 %
2	0.4 %	0.2 %
3	1.5 %	0.3 %
4	5.7 %	1.0 %
5	13.6 %	2.1 %
6	24.2 %	0.6 %
7	39.6 %	4.5 %

20.4.5 High-level metrics and key performance indicators

An important part of the game analytics field includes the measurement, monitoring, and presentation of metrics that are independent of the game mechanics themselves. These metrics include what are often called key performance indicators (KPIs), but are not limited to them.

The term KPI should, in theory, be strictly used for metrics that are essential to the company. In practice, it is often used to designate a set of industry standard metrics. Small studios often neglect to measure and monitor these metrics. Their limited resources make it hard for them to justify using a programmer's time to implement a piece of code that will have the sole purpose of telling them how many people play their game on a daily basis, for instance. However, as soon as they meet with a potential investor or a publisher, they quickly realize that high-level metrics matter. They form a common and standard way to communicate how good a game is with anyone in the industry. Most publishers will invest in a project if and only if the studio developing it can present good retention or engagement metrics.

This section gives a short introduction to some of the most important high-level metrics in the games industry. While some of these metrics do not apply to premium titles, many of them are still valid metrics, and maximizing engagement and growth has a big impact on any game, regardless of its business model.

20.4.5.1 HIGH-LEVEL BUSINESS-ORIENTED METRICS TO MONITOR

The following metrics should be monitored closely during and after the launch or soft launch.

- downloads/installs/new users
  - Downloads and installs figures are often made available by the platform holders. New users need to be tracked the first time the player launches the game. All third-party services provide a way to get this metric out of the box.
  - The three metrics will yield similar results. An important discrepancy often indicates that users are having trouble with installing (downloads >> installs) or launching the game (downloads or installs >> new users).

- active users
  - An active user is someone who launched the game in a given period. It is often measured daily (DAU), weekly (WAU), or monthly (MAU).

- number of sessions, median session time or average session time
  - The definition of a session can vary from one game to another and one tool to another, but in general it can be interpreted as a play session. It can potentially include short pauses.
  - Some games are designed to generate multiple short play sessions while others are designed to keep the players engaged for fewer but longer sessions.

- revenues and related metrics
  - ad revenue
    - provided by the ad networks
  - IAP and download revenue, number of transactions and refunds
    - provided by the platform holders
    - these figures will be slightly different than what the in-game analytics track. A significant discrepancy could indicate that players are cheating and creating false transactions.

20.4.5.2 HIGH-LEVEL METRICS TO BENCHMARK

The following metrics are useful to benchmark a game against other games but also to compare different iterations of the same game to make sure it is always improving. These metrics are often broken down by country, version, or platform.

- retention Day X (1, 3, 7, 14, 30)
  - The daily retention for Day X is the proportion of new players active exactly X days after they first played.

- Retention metrics are important after the launch to understand if people come back to play. This metric is an industry standard, and benchmarks for it can be found on various sites.

- average revenue per user
  - The average revenue per user (ARPU) is measured as the total revenue divided by the number of users for a given period. It includes revenue from downloads, virtual goods, and advertisement. The ARPU is often broken down by day to give the average revenue per daily paying user (ARPDAU).
  - The ARPDAU is an industry standard, and it is useful to compare the monetization for two different titles or periods.

- average revenue per paying user
  - The average revenue per paying user (ARPPU) shows how much, on average, each paying user is spending for a given period. It is often measured monthly but can also be measured daily or weekly.
  - The ARPPU can vary a lot from one game to another and is useful to get an idea of how good the game is at monetizing the paying users.

- percentage of paying users
  - The percentage of paying users can be measured per day, week, or month.
  - This metric is an industry standard, and it is useful to compare two games or periods. Benchmarks for this metric can easily be found.

20.5 Conclusion

Independent game studios and micro-studios can get a lot of value from using analytics throughout the development of their games. Because their resources are more limited than bigger studios, it is vital for them to plan ahead and make sure that they use analytics in a way that brings the most value without requiring substantial financial resources or specialized knowledge and competencies.

By starting small and increasing their use of analytics through each iteration of their games, they can achieve great results without putting too much pressure on the development team. The simple examples presented in this chapter are a good starting point to make sure to cover the main areas where analytics can bring them the most value. Techniques not presented in this chapter are also important to mention: predictive analysis and A/B testing in particular. These methods can be very effective when the number of players is high enough to yield significant results. However, they require such a big amount of work regarding both analysis and development that the return on investment is rarely positive for smaller studios, even when using third-party tools that promise the opposite.

Whether a game is still in its conceptual phase or if it is already on the market, it is always time to implement or use analytics. An increasing number of small studios are starting to use analytics in their day-to-day design decisions. Data can be a decision aid to improve game design, user experience, and monetization. It can also serve as an additional QA resource to detect bugs, and is an essential source of information for current and potential partners, including investors.

Further reading and external links

- www.gamesbrief.com
  This website primarily focused on F2P games is full of articles about analytics and design for F2P. Most of the articles are also pertinent for premium games.

- Hot failure: tuning gameplay with simple player metrics. http://www.gamasutra.com/view/feature/6155/hot_failure_tuning_gameplay_with_.php?print=1
  This 2010 article will never get old. 'In this article taken from Game Developer magazine's September 2010 issue, Google game developer advocate Chris Pruett describes how he quickly and cheaply implemented useful metrics into his android game, Replica Island.'

- Fields, T. V. (2013). Game industry metrics terminology and analytics case study. In M. G. El-Nasr et al. (eds), Game analytics: maximizing the value of player data (pp. 53–71). New York: Springer.
  In the fourth chapter of the book, Timothy Victor Fields gives an overview and definitions for industry standard metrics as well as a complete case study.

CHAPTER 21

Affordable and data-driven user research for indie studios

PEJMAN MIRZA-BABAEI, *Execution Labs and University of Ontario Institute of Technology*

THOMAS GALATI, *University of Ontario Institute of Technology*

Highlights

User research does not have to be expensive and time-consuming. In this chapter we focus on the specific situation where the resources, expertise, and time available for user testing is limited, as is usually the case for indie studios. This means adapting affordable and accessible user testing processes for indie studios. We emphasize the contribution of analytics techniques in this adaptation process, and describe different methods of how to incorporate analytics into other Games User Research (GUR) methods.

21.1 Introduction

We define *user testing* as a process by which developers will test their product (a game), or a prototype of their product, with a set of representative users. The goal of these tests is to evaluate if the product meets certain goals or design

Games User Research, Anders Drachen, Pejman Mirza-Babaei, Lennart E. Nacke (Eds).
© Oxford University Press 2018. Published 2018 by Oxford University Press

objectives as intended by the development team (Zammitto et al., 2014). The scale of these tests may vary, from testing enjoyment of the entire game, to something much smaller, like testing the effectiveness of a single tutorial level. A person designing, conducting, analysing, and reporting these tests is referred to as a *user researcher.*

User testing varies from product to product, and even varies depending on the stage of development. Small studios (often indie developers), with arguably limited resources, may find that user testing is difficult to conduct and question the return on investment (Mirza-Babaei et al., 2016). This can be due to a number of reasons, most notably because of a lack of knowledge on this topic, or as a result of limited manpower. A report by the Entertainment Software Association (see http://www.theesa.com/ for more details) indicates that almost a third of all gaming firms have four or fewer employees. It is unlikely that these small studios can afford to retain a dedicated user research specialist.

However, with an understanding of different adaptations of user testing approaches, as well as a breakdown of their advantages and disadvantages, user research can be optimised and made more affordable, without the need for a dedicated user research specialist. Understanding what tools and resources are available to small studios to conduct testing can be a huge boon to a product.

User testing is not a spontaneous activity it requires preparation and planning in order to maximize effectiveness. To begin with, it helps to have a goal in mind for a given test session. Knowing what to test for is as important as the process of testing itself. The goal of a user test will vary depending not only on the product at hand but also on the product's stage of development.

21.2 A typical usertest protocol

Testing starts with a build of a product that could be anywhere from a demo, to alpha build, to a near-final version. As a team or producer, it must be decided what the build is going to be tested for. Or, to put it differently, what is the goal of the user testing session? With the goal of the session in mind, the next step is to design the structure of the test. This involves describing the methods that will be used, as well as outlining and gathering participants. After this, the study can be run.

Depending on the methods chosen for testing, the data may be quick to analyse or require a period of time to sort through. From this data, a concise list of problems uncovered through the testing session should be made. This is in preparation to present or discuss the data with the development team. The data must be concise and easy to understand in order for the development team to make impactful changes and produce fixes to the current build (see Chapter 18 for more details on reporting user research findings). Once this has been completed, future play sessions with the adjusted build may be conducted.

21.2.1 Before planning a usertest session

Before planning a testing session, the objective of the test should be determined. Developers often struggle deciding what it is they want to test for. One way to help determine the objective of the test is to consider the potential player base. What are the player profiles? Knowing who is going to be playing the game can help narrow down what needs to be tested. Additionally, ensure the testing build can reliably answer the developers' questions. The goal of the test must be reflected in the capabilities of the current build.

21.2.2 Usability vs opinions

A common mistake when studios begin user testing is confusing a usability issue with an opinion-related issue. For example, usability issues could range from a player not using an intended mechanic to constantly skipping or missing areas in the game. Opinion-based issues deal with what the player wants the game to be like or how they feel about the game. This refers to what they think, feel, or state about the game. It is important to differentiate between these types of questions, as we need to design different test sessions for answering each.

21.3 The evaluation process

As mentioned earlier, knowing the goal of the testing session is an important step before testing begins. It dictates what testing methods are viable for the session.

21.3.1 Set-up

The next step is to set up the testing environment. A location is needed, and a protocol to follow for testing. Testing can be done in a controlled environment, such as a lab or testing room, or as simple as a room that only has the game and recording devices. A controlled environment is often ideal for a testing session to reduce the amount of interference possible, which may influence the feedback from the players.

21.3.2 Recruitment

The target audience of the game is who should be recruited to participate in the playtest. As game developers, those around you are mostly likely also game developers, so it is not sufficient to simply ask nearby developers to test. A player will have different views on the game than a developer. It is important to look beyond friends and family for testing a game. Advertising on various social media can help reduce the difficulty in recruitment. Larger studios have player recruitment application forms online that can be used as a reference for making custom recruitment forms.

Keep in mind that testers should be compensated for their time. Users who are compensated are more likely to return to help test again. As a long-term strategy, it is beneficial to create a database of players who are willing to come and test on future projects.

21.4 Methods for testing

The methods used for testing a product can vary greatly, as there are many options available. Different methods will be better at producing different information. Combining multiple testing types with a build or running different session types at different times can often provide better results than a single method. Earlier chapters have discussed user research methods in detail; here we provide a brief summary of the methods we utilized in our case studies. These include observation, interview, focus group, and game analytics.

21.4. 1 Observation

Observation is one of the more common user research methods. Observation involves members of the user research team or development team viewing (or reviewing) users' gameplay and interactions. This can be implemented in many ways, with the team watching a recording of a play session, a team watching a live play session from a separate room, or a team in the physical location of the session.

The observation method is easy to conduct and gives a large amount of data for the testers. The team can take recordings and notes at the time of testing. However, this method often feels intrusive to the user if the researcher is observing the session in the same room as the player. Another issue with this method is that although a large amount of data can be collected, it can be time-consuming to analyse large amounts of video data (see Chapter 11 for more details).

21.4.2 Interview and focus group

Interviews and focus groups are other common methods in user research. They allow for a deeper understanding of how players felt and the reasoning behind their actions during play. Interviews can give the team insights into how the player felt during play, why they performed certain actions, or problems they encountered that may have not been seen in other sessions. A focus group can be thought of as fairly similar to an interview, only with multiple people in the interview. The benefits of this method are that it allows for a largegroup discussion, where multiple users can collectively discuss topics and answer questions asked by the researcher.

Both methods have their own challenges. Both must be planned carefully, and questions asked have to be outlined so they are not *leading* or *loaded*. The researcher must be careful not to influence the user's responses. The user needs to feel they can respond freely. A downside of focus groups is that they are prone to a single person dominating conversation, with others simply going along with the loudest voice. Focus groups are also vulnerable to *groupthink*, which may be described as a desire for conformity when discussing a topic with a group of people. This could result in a flawed outcome, as group members try to minimize conflict within the group by suppressing contending viewpoints (see Chapter 10 for more details).

21.4.3 Game analytics

Game analytics is a broad topic, but essentially deals with the gathering and analysis of data towards driving decisions in game development. From our perspective, the focus is on recorded gameplay data, generally referred to as telemetry.

Behavioural telemetry typically involves in-game systems or third-party tools during play. These methods of gathering information are less intrusive than observation, and can provide a large range of data from the participants. With this method it is possible to access information that may be hard to uncover from an interview or questionnaire. Previous chapters (particularly Chapter 20) have discussed different methods of integrating analytics solutions with games, and how we can use collected data to draw conclusions.

Behavioural telemetry from games can be analysed in a variety of ways for different purposes. An example is heat maps, which show the distribution of something across a geographical area, for example, how long time people spend in specific areas or how often players die in specific locations. Another example is time-spent graphs, which show how long a player spends in a specific game mode, location, or other segment of a game (e.g. a graph could show the average time spent in different levels of a game). Analytics does not only deal with behavioural data, but can also integrate measures from user testing. There are hundreds of examples of analyses from games contexts available; they all provide data-driven information on game design and production.

Analytics, while certainly effective if used after game launch, can also be used to great effect during the testing phases of a product. In fact, analytics can be used from the earliest design phases, where, for example, quantifying the intended player behaviour can drive later comparisons with actual player behaviour.

21.5 Case studies

By way of examples, we discuss two case studies where we designed and conducted a number of user tests on two commercial games under development. Understanding that, as mentioned earlier, each user research method has weaknesses, we attempted to circumvent these limitations by combining different methodologies. The two games were a puzzle/platformer and a multiplayer online game.

21.5.1 Case 1: Puzzle/Platformer

The puzzle/platformer game was a linear, level-by-level game experience. Early in development, we were tasked with ensuring that there were no major usability issues and determining if the challenge of the game scaled appropriately with the introduction of new mechanics. The game was still fairly early in development, so to reduce costs we decided to limit the number of testing participants but would conduct multiple rounds of testing. Research suggests that majority of usability issues in a given product build can be uncovered by fewer than ten users. By the same token, more important issues are identified more easily than less important ones, allowing us to find issues more efficiently (see Chapter 13 on the RITE approach for more details).

As a goal of the user test sessions was to highlight major usability issues, we decided to test the first hour of gameplay. Using the resources we had, we conducted our sessions with one user at a time. Hence, we determined that one-on-one interviews after a play session would be an ideal method to combine with our gameplay observation. Problem arises, however: after a long playtest of several levels, it is difficult for users to remember if they encountered certain issues on given levels. Our challenge, then, was to come up with a way to identify users' issues in the game without demanding players to recall all of them.

In this game, as is typical of a platformer, players fail the level when coming into contact with hazards. Introducing mechanics to navigate around those hazards is what allows for fun gameplay. We wanted to test if each of the mechanics for avoiding the hazards was well received by players, or if users might be experiencing too much difficulty with the mechanics. We determined if the mechanics that are added were done well, players would not die as frequently while using them. Therefore, we chose to record where (the x, y coordinates) in a level a player died (to see if the mechanics are being taught properly) and how many times a player died in a given level (to see if any levels seem more difficult than others). As an extension of this, we can record the time spent on a level, to see if any individual levels are more problematic than others (i.e., do they take significantly more time to complete than the other levels?).

An extension of what we can consider a failure or difficulty spike in this game are locations where the player repeatedly tries to perform a jump spike in the same area. This is, after all, a platformer game, so jumping in the same area a lot might mean that the user is failing at a jump that is not around hazards—so it will not trigger our death events, but could still indicate difficulty. For this reason, we chose to also record the location (x, y coordinates) of a player's jump. All together, these are simple metrics which can be logged and uploaded to a server.

We determined first if any levels were particularly out-of-line with respect to number of deaths (see Figure 21.1). In those out-of-line levels, we considered heat maps of the player deaths and jumps (Figure 21.2), to identify the most difficult areas of the level. The heat maps showed if users were properly learning new mechanics, or if perhaps a level had just been designed to be too difficult.

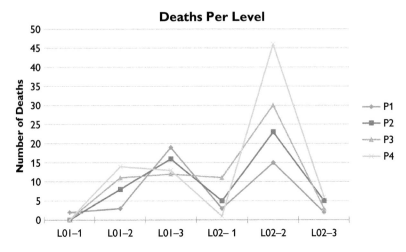

Figure 21.1 Number of deaths per player per level. Note in Level 02–2 (second from the right), there is a disproportionate number of deaths.

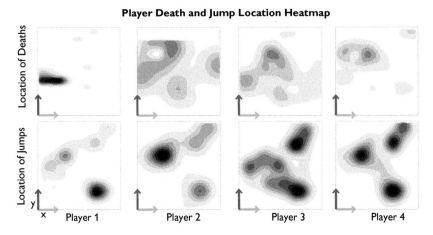

Figure 21.2 Location of player deaths (top row) and player jumps (bottom row) for the playtesters on Level 02–2. Certain areas show repeat failures, and may be worth closer investigation.

Takeaway: Combining metrics which were relatively simple to collect and analyse (number of deaths per level, location of deaths, location of jumps) with the reviewing of recorded gameplay videos and post-gameplay interviews helped us to optimize our time when we analysed the data. For example, rather than reviewing all recorded videos, we could use the number of deaths per level to identify potentially problematic levels. Then, we could use location of deaths and jumps to narrow down our focus to the areas with potential issues in those levels. Finally, we could review gameplay videos for these selected areas to identify possible causes of each issue. These potential issues could be discussed with players in the post-session interviews to help us identify the main flaws underlying problematic areas or scenarios.

21.5.2 Case 2: Stream Game

The next case study is a multiplayer online game. Player interaction was through the use of a specific currency, which could be used to purchase items that would impact the gameplay. Currency management was the main mechanic for the players. The goal of our user test was to evaluate the currency system of the game and user spending habits.

We wanted to evaluate how impactful it was for a player to make purchases. As this was an online game, which was to be played over a set play time, we knew all of our participants would be playing at the same time. Because of this scenario, we chose to have all the users in our test session play the game in the same general area as other online players. We then conducted a focus group to gather collective feedback with all users participating in the test session. We had to ensure that the focus group discussion would be centred on the main research question (currency management). To accomplish this, we tracked user information, time, and purchase information for every single change-of-currency event

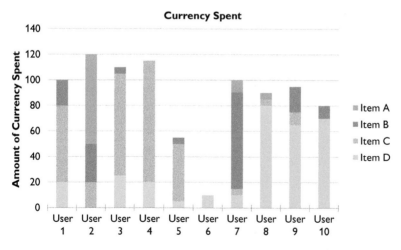

Figure 21.3 Amount of currency spent per player per item. This lets us know the spending habits of the different users.

in the database. It was very important for us to know the total amount spent by users and the breakdown of spending between items. We then created database queries that would format the data in various pivot tables (see Figure 21.3). These prepared queries allowed for short-term rapid analysis of the data.

Takeaway: Rapid analysis helped us form effective, targeted questions about player spending habits, and we were able to modify the focus group script on the fly. As an example, User 2 was the only one who did not buy Item D but did not comment on this until it was brought up in the analysis. This opened up more discussion on what the players felt were the most impactful items, as we could ask them very specifically about their purchases.

21.6 Conclusion and recommendations

The case studies highlight the benefits of combining analytics with other research methods. Understanding this, we now discuss general approaches that user researchers might take to adding analytics to typical evaluation methods.

21.6.1 Focus groups + analytics

As mentioned earlier, the weakness of focus groups is that there is the potential for one member of the group to dominate the discussion. As in the case study described earlier, we recommend having recorded metrics on hand in order to help guide discussion and reduce the effect of groupthink. The use of analytics can help eliminate bias and potentially reduce the effect of one speaker influencing the opinions of others. For example, if the majority of a group states that an item in a sample game was useless, but metrics indicate that one or more users made significant use of that item, we can inquire further with those users. In a setting without metrics, we may not know how frequently a player used an item, and the user may have remained quiet.

21.6.2 Interviews + analytics

Metric analysis for an individual user's gameplay session can be used to improve targeted feedback. This is beneficial because, even if a user may forget specific issues they had when playing the game, data would still capture those issues, and a user may be reminded of any difficulties. This is true for all different interview types.

Collecting metrics could simplify some of the questions that might be asked of a participant by using the data to extract partial answers for certain questions. This can also be used to see if the user fully understands the systems that are being evaluated, by contrasting an answer they may give with the facts revealed by the metrics. Using metrics, researchers can come up with questions that can be used in the interview to get more specific and impactful feedback.

21.6.3 Observation + analytics

Observation is, as discussed earlier, potentially a very time-consuming method in reviewing recorded gameplay videos. Consider the case of several recorded gameplay sessions, and the extensive amount of time required to watch and annotate these sessions for actionable feedback. While this traditionally would take several hours of labour, analytics can be used to significantly reduce this time by highlighting key moments in a playtest where a user may deviate from the norm or designer intention. This narrows the scope of the observation down to much smaller segments, reducing cost and time for developers.

As showed in the first case study, a simple implementation of this for a typical game would be to measure and record the time passed between game checkpoints. If a segment of a given user's playtest is significantly longer than the intended design (or significantly shorter, for that matter), then that highlights a specific portion of the playtest worth observing. In this respect, the use of analytics can significantly cut down on the time to effectively generate actionable feedback.

References and further reading

Mirza-Babaei, P., Moosajee, N., Drenikow, B. (2016). Playtesting for indie studios. In Proceedings of the 20th International Academic Mindtrek Conference (AcademicMindtrek '16) (pp. 366–374). New York: ACM. doi:10.1145/2994310.2994364

Zammitto, V., Mirza-Babaei, P., Livingston, I., Kobayashi, M., Nacke, L. E. (2014). Player experience: mixed methods and reporting results. In CHI '14 Extended Abstracts on Human Factors in Computing Systems (CHI EA '14) (pp. 147–150). New York: ACM. doi:10.1145/2559206.2559239

CHAPTER 22

'Play as if you were at home': dealing with biases and test validity

GUILLAUME LOUVEL

Highlights

The present chapter discusses the inevitability of biases when testing under lab conditions. It describes the difficulties obtaining the data needed by researchers and the difficulties projecting them to everyday situations. Lastly, it provides advice and guidelines to reduce biases in the study to increase its validity and obtain more useful and meaningful results.

22.1 User test validity and what it implies

The role of Games User Researchers is to help the development team build a game with a good—if not the best—user experience possible. To do that, Games User Researchers will conduct one or several tests to assess the players' experience and identify usability and gameplay issues which may occur (see chapter 5 for more on maturity levels in user testing and chapter 7 for an overview of GUR methods). They will be also in charge of assessing the appreciation of the multiple features the game offers, or even of the game as a whole. Since the work of the Games User Researchers is not without consequences on the game's design, their studies need to be valid and ecologically sound. In other words: does the test measure

Games User Research, Anders Drachen, Pejman Mirza-Babaei, Lennart E. Nacke (Eds).
© Oxford University Press 2018. Published 2018 by Oxford University Press

what it is supposed to measure and are the results in tune with a real-world situation? These two dimensions will be referred to as 'validity' through this chapter.

The psychologist Neisser (1976) said, 'Observations made in the laboratory have to (or are meant to) mimic everyday life phenomena'. Unfortunately, we can't recreate the reality of players sitting in their room, playing a game they just bought for $70 whenever and how many times they want, with no one looking over their shoulders or asking them questions from time to time. Mook (1983) argued that a lab situation was more about 'what could happen' than 'what does happen' in a real-world situation.

Let us say that you want to test the end-game of your game. Would it be reasonable and doable to observe dozens of players for 70 hours? It would cost money, resources, and time. Besides, you would have too much data in the end. There are choices to be made. You could re-invite players who already played several hours of the game during a previous user test or let players play the introduction of the game, then jump to the end-game, for example. But each solution has its flaws. On the one hand, the players you already invited now know each other, which impacts their behaviour. On the other hand, playing the beginning then the last sections of the game will give you very little feedback on how the difficulty curve is handled.

As we are working on unfinished products, mimicking everyday-life phenomena is hard to achieve. Mook seems more reasonable than Neisser here, but looking for 'what could happen' could lead to false negatives and false positives in your observations and results.

A false positive (or false alarm) is when you observe something which is very likely tied to the context of the test and that would not have the same impact in a real-world situation. For example, the majority of your players reported that the customization lacked variety in the test build. They had five models of hats, gloves, and glasses. However, in the final version of the game, they will be able to change their bags, jackets, shoes, etc. So the initial feedback was mostly a false alarm.

A false negative is when you miss something in the context of the test which could happen in a real-world situation. For example, you recruited players who were really interested into your upcoming game which already had press coverage. In this coverage, some key features were detailed so playtesters already knew what they could do as soon as they had the controller in their hands, so everything went smoothly during the tests: no flag had to be raised about the features introduction. The problem is that the majority of final users may not be fully aware of these features, and the tutorials may be not enough on their own.

The validity of a test depends essentially on its goals, the hypothesis, and the type of gathered data. The user experience has many facets. You can be interested in the usability of some features of the game, its challenge, or the overall appreciation. Two user tests with very similar experimental conditions may not share the same level of validity. For example, a development team wants you to test an unfinished game in which only 50% of the game is available. If the main goal is to test the usability of each feature, your study can have strong validity. However, estimating the overall appreciation of the final game will be very hard. The only appreciation data which will be valid is the appreciation of the available content of the game you test. It means that the work of Games User Researchers is sometimes to define (or redefine) the goals and the hypotheses of the user test regarding the constraints of the experimental conditions to maintain the validity of their test.

If a test has a poor validity, there are risks that its results will be misleading or useless. Of course, this is something we want to avoid. As said earlier, Games User Research (GUR) costs money, time, and human resources. Plus, it could greatly impact game design choices. Unfortunately, there is no such thing as a perfectly valid user test. Yes, it hurts, but it is okay as long as you know what the biases of your test are.

To help you evaluate the validity of your tests, we will try to identify the most common biases that could impact the validity of a user test and, as a consequence, your data and analysis. We will discuss their impact and propose some solutions to control or minimize them.

22.2 Things that could hurt the validity of your test

What follows is a list of the main biases and external events that could affect the validity of a test. Think of them as guidelines to conduct your user tests, things that you should be aware of when doing GUR. Some items may have a straightforward solution while others may be more complex to deal with. Most of the items are based on empirical evidence but we will refer to certain psychological concepts which you can learn more about from the references at the end of the chapter.

Again, there is no such thing as a 'perfectly ecological study'; the goal here is to try our best to gather data with as little noise as possible. Their impact is relative to your test goals. For example, if you are leading an appreciation test, an instructions bias would cause less damage than in a test focused on usability (this bias will be explained in Section 22.2.2.2).

22.2.1 Around the test

22.2.1.1 RECRUITMENT

When recruiting, be aware of your playtesters' background. Expert playtesters (like game designers) will most likely pinpoint micro issues, while novice players could have a hard time acknowledging consistent interactions or control schemes. Either way, it will add noise to your data and therefore will be time-consuming to filter the feedback. Another thing to avoid is inviting your friends and family. They may lack objectivity when asked to give their opinion and will often behave less naturally (Chapters 2 and 3 talk more about recruitment).

22.2.1.2 LANGUAGE

This advice could seem obvious, but make sure that your players understand what they read. If you suspect your players do not understand the language the game you are testing is in, ask your players right away and let them know that you could translate some words they do not understand. The same thing applies to your surveys and technical terms in-game. Be aware that 'D-pad', 'cover to cover', and 'kiting', for example, may not make sense for everyone, even veteran players. If you have to use technical terms in your surveys, we recommend defining them in lay terms to avoid misunderstandings.

When recruiting, explicitly ask your participants their mastery towards the language the game is in. You could ask about how often they watch TV shows in this language, with subtitles or not, or if they play games in this specific language, etc.

22.2.1.3 REWARDS

If you plan to compensate your participants, make sure they understand that their reward will be given regardless of their performance and that its role is to pay for their time. It doesn't necessarily have to be a monetary compensation: goodies, physical games, or digital keys of your games' company will do just fine. You could even sign your participants up for an early access of the game they just tested. Openly telling them, before the test, what the reward will be may influence them, so unless you are explicitly asked, just let them assume you will be fair regarding their reward—and then be fair.

Not rewarding your participants exposes you to two problems. Firstly, you lower your chances to recruit players. Secondly, the reward serves as a justification for players to come to your lab (social psychologists would call the reward 'extrinsic motivation'). If their experience turns out to be negative, they will be more likely to be objective (i.e., not giving extreme ratings), as they would not rationalize their participation solely based on their 'intrinsic motivation'. In short, the reward is here to lower the cognitive dissonance of the participants in case something goes bad.

22.2.1.4 TEST ROOM SET-UP

Unless the game you are testing is a local multiplayer game, players should not see other players' screens. That way, they will not be tempted to look for information (path, hidden secrets, gameplay mechanics, etc.) that they could not have obtained if they were playing alone. The same goes for sounds: we recommend giving headphones to your players. Plus, it will keep your workplace a quiet environment. And last, step back from your players so you will not be in their field of view while they play (Chapter 6 covers more about setting up labs).

22.2.1.5 PRIMING EFFECT

In psychology, the priming effect happens when a person's decision is influenced by a previous exposure to a stimulus. In a GUR context, players arriving at your lab may be exposed to video games media such as game posters in your studio, magazines, or even your clothes. These video games media are stimuli that will remind them with subtlety how good (or bad) those games were and could affect their mindset, their expectations, and how they perceive your game or company as a whole. Wherever the user test is happening, consider making the place as neutral as possible. The less influenced your players are, the better your data. As this effect might be subtle and unconscious, the following example is a caricature of what a player who is subject to a priming effect could think. Let us say that she is in your waiting room with your games company posters:

> Oh right, they're the guys who made this game. . . . I didn't even know it but I really loved it when I was a child! Oh and they made this game too? I'm sure the game I'm gonna play today will be awesome as well!

Again, this is a caricature, but by exposing your players to those stimuli, it is safe to say that you influenced them in a certain way.

22.2.1.6 HARDWARE

Be assured that all your test participants play with the same hardware (controllers, screens, headphones, etc.). This is basic standardization of your test procedure but it is an important thing to check! If one player has a cheap controller with worn-out triggers while another gets a brand new elite one, you will have a hard time comparing their data. What you will observe are differences of behaviour mostly caused by the controllers and not because of the game itself. To use the terminology of the Introduction, we can assume that you will get false positives in your observations if your players have different equipment.

22.2.2 During the test

22.2.2.1 SOCIAL PRESSURE AND SOCIAL DESIRABILITY BIAS

Make sure players feel comfortable about having a stranger looking at what they are doing and that they understand that this person is not there to judge them. Let them know that you are not directly involved in the project as a developer could be, so they can criticize without giving it a second thought. Explain that the goal of the test is not to complete all the available content. Do not make them compete against each other (at least if your game is not competition-oriented). Reassure them by telling them that if they have a hard time succeeding, it is very likely because of the game, not because of them. During observation, try to be as invisible as possible. Interrupt the player only if necessary and remain neutral in your behaviour and tone.

If you intervene every time you think your players are in trouble or would not succeed in a task, you will miss lot of observational data (what really caused the trouble? how did they find a way out of it? etc.), thus creating false negatives. Plus, you will most likely break their flow. Before your test, consider setting a criterion like 'If my players struggle for less than five minutes, then I will not help them, even if they are explicitly asking for help'. However, when they do, it does not prevent you from telling them that you know they are in difficulty and that you would like them to keep looking for a solution by themselves for a little more. Saying that with a smile will help a lot, but remain neutral in your attitude and language. If you appear too friendly, your participants may change their behaviour to 'show off', talk to you often instead of being focused on the game or on the task you asked them. However, if you seem too strict, they will most likely feel judged and ill-at-ease, and they will not dare tell you that they do not understand something.

22.2.2.2 INSTRUCTIONS BIAS

As a Games User Researcher, it is important to explain the same thing to all of your participants, and in the same way. This is even more important if the game does not yet have its tutorial or if it is incomplete. The best way to make sure that everyone gets the same instructions is to write them down and check if you did not miss any as you read them. However, if you forget to mention some information (e.g. players cannot equip hats because of a technical issue) and a player asks you directly if it is normal, give the information to everyone. If a participant did not understand the instructions, try your best to stick to the original ones by reformulating your sentences.

Be wary not to give too many details on what you expect from participants. For example, compare the following:

1 'Feel free to explore the controls by yourselves before starting your first mission.'
2 'Feel free to explore the controls, especially the cover system, before starting your first mission.'

The first sentence leaves room for participants to discover the controls by themselves, while the second may change their behaviours, unconsciously, to match your expectations. This statement may seem obvious, but slipping out details on what you are looking for can easily happen, so take time to prepare your speech before your test!

22.2.2.3 PLAYERS' INFLUENCE ON PLAYERS

Be aware that players will most likely talk to each other during breaks or lunchtime. They could exchange usability tips and game mechanics, or tell each other where they are in the story, and so on. During those conversations, a group leader could emerge and influence everyone's opinion about the game. What you risk here is a levelling of your appreciation data and the usability of your game's features. For example, on the usability side:

> You have been observing a player struggling with a puzzle for several minutes now, and he seems far from finding the solution as he is not looking in the right place for clues. It's almost lunchtime, so you decide that you will give him a hint about where to look right after lunch. Once lunchtime is over, your player comes back, sits in front of the game, grabs the controller, and solves the puzzle right away. . . . And you just stand there in awe, wondering what other information players shared during the break.

It is hard to control what happens outside the test room, so the best you can do is to kindly remind your players that it is important for you that they do not talk about the game to each other. Make sure they understand that everyone has to discover the game by themselves. One thing that could prevent or at least reduce talk about the game being tested is to give your participants something to do not directly related to video games (magazines, quizzes, foosball, etc.).

22.2.2.4 SESSIONS' LENGTH AND BREAKS

You should consider having game sessions of reasonable length to manage your players' fatigue, attention, and well-being. The average time before players take a break is surely not the same whether they play a turn-based strategy game or a hardcore fast FPS.[1] Keep in mind that if your game is demanding, your testers will need more breaks, or at least longer ones, than if your game is more slow-paced. Based on empirical observations, your players should be doing fine even after one hour of test on a mobile game, but do not expect the same length of time for a VR session (which should be around 30 minutes). For a narrative-based game, one play session could last two hours. However, if your game is more demanding (e.g., a competitive one or a die-and-retry[2] game), you should aim for sessions of one hour maximum.

Ideally, players should be able to take a break whenever they want, but it may be difficult to fit each break in your schedule.

22.2.2.5 BUGS AND CRASHES

Technical issues may happen, too! Make sure your players are aware that they are not here to go bug-hunting, and that they should try their best to ignore them. Now, if your build has too many bugs or crashes too much, the validity of your appreciation data is at risk. Series of crashes and bugs cause frustration, despondency, and anxiety as they break immersion. In the end, players would not rate their gameplay experience but the context. You may be able to isolate a few usability issues that occurred while the game was running fine, but the user experience would not be representative of a final one.

Playing the build a few days before the test will help you anticipate technical issues and prepare some ways of getting around them during the test (e.g., through cheat codes or by skipping parts of the game that are too unstable).

---

[1] FPS: first-person shooter (e.g. Doom, Counter Strike, Call of Duty).

[2] Die-and-retry: a game where the progression and mastery of the gameplay are mainly based on a succession of trials and errors (e.g. Super Meat Boy, Spelunky, Risk of Rain, Rogue Legacy).

22.3 Conclusion

The aim of this chapter was to give you an idea of how crucial test validity is and how it lies everywhere in a test session. For each decision you make while testing, you should ask, 'How does it impact the test validity?' The number of parameters is huge and attempting to totally suppress them could be to your disadvantage. If you try to suppress them all, your test will be more like a 'lab test'—cold, impersonal, and far from the reality of a player playing a game at home. However, if you are too careless about test validity, noise will cloud your data, and extracting viable results will be hard. By presenting impactful biases and by giving you ways to reduce them, our goal was also to help you be more aware and confident while presenting your test results.

Now, keep in mind that what we talked about here was user testing through direct observation. There are other methodologies that could complement this kind of user test. For example, you could run diary studies to keep track of what your players are doing at home with your games. You could use non-invasive biometric methods to learn more about what your players feel while they play without interruption. Or you could collect much information about what players do through data tracking in a transparent manner. You will learn more about those methodologies in other chapters of this volume (for example chapters 7–19).

References

Neisser, U. (1976). Cognition and reality. New York: Freeman.

Mook, D. (1983). In defence of external invalidity. American Psychologist, 38(4), 379–387.

Further reading

Priming effect

Yi, Y. (1990). Cognitive and affective priming effects of the context for print advertisements. Journal of Advertising, 19(2), 40–48.

Cognitive dissonance

Festinger, L., Carlsmith, J. (1959). Cognitive consequences of forced compliance. Journal of Abnormal and Social Psychology, 58(2), 203–210.

Extrinsic and intrinsic motivation

Ryan, R., Deci, E. (2000). Self-determination theory and the facilitation of intrinsic motivation, social development, and well-being. American Psychologist, 55(1), 68–78.

Biases in user testing and validity

Podsakoff, P., MacKenzie, S., Lee, J., Podsakoff, N. (2003). Common method biases in behavioural research: a critical review of the literature and recommended remedies. Journal of Applied Psychology, 88(5), 879–903.

Hughes, M. (2011). Reliability and dependability in usability testing [online]. Retrieved 7 November 2017 from http://www.uxmatters.com/mt/archives/2011/06/reliability-and-dependability-in-usability-testing.php

Sauro, J. (2012). 9 biases in usability testing [online]. Retrieved 7 November 2017 from http://MeasuringU.com. http://www.measuringu.com/blog/ut-bias.php

Sauro, J. (2014). Assessing the validity of your research [online]. Retrieved 7 November 2017 from http://www.measuringu.com/blog/validity-research.php

CHAPTER 23

Dissecting the Dragon: GUR for Dragon Age™: Inquisition

JAMES BERG, *Electronic Arts Canada*

Highlights

This chapter describes challenges involved in the development of Dragon Age™: İnquisition, in particular, problems arising from the size of the game world, as well as combat mechanics and player classes and playstyles. It shows how Games User Research (GUR) directly contributed to game design decisions, for example, in terms of menu and UI design.

23.1 Introduction

This chapter will provide a case study of the research conducted for Dragon Age™: Inquisition. It will explain a few of the key challenges and approaches to resolving them, the core research foci, and some of the impact that research had on the game design.

Dragon Age™: Inquisition is a party-based Role-Playing Game (RPG), the third instalment of the highly successful Dragon Age™ franchise. The player takes on the role of the Inquisitor, who is cast unwillingly into incredible events occurring within the world of Thedas. Throughout the game, the player must

Games User Research, Anders Drachen, Pejman Mirza-Babaei, Lennart E. Nacke (Eds).
© Oxford University Press 2018. Published 2018 by Oxford University Press

lead a party of companions in battles both physical and political, and player decisions will have major effects on the state of the world.

When working on a game the size of Inquisition, being flexible with methodology and providing multiple streams of research maximized my ability to assist the game team, and minimized downtime between full research sessions. Unless otherwise noted, all research mentioned was conducted via survey-driven, group playtesting.

The primary method for the project's playtesting was single-day group sessions (12–18 players) (chapter 7 provides an overview of GUR methods). For exploration-focused sessions, participants provided qualitative and quantitative answers to survey questions during and after the sessions, usually after exiting each exploration area, or after a fixed time period within the session. Players almost always had the option to provide open-ended written feedback at any time, which helped avoid players' forgetting things, and often provided useful stream-of-experience feedback. This open-box approach is always unpredictable, but it can gather feedback that would not be recorded any other way.

For multiplayer sessions, which consisted of groups of four players playing cooperatively with verbal communication, participants provided feedback after each match. Qualitative and quantitative approaches were similar between single-player and multiplayer research sessions.

In addition, an eye tracking session was conducted for menu research, and some multi-day, single-player sessions gave players a longer time period to progress through the game in a more naturalistic fashion. Throughout the project, I also provided informal expert evaluations of menu usability, advised on-demand about feature planning and changes, and helped the team identify risks.

23.2 Key project challenges

Research on Inquisition was particularly interesting because the team had the time and freedom to experiment with different ideas throughout development. This allowed us to design, conduct research, and iterate based on research results and internal team feedback.

23.2.1 Scope: the game is *how* big?

The most pressing challenge for Inquisition research was the sheer scope of the game (Figure 23.1). The first time someone explained to me that the Hinterlands was larger than Dragon Age: Origins and Dragon Age II combined,

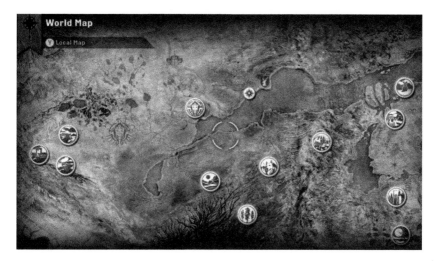

Figure 23.1 Game world map

I thought that was going to be the entire game. In actuality, the Hinterlands is one of ten exploration zones in Inquisition, and not even the largest. Scope was a continual concern for research—as the game changed and grew, it was impossible to keep track of all the design additions and changes, leading us to rely more and more on Bioware designers and producers to proactively ask for research on their game areas. Constant communication allowed us to address new priorities and evaluate changes to ensure they improved the game. It is important that you, as a researcher, ensure you budget enough time for phone and email conversations and meetings during your project planning. Being located in a different city than the development team prohibited having regular face time with the team, but flying out to meet the team and discuss things helped alleviate that lack of direct connection. Videoconference chats are another good way to stay personally connected with your development partners.

Games the size of Inquisition are typically built in pieces, any one of which can derail research if it is broken. We must be prepared to thoroughly play through our research areas with a sharp eye out for issues that would hinder our research. Quality assurance (QA) is a valuable ally for finding issues, but their priorities are often different than ours—play your own game to evaluate builds for research suitability! Throughout Inquisition, the research focus had to be adapted or changed based on what was testable. This required setting aside a substantial amount of time to play, understand, and verify the functionality of the game builds prior to any research playtests.

Trying to provide deep research on all exploration areas would have resulted in shallow coverage of each. Players needed quite a bit of time to explore and experience each area in a way that was representative of the intended experience. A player can very easily play for 20 hours just in the Hinterlands alone, for example. Instead of opting for this broad, shallow coverage, I worked with the team to identify game areas that were representative of 'what good looks like' for various areas. Single-player, survey-driven research playtests were then focused on these, providing deep, actionable research data whose findings were then applied to other areas as appropriate. This allowed Bioware to compare areas to each other at a meaningful depth, ensuring each area met design goals. These crossover pieces could be something as granular as establishing how players reacted to certain density of enemies or gatherable resources, but also higher-order organization for how they reacted to certain mixes of exploration and story, or specific questlines. As an example, an early playtest had players dropped into the Storm Coast without any of the core narrative story, so that we could understand how players would react in an environment that was challenging to navigate, and what they would be inclined to do without core story driving some of their actions.

Four examples of areas that received deep focus were the Hinterlands, Crestwood, the Emerald Graves, and the Storm Coast. The Hinterlands was the quintessential high-density exploration zone, with loads of story and exploration content, and was also the first major zone the player encountered—it received more testing than anything else because of these factors. Crestwood was a highly story-driven area, and was playable early, so it was the main stand-in for that type of play. The Emerald Graves was a mix—some story, but the zone also encouraged a lot of open-ended exploration. The Storm Coast was light on story, but heavy on what is-around-the-next-corner exploration. Also, Iron Bull is recruited there, so clearly it was critically important (Figure 23.2).

Figure 23.2 Iron Bull – a companion of the player character

The large scope of the game meant some long playtests, which in groups of up to 18 players resulted in a large amount of qualitative data. With timelines of ten business days from the end of one session to the start of the next one, the qualitative information that was actively reviewed and reported on needed to be heavily prioritized. We would frequently gather substantially more data than could be reviewed, so that it was on hand in case the development team wanted to look at something specific. Identifying key performance indicators and using these as repeated measures throughout the research process helped to identify where actual issues were occurring in the user experience, and this helped to further refine the list of things to make time to review.

23.2.2 Combat—utilizing a wide array of pointy, burning, exploding things

We specifically tested encounters and mechanics in areas that were designed to represent both set-piece battles and the more frequent open-world battles. Set-piece battles had to be tested to ensure that they were both enjoyable and understandable—for example, defeating the Pride Demon at the end of the Prologue requires the player to notice and activate a rift that opens and closes. Our research helped ensure the game taught the players this in a way that did not feel intrusive, without specific tutorials, while minimizing non-diegetic elements.

Some set-pieces were also set up to give a tactical advantage—a chokepoint with terrain above where clever players could rain death down upon their enemies. For these, Bioware wanted to know if players actually used them (many did) and what they thought of them (great!). Similarly, open-world battles could begin at different ranges—determining how players reacted to this was important. Typically, players engaged at the maximum range possible, opening the engagement with their mages and archers. Players also enjoyed the surprise and intensity of battles beginning at short ranges, such as through opened doors, or enemies appearing around blind corners. Alternatively, some players just charged forward all the time, heedless of range—ensuring the game handled different styles was key to ensuring everyone enjoyed the combat. We also learned a lot about how players disengaged. If you have played Inquisition, you will likely know that bears will chase you through the Hinterlands for a very long time. (You are welcome!) Most of these observations were gathered through observation of recorded player video, which allowed an evaluation of players in the same combat area regardless of the time it took them to reach that specific point. Doing it this way also allowed an examination of their quantitative responses from game surveys, allowing identification of both behaviour and perception.

Another key example of focused combat testing was the pause-and-play tactical combat system. The interface and controls were powerful but complicated. We discovered that some players simply did not want to use the system, and others could not figure it out, even after iteration and tutorials. It was key for players to still be able to succeed at combat without using it, so the team opted to avoid simplifying it, as that would reduce its utility to those who wanted to use it. Some players played Inquisition almost as a turn-based game, consistently pausing and playing in tactical mode.

The system allowed players to advance time at their own pace, but this was considered highly advanced user behaviour, and while extremely valuable for a subset of players, it was not common. Most players would occasionally use tactical mode, mostly for tough fights such as dragons. Starting tactical mode to give commands, then exiting it, was more common than advancing time slowly using the system—this was simpler for players both in terms of a mental model and in remembering how to use the modes' controls, as they only had to remember a few. Much of this was identified through survey responses, followed up with video observation.

Ensuring combat was learnable was critical to the game's success. Control sheets available on playtester desks were absolutely required for most sessions. Tutorials did not make it into the game early in production, so I frequently wrote out my own basic tutorials for players, with mixed success. Control sheets turned out to require a high level of detail—players who felt they would 'figure it out' did not read the simple *or* the complicated ones, and players who wanted the full controls were frustrated when provided with simpler sheets. Also, I learned to ensure that players were explicitly told to review the controls, with session time budgeted for this—despite the presence of physical pages sitting on the desk, some players did not read them otherwise. This process was helpful in preventing them from rushing through looking at the sheet—players often want to get to the game as fast as possible, so gating their session experience helped them focus.

When we needed to test combat in later levels of the game, things became particularly challenging for everybody—a mid-level party can have 32 different active abilities available, plus consumables and various other systems to first learn, then utilize. Whenever possible, I ensured players first played through something fairly straightforward to give them a chance to learn the controls and gameplay flow. It was not something that could be completely avoided given the size and complexity of the game, but it required a great deal of care in identifying whether complaints and difficulties stemmed from game design or from a player's playing a mid-game area with only a few hours' experience. Bringing players back for multiple sessions was another tactic we used, but this was very challenging for recruitment, and dividing demographics too thinly was a constant concern. Longer-term playtests were used as often as possible to provide a natural learning curve. Towards the end of the project, when the game was fully playable, some of our playtests lasted three or four days.

23.2.3 Class and player agency—can they play it their way?

The single-player game has three classes available, with a large variety of character builds and progression options, as well as two genders and three races (Figure 23.3). A common occurrence early on in single-player testing was that participants would have to create a character with a class or gender that they would not normally play, because abilities, art, or audio were not implemented for those yet. Agency over class and gender were important to players, which had to be factored into interpreting research results. Our research never had sufficient sample sizes to determine an effect size, if any, with quantitative statistics, but qualitative feedback strongly suggested that the inability to select class and gender had the effect of raising frustration and decreasing engagement.

Figure 23.3 Character creation screen – class selection

Researchers should be prepared for this kind of development reality—if possible, plan deeper testing with immersion- or agency-driving features at a stage when these options are available. Before that is possible, focus on testing usability or functionality rather than engagement or enjoyment of this particular feature set.

The players' chosen character class also changed their experience substantially. Classes are asymmetrically balanced, and during development, classes were frequently not kept well-balanced, resulting in the potential for players to have substantially different experiences. It was a constant balancing act between allowing players' agency and constraining their options to a smaller option set, or single choices, to reduce variables impacting the research.

The 'right' choice depended heavily on what the research focus was—for combat tests, it was usually necessary to constrain the variables by limiting choice, but for exploration, we could let players choose whenever things were relatively comparable.

Multiplayer mode was even more challenging—we knew there would be at least ten character classes with multiple skill trees, with four players simultaneously playing on the same team. For character classes, Keeper, Elementalist, Archer, and Legionnaire were the early choices used to represent a balanced four-player party. Because of the immense variety of multiplayer class mixes, it would have been impossible to test even a fraction of the combinations, so we opted to restrict class choices to those that were archetypical of their role—Tank, Utility Mage, and Damage Dealer. So long as the design team balanced classes by role, everything would be viable. Proving this via large-scale research would have been fantastic, but was not doable. Sometimes you just have to trust your development team!

In multiplayer, the design intent was to require a class-balanced party, with at least one defensive warrior among the four players. This required careful monitoring of group composition, evaluating how it affected the overall experience. In practice, player teams would frequently attempt to play without a defensive warrior to Tank enemies, and always eventually fail. This created a disparity in the data—a player playing as a Keeper in a group with a Legionnaire could have a great time, but a Keeper in a group with three Archers was far less likely to have a good experience. Ensuring the ability to tell the difference between these situations required detailed planning ahead, such as making sure to record the class composition for each match and how far they progressed, and using a variety of Likert-type scales to evaluate individual aspects of player perception. For example, asking both how they felt they performed and how their team performed allowed us to identify if they felt their team was letting them down. All of these measures were repeated, building up an ever-improving baseline for the data of each individual session to be compared against. As usual, this was done via survey.

23.2.4 Player playstyles—seriously, no two are alike

It should come as no surprise that players will play an open-world RPG like Inquisition in varying ways. However, consider this in the context of playtesting: one player enjoyed hours of running through utterly empty mountains 'exploring', other players voraciously read hours' worth of unvoiced companion dialogue to the exclusion of gameplay, and the spectrum of players ran from completionist explore-everything players to speedster no-time-for-plot players. These players would frequently co-exist in a single playtest session, and it was our job as researchers to determine if our game catered to all of those players, and if not, to understand the how and why of it.

One straightforward difficulty this created was simple pacing—players could complete an area to their satisfaction in two hours, or need eight, but session timelines could not always accommodate the more thorough players, and the speedsters sometimes completely missed things that needed feedback. One successful approach was to sacrifice naturalistic player behaviour by directing players to specific areas, or instructing them to engage with certain features in order to ensure that feedback was gathered about those specific things. Once feedback was focused on an area or feature, the same content could then be retested with naturalistic gameplay. In other cases, I allowed naturalistic behaviour, and differentiated through careful survey questions between players who had seen content but not engaged, and players who did not encounter the content at all (see chapter 9 for more on surveys). For those who found content but did not engage, we asked about why they chose not to, which provided different, but still useful feedback to the development team. Be mindful of sample size when taking this approach—if only a few players are providing feedback about something, always remember that there is a high probability that it is not going to be representative of a broader population group. Whenever possible, I recommend utilizing the multiple-test approach of first gathering directed feedback, and then measuring engagement with undirected feedback. This has also worked well in research conducted since Inquisition.

To evaluate their engagement with features like quests, gathering, and crafting, a simpler method suffices—copying their save files, and loading them up to personally take a look at what they picked up, crafted, quests completed, and the like. The combination of their written opinions and feedback with the hard data of what they actually did gave us a good picture of overall player behaviour and engagement. This was, however, very time-intensive. This can be an effective method of gathering data prior to telemetry being fully implemented, which on your projects will hopefully automate much of this data gathering.

Researchers need to be very careful about making any assumptions about how players would engage with content during a playtest. When building your test plan, ensure it is either flexible enough to accommodate player agency or has watertight directions to direct feedback gathering.

23.3 Examples of research contribution

On a project as large as Inquisition, research was never the one deciding factor for decisions being made, but the voice of the player is critically important to Bioware, so research was always taken seriously. Provided here are additional examples of research impacts on the final game.

23.3.1 Weapon crafting screen—pretty, pretty useless axes

Figure 23.4 is a screenshot from eye tracking research conducted on an early version of the crafting interface; Figure 23.5 is the same screen in the retail game. In the first screenshot, note the gaze path (lines connecting saccade points) and the visual fixation points (circles, with a larger circle indicating a longer fixation time). The player selects a material from the left-hand menu, which changes

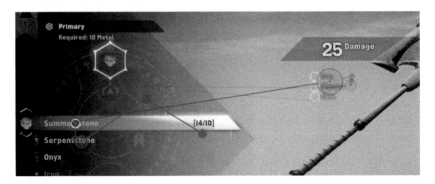

Figure 23.4 Gaze tracking on the in-development Crafting screen

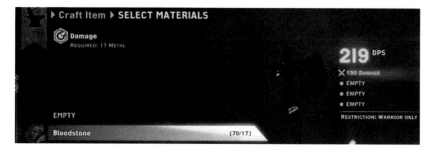

Figure 23.5 Retail Crafting screen, after iteration

the weapon appearance and damage. A key problem we found was that some players were creating weapons without visually fixating on the damage of their weapon, shown in the top right—they were deciding what material to use based purely on the appearance change, without ever realizing it affected the weapon statistics. Our research demonstrated that some players were literally not looking at the damage stat.

As a result, observe the changes in the retail screenshot (Figure 23.5). The development team ensured the damage per second stat was a bright orange, and that it pulsed when players changed the material selection, adding to the likelihood that players' eye would be drawn to it. Grey text was brightened to white to provide better contrast, and the orange background of the damage helped draw the player's eye to that critical statistic.

This is the kind of feedback that would be extremely hard to gather any way other than eye tracking. If you have access to it, there is nothing more definitive for menu usability than a solid eye tracking research session .

23.3.2 Navigation—the hitchhiker's guide to Thedas

Originally, Inquisition used a ribbon-style compass (Figure 23.6a) instead of the final radar (Figure 23.6b). Playtesting showed that the players had trouble

Figure 23.6 Navigation options changed during development

differentiating icons due to overlap, that they had difficulty orienting themselves with the compass while rotating the camera, and that it was frustrating to players having only 180 degrees of visibility.

The development team switched to a radar, and the reception was far more positive. Players expected it to show terrain, acting as a minimap, but otherwise it met player expectations, and substantially improved player experience compared to the 180-degree ribbon. Complaints about navigation dropped off substantially.

23.3.3 Locomotion—being able to leap tall logs in a single bound

One of the most interesting design iterations and progressions that I was able to contribute to was the locomotion system (Figure 23.7). Early on, the player characters were effectively locked to the ground—jumping over even small logs was not possible. Unsurprisingly, this was unsatisfying for players who wanted to explore the gorgeous 3D world, and Bioware designers wanted to give those players greater freedom to do so.

The Bioware team then prototyped a mantling system where players could approach climbable objects/terrain, and press a button to do so. One-on-one research was conducted to test this, by giving players a few specific locations they had to get to in the Hinterlands, and asking them to try to run and climb

Figure 23.7 Player freedom was a core design goal, including locomotion

their way there. Their expectations varied wildly—some players felt they could only climb things waist-high, while others expected to be able to climb anything that their character could reach up and grab the lip of. The system worked, but was not providing the level of freedom Bioware wanted, and although players enjoyed not being stuck to the ground, it also added confusion and uncertainty about what could be climbed. The overall user experience of the system was unsatisfying for everyone.

Bioware continued to work on the system, adding the ability for players to freely jump, allowing full-fledged exploration and a consistent player experience. Player avatars now behaved the way players expected them to, and the many exploration-focused players greatly enjoyed the ability to find all sorts of new trouble. Bioware designers also took advantage of the improved locomotion by hiding Easter eggs in areas accessible only by the leaping explorer. (Anyone for some cheese?)

23.3.4 Character portraits and status bars—not just for Orlesian dating profiles

Figure 23.8 shows an early version of the player portraits and status bars (Figure 23.8a), and the final version (Figure 23.8b). The HUD and UI was

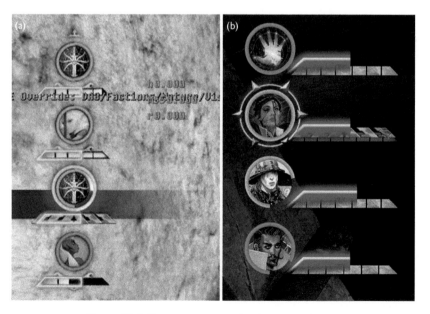

Figure 23.8 Player portraits – in development and at retail.

something that the development team did an incredible amount of iteration on and refinement of, and this is a great example.

In the game itself, remaining health is represented by green bars, Guard by silver overlay, and Barrier by blue overlay—both Guard and Barrier absorb health damage for the player, until depleted. Testing on the early versions showed that players had trouble realizing they were at low health when they had Guard—did you notice the third player on the left is almost dead? This screenshot was shown to players, and they were asked to describe their character's status. Even with a red stripe behind the portrait, most players were not noticing when their heroes were at low health.

In the final version (Figure 23.8b), the player depiction in their portrait updates with damage, and the bars are only partially overlapping, providing better visibility. For example, Cassandra, second from the top, is now more clearly not having a good day.

23.4 Takeaways

The Inquisition project held distinct challenges due to its scope, and extensive combat and player class systems. The ways that GUR contributed to problem solving and design decisions may be helpful to other games developers and researchers:

- Particularly in large-scale games, constant communication is necessary, ideally including face time.
- Gather as much research data as you can, then prioritize the leveraged data, and keep the rest at hand.
- When researching with iterative game builds, test thoroughly before research playtests, provide highly detailed control sheets, and budget session time for playtesters to review controls.
- Game mechanics such as character classes may force a trade-off between forcing choices to constrain variables and letting players choose.
- Make sure the playtest session plan is robust enough to deal with player agency, or has clear directions for gathering feedback.
- Multiple-test approach: gather directed feedback first, then measure engagement with undirected feedback.

CHAPTER 24

Running user tests with limited resources and experience

JULIEN HUGUENIN, *Ubisoft Paris*

Highlights

In this chapter I give ideas on how to run user tests (aka playtests) with limited resources. You may be a developer trying to test your game on the side, or someone trying (or who has been tasked) to test a game. We will ramp up from almost no resources whatsoever to the basis to create a dedicated lab space (chapter 25 also delves on the topic of GUR on a budget, chapter 5 discussed GUR maturity levels and chapter 6 contains additional information on lab space setups).

24.1 Introduction

You know that you can improve your games by making playtests. That is a great start. After all, playtesting is becoming more and more the norm and an essential part of the development process. Moreover, getting feedback on how well your design vision translates into the player's experience is a very appealing notion for any designer, and it is the recipe for consistently making better games. You have, however, little experience and not much time to run those tests. But there is still hope! Regardless of the size of their structure, researchers always have to make the best of their time and dedicate an appropriate amount of resources to each test. While using an external structure to playtest your game is very much

Games User Research, Anders Drachen, Pejman Mirza-Babaei, Lennart E. Nacke (Eds).
© Oxford University Press 2018. Published 2018 by Oxford University Press

a valid option (and one that is often overlooked by a developer's company, big or small), it is entirely feasible to implement a playtest process in a company or development team of any size. The key factors are, first, to properly identify what would benefit your game the most with the amount of resources you can dedicate to playtesting, and, second, to take the most efficient course of actions to prepare, run, and report on your test. While experience obviously helps, this chapter gives an overview of the basic options depending on your resources, and introduces the notions that dictate those choices.

24.2 Little experience, little resources—getting started

For that first part we will focus on minimizing the amount of time you must devote to the test itself.

24.2.1 Test preparation

The incompressible part of your test session: you need to decide what to focus your test on, and decide when, where, and how to run it.

24.2.1.1 DETERMINE TEST OBJECTIVES

Exploratory research is great, but costly. Instead, determine strict goals for your test session. It could be getting feedback on a hot topic for the team, having the players enjoy the game in its entirety and giving you overall feedback, or letting them experiment with a new feature. By restricting the size and the number of focuses, you will be able to produce feedback of greater quality (it is much easier to analyse data with a clear question in mind), and you will spend fewer resources (i.e., time) to set up, run, and analyse the test.

You will then tailor your session to address those objectives: each objective should be reflected in a portion of your test plan. For example, you want to see if the players enjoy the game (Objective A), understand how to use the jet pack feature (Objective B), and check if Level 4 is hard enough (Objective C). For Objective A, you will ask players to fill in a general questionnaire ('Did you like the game?') at the end of the session. For Objective B, conduct a small interview after the level where the jet pack is introduced ('What was new in this level?' 'The jet pack? Could you explain to me how it worked?'). For Objective C, ask at the end of each level if it was too hard or too easy.

Test goals for a game usually revolve around three broad axis. The first and most 'actionable' one is to evaluate the usability of your game ('What Is Usability?', 2006). Whether it is through think-aloud sessions, interviews, or direct observation, the goal is to check if your players are able to interact with the game as designed. Do they understand the rules and objectives? Is the tutorial of X or Y feature doing the job? Are the UI elements understandable enough? This process often leads to easily actionable findings ('Objective X is hard to understand, reword it', 'Icon Y is hard to differentiate from icon Z, change its shape'). Testing usability ensures that your players can enjoy the game without any hurdles, improving the quality of the overall experience (a subset of this is to check if your game is accessible: e.g., is your UI colour-blind friendly?). Examples of classic methodologies in usability testing include think-aloud sessions (where players talk as they play) and usability interviews (where you evaluate the usability with direct questions at key moments) (Theodorou, 2010) (see chapters 7–19 for more on GUR methods).

The second axis, and in a way the most important one and often the hardest to act upon, is to measure how satisfying the experience is for your players. Basically, you want to know how they feel about the game by collecting their appreciation through questionnaires, interviews, and focus groups ('How was the game?' 'How were the controls?' 'Was the game too easy or too hard?' etc.). Players are good at pointing out when something feels wrong, but much less so at explaining why and how to fix it. This is why observing your players or running additional tests to investigate the issues raised is often a must to improve your game.

The last axis, and one that often runs in parallel with the two others, is taking general measures of what your players do in the game. Do they use the stone of town portal? Do they use the fast travel feature? How much money do they have after Chapter 4? How much time it takes them to complete Level 3? All of this can help to fine-tune the game or investigate known issues. This can be done by either manual note taking, telemetry, or a mix of both.

24.2.1.2 MANAGE YOUR RESOURCES

Several factors tend to inflate the amount of resources involved in your test. The number of players increases the time you need to recruit them and the amount of data generated that you need to analyse afterward. This is especially true in the context of appreciation testing, and doubly so if you have a long questionnaire with a lot of open-ended questions. Similarly, reviewing what players say during interviews and focus groups will take a while. As a rule of thumb, if your number of test focuses increases, so will the time needed to complete your test, especially if you have varied sources of data (questionnaires, videos, interviews, etc.). Thus, small and manageable tests will need to have a very limited focus (e.g., test usability of Feature X *or* collect appreciation on the first hour of the game *or* check the appreciation of the difficulty and the number of deaths by level). You will find later in this chapter several examples of test protocols, from modest ones to more resource-intensive ones.

24.2.1.3 DETERMINE PLAYER PROFILES

While extensive methodology exists to assert who your players are (or should be), at that point just try to check with the team what should be the gaming habits of your game's target. Focus on recruiting players familiar with the genre and the support of the game rather than ethnological consideration (precise age, gender etc.). The idea is to focus on the type of players who are the most likely to play: your test will highlight what impairs their experience, and correcting those issues will improve the game itself. Avoid members of the industry except in certain specific tests: testers should not make or talk about video games for a living.

24.2.1.4 RECRUIT THEM

The main benefit of organizing a user test is, as implied, to get feedback from the ones the game is designed for. Recruiting players willing and available for test sessions can be a challenge, especially without the help of a pre-existing community for your game. Fortunately, it is very feasible to organize tests outside of established pipelines. The first step is to involve your own network, or the one of your company, colleagues, etc. A common alternative is to look around for a place to go and physically recruit players. Most public spaces work, but universities and schools are a great source of players: they generally have some flexibility in their schedule, fit most target player profiles, and are generally enthusiastic about testing games. Try to make a list of all the interested players, even if they do not make it to the test session, for later use.

24.2.1.5 SAMPLE SIZE

The number of people you need to run a test is usually one of the first things a person exposed to user research asks. The bottom line is: not as many as you think. Usability testing norms can require as few as five users (Nielsen, 2000) (but repeated tests are highly recommended), while having a good chance to highlight representative trends of player comments. Appreciation, however, often implies a slightly higher number (around 20 is a good threshold to aim for, but in this case, the more the better). This is why small test structures usually focus on usability testing, but if you have access to a large pool of players, big sessions with little direct observation can be more economical in terms of time spent. Of course, a combination of both is the best way to cover everything your game needs in term of testing (chapters 22, 23 and 25 also discuss sample sizes).

24.2.1.6 ORGANIZE LAB SPACE

You are now ready to welcome your first player. This is often a great experience for them, but you want them to be able to focus on your game or else you will not get the feedback you are looking for. Therefore, isolate part of your workplace. What you want is somewhere shielded as much as possible from the distractions of a crowded open space. This could be a break room that you steal for a few hours, a meeting space, or even just a quiet corner with a desk facing a wall, for example. Providing good headphones also goes a long way to immerse players in the experience you want them to give feedback on. If you are unable to observe/monitor closely, make sure that you are available at any moment to help. Working a few metres away from your test space can do the trick, but you need to be sure that your players never feel alone: being abandoned in a foreign workplace can be very disturbing and could prevent them from relaxing and enjoying the game. Moreover, they might be unwilling to risk disturbing someone if they have an issue or need something.

24.2.2 Running the session

Let us assume you do not have the time to directly observe the player for the whole duration of the session.

24.2.2.1 WELCOME THE PLAYERS

After greeting the player(s), make sure they are comfortable in your test space (a water bottle and some snacks universally help). Moreover, remind them that they are here to play the game as if they were at home, and that you are testing the game, not them. Explain to them that they must relax, and that you are available if they have any question or need help for anything.

24.2.2.2 COLLECTING DATA WITHOUT DIRECT OBSERVATION

Not being actively available for the test session limits the amount of data you can collect, but self-administered questionnaires allow feedback on basically any aspect of your game. Great free or cheap tools exist to do just that (SurveyMonkey and the like), but limit the number of questions to what is relevant to your focus:

bigger questionnaires require more time to fill, compile, and analyse. Also limit the number of open-ended questions: one per facet of your game might suffice. There are also tools that allow you to record a video of your sessions, such as OBS and Fraps. However, keep in mind that watching videos later will probably take as much time as participating in the session in the first place, without the possibility to interact directly with the players.

Another way to collect information during a test without direct observation is to ask the testers to report data by themselves. For example, you could ask them to write down their score at the end of each level or add a note each time they are killed by a specific enemy. While this greatly risks skewing players' behaviour (e.g., by making them too self-aware of their performance), it can help answering specific questions (how many times do players die during the first hour, on average?). Moreover, this method should not be used to collect data that could get the player out of the game's flow (e.g., writing down each time they collect a power-up). All in all, ask for a self-report only if what you ask them is the only thing of interest to you.

In-game telemetry (i.e., making your game collect data on the players' behaviours, such as number of death per level, time spent before reaching Level 4, drop ratio after two days, or whatever you identify as key performance indicators) can do the heavy lifting in terms of data collection (Drachen, 2012). However, it requires some precious development time and is often implemented late in the production cycle, if ever. If you can, work with the person in charge of implementing telemetry in your game: you can help them by 'testing' the telemetry way before launch and they can help you by providing a way to keep track of valuable data without too much work and with a level of granularity difficult to reach by hand. Useful data often include anything related to the challenge of your game (number of retries or completion time for each level, etc.) or data that inform you about the behaviour of your players ('they played this type of activity in average time', etc.)

Regardless of the way you collect data, keep in mind that data are much harder to correctly interpret without the context given by direct observation.

24.2.3 Compiling data and reporting

24.2.3.1 COMPILE DATA

The very basis of user research in general lies in the ability to support observation with reliable data. To that effect, compiling the collected data is the first step in reporting your findings. Put together charts with your ratings, compile answers and trends that appear in the players' comments, etc. Try to ignore outliers not very representative of appreciation trends; cross that with the trends observed during the post-test interviews or focus groups. Now confront your findings with the pre-established hypotheses and known issues, and build a list of the issues highlighted by the players.

24.2.3.2 REPORT FINDINGS

The best way to report findings highly depends on how you work. Reporting to a small team could be done with a simple presentation highlighting the issues observed during the session. On the other hand, communicating the results to a larger team or spread across different locations might require you to write down your report in a more detailed fashion. Regardless of the format, describe the issues observed, citing probable causes, and backing your assertions with players' comments or any source of data you collected and related to the issue. Whichever format you choose to report your findings, it is good practice to create a backlog of those issues, or, even better, enter them in the team's to-do list. Moreover, debrief those the test is intended for, making sure everyone is on the same page, and check their action plan for the issues raised (chapter 18 goes into depth on the topic of reporting GUR work).

24.2.4 Test examples—short sessions, or no access to players, or no direct observation

Test A: Between five and eight think-aloud sessions with colleagues or friends (but not from your project if they were already exposed to what you want to test); focus on the usability of the first hour of the game. Observe each player one-by-one as they play the game for the first time, and write down anything related to their understanding (or lack thereof), their ability to interact with the game, and frustrations that arise while doing so. Debrief with each player to have a better understanding of what went wrong, then report to the team the most common and severe issues. Can be done on early prototypes.

Pro: Actionable feedback on micro elements of the game that will make the experience go more smoothly if addressed; works on games at the early stages of production.

Con: Impossible to get feedback from real users; some issues might be overlooked, especially if the intended audience is significantly more mainstream than your team members.

Test B: Self-administered questionnaires centred on a representative portion of the game. Prepare a questionnaire focused on what they played. A typical questionnaire could include the following questions:

- 'On a scale of 1–5, how much did you like the game?'
- 'What was your favourite moment?'
- 'What was your least favourite moment?'
- 'What did you think of Feature X?'

If you test your game on a large pool of players you should see trends appear above ten people, but very polarizing eelemtns should stand out before that. You can also run shorter tests outside of the lab, in coffee shops, events or elsewhere, to get impressions from people outside your organization.

Pro: Allows to evaluate how satisfying the first contact with your game is and see the most salient issues; requires little work outside of recruitment as long as you limit the number of open-ended questions. Also works on games at early stages of production.

Con: Only gives large trends and misses a lot of small and easily actionable issues; requires access to a large number of players.

24.3 Dedicated resources

This section assumes that you are willing to dedicate a larger amount of time to the test session. Indeed, running an entire test session, from preparation to reporting, while being present during the session—to do all that in less than a week is difficult.

24.3.1 Running the session

24.3.1.1 DIRECT OBSERVATION

Now that you have more time allocated to running the test, the next big step would be to directly observe the players as they play. This allows you to spot a lot of usability issues the game might have, to directly observe playing behaviours (thus giving precious context to whatever they might then say in the questionnaires), and to see how players interact with the game in general. Limit your direct observation to one or two players at the same time. More than that, and you might miss too much to make your observations reliable: not having the context of what you see limits your ability to understand the situation and spot issues. An alternative is to record everything to watch later, but, again, you miss the opportunity to interview the players.

24.3.1.2 ATTITUDE TOWARDS PLAYERS

It is crucial to keep some distance with the player, especially while directly observing them play: we obviously want the players to feel welcomed and at ease during the session, but being too friendly increases the risk of skewing the player perception favourably towards you, and, by extension, your game. The optimal result would be for the player to completely forget your presence and experience the game as it is. Some indicator of a player being too friendly would be that they constantly stop playing to interact with you (seeking validation for their performance, joking, or speaking about things completely out of the test focus). It is most often easy to bring back the player on track by simply asking them to focus on the game. At the opposite end, a player who looks hesitant to share their feelings (during interviews or the test session itself) might need some reassuring: 'We are here to evaluate the game, not you.' 'Do you want to take a break?'—or any other 'icebreaker' should be enough.

24.3.1.3 SHOW TO THE TEAM

One of the greatest benefits of playtesting your game is that it gives you the unique opportunity to show the team the reality of the experience they are working hard to build. This might shock them out of what they perceive their game is and face the reality of it (for better or worse). The most effective way to do that is to witness a live test session. No 'I'll look at the video'; no 'I'll read the report': just look. This can be done in a number of ways, the easiest one being to invite key people to attend the test session, give them context, and have them watch the players without interfering. There are also very accessible ways to stream the video of the players so everyone can watch (such as YouTube streaming service, or software like OBS to easily manage video feeds).

24.3.1.4 GET THEM INVOLVED

One great way to combine limited resources and involve the team in the test process is to get help to run the test sessions, especially from the design team (or, more generally, from those whose work is the closest to the focus of the test). They can help to recruit players or participate in the observation session itself. Keep in mind, however, that they might not have a grasp of user research as good as yours, or of the attitude required or the specifics of a test session. To counteract that, you might want to be the one interacting with the players (if they have an issue or need something), and limit the in-session involvement of the members of the design team to note taking and silent observation of one or two players each. Moreover, keep in mind that they might be (understandably) more biased than you are: they have pre-existing ideas of how the player should or will play. They might also focus on things relevant to them to the exclusion of everything else, whereas good researchers actively try to be more objective in their approach. As such, you should consider getting help from the team only as a last resort.

24.3.2 Test examples

Test A: Full usability review, 5–8 external players who play the full game (or close to it: you want them to have access to all the features of the game) while being observed and interviewed at key moments (i.e., a fixed time when you deem that a certain element of the game should be mastered: e.g., 'after 1 hour, players should know that collecting diamonds gives them life'). The objective is to validate with each participant their understanding of the controls, UI elements, and rules of the game.

Pro: In-depth details of the most common usability issues of the game, as well as a good portion of the less common ones; actionable feedback and a lot of quick wins to improve the experience ('change colour of X element to improve understanding of Feature Y').

Con: No real insight as to how the experience is perceived by the players. If you really need to assess player appreciation after such a session, keep in mind that (1) the small sample limits your ability to see any meaningful trend in the responses, and (2) any interview increases the risk of skewing player appreciation. Do that only if you already have already run a full appreciation test to put your data in perspective (see later).

Test B: Full appreciation review; 15–20 external players; focus is on appreciation of a significant portion of the game; no direct observation (as there are too many players to observe without inflating the test's cost). Each player simply comes in, plays the game, then answers a detailed questionnaire. You can increase the granularity of the feedback with intermediate questionnaires at key moments of the game, without breaking the game's flow (end of each world, every five matches, etc.). You can run the test over a week or two as the players come in small groups (or alone); you compile the answers at the end for analysis. Reporting could consist of a review of the most-cited positive and negative points, with appropriate quotes from the players.

Pro: Direct access to players; first-hand account of what they think of the game; surprisingly time effective if you can recruit players easily.

Con: Requires access to a large number of players; little actionable feedback (players tend to agree on macro elements rather than specific, actionable ones, and to speak with their own words); lack of context on the feedback given. The game needs to be rather polished so the players can assess the full experience.

Test C: Hybrid test; mix of think-aloud and full appreciation tests; works great on small games. Recruit around 25 players, run a think-aloud session for around an hour with six of them and write down any frustration points, understanding issues, and weird behaviours. Let the others play the game for a few hours without interference, then have them complete a questionnaire about the game.

Pro: Resource-efficient; gives reliable insights on macro and micro issues; a representative snapshot of the state of the game.

Con: Generates a large amount of data of varied type which might take a while to compile and analyse.

24.4 Ramping up

This section gives guidelines on how to build your very own dedicated and in-house test lab.

24.4.1 Building a test database

Building a dedicated tester base is a big step towards a streamlined testing pipeline and is the backbone of any long-term user research endeavour. This often takes the shape of a database which includes the coordinates and gaming habits of your players. At the beginning of each test, you will simply have to pick the right profile and check their interests and availability by mail or by phone. There are a variety of ways to make that database grow, but a mix of word-of-mouth (with the help of flyers strategically distributed or given to players during sessions), social media presence (using the channels by which your game is promoted), and paid, targeted ad campaigns is usually the way to go.

24.4.2 Convenient and adaptable test environment

Building a test lab largely depends on your resources, time, and needs. A developed lab usually consists of several polyvalent test stations (test stations that can be used for a variety of purposes/tests) that include a variety of devices. Even if you focus exclusively on mobile games, you still need a computer of some kind to fill in questionnaires. Most of all, they should be comfortable for players, in a quiet environment, and with enough separation to prevent one tester seeing what is happening on adjacent stations' screens. Alternatively, having a lounge-like room with a couch and a single screen, with carefully placed cameras and mics is the typical think-aloud session set-up.

24.4.3 Improve data collection

Observations can be improved in a number of ways (and often they are cheap to carry out). Screens with the video and audio feeds of the players can be installed either in the test room or close by to maintain distance from the tester. Strategically placed cameras or even one-way mirrors are great ways to perfect your test conditions. Install a secondary screen for the sole purpose of questionnaires, making them easy to complete without cutting the main game from the primary screen. Making the video and audio feeds from test stations available to visitors is key to your lab being more accessible to visitors (e.g., from the developmental team). Note that it is possible, and good practice, to push the video feed of mobile devices onto a big screen (for your convenience if you are running a think-aloud session, or for the convenience of visitors or note takers posted outside the test room).

24.4.4 Build a team

As your resources increase, so will the amount of work required to run the tests. Creating a dedicated user research team is a major step to have a fully fledged user research lab, and most teams benefit from having people from different specialties. Graduates of programs in human-machine interaction, ergonomics, or similar academic areas can work along UX designers and game designers interested in testing. If you end up being involved in the recruitment of new lab members, the skills that you are looking for are fairly broad. Good-to-great analytical skills and the ability to apply critical thinking to video games are a good start, but being able to interact in a convincing fashion (soft skills) with the team should not be underestimated. After all, our research is only useful when we are able to convince the team to implement changes in the game!

24.4.5 Create a user test strategy for your game

Once you have some experience, you can start envisioning the testing of your game from the beginning to the end with a coherent and long-term strategy. What is your development plan? When can you schedule tests to best help your team? For example, you know that Feature A or B will be implemented in two months. Test them. You know that the game will be in soft launch in six months. Plan sessions for testing the game's appreciation at least three months before that. New, never-seen-before feature? Test it as early as the prototype phase. By anticipating your testing needs six or more months in advance, you will be more efficient resource-wise and will have more impact on the game.

24.5 Takeaways

The point of this chapter is that you can run tests in your organization regardless of its size and with very few resources. The key to achieve that is to assess what needs testing the most and focus on that. Remember that multiple small tests across time are better than a single big test. Moreover, testing will become increasingly more efficient as you acquire experience, build a tester base, streamline test processes, and involve the design team. All in all, any resource you involve in testing will generate significant return on investment as you help the team take more informed decisions with user-generated data.

References

Drachen, A. (2012). Intro to user analytics, Gamasutra, Retrieved 15 September 2017 https://www.gamasutra.com/view/feature/193241/intro_to_user_analytics.php?print=1

Nielsen, J. (2000). Why you only need to test with 5 users. Nielsen Norman Group. Retrieved 20 October 2017 from http://www.nngroup.com/articles/why-you-only-need-to-test-with-5-users/

Theodorou, E. (2010). Let the gamers do the talking: a comparative study of two usability testing methods for video games [master's thesis]. London: University College of London. Retrieved 21 October 2017 from https://www.ucl.ac.uk/uclic/studying/taught-courses/distinction-projects/2009_theses/TheodorouE.pdf

What Is Usability? (2006). UsabilityNet. Retrieved 26 October 2017 from http://www.usabilitynet.org/management/b_what.htm

Further reading

Long, S. (2013). User research for indie games: playtesting on Morphopolis. Gamasutra. Retrieved 26 October 2015 from http://www.gamasutra.com/blogs/SebLong/20131115/204909/User_Research_for_Indie_Games_Playtesting_on_Morphopolis.php

Schanuel, I. (2013). User testing with limited resources. The Thinking Zygote. Retrieved 26 October 2015 from http://www.thinkingzygote.com/2014/04/user-testing-with-limited-resources.html

Starting from scratch: pragmatic and scalable guidelines to impactful Games User Research

JOHAN DORELL, *EA DICE* *(formerly of Paradox Interactive)*

BJÖRN BERG MARKLUND, *University of Skövde*

Highlights

In this chapter we will provide a pragmatic description of how Games User Research (GUR) processes can be employable and impactful even with limited resources and prior user research experience. We will also provide guidelines for how GUR processes can start small and be iteratively expanded to become an integral part of a developer's working processes. Included are step-by-step guidelines for starting to work with GUR (chapter 24 also discusses GUR on a budget, and chapter 5 covers an overview of methodological maturity).

25.1 Introduction

For many developers, GUR may at best seem unreasonably cumbersome and too time-consuming to be worth the effort, and at worst it might seem downright antithetical and obstructive to game development processes—especially so for

Games User Research, Anders Drachen, Pejman Mirza-Babaei, Lennart E. Nacke (Eds).
© Oxford University Press 2018. Published 2018 by Oxford University Press

smaller studios. 'Research' in particular is not something that is strongly associated with efficiency and immediate applicability, and might thus be regarded as unnecessary or at odds with the more pragmatic, pressing, and tangible goals and requirements that developers work towards.

The first step in starting to work with GUR is to tackle these misconceptions at a company level: GUR simply means making a concentrated and systematic effort to better understand how different design decisions change a player's impression and enjoyment of your game, and whether the game achieves what you intended. But, more importantly, GUR also gives you the tools to translate this understanding to actionable development guidelines that ensure subsequent iterations amount to the right types of game improvements.

This chapter provides practical guidelines for integrating GUR processes in small- and medium-sized development projects. Specifically, this chapter aims to provide an entry point for developers who may be interested in user research, but who may be unsure of how to take their first steps into it or are intimidated by the investments it might require. While there are many different types of GUR frameworks already available, their depth and scope can seem somewhat unapproachable for someone who wants to see how GUR may fit into their development processes and how it can impact the quality of their games.

With this in mind, using examples of how Paradox Interactive (henceforth Paradox) went from ad hoc playtests to more refined testing processes, this chapter will provide some pragmatic and scalable guidelines for developers who either want to start out small and try out GUR, or who want to expand their efforts and have it become a more ingrained aspect of their development team's praxis. Doing so in a way that starts providing valuable contributions to development processes does not necessarily have to involve massive resource investments, a high level of expertise with experimental research methods, or knowledge of esoteric data handling processes. Efficient and impactful GUR can be conducted at many different levels and, as the examples provided in this chapter will show, any developer has the capacity of making good use of it by letting research processes organically grow in their working environment.

The chapter will conclude with some guiding principles for how to approach GUR as a smaller development team by starting out with small-scale research scenarios and by cultivating a research-conducive dialogue. The chapter will also provide a description of characteristics and skills that we consider make up a good, pragmatic, and ultimately impactful Games User Researcher. The challenges involved in conducting valid and useful GUR has to do with fostering team communication as well as devising good research methods. Good GUR is about asking relevant questions, figuring out metrics with which to answer them, and communicating results back to colleagues as actionable advice. Thus, it not only involves knowledge of research methods, but it involves the cultivation of a research-oriented dialogue in the entire development team.

25.2 The case of Paradox's Games User Research

This chapter is based on experiences gained from the two-year-long process of incorporating GUR into Paradox's development processes. By examining documentation from our test cases, research reports, post-mortems, issue statistics, and email conversations gathered throughout our two-year working process, we aim to describe what aspects and procedures have worked well and the different challenges we faced throughout our GUR initiative.

The overall GUR initiative started out with small-scale explorative research on the periphery of the studio's development projects. Over time, the efforts iteratively grew larger and became more closely intertwined with the studio; Paradox currently has a department with five full-time employees dedicated to GUR. During this process, we have worked with many different types of developers and projects. We have worked with smaller development teams of two employees up to larger teams of 70 employees, though most have ranged between 10–20. We have worked on internal projects headed by Paradox as well as projects headed by developers at external studios. The genres and target audiences of the different projects' game titles have been equally diverse: we have worked on titles ranging from city builders and grand strategy games to role-playing and Multi-Player Online Battle Arena (MOBA) games similar to League of Legends and DotA 2.

Paradox is a developer and publisher focusing on PC games; they have produced a large number of diverse titles. The best way to sum up all of them is to say that they are made for an audience that can be defined as 'dedicated gamers', an audience that is not averse to spending a lot of time and effort to explore and master complex game systems. Thus, Paradox's core ethos is that games should be interesting and challenging in the long term rather than easily digestible and immediately gratifying experiences. Paradox consists of a collection of several development studios that work on different types of projects. Paradox Development Studios, the largest and most prominent division of Paradox, are responsible for the grand strategy titles such as Europa Universalis, Crusader Kings and Hearts of Iron. Smaller studios such as Paradox North and Paradox Arctic work on titles such as Magicka: Wizard Wars and Magicka 2. Due to this studio division, Paradox projects can vary in size significantly, ranging anywhere between teams of 2–50 developers. In this chapter we will refer to Paradox as a single entity for easier reading.

The wide variety of projects we have been working on, and the many stages on which we've conducted research, allows us to describe GUR on many different levels—and, perhaps more importantly, to describe them from a pragmatic perspective. The studios we worked with were typically small- to mid-size (i.e., 10–20 employees). As we began this initiative, we also lacked many of the resources that many other large studios involved in GUR often possess (e.g., dedicated lab space, elaborate testing equipment, a database of available participants). We also had little previous knowledge of GUR at the outset, and had to do extensive research on what it was in order to find out its relevance to us, and to examine how we could make it useful for our studio. Many practitioners and researchers have already built frameworks and processes for how to incorporate GUR into the game development process, and we had to explore, remodel, and reinvent their models to make them suitable for our own organization. We think these are challenges that many fledgling user researchers might be familiar with, and thus we hope that our experiences can serve as pragmatic and applicable advice for how one might go about constructing GUR processes from scratch.

25.3 Games User Research examples

To describe the iterative growth of Paradox's GUR processes, five primary 'milestone' projects will be used as examples. These projects (numbered 1–5, in chronological order) exemplify how our experiences of different types of working structures and conditions informed the ways in which our GUR processes changed throughout the past two years. In initial projects, playtesting usually happened on the periphery of the core development process. But with each passing project, GUR processes became more rigorous and structured, and as our proficiency in execution improved, they also became a more integral quality-improving asset to Paradox's development processes. In Figure 25.1 the projects' place in the overarching iterative improvement of the GUR integration at Paradox is shown. The projects are grouped into three phases which characterize the distinct stages we progressed through when establishing GUR processes and integrating them into the company's development pipelines.

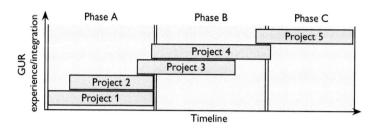

Figure 25.1 The projects' place in the overarching iterative improvement of the GUR integration at Paradox

Paradox's propensity to work with a wide variety of titles is very much reflected in the chosen examples. Project 1 was a Real-Time Strategy Game (RTS) with a strong emphasis on its story-driven game campaign set in a sci-fi universe, whereas Project 2 was a third-person historic combat game with a strong multiplayer component. The subsequent examples are also scattered all across the genre and gameplay spectrum: Project 3 was an RPG with an in-depth, turn-based tactics combat system; Project 4 was a fairly straightforward city builder with heavy emphasis on the simulation of citizens' natural needs and behaviours; and Project 5 was a pen-and-paperesque Role Playing Game (RPG) for mobile platforms.

With the exception of Project 3, all examples were primarily developed at external studios, and Paradox's role during development was as publisher and producer. In that capacity, we assisted the development projects with production support and testing (which is where our user research processes come in). All of the development teams were fairly similar in size, ranging between 10 and 20 people working on the projects at any given moment. The various ways in which the projects practically differed from one another, and in which our own experience and the projects' structures and conditions informed the conducted GUR, will be outlined chronologically in the following sections.

25.3.1 Phase A—GUR on the fringe

The first two projects (the RTS and the third-person combat game) were our first experiences conducting something that resembled proper user research. As such, they served as very valuable learning experiences where our initial, largely untested and unstructured working processes were put to the test. These projects were conducted before GUR was a recognized component of Paradox's development pipeline, and had thus both started out without much consideration of including user research processes in development. We came into the development processes rather late, when most assets and mechanics had been finalized and the games were already mostly playable.

For both projects, we started doing playtests as soon as we got access to game content. Due to the lack of premeditation, research subjects were found through convenience sampling—which in reality meant that we pulled in people at our office who had reported that they enjoyed other games of the same genres. We booked a meeting room in which we hooked up one of our own computers with screen-capturing software, and used a handheld camera to record the player during the session. The immediate issue with this haphazard test set-up was that the camera recordings and the screen recordings were difficult to synchronize properly to produce useable test videos. This forced us to simply have both developers and producers sit in the back of the room and observe the test sessions directly. Needless to say, participants were not particularly comfortable with playing in front of an audience consisting of developers involved in the project. Even so, the testing yielded a lot of useful results and takeaways, and it was the first time that developers and producers had the opportunity to directly observe a completely new player engage with the first part of the game, which in itself is a very useful process for developers. Watching these interactions occur live, as compared to a recorded video, made some gameplay issues more tangible for the development team. However, having this many people in the same room observing one participant at a time is generally not advocated. It tends to make players feel scrutinized, and they will interact with the games in different ways than they might if they were playing in a more natural setting. Some players, we noticed, also tended to become very nervous, especially about making gameplay mistakes that would make them, in their mind, look bad in front of the development team.

The late inclusion of GUR limited us to primarily rely on ad hoc sampling and testing methods, and made it challenging to make meaningful contributions to either game. Shortcomings and design issues could be identified during testing, but due to the rigid project schedule, and the limited time left for development, they were difficult or deemed unfeasible to resolve, as it would require significant revisions that would either be too time-consuming or that would jeopardize the games' overall stability. The dilemma that both development teams ultimately encountered was to either smooth over problematic parts of their games to the best of their abilities, or completely remake large portions of their game from scratch. Neither position is comfortable to be in as a developer, as you are stuck either with creating a game cobbled together of troublesome mechanics, or with significantly inflated development costs.

Both of these early projects were thus important lessons of the maxim 'the later the test, the costlier the fix'; a lesson we tried to take with us to our next development projects. Furthermore, the projects showed us that while just a limited amount of GUR might not be an ideal scenario, it still served an important role in improving aspects of the games. For example, the lack of playtesting earlier in the project led to a traditional issue of nearsighted design choices; the developers' expertise in their own game made it difficult to identify parts that were difficult to grasp for newer players, and our GUR tests helped to effectively highlight those issues.

25.3.2 Phase B—working towards established GUR processes

The third project we worked on was a turn-based RPG in third person. As this title was developed internally at Paradox, we worked directly with the developers when creating the research questions, research design, and so on. As a project, it shared some similarities with the earlier-mentioned RTS and historic combat game in that we started working on it after it had been in development for a while. As opposed to the previous projects, however, GUR was initiated well before the game's supposed release date. With more time to work with the title, more extensive forms of user research processes could be employed, and they were also given time to become a more natural part of the development team's working structures. Repeated playtests could be conducted on earlier versions of the game, and test hypotheses and results could be discussed more directly with the development team. As a result, we could start establishing and refining the core research questions that we aimed to evaluate during each playtest, as well as plan ahead to make sure we covered all pertinent aspects of the game. This pre-planning made it possible for us to not only test the first parts of the game, but also to conduct testing on mid- to late-game portions of the game. We also managed to test different content in terms of levels, races, and units, to ultimately start seeing the contours of the game's 'meta' layer. As we tested further iterations, we could also see if issues that we had previously found were fixed or not, which made it easier for the developers to know if the work they did had the intended effect.

During this time we had also acquired a PC dedicated for playtests, which reduced the amount of time spent moving computers between meeting rooms and installing software on new equipment. We also invested in other hardware, such as a decent web camera and microphone. This raised the quality of our test outcomes, and as we now had the same set-up during every playtest, we encountered fewer hardware and software issues.

For most playtests, the basic needs are easy to cover, especially if your game works on PC. You want to record the game and the participant playing. It is cheap to get a webcam and stand-alone microphone that yields great results. The following gear is what we have used and would recommend to others:

- a PC that can run your game and screen-recording software simultaneously
- mouse, keyboard, gamepad; whatever peripherals your game may utilize
- camera equipment (we used a Logitech C920)
- audio recording equipment (Blue Microphones Snowball)
- external video capture card for consoles (AverMedia external capture card)
- camera to record mobile play (flexible tripod with the above camera)
- video broadcasting software (XSplit or Open Broadcaster Software)

The fourth project, the city-builder game, was the first full project we saw through from start to finish. Being present at the outset of development significantly improved the user research processes as it enabled hands-on playtesting on early prototypes. This made it possible for us to immediately establish testing methods that were suitable for the game and the development team, and that would easily accommodate newly added features as well as improvements to previous builds. It provided us with a good understanding of the state of the game and especially what the main issues were throughout development. As we were looped into the overall scope of the game and the schedule of when things were to be implemented, we could also plan the ensuing research. This enabled us and the developers to continuously receive feedback on core mechanics that were iterated upon heavily. We were also able to create a test plan so we knew that we would have time to test the most important aspects and we also knew what we would not test, or what was at the risk of not being tested. As such, we were able to test the long-term progression and unlocks of new buildings later in the project. We were also able to conduct tests on the more complex simulations in the city builder.

On the topic of complexity, another benefit of conducting research along the whole project is that you as a researcher have the time to get much more familiar with the game. Complex games, especially early in development, require large time investments to 'grok'. Understanding the game you work with enables you to create more accurate research designs and focus on the parts that are most important to the gameplay experience. Had we not had this time, we would likely have missed testing the deeper simulation aspects, as we would not have understood how deeply they affected the game. After trying out this process, we have implemented it for all our projects and have since been trying to conduct continuous testing as early and often as possible. The insight this gives on every milestone is important for our producers and developers, so that they are able to make better long-term plans and decisions about the overall scope of the projects, and how likely it is that we need to make adjustments in term of scope, time, and resources.

25.3.3 Phase C—fully GUR integrated development

The last project example, the mobile RPG-esque game, exemplifies how GUR was conducted when our working processes and methods had become more refined and embraced as an integral element of Paradox's projects. During the game's development, we had the opportunity to implement our previous experience with user research in a more deliberate and premeditated manner. As we had become more experienced in conducting continuous playtests, we were able to set up a semi-structured process for when to do playtests at the beginning of the project, and it even made it possible to plan tests before any development had started. For example, we included an external partner who conducted a competitive analysis in the beginning of the project. This was helpful in comparing the planned game title to the identified core competitors and their respective strengths and weaknesses (see the end of chapter for readings on the topic). Since we also had a set plan for all tests on certain milestones for most of our projects, we were able to identify points in the development process that placed higher demands on our GUR and could thus plan to pull in extra resources, working hours, and personnel as they became necessary. The ability to work with the user research processes as an integral part of development was thus a far cry from the earlier experiences where they were conducted as peripheral activities, and where we had to scramble to set up haphazard ad hoc tests.

25.4 Five processes involved in successful home-grown GUR

From our experiences with transitioning from the haphazard, ad hoc approaches to GUR used during initial projects to established working processes and methodologies, we have identified five key processes that led us towards establishing impactful GUR practices. This section will outline these processes (and some of the more common pitfalls we encountered while enacting them).

25.4.1 Starting out, and starting to grow: learning to work with small data

Starting out small ensures that GUR is allowed to naturally 'grow' into a studio's development processes, as it will naturally adapt and evolve in accordance to the studio's scale and workflow. Superimposing large and overly ambitious GUR processes and tools that are not a good fit for a studio will likely end in large investments being made with little return, and can make a development team resistant to the concept. It also tends to be easier to "convert" people in charge of the budget to becoming GUR proponents with cheap tests that yield easily digestible results quickly. Start by tackling relatively low-level design problems, and utilize the cheapest tools and methods to implement and experiment with. For example, small-scale, one-on-one playtests with four or five participants that rely on think-aloud methodologies or video analysis do not require any particularly extravagant or esoteric equipment or software to set up. A meeting room, a gaming computer, a decent webcam, along with a couple of days to prepare and execute tests and to compile a results report is all that is needed.

Doing these types of tests are relatively minor investments and should be possible in most studios. While it is always preferable to run test sessions with external participants (or other subjects not chosen by convenience sampling), early GUR efforts will often need to rely on ones that are easy and cheap to access. Friends and people from the company that do not work on the project can be useful subjects when identifying major usability issues. But it is important to acknowledge that these kinds of subjects can be less likely to give negative feedback than subjects that have no personal ties to the development process. This drawback makes any type of post-play evaluation method (e.g., surveys or interviews) unreliable. However, from our experiences with the early game titles, analysing and discussing videos or live streams of participants running through core parts of a game can provide valuable information to the development team (in terms of usability, learnability, efficiency, accessibility, and general difficulty levels). While these cheap and quick methods of GUR might seem limited in their usefulness, they are worth a whole lot more than no GUR at all. The most important value that these types of tests provide is not only to heighten the quality of your game, but also to introduce the idea of GUR processes to your studio's development pipeline and to experience first-hand what is involved in conducting them. So, even though it is almost guaranteed that your first tests will have a lot of room for improvement, they are necessary, albeit somewhat painful, first steps.

After a while, the limitations of the first types of convenience-sampled play-tests will likely make you want to progress to something bigger. But it is important not to transition too quickly into large tests—progress should be made in service of producing the *right* data that is of use to you and your team, not merely producing *more* data. From our experiences a good way to progress is to start conducting smaller-scale expert reviews or heuristic analyses. While these methods are fairly superficial and only result in feedback from the perspective of a small subset of potential players, they are cheap and effective. They primarily require an investment of your time and access to a computer that can run the game and a somewhat stable build.

Expert reviews and heuristic analysis typically involve polling 'experts' (e.g., members of the development teams, researchers, or highly proficient fans of a game series or genre) for advice about usability aspects of different parts of the game, based on recommendations and heuristics drawn from their experiences with other, similar games. These methods are useful for catching general usability issues early on that are cheap to fix, and are used throughout the industry, from smaller studios to AAA equivalents. There are plenty of articles available that exemplify how you can use these methods written by members of the GUR community. (See end of chapter for further information.)

25.4.2 Solidifying skill sets: establishing, refining, and expanding your repertoire

When you have started implementing the earlier relatively cheap and easy methods, you will immediately start noticing things about your testing processes and methods that you wish to tweak and improve upon—and you will thus also start looking for ways to do so (we have included some fundamental references and resources in the links section). But, as always, it is important that these improvements are made in service of your development team's needs, and not in pursuit of reaching a general industry standard (that might be inapplicable to your studio's situation) or what would come across as being the most impressive. Changes need to mirror the needs and capabilities of your studio, otherwise you will be conducting advanced tests that generate data that, while perhaps cool on its own, is difficult to apply to improve a game's quality. Building upon your initial experiences from earlier projects, talk to your colleagues and stakeholders and try to do short post-mortems; use these to identify and prioritize aspects of your process that should be improved for the next tests. Then you can focus on making your research more efficient, reliable, and integral to development projects. The modest steps described earlier were the ones we first took when implementing user research methods across the organization. Identifying ways in which our GUR had provided value to our first projects, and ways in which that value could be increased further, allowed us to find better ways to work with development teams and stakeholders, and to manage the conditions we worked under while yielding a lot of relevant and actionable results for the development team.

Finding someone who can act as your mentor regarding GUR methods and working processes can be an efficient way to improve your skill set. There is a lot of literature written on the topic of user research, but the finer details on how to apply GUR methods are not always clear. Having someone experienced that can help you with these questions will save you a lot of time and headaches, and you will avoid reinventing the wheel. (For further information, see the references at the end of the chapter.)

When you feel that you have established your presence in the organization, and that you have developers who will function as evangelists for you because of your contributions to their work, you can start planning for ways to expand upon your GUR processes. As we did during our transition from the first projects to the later ones, try to figure out a process in which you can do user research for your stakeholders in a structured and iterative manner. It is imperative that you align this to your developers' working processes, whether it's in milestones, sprints, or something else. Preferably, you can also discuss this with them, so that they are aware of what you are going to do and when, which gives them the opportunity to react to your results in an effective way. It would not be as easy as we perhaps have made it sound, and various obstacles will almost definitely emerge. Project budgets and scopes change, and so does the development team and the timeline of the project. As you face these issues, however, you will learn how to adjust for these things and you will be much better prepared to do continuous testing on your projects. This will free up a lot of time and you will also know when you have low-activity periods. It will enable you to research more advanced methods and to start conducting tests that you feel are appropriate. The methods depend largely on the types of projects you work on and what resources you have, but some examples are telemetry, eye tracking, large-scale playtests, cognitive walk-throughs, and competitive analysis. These methods either cost more to use or have more limited scopes of application but they are still valuable complements to the more essential processes you have already established.

You can also start delivering results that are more high-level and useful for more executive people, who are not necessarily interested in the nitty-gritty. This helps them as well and it also helps you in showing a larger part of the organization what you are delivering. Convincing executives why you make important contributions to the quality of the final game product is also a good way to receive more resources for things you find important.

25.4.3 Show your value: communicating user research results

As a last step when conducting any type of research, efficient delivery is essential for actually having an impact on development processes and a game's overall quality. Speaking from experience, there are very few developers, producers, or other stakeholders that have time to read through long reports, especially when only small segments of the reports are relevant for their individual interests. You should, of course, focus on delivering thorough and comprehensive results. However, just as your work should strive to produce the *right* data, your reports should be structured in a manner that makes sure that it reaches the *right* people and that it is presented in a way that is accessible to them. As a general rule, you should keep research methodologies, tools and software used, processes of participant sampling, and similar descriptions at the end of the report as optional reading. The top priority should always be an executive summary of the results with the key findings, followed by specific issues. The subsequent categorization and presentation of issues then need to be done differently depending on whom you are testing for. Identified issues that severely impact game quality should be summarized and presented first, as they can require restructuring of the team's short-term development pipeline. Subsequently, lesser issues should be categorized and specifically conveyed to corresponding team members; issues that only relate to UI design can be sent directly to the team's UI person, and so forth.

Figuring this process out takes time, and we only started seeing it as an important part of our procedure somewhere between our work with the first and second example projects—and we had started figuring it out around the time we started working with the last example project, the RPG-esque mobile game. In our first projects, we continuously delivered a 40-page report to whomever ordered it. This worked fairly well for teams that had someone around with the time to read through it and deliver the key identified issues to whomever was suitable for fixing them. For others, however, the lengthy reports quickly became a chore and deemed too time-inefficient to engage with. Our solution to overcoming this barrier was to lift all identified issues from the document and instead report them among all other bugs in the issue tracker already used by the company, JIRA. This naturally aligned the research outcomes with development processes as test results were worked into the pipeline similarly to how other game issues were treated (e.g., bugs discovered by QA, or certification demands). JIRA-implementation also made it possible to directly assign issues with their corresponding developer, and we could attach short video clips directly from test sessions for each issue to clarify them further. We then tailored the reports to only include a brief summary of the key test findings, as well as specific answers to the research questions posed at the start of the test. This made the reports more efficient for people who wanted to get a general idea of research outcomes, while team members who were only interested in specific issues could easily navigate the report to find information relevant to their working process.

A simple and efficient way to present your results to developers is through the use of videos. A short video summary of the key takeaways from playtests (with accompanying in-game footage) can communicate your results very effectively and is easy to distribute throughout a development team. You can do similar presentations of your expert review results by talking through your results. The main benefit this has is that developers can watch these summaries at any convenient time, and also scroll through the video to find issues relevant to them (chapter 18 contains additional information on reporting).

25.4.4 Learning to plan: intertwining research and development

While premeditated working processes are always preferable to ad hoc ones where you scramble to set up playtesting scenarios, the ability to thoroughly intertwine GUR into development projects is an acquired skill. While successful research/development merger can take on many shapes and forms (depending on the details of the project in question), we have identified some general work structures that have produced positive outcomes in our projects. In the process of identifying those structures, we have also naturally experienced some that you will definitely want to avoid. One of the more common examples of the latter is when testing starts as a late afterthought in a project's pipeline, which is not all that uncommon. In our earlier projects, passion and resources had been spent on creating an experience that we hoped players would enjoy in the way we intended them to—but when we initiated tests shortly before the game's launch, issues quickly emerged that pulled the rug out from under the team. The importance of planning tests as an integral part of a development project is often learned the hard way (we learned that in the transition from the first few projects), and constitutes an important step in starting to solidify GUR processes. One issue you might face is thus that early negative experiences with user research might sour your team on the concept, which leaves your hard-learned lessons dead in the water. But, if you manage to persevere and keep pushing the envelope for how research is integrated into your team's development processes, you have already managed to pass a big hurdle.

At the initial stages of using GUR, your research will likely have to be conducted in fairly late stages of the production pipeline (as was our experience in our first projects). This may limit how extensive and in-depth your testing can be, as the game has already started to ossify, and many game features will already be locked down. This is still, however, a good opportunity to start experimenting with rapid ad hoc playtests that, while perhaps not particularly resource-efficient and precise, can produce some important insights into how certain game features can still be improved.

As you and your colleagues become more familiar with GUR, your processes can hopefully expand and be integrated more deliberately into other parts of the production pipeline in subsequent projects. If you manage to devise and implement applicable GUR processes, and get adept at working with them, you will quickly gain experience in both long-term planning and rapidly executing important core tests if time is limited. You should also have had time to explore research methods that might have more specific areas of application; whereas ad hoc tests based on more intuitive methods may be useful to explore general game issues, specific methods can be applied to examine individual aspects of the game in more detail. With this expanded toolbox, you can iterate and expand your GUR processes and offer relevant feedback at more stages of development (as we started doing in Phase B) (Figure 25.2) (chapters 2 and 3 also talk about GUR across game production).

One thing in particular that you will be able to improve with better organizational integration is the sampling processes behind your playtests; being able to have a varied group of participants is a large part in improving the usefulness of your research. When time and resources are limited, you will often have to employ quick and easy means of sampling: asking peers or colleagues to try the game themselves, or asking friends and family to come in for some playtests. With more time for playtests, and with the ability to familiarize yourself with the game project and its intended audience, you can start using more elaborate

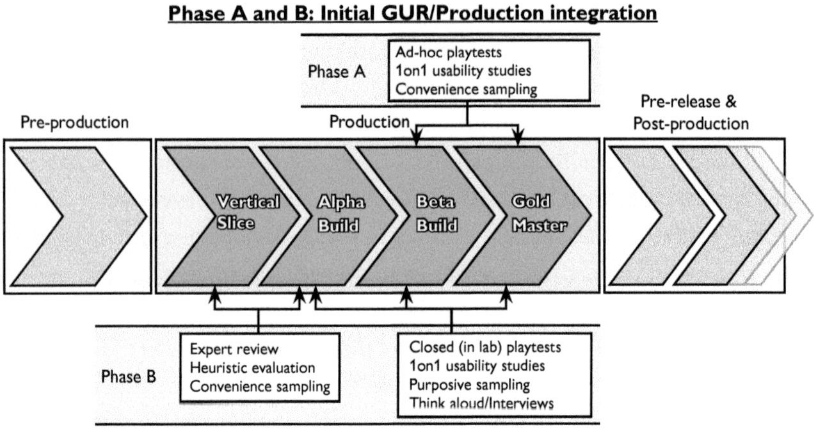

Phase A and B: Initial GUR/Production integration

Figure 25.2 Our own GUR work had humble beginnings, but could iteratively be expanded and more closely integrated with development processes as our own and our colleagues' understanding increased as to how GUR could be used to benefit our projects

sampling methods (such as purposive or dimensional sampling). It is, however, important that your sampling methods grow in proportion to your research tools and analysis methods—larger and more elaborate samples require more rigorous documentation and planning, and just increasing the number of test subjects does not necessarily mean better research outcomes if you are not ready to execute the playtests well or process the increased amount of data.

Purposive sampling is a broad descriptor of subjective sampling processes. In a typical purposive sampling, you choose playtesters based on whether or not they possess qualities you can directly identify as pertinent to your project or testing hypotheses (e.g., a 'type' of gamer that fits the game's target demographic, or members of an age group that your studio has had trouble resonating with in earlier projects). Dimensional sampling is a bit more involved, and is done to minimize the risk that tests fail to identify unknown issues and ensure that all demographics are represented by first identifying characteristics (or 'dimensions') of relevant testers (e.g., age and prior gaming habits) and ensuring that at least one tester representative of every conceivable combination of these characteristics is included in the playtests.

As your testing experiences and skill sets will continue to expand and improve, their applicability will start creeping into even more stages of the development pipeline: you can be an asset during pre-production by conducting competitor analyses or expert reviews on similar titles to establish best practices and report on common pitfalls. You can also do valuable tests on early mock-ups, contribute to UI flow charts, and do focus groups on what people want to see in your next project (Figure 25.3).

You can also focus on expanding the tools you use for your core tests and enhance them. Eye tracking, for instance, is getting cheaper and cheaper and can provide very valuable feedback, especially for UI-heavy games. For the later development stages, you can tweak your playtests so that they focus on providing feedback on the few things that still can be changed. For example, balance and difficulty levels are things that can often be tweaked very late in projects. During the final post-production stage, you can also analyse the reviews your game received and do a post-mortem of what reviewers found to be positive or negative aspects of the game. The specifics of carrying out these methods are detailed in many other texts, and also in other chapters in this book (for some specific recommendations, see the resources listed at the end of this chapter).

25.4.5 Putting it together: testable design queries and useful research outcomes

As described previously, the work involved in conducting GUR is not limited to the methods and tools that you employ in your playtesting environment—it also involves effectively communicating research in an impactful way to other team members. What all the previous examples allude to is that impactful GUR requires development and testing processes to interface well with one another. Just as it is difficult to devise ways of testing vague design problems, it is difficult

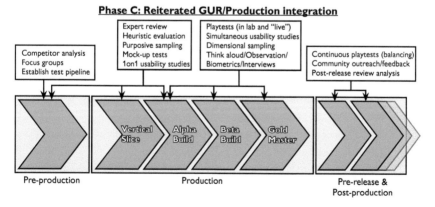

Figure 25.3 This figure depicts where some suggested methods are most commonly used, but they can be applied at any stage where you find them to be applicable. For example, expert reviews can continue into alpha if new mechanics are being tested

to actually apply vague research results during design decisions. This aspect of GUR is something you need to make into a fundamental part of your own mindset and working processes, as well as something you cultivate in your studio's working culture.

One of the major challenges we faced at the outset of our own efforts was cultivating a dialogue between ourselves and our colleagues that was conducive to impactful GUR. This challenge is not something that can be boiled down or related to practicalities or research methods, but rather a thought process that needs to be iteratively established in a working environment. For many studios, there is a gap between development and research; the latter can often be seen as an unnecessary hindrance to development, and designers sometimes close themselves off from research as it can be seen as intrusive to their vision. While direct aversion to GUR is a worst-case starting point, it is not unheard of. Developers want to focus on progressing towards completing their game vision, and research can seem rather pointless or counter to that end. But if you are able to start conducting impactful tests (on however small a scale) that produce relevant data, and present it in a meaningful and applicable way to your team, the positive influence GUR can have on their work towards achieving their game vision will start becoming apparent. Working with GUR thus entails acting as a conduit between development and research processes, and successful and impactful GUR constitutes a dialogue between the two that is mutually constructive (Figure 25.4).

While our own initial experiences were not too arduous when it came to establishing a dialogue between research and development, we certainly did not hit the ground running. As previously described, a large part of our early GUR work consisted of translating reported design and development issues into

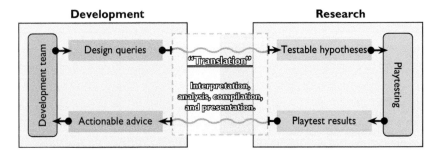

Figure 25.4 Impactful GUR requires that you are able to act as a conduit between development and research. You need to be able to translate design queries to testable hypotheses, and outcomes from the testing of those hypotheses into actionable advice for the development team

what we felt were executable test scenarios that would answer questions in the same general ballpark as the reported issue (resulting in overly lengthy post-test reports). As our working processes improved, and our colleagues became increasingly familiar with GUR processes and what type of information user research could provide, the dialogue became more honed and efficient. It is important to acknowledge that this honing did not just involve us becoming better researchers, but also our colleagues becoming better at presenting design queries as testable scenarios.

This system of communication is crucial, but it is hard to suggest a definite step-by-step working process to achieve it since it is unique for every studio environment. As a general rule, however, your ability to act as conduit will often dictate the system's success. Being a good conduit involves being flexible, as what needs to be conveyed between development and research changes throughout a project's progression. It is thus important to understand at what level development ideas and issues should be discussed, how tests should be described, and how their outcomes should be analysed and presented. GUR's role in a project changes, oscillating between being explorative and descriptive many times throughout a game's many development phases. At certain stages, more open-ended exploratory testing, largely independent of specific design queries, can be valuable to discover issues that the developers might not have been aware of. At other stages, there will be a higher need for directed tests that are specifically designed to identify and describe why certain parts of the game are problematic.

25.5 Summary

Impactful GUR entails more than just conducting research—it requires a prag-matic outlook, where a development team's needs and capabilities are taken into account when user research is planned, conducted, and analysed (Table 25.1). One issue that many face when starting out their journey into GUR is that the guidelines, methods, and tools that are available are often quite daunting and resource-intensive to implement. Thus, the whole endeavour can come across as a luxury reserved for AAA studios that can afford the high barrier to entry. In our experience, however, GUR can be a valuable and applicable tool even in smaller studios.

In order to be impactful, and to provide value to your team, you need to be a good communicator, developer, and researcher. A good way to start working with GUR is to experiment with small-scale research endeavours. During these you can start developing your own research skills simultaneously as the added

Table 25.1 *Summary of the GUR Implementation Process*

Just do it – Identify important stakeholders and conduct key GUR methods that quickly yield actionable results. Use any resources and participants available. Playtests late in the development process and expert reviews are methods that are easy to implement.

Establish and solidify your skills and research methods. Refine your playtesting process: experiment with hardware set-ups, test procedures, report structures, and participant sampling processes.

Establish your key stakeholders and improve the process of communicating findings. Now you know your organization and what you can deliver. Use this information to reiterate whom to present what findings to. Together with stakeholders, refine your research priorities.

Integrate research with the development schedule. Start planning ahead and schedule GUR tests based on what will be delivered at what time. You will quickly realize the scope of what you can test and how you need to prioritize.

Cultivate the dialogue between research and development. Depending on how communication works in your organization, establish processes for how to communicate about research and what needs to be communicated to whom. Educate stakeholders about research so they can participate in the process more and understand what is required to conduct tests.

Finally: *reiterate, reiterate, and reiterate.* After each project and each test, engage in a short post-mortem to find dos and don'ts and improve your process continuously going forward.

values of the process are made noticeable to your team. Over time, you will become more efficient and confident in your research methods and in your ways of communicating research outcomes to your team in an appropriate manner. Eventually you will be familiar enough with the relationship between research and development that you can foresee and pre-plan research processes for entire game projects.

25.6 Key takeaways

- *Start out small.* It is easy to become fixated on the finer details of GUR processes, and to want to ensure that everything is set up correctly and accounted for. However, the important thing when first starting out with GUR is not *how* you start, but rather *that* you start. GUR is a skill that one develops through practice and experience. Working with rapid ad hoc methods is, while sometimes messy, chaotic, and often decried by career researchers, an excellent way to start understanding the intricacies of GUR. So do not wait for everything to be perfectly aligned before you start your first tests—start testing, iterate, and improve your processes from experience.

- *Iterate often with your stakeholders on how you can best give them the information they need.* For some organizations, longer reports are okay and work well, others will want shorter reports and summaries and more video examples. This differs depending on how the organization is run and what roles you are reporting to, as well as on individual differences in how different people like to work. You will need to figure it out in your specific circumstances and tailor your reports to the people you work with.

- *Resist the urge to go for fancy equipment and overly complicated methods.* Fancy equipment and complicated methods are good and can provide valuable results, but you need tailor your working processes to your team's needs and your studio's available resources. More advanced GUR tools and methods are often costly, as they require a lot of time to start using and to tailor them for your organization. A lot of GUR-specific software costs a substantial amount of money. You can definitely be impactful and efficient with cheap and free alternatives.

- *Level with the audience of your research—get to know the people that work in and with your company.* Talk to them about what they do and what their usual tasks are. This is a powerful tool for you to understand how people in your organization actually do what they do on a day-to-day basis, and in the long term you will get to know how, when, and by whom different decisions are made. Who creates the UI? Who implements it? There is no better way to get information on how to tailor your tests and results for your organization than knowing who the ultimate recipient of your research might be.

Literature

Desurvire, H., Caplan, M., Toth, J. A. (2004). Using heuristics to evaluate the playability of games. CHI '04 Extended Abstracts on Human Factors in Computing Systems (pp. 1509–1512). Vienna, Austria: ACM.

Desurvire, H., Wiberg, C. (2009). Game usability heuristics (PLAY) for evaluating and designing better games: the next iteration. In A. A. Ozok and P. Zaphiris (eds), Online communities and social computing, Vol. 5621 (pp. 557–566). Berlin and Heidelberg: Springer.

Lectures

Hodent, C. (2014). Developing UX practices at Epic Games. Lecture given at Game Developers Conference Europe 2014, Cologne, Germany.

Livingston, I. (2014). Where are the sharks? User research in the Far Cry production pipeline. Lecture given at Game Developers Conference 2014, San Francisco, CA.

McAllister, G. (2012). Implementing an in-house playtesting process. Lecture given at Game Developers Conference Europe 2012, Cologne, Germany

Steury, K. (2011). Games user research: tips and techniques for projects of all sizes. Lecture given at Casual Connect 2011, San Francisco, CA.

Resources

Finding a mentor: The community is small but eager to help out newcomers; knowledge spreading is something that many of us are eager to work on and why this book initiative was started in the first place. We recommend you to head to gamesuserresearchsig.org and to find the LinkedIn group.

Heuristics: Nielsen, J. (1995). 10 usability heuristics for user interface design. nngroup.com/articles/ten-usability-heuristics/

CHAPTER 26

Strategies for understanding and researching mobile games in context

STEVEN SCHIRRA, *Twitch*

BROOKE WHITE, *Yahoo*

Highlights

Mobile games are deeply integrated into players' everyday lives. In this chapter, we introduce methods such as paper prototyping and diary studies that consider both the unique form-factor of mobile touchscreen devices and the need to understand users' context for gameplay. We consider the constraints of lab-based research for mobile games, and discuss strategies for conducting mobile studies in and out of the lab.

26.1 Introduction

In Games User Research (GUR), context is crucial. Knowing *where* users will play your game, *who* they will play with, *what* equipment they will use, and *how* they will use it can say a lot about which user needs should be supported. These needs can vary by platform. A user firing up their PlayStation 4 on the couch

Games User Research, Anders Drachen, Pejman Mirza-Babaei, Lennart E. Nacke (Eds).
© Oxford University Press 2018. Published 2018 by Oxford University Press

would have many different constraints than, say, a user swiping through their smartphone on a crowded bus.

Peering into the user research labs at most major game studios, you may be surprised to find that most look more like living rooms, home offices, and Internet cafes than sterile research facilities. Creating a naturalistic setting not only helps put participants at ease during a study, but also allows researchers to study user behaviour in environments that mimic their real-world counterparts. This strategy can be particularly effective for console and PC game research, where users tend to be tethered to dedicated hardware and spaces to participate. However, when we think about 'typical' mobile gaming environments, creating an ideal research space can get more complicated.

To start, what is a typical mobile environment? Is it a doctor's office? An airport? A beach? A comfortable armchair? Is a typical gameplay session 30 seconds? Thirty minutes? For many mobile users, the answer may be all of the above. Because the context for mobile gameplay can shift drastically as users engage in daily activities, it's important that we consider these ambiguities in research planning.

To that end, researchers may draw from a variety of methods across a mobile development life cycle. Lab-based research allows for the collection of deep observational data around mobile device use and interaction, while 'in-the-wild' research helps researchers understand player behaviour across many game sessions—and in the context of their day-to-day lives. Taken together, these approaches allow us to gain a deeper understanding of the user experience, and provide game teams with data they need to create successful games.

In this chapter we will discuss strategies for studying mobile games in and out of the lab that consider the complexity of mobile gameplay. Firstly, we situate some unique challenges of mobile game design from a research perspective. Then we introduce a framework and methods for studying mobile games throughout the development process.

26.2 Challenges for mobile games

In our experience, there are three broad categories that encapsulate the differences between researching traditional games and mobile games. In what follows, we define each area and discuss why mobile games may require different research considerations than their PC and console game counterparts.

26.2.1 Learnability

Learnability describes the extent to which games can communicate game goals, rules, and mechanics. This communication is crucial to users' understanding of—and enjoyment in—the game. In designing for a small screen, there is little room for complex menus or other UI elements, and written instructions can be difficult to display as well as fit into the short attention span of the mobile user. Users are often short on time and want to be placed into the action immediately. The user interface, navigation, and onboarding process needs to help players quickly become familiar with the game's core rules, mechanics, and structure.

26.2.2 Physical interactions

Mobile games are unique in that they have almost unlimited methods of user input. Users can tap, scroll, pinch, swipe, draw, shake, rotate, and tilt to interact with a game. And unlike inputs for traditional console and PC games, mobile devices provide little opportunity for physical interaction through buttons, keyboards, joysticks, d-pads, and triggers. Development teams must create unique sets of touchscreen inputs and menus to suit each game, make users aware of these new inputs, and help the user understand whether their on-screen interactions were successful. On top of this, a single user interface must work effectively across a multitude of mobile devices, screen sizes, and pixel densities—and sometimes integrate with cameras, GPS, accelerometers, or other mobile sensors.

26.2.3 Progression

Many mobile games are meant to be played over a series of days, weeks, or months—and, in some cases, years. Although mobile games are played over long periods of time, individual session lengths are short. (For example, a study of 1242 UK smartphone users revealed that the average mobile game session lasted only 5.3 minutes; 'In the UK', 2015.) To keep players engaged, games may slowly increase in difficulty to provide new challenges, or novel gameplay modes may be introduced. New stories may unfold to keep the narrative fresh. Developers may also intentionally incorporate mechanics that control how much progress players can make each day, such as wait-timers, limited numbers of daily moves, or player actions dependent on the time of day. This means players' sense of fun, challenge, and accomplishment can drastically change over time as they progress in the game.

Games User Researchers employ a variety of methods to focus on these key areas. Whereas PC- and console-based testing tends to rely heavily on traditional lab-based testing (albeit in comfy living room–style labs), mobile games have many elements that are best studied in the context of users' day-to-day lives. Therefore, we must also incorporate in-the-wild field-testing methods alongside lab research.

26.3 Early-stage mobile research

Unlike console games where the development process may take years, mobile games have more aggressive development schedules, so uncovering issues early in the process can save valuable development time. Early-game concepts and workflows can be tested with users in the lab using methods such as *paper prototyping*. With this method, key interfaces, storylines, or workflows are hand-drawn on paper (we prefer blank index cards), and users are asked to think aloud and interact with the cards as though they are using a mobile device. Multistep workflows are drawn out over a series of cards, and swapped out by the researcher (who acts as the 'computer') based on the user's interactions. Mobile games are well suited for paper prototype studies, particularly because of their flat form-factor and lack of external affordances, such as buttons and joysticks. It's interesting to observe users almost immediately suspend disbelief and interact naturally with the paper cards by tapping, swiping, and pinching the 'screen'.

In our own work, we have found paper prototyping useful in a variety of contexts. For example, a mobile strategy game team wanted to understand how effectively their tutorial would teach players the game's core storyline and objectives. The team wanted to introduce players to the game through a series of character dialogue boxes and simple drag-and-drop interactions. To evaluate this process, we created a paper prototype that included one card for each tutorial screen and interaction, then brought users into the lab for testing. In observing just a few sessions, we found that not only was the tutorial long and clunky—taking nearly ten minutes for participants to complete—but also that many of the instructions were difficult to understand. Because the testing material was simply paper note cards, the game team quickly removed superfluous information and between sessions rewrote confusing passages. Similar paper prototyping studies can be effectively conducted on early-game menus, user interfaces, and workflows as well.

As teams move further into their development process and begin producing *digital prototypes*—interactive or semi-interactive digital representations of a game workflow or system—further lab-based studies can be conducted to test their intuitiveness, delightfulness, and overall usability. When we study digital prototypes in the lab, we pay particular attention to the deep behavioural data that is best collected through direct (and close) observation of players. In observing the way users interact with the game on real mobile devices, we may uncover parts of the user interface that are difficult to tap or interact with, gestures the user attempted that are not registered by the game, and mistakes the user makes as they input specific game commands. We also want to understand users' cognitive processes as they play—how they learn and make decisions in the game—and how well the game's design supports this process. Having users in the lab allows researchers to ask pointed questions and collect user feedback in real time.

Recordings of lab sessions are particularly useful when researchers want to examine mobile users' on-screen interactions in more detail and document their findings for the game team. To properly document a mobile gaming session, it's important that the recording device be able to continuously capture both the mobile screen and the user's fingers and hands. At the same time, the camera set-up should encourage users to hold their devices in a completely natural position. Documenting a lab-based session can sometimes be at odds with giving players the full freedom of movement they would enjoy in everyday life, but is often necessary in order to observe nuanced touchscreen interactions on small screens.

Few commercial camera set-ups are optimized for recording mobile devices, so many researchers have invented their own solutions. For example, we have talked to one research team that duct-taped a tall tripod, a GorillaPod tripod, some chopsticks, and a camera together to document their sessions. Small camera sleds that attach directly to a mobile device are also widely used in mobile GUR labs and can be the best option to see screen, fingers, and hands while still allowing the user to hold the device naturally (Abney et al., 2014).

26.4 Late-stage mobile research

Later in the development process, a beta version of the mobile game may be developed. These pre-release builds, while unfinished, contain all the features, systems, interfaces, and instructions users need to play through a self-contained game experience. As builds become more fully featured, lab-based studies may become more limited in their usefulness because they cannot provide *ecological validity*. That is, in the superficial space of the lab session, the researcher cannot understand what it's like for a mobile user to play the game in the wild.

Let's imagine we wanted to study the fictional mobile game *Sanic's Universe*, a building game where users create and customize their own city. Each day, players receive a quest from the mayor, and must complete all the quest objectives by the next calendar day to level-up their city and unlock new buildings. Tasks such as building construction and resource collection take time to complete—ranging from a few minutes to several hours. Players must effectively manage their time and return to the game multiple times each day to ensure the objectives are complete.

In researching such a game, we may have many questions about user behaviour and attitudes that are difficult to answer in the lab, such as Can users easily manage the requirements of the game alongside other mobile activities? Does the daily quest structure remain engaging over time? Do users experience game issues in everyday mobile contexts (texting and playing, playing with weak mobile signal, etc.)? At the core of these questions is a desire to know about gameplay in the context of users' daily lives. There are many fieldwork strategies that mobile Games User Researchers use to answer these types of questions and collect data in the field.

26.4.1 Designing a mobile diary study

One such method to capture gameplay data in context[1]—and across several days or weeks—is a *diary study*. In a diary study, participants remotely document their mobile gameplay activities and behaviours as they occur and send reports back to the researcher, providing contextual learnings (information) that are difficult—if not impossible—to collect in the lab. There are many ways to frame a diary study, and researchers should strongly consider the game's structure in their design plans. Some key considerations include the following:

- **How many users should be included?** This is largely dependent on the researcher's timeline, resources, and research questions. We want to

---

[1] There are many other methods for understanding the user experience in context that can be applied to mobile games. For in-depth discussions of contextual user research methods, refer to Bentley and Barrett (2012) and Beyer and Holtzblatt (1998).

collect data about a variety of experiences to identify themes and patterns—while also being mindful of the vast amount of qualitative data we are collecting. As with most qualitative research, large sample size is not a virtue; we have collected meaningful data with as few as five users, but have seen many studies include 10–20 users to ensure a diverse participant pool.

- **How will users gain access to the game?** This can be accomplished by inviting participants to the lab to have the game installed on their mobile device in person, or through an over-the-air remote distribution service such as TestFlight for iOS or Google Play for android.

- **How long will the study run?** The length of the study can be firmly structured around calendar days (e.g., one week, two weeks), or loosely structured around game milestones (e.g., the study is complete when the user reaches Level 10).

- **How will users document their behaviour?** Users can report on their game sessions through a paper activity log or an online survey—or mobile-centric methods such as text messages, mobile video entries, or voicemails.

- **What will users document?** Data collected could include the physical location of the session, what users did during their session, how they felt about the session, what technical issues they may have encountered, and other relevant details. In addition, it is most useful for the development team to have accurately instrumented the beta build to capture data like session frequency, duration, and game progression.

- **What is the frequency for entries?** The cadence of diary entries should give researchers the contextual information they need without overwhelming participants. Participants can be asked to report after each game session, after each day of gameplay, or upon reaching certain milestones.

Researchers should also be mindful of the limitations diary studies. These studies require lots of active management from the researcher throughout the data collection phase to keep participants engaged and submitting their entries. The amount of data to sort through and analyse can be significant, and require many hours of analysis, which can be difficult in a fast-paced research setting. However, the data collected through a diary study can provide rich contextual findings that would be difficult to understand in the lab.

26.4.2 Thinking through a diary study: Sanic's Universe case study

Let's imagine we are designing a diary study for our fictional building game Sanic's Universe. In our lab research, we validated that our menus and user interface are intuitive and easy to use. We have also completed several rounds of lab-based testing on the first-time user experience and made improvements to increase the game's learnability. We feel confident that most users who complete our onboarding flow will have a strong understanding of the game's story, structure, and goals. But now we want to focus on the daily quest structure and understand whether we are setting achievable goals for the player, and seeing whether completing those daily goals continues to feel fun and rewarding over time.

We invite 15 local users from our target demographic (e.g., smartphone users; affinity for building games) into the lab to install our beta build of the game onto their personal mobile device. With users on-site, we can evaluate their first-time user experience with the game. We also interview them about their recent mobile gameplay experiences to better understand their backgrounds, and explain the requirements of the diary study. Since we are most interested in the daily quest structure in this study, we ask participants to submit an entry after their final gameplay session of the day, including a screenshot of their current city. The study will span two weeks so we can understand differences between weekday and weekend gameplay—and also give participants ample time to level-up in the game, unlock new buildings, and see their cities grow. Participants are required to keep push notifications turned on for the study so they are informed of new quests, but there are no other gameplay requirements, so we can understand their natural behaviour. For each of the daily entries, participants will answer the following questions:

- When did you open the game today? What was your physical location for each session? What else were you doing while playing the game?
- Describe your overall experience in the game today. What did you do in the game? How do you feel about your sessions today?
- What was today's daily quest from the mayor? Were you able to complete the quest? Why or why not?
- Were there any memorable moments in today's gameplay session? If so, please describe.
- Did you find anything frustrating or difficult in the game today? If so, please describe.

- Did you run into any technical issues with the game today? If so, please describe.
- What does your city look like today? Please text a screenshot along with your entry.

To make reporting mobile-friendly, we instruct participants to submit daily reports by recording a video response on their smartphones and sending that video to one of the researchers via text. Throughout the two-week study, participants receive daily text messages reminding them to make their video entries. As entries are submitted, they are transcribed and logged by the researcher— both to track participants' progress in the study and also to surface critical issues to the team as they arise. At the completion of the study, participants are invited back for a final in-lab interview where researchers can follow up on their experience with the game, and ask detailed questions about specific diary entries and responses. We can also see the game progression itself on the user's mobile device.

With the data we collected, we can apply traditional qualitative data analysis techniques to understand the themes and patterns in the data (see also chapters 8–10 and 12 for more on qualitative data evaluation from the perspective of particular methods). We can gain information about where participants used the game and what other activities they were engaging in at the time; we can discover patterns in user pain points and delights and tie those responses back to specific quests and sessions; we can see how users' attitudes change as they make progress in the game; and we can highlight technical issues and constraints that arise in the context of participants' mobile lives. Pairing this contextual data with our learnings from the lab helps create a more comprehensive understanding of the mobile experience so we can validate which parts of the design support the needs of our users, and which parts need further iteration and revision.

26.5 Takeaways

As the smartphone market continues to grow, so too does the need for industry Games User Researchers to understand mobile games and their users. In industry contexts, we draw from a variety of research strategies and methods to allow for the close observation of nuanced touchscreen interactions, to provide a deeper understanding of mobile gameplay in everyday contexts, and to understand how user attitudes about mobile games change over time.

In this chapter we have discussed a few unique challenges to mobile game research. Here are some key takeaways that you can use immediately with your own games.

Challenge: Providing research that explores both users' mental models and game learnability early and iteratively throughout an aggressive development cycle.

Takeaway: Leverage paper prototype studies with mobile gamers early in development process to evaluate learnability of key navigation, UI patterns, and conceptual game mechanics. As teams are just beginning to think about possible game mechanics, UI, and navigation, encourage the designers to sketch these ideas on paper cards, and present them to users to validate concepts and discover issues. Once the game is more fleshed out and the team develops onboarding or tutorial screens, again use paper prototypes to enable rapid iteration (even between sessions).

Challenge: Evaluating users' physical interactions with prototypes and early builds of the mobile game interface.

Takeaway: Ensure you and the design team have appropriate recording equipment to observe both the mobile screen and the user's fingers and hands interacting with the game, while encouraging users to hold their devices in a natural position. Mobile sleds are currently the most effective tool for this (Abney et al., 2014); you can buy one or build your own.

Challenge: Evaluating mobile game usage in context; understanding players' progression in the game over time.

Takeaway: As soon as core gameplay and progression are in place, get real users to play the game in the wild. Set up a diary study (and ensure the team instruments core elements) to gain insight into daily usage patterns, progression, and insights around user satisfaction and pain points—all well before launch. You can even set up diary studies post-launch or during larger betas to gather qualitative feedback to map onto data analytics for live games. Arranging a diary study on a live game can also allow you to experiment with the best protocol and format for you and your teams to evaluate progression for your specific game genre.

In the end, having good instincts for mobile GUR is less about learning a new set of research methods and more about developing an evolving mental model of the mobile user experience, and focusing your work on the unique opportunities and challenges that mobile games hold.

References and further reading

Abney, A., White, B., Glick, J., Bermudez, A., Breckow, P., Yow, J., Tillinghast-Trickett, R., Heath, P. (2014). Evaluation of recording methods for user test sessions on mobile devices. In Proceedings of the First ACM SIGCHI Annual Symposium on Computer-Human Interaction in Play (pp. 1–8). New York: ACM.

Bell, M., Chalmers, M., Barkhuus, L., Hall, M., Sherwood, S., Tennent, P., …, Hampshire, A. (2006). Interweaving mobile games with everyday life. In Proceedings of the SIGCHI Conference on Human Factors in Computing Systems (pp. 417–426). New York: ACM.

Bentley, F., Barrett, E. (2012). Building mobile experiences. Cambridge, MA: MIT Press.

Beyer, H., Holtzblatt, K. (1998). Contextual design: defining customer-centered systems. San Francisco, CA: Morgan Kaufmann.

Brandt, J., Weiss, N., Klemmer, S. (2007). txt 4 l8r: lowering the burden for diary studies under mobile conditions. In CHI '07 Extended Abstracts on Human Factors in Computing Systems (pp. 2303–2308). New York: ACM.

De Souza e Silva, A., Hjorth, L. (2009). Playful urban spaces: a historical approach to mobile games. Simulation & Gaming 40(5), 602–625.

In the UK, app users have longest sessions with games. (2015, 20 November). eMarketer. http://www.emarketer.com/Article/UK-App-Users-Have-Longest-Sessions-with-Games/1013257

CHAPTER 27

Involving players with special needs in Games User Research

KATHRIN GERLING, *KU Leuven*

CONOR LINEHAN, *University College Cork*

REGAN MANDRYK, *University of Saskatchewan*

Highlights

This chapter provides an overview of challenges that emerge from the involvement of players with special needs in game development, focusing on user involvement in early design stages and challenges that emerge during playtesting. Through three case studies focusing on young children, people with disabilities, and older adults, we offer insights into appropriate methodology for GUR with diverse audiences. Additionally, we discuss strategies to establish a respectful and empowering process for user involvement.

27.1 Introduction

Player involvement in the development process through Games User Research (GUR) is a crucial step in adapting games to the needs of players. Working collaboratively with diverse audiences can contribute to the design of more inclusive games and assist in the development of not only entertainment-focused but also of serious and educational games wishing to target specific groups of players.

Games User Research, Anders Drachen, Pejman Mirza-Babaei, Lennart E. Nacke (Eds).
© Oxford University Press 2018. Published 2018 by Oxford University Press

However, involving special populations in GUR can be challenging: participants may have a different experience with many technologies in terms of accessibility and usability, and some impairments and disabilities influence participants' abilities to engage with some of the standard tools in GUR, such as questionnaires on player experience. Therefore, involving diverse audiences in GUR requires a detailed understanding of the following:

- The needs of that specific groups of players.
- The impact that engagement with games in a user research context can have on players.
- Common challenges that arise throughout the research process when working with participants who have special needs.

This chapter provides an overview of challenges that emerge from the involvement of players with special needs in game development. While the present chapter cannot cover everything there is to know about how to involve players with special needs in GUR, it provides a starting point. At the end of the chapter, several suggestions for additional reading are included, including resources that discuss the case studies included later in detail.

We provide an overview of four case studies that illustrate common challenges and opportunities when engaging audiences with special needs in GUR, focusing on older adults and young people with disabilities. For each case study, we provide an outline of the characteristics of participants involved in the research, methodological approaches, and challenges and opportunities that were observed. While these case studies were carried out in an academic context, the approaches and considerations used in an industry setting would be similar, and the lessons learned from them transfer directly to any commercial development context.

27.2 Case Study 1: Games User Research for a movement-based game with older adults

Older adults are a growing demographic among the global player population, not only due to the natural effects of populations' ageing, but also because this section of the population is becoming increasingly engaged with game playing. Catering to this audience offers game developers access to new markets and new commercial opportunities. Moreover, game playing offers older adults in, for example, residential care the potential for entertaining new types of cognitive, social, and physical exertion, thereby contributing to their quality of life.

However, when designing for this audience, the impact of age-related changes and impairments can introduce challenges for prospective players, increasing the need for careful and well-designed user involvement throughout the development process.

27.2.1 Movement-based games for older adults in residential care

Movement-based games hold the promise of providing cognitive and physical stimulation for older adults in residential care. This case study explores the design of movement-based game interaction for older adults who experience age-related changes and impairments through the development of a gesture-controlled game, implemented using the Microsoft Kinect camera (for details of the project, see Gerling et al., 2012).

27.2.2 Approach and participants

The study was carried out together with the Sherbrooke Community Centre in Saskatoon, Canada, a care facility that caters to older adults who experience a wide range of age-related changes and impairments. It was conducted in two steps, first assessing the suitability of different gestures through an analysis tool, and then integrating a set of movements into a gesture-controlled gardening game. All sessions took place in the media room of the care facility. Each session lasted about 30 minutes, including five to ten minutes of interaction with the analysis tool and game. Participants took part individually, and were accompanied by a staff member, who was also involved in their recruitment.

Fifteen older adults participated in the first step of the research. The average age was 74 years (range 60–90, 7 female). Out of all participants, 13 older adults used wheelchairs, and one person relied on a cane as walking support. Six participants reported hemiplegia as a result of stroke. Eight had previous experience playing video games. Twelve older adults were involved in the evaluation of the final game. The average age was 77 (range 60–90, 5 female), 11 participants used wheelchairs, and 6 had hemiplegia.

27.2.3 GUR methodology

The case study adopted a quantitative approach to explore accessibility, usability, and player experience. Both steps of the research involved a standardized questionnaire to explore participant mood (using the Positive and Negative

Affect Schedule, PANAS; Watson et al., 1988), and a questionnaire specifically designed to gain insights into players' experiences carrying out gestures and playing the game. Additionally, metrics and observations were included to give further insights into overall performance and instances in which player characteristics had an impact on their engagement with the game.

27.2.4 Challenges and opportunities

Through the research, we identified a number of challenges that must be considered when engaging institutionalized older adults in GUR. It should be noted that we worked with a physical therapist to identify suitable movements for the target audience, including a calibration routine in the game that adapted the interface to a player's range of motion and adjusted difficulty levels to player speed. Nevertheless, despite catering to a broad range of skills and abilities in our initial game designs, some participants still struggled to carry out the movements required to play or found it difficult to understand in-game tasks. In some cases, this prompted participants to reflect upon their abilities, or led to frustration when they could only complete the game after the second or third attempt, suggesting that levels of challenge required to interact with and successfully complete games needs to be considered at a very basic level.

We observed that older adults diagnosed with cognitive impairments particularly struggled, not only when learning how to interact with the game, but also when completing other parts of the research process. We observed that some participants required additional time to complete questionnaires and sometimes experienced difficulties when following instructions (e.g., when trying to quantify their emotional state as required by the PANAS questionnaire), underlining the importance of investigator support throughout the entire process. Likewise, some participants who had little previous experience with technology in general and games in particular found it difficult to find the correct words to refer to elements of our study to describe their experience. Additionally, not having played video games before might influence their perception of the game, leaving participants without a comparable previous experience or expectations of what engaging with a game would feel like. From a methodological perspective, since verbal communication in this study often allowed only a small window on participants' experiences, observations and metrics were immensely helpful. They offer an alternative view of the play experience, and deepened our understanding of instances where players experienced difficulty, accomplishment, and joy.

27.3 Case Study 2: exploring the value of social play for older adults in residential care

This case study explored how older adults in long-term care engage with games in a social setting. It compares results from two care facilities: a seniors' residence catering to independent older adults, and a care home offering high levels of support. Studies were carried out over the course of three months in both locations to gain insights into similarities and differences in how both groups engage with games 'in the wild' (for details on the work, see Gerling et al., 2015).

27.3.1 Research approach and participants

The study focused on weekly hour-long gaming sessions that were offered at both care facilities over the course of three months. Video games were advertised on the official activities schedule, similar to other leisure activities offered at both facilities. Older adults were recruited with the help of staff, and encouraged to get together in groups to play both custom-designed and commercially available (e.g., Kinect Sports Bowling) movement-based games.

Sessions were facilitated by a researcher. At the beginning of the study, all participants received a comprehensive introduction to the Kinect system and all games. At the seniors' residence, facilitation of the sessions was gradually transferred away from the researchers to the residents themselves. During the sessions, participants took turns playing the games and were given the opportunity to compete with each other (e.g., in bowling). Gaming sessions at the seniors' residence continued in a group setting throughout the study. In contrast, after the first month, gaming sessions at the care home were changed to individual activities at the request of residents, who felt that engaging with games in a social setting was problematic.

A total of 16 older adults (eight female) participated in the study, 10 at the seniors' residence and 6 at the care home. The average age was 79 at the seniors' residence, 74 at the care home. Four participants at the seniors' residence used walkers for assistance, one participant used a wheelchair, and five were able to walk independently, whereas all participants at the care home were using wheelchairs. A screening of cognitive abilities (see the following section on GUR methodology) revealed that all but one of the participants at the seniors' residence had no cognitive impairments, whereas all participants at the nursing home had already experienced severe changes in cognition.

We gathered written consent from participants at the seniors' residence, and oral assent witnessed by a guardian from participants at the care home.

27.3.2 GUR methodology

The study adopted a qualitative approach, combining observations made throughout the gaming sessions with monthly group interviews exploring player perspectives on games in general and as a social activity in particular. Following changes at the care home, individual interviews were carried out to accommodate the needs of older adults experiencing severe age-related changes and impairments. At the beginning of the study, participants were screened for cognitive impairment using the Mini-Mental State Exam (MMSE; Folstein et al., 1975)

27.3.3 Challenges and opportunities

While working with both groups of older adults, we identified challenges and opportunities associated with their experience with games, along with the impact of skills and abilities prevalent in both groups. The study revealed a strong impact of combined cognitive and physical impairment on their interest in engaging with games in a social setting. Particularly at the nursing home, we found that delays in turn-taking caused by physical impairment, long periods of time required to engage with the games, and difficulties among participants communicating with each other as a result of cognitive impairment created instances of frustration and vulnerability. Observation of play sessions demonstrated that it was very difficult to design accessible yet interesting experiences for participants who had a wide range of skills and abilities. Most surprisingly, the social setting in which games were played introduced additional challenges. The social setting was unexpectedly problematic, as it enabled players to observe the performance of others and to reflect upon their own abilities and the impact of ageing. While most participants started out on a level playing field, the long-term nature of the study revealed that some players developed their skills faster than others, sometimes leading to frustration among participants struggling to engage with the games if, for example, the impact of age-related changes was stronger on a certain day. From a methodological perspective, long-term observations provided valuable insights, as these allowed us to study experience over time, which also helped participants overcome challenges associated with a lack of familiarity with games and, on the other hand, allowed us to overcome any novelty effects that may have been present in a short-term study. When working with older adults at the seniors' residence, questionnaires were effective, and focus-group interviews gave an opportunity to tease out emergent ideas from the group. In contrast, participants at the care home with significant cognitive impairments were interviewed individually to account for their situation.

27.4 Case Study 3: games for young people with neurological vision impairment

Involving people with disabilities in GUR is the first step towards creating interactive experiences that are tailored to their needs and ideas. However, there are a number of challenges that need to be considered prior to player involvement that we discuss through two case studies focusing on the involvement of young people with complex needs in game development.

Neurological vision impairment (NVI) is a term that describes vision impairment caused by injury to areas of the brain that are responsible for visual processing. NVI detrimentally impacts upon quality of life. Recently, therapy strategies that focus on training peoples' eye movements have been demonstrated as effective at improving functional vision for people with NVI. These therapies require participants to repetitively search an array of monochromatic on-screen stimuli in order to find target stimuli. Therapy must be undertaken in 30-minute sessions multiple times per week for a number of months. While adult stroke patients have previously demonstrated adherence to these types of interventions, this has not yet been demonstrated with children, nor, we would argue, is such a demonstration likely, due to the repetitive and boring nature of the task. We report on a project that explores a game-based vision therapy program to support participant engagement and adherence.

27.4.1 Research approach and participants

This project was carried out in close collaboration with the WESC Foundation in Exeter, UK, which is a specialist education centre for people with visual impairment. The project involved a highly iterative design and evaluation procedure. Beginning with a basic prototype that closely resembled the tasks used with adults, fortnightly design sessions were held over a six-month period, in which participants were observed playing the game and were asked to provide feedback. Information gathered from these sessions was used to gradually improve the design of the game, through collaboratively selecting activities and features that were most appealing to players.

The primary group of participants, with whom we worked closely, were four people (3 female, 1 male), aged 18–20, recruited through a specialist education centre for learners with vision impairment. Two participants had an undiagnosed neurological presentation with associated developmental delay, and learning, speech, and language difficulties. One participant had been diagnosed with a tumour on the optic chiasm at six years of age and had associated optic atrophy at the time of participating. The fourth participant had a confirmed diagnosis of cerebral palsy and left hemiplegia and unconfirmed NVI. Two participants were legally blind and two were described as having low vision.

A second group of participants consisted of three young people with acquired brain injury and suspected hemianopia who were part of a local community group organized by an occupational therapist. Each person in this group had relatively minor cognitive and physical impairments, thus more traditional co-design activities were possible. Data were collected from these participants during a one-off design session that lasted approximately two hours.

Note that the initial approach to potential participants was made by their college tutor. Candidates were informed about the study by a researcher who dictated a verbal information sheet, and gave formal consent by initialling (or placing a cross) in a large bold box under a transcript of the information.

27.4.2 GUR methodology

We began the project intending to undertake a participatory co-design methodology (similar to that described in Case Study 1). That is, in order to ensure that the game best fulfilled the needs of users, we intended on involving those users centrally and collaboratively within all design activities and decisions. We held regular design sessions with participants every two weeks over a six-month period. Each session typically involved participants playing the latest version of the game, for varying amounts of time, and providing feedback to the researcher. The researcher both engaged in the session and took notes. In earlier stages of the design process, when only rough prototypes were available, these play sessions were typically quite brief (5–10 minutes). In order to assess player preference, multiple prototypes were created and the researcher noted which version was most enthusiastically engaged with by participants. These comparisons facilitated specific design decisions, such as whether to include borders on shapes, or whether to include animations. Towards the end of the six-month period, when a complete game was available, sessions lasted 30–45 minutes, with participants attempting multiple playthroughs of the game.

In practice, there were a number of factors that significantly undermined our ability to undertake a genuinely participatory design in this project. Firstly, there are significant constraints when working in the health domain. Our intervention strategy—treatment of NVI through compensatory eye movements—is based on an existing intervention, which has already been demonstrated as clinically useful with adults. The long-term success criterion for our project is the demonstration of significant improvements in the functional vision of participants, brought about through playing of the game. In order to demonstrate such an improvement, and provide evidence of the standard acceptable to health practitioners, a randomized controlled trial (RCT) must be undertaken. However, the research ethics committee for the health service, quite rightly, does not allow speculative projects to undergo RCT. There must be some logical justification for why the therapy should work. In this case, this meant that some of the features of that original therapy, such as the repeated searching of the entire visual field, were non-negotiable features of the final design, regardless of anything that happened at design sessions. Thus, our work is not strictly participatory, nor collaborative, since there were non-negotiable features of the final game.

Secondly, there were significant challenges in communicating constructively with participants about design work in this project. Participatory design requires constructive, empathic dialogue between designers, users, and communities. It requires the participants to own the process and to hold researchers to account for decisions made. There is always a concern in working with participants with cognitive, verbal, and social disabilities that the same two-way dynamic is not present and, regardless of intentions, the researcher can be seen as using the participant as a resource, much like in a more traditional user-centred design context. Indeed, in our project, we found that participants almost never complained or expressed frustration with our game as long as they were able to play it with even the most basic level of success.

A further difficulty arose in our study in that our participants refused us permission to have their voices recorded or the sessions video recorded. Thus, design sessions were recorded only via notes made by the researcher. This is a limitation of the work, as it renders findings open to bias from that one individual.

27.4.3 Challenges and opportunities

The key contributor to the success of these sessions was the relationship and trust that had been built up between the researcher and participants over the course of his two-year placement at the centre. We suggest that it would have been very difficult to facilitate productive design sessions if the researcher simply visited the centre on a fortnightly or weekly basis to gather information and leave. By undertaking this project we found significant challenges inherent in delivering therapy programs through the format of a game.

Designing 'challenge' in therapy-specific games is more complicated than in other games, as it is difficult for the designer to understand which activities participants will find too easy and which they will find almost impossible. Moreover, there are two distinct types of challenges presented by a therapeutic game to the player. Firstly, the therapeutic task itself will represent a challenge for the player to undertake. Therapy necessitates repetition of skills or behaviours that the player is not proficient or comfortable in performing. Secondly, in order to present engaging and meaningful experiences for players, games must present appropriate levels of game challenge to participants. These in-game challenges are the central means through which games generate the motivation and engagement that is valuable in the context of therapy. Players get bored with and lose interest in games that are too easy, while they become frustrated with games that are too difficult. Indeed, in our study, some participants who were legally blind with very poor visual acuity had little difficulty playing the game. At the same time, games that are too difficult for the player are potentially de-motivating. Both of these types of challenge can function as a source of frustration for players and have the potential to undermine the engaging qualities of the game.

The use of a visual medium for the purposes of vision therapy presents notable challenges. Research on design for people with vision impairment typically focuses on the substitution of visual interface elements with stimuli that address other senses (e.g., hearing, touch). This approach is not appropriate in the context of vision therapy. Functional vision rehabilitation builds on the presentation of visual cues to encourage people with vision impairment to develop compensatory strategies such as eye and head movements to improve the effectiveness of visual scanning. To achieve this goal, players must complete search tasks using their visual skills, and displayed images should not be completely replaced with haptic or audio interface elements.

27.5 Case Study 4: games for children and teenagers who use powered wheelchairs

To explore opportunities in motion-based game design for children and teenagers who use powered wheelchairs, we worked with a school that provides education for young people with special needs. Throughout the game development process, our goal was to better understand how young people using wheelchairs perceive themselves with respect to video gameplay, their perceptions of motion-based games, and their thoughts on wheelchair-based game input (for more on this topic see Benton et al., 2014).

27.5.1 Research approach and participants

The project was carried out in collaboration with a local school, and included two steps. Firstly, over the course of two months participants were invited to attend four focus groups that were designed to give them an opportunity to share their perspectives on gaming, disability, and movement-based play. Based on these focus groups, which included a co-design component during the later stages, three movement-based games were developed, and evaluated in the second step of the project, during which participants were invited to engage with the games either in pairs or individually.

Participants of this case study had a wide range of physical and cognitive abilities. During the first phase of the project, we worked with two groups of children and young adults over the course of four months. In total, nine participants, 13–22 years of age (three female), took part in this phase. All used powered wheelchairs; medical conditions ranged from spinal cord injury as the result of accident to progressive neurodegenerative diseases and developmental conditions such as cerebral palsy. While most participants could express themselves through speech, one participant was non-verbal and required the assistance of staff, and another participant applied assistive technology (iPad application generating speech) to participate in our design sessions. During the second phase of the project, we worked with four young people (ages 16–18) using powered wheelchairs; participants again had a wide range of physical and cognitive abilities. Additionally, other students were given the opportunity to try the games, but their data were not included in the study because they did not match the inclusion criteria (e.g., no use of powered wheelchairs).

Note that we obtained written consent from participants' legal guardians, and followed up with an oral assent protocol in which participants were informed about the goals of the study and asked to verbally consent to participation.

27.5.2 GUR methodology

Within the focus groups during the first part of the study, we applied different methods to encourage participants to reflect upon themselves, their relationship with games, and disability (see chapters 7 and 8 for overviews of GUR methods).

For each focus group, we prepared guiding questions, and additional props and approaches if necessary. For example, we applied methods from visual sociology (Pauwels, 2010) to create drawings that represented participants in order to explore which aspects of themselves they considered important, and we included props, screenshots, and short game descriptions to help guide group discussion during later stages. Sessions were audio-recorded and transcribed. During the second part of the study, we adopted a qualitative approach that allowed us to explore in depth the experience that players had with the resulting games during gaming sessions. We developed three games of varying complexity: Speed Slope, a downhill skiing game, Rumble Robots 3D, a robot boxing game, and Rainbow Journey, a playful sensory experience without set goals. Observations were made by one researcher while another provided assistance throughout play, and followed up with participants in short post-play interviews exploring their experience. Again, all sessions were also audio-recorded, and transcripts and observations were combined into a document allowing us to arrive at a comprehensive understanding of the gaming sessions. All sessions were accompanied by at least one member of staff.

27.5.3 Challenges and opportunities

There were a number of challenges that emerged throughout this case study, some relating to the cognitive and physical abilities of participants and others emerging from the research context in a school setting. Specifically, during the focus-group stage, hosting a group of young people with mixed abilities comes with a number of unique challenges. There were many occasions where the investigator had to intervene to encourage the group to stay on topic, and there were some instances of frustration if participants required a lot of time to express their opinions (e.g., because they experienced difficulties speaking). Additionally, there were many instances of participants talking at the same time, along with background noise and other sounds that impacted the transcription stage of the project. Regarding the testing stage, participants' cognitive and physical abilities impacted the research process. Often, individuals with cognitive impairments required continuous assistance when playing the games, and some experienced difficulties engaging with more complex game concepts (e.g., hitting goals in Speed Slope). Similar to the first stage, eliciting feedback from some participants took more time, requiring a flexible scheduling system. Likewise, players with severe mobility impairments experienced difficulty when trying to excel at the games, as differences in their level of upper body and wheelchair control influenced in-game performance. To this end, we developed two tracking solutions that could accommodate a range of abilities (see Figure 27.1); further, working with a broad range of games in terms of complexity and difficulty was beneficial as it ensured that all players would be able to interact with at least one of the games. Another challenge that emerged from the setting—testing the games at a school—was that word-of-mouth spread about the study, and students who did not meet the inclusion criteria for our research (e.g., students using manual wheelchairs) became interested in playing the games. With the support of staff, we decided to facilitate gaming sessions for individual students without including their data in our study to avoid disappointment and a negative impact on relationships among students. Similar to previous studies, we found that making observations in combination with interviews was an effective means of eliciting detail on participants' experience and opinions. In

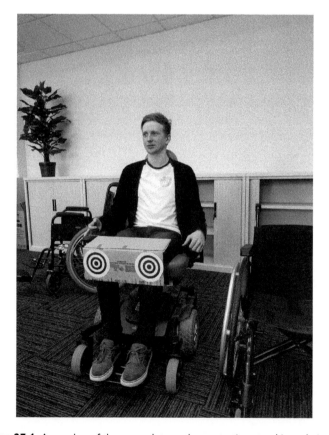

Figure 27.1 A member of the research team demonstrating a tracking solution that enables power wheelchair users with little upper body control to participate in play

this context, the presence of two researchers for all sessions was beneficial as it allowed us to make extensive observations while flexibly adapting our processes to individual participant needs.

Generally, these case studies illustrate some of the challenges and opportunities that emerge in the context of GUR with audiences with special needs. In the following section, we discuss emerging themes, and provide recommendations for GUR with diverse user groups to help researchers and practitioners address the most common challenges.

27.6 Recommendations for Games User Research with diverse user groups

Based on the insights from the case studies, we provide a set of recommendations for researchers and practitioners wishing to carry out GUR with diverse audiences. We focus on four core aspects: considerations that are necessary to reflect (1) the needs of participants, (2) methodological and procedural requirements, (3) the special nature of game development, and (4) the impact that the research setting can have on GUR with special populations (Figure 27.2).

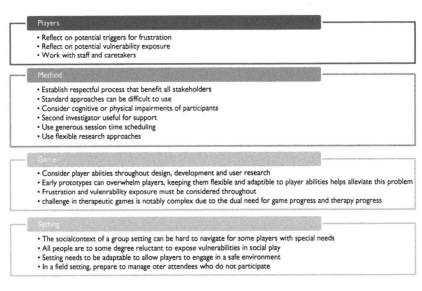

Players
- Reflect on potential triggers for frustration
- Reflect on potential vulnerability exposure
- Work with staff and caretakers

Method
- Establish respectful process that benefit all stakeholders
- Standard approaches can be difficult to use
- Consider cognitive or physical impairments of participants
- Second investigator useful for support
- Use generous session time scheduling
- Use flexible research approaches

Game
- Consider player abiities throughout design, development and user research
- Early prototypes can overwhelm players, keeping them flexible and adaptible to player abilities helps alleviate this problem
- Frustration and vulenrability exposure must be considered throughout
- challenge in therapeutic games is notably complex due to the dual need for game progress and therapy progress

Setting
- The socialcontext of a group setting can be hard to navigate for some players with special needs
- All people are to some degree reluctant to expose vulnerabilities in social play
- Setting needs to be adaptable to allow players to engage in a safe environment
- In a field setting, prepare to manage oter attendees who do not participate

Figure 27.2 A summary of the key recommendations the four case studies give rise to. For additional detail, please see the suggested further readings

27.6.1 Considerations regarding participants

Impairments and disabilities can have a strong impact on participants' ability to engage with games and GUR. It is important that researchers reflect upon potential triggers for frustration throughout the design of their research, and understand difficulties that are associated with certain participant groups, for example, persons with complex needs.

One of the drawbacks to the involvement of players with special needs is the significant potential—as a by-product of the process of exploring and testing activities that participants find challenging—for the exposure of participant vulnerabilities. For example, during design sessions to create games for young people with NVI (Case Study 3), we had to ask questions of our participants regarding whether they could see on-screen items and whether they could discriminate between different shapes, because this is the goal of the scanning task. Designers in this situation, as in any situation working with vulnerable participants, cannot avoid reminding participants of the limits of their abilities, something that has the potential to cause upset. Likewise, our work with young people using powered wheelchairs (Case Study 4) explored questions around physical abilities and assistive devices, both of which had potential to encourage participants to reflect upon their own situation.

To this end, involving staff in participant recruitment offers an opportunity of ensuring that only those individuals able to cope with the research process are invited to participate, reducing the risk of vulnerability among prospective participants who would have experienced frustration as a result of procedural requirements of the research.

27.6.2 Methodological and procedural considerations

From a methodological and procedural viewpoint, participant abilities need to be considered to establish a respectful research process that benefits all stakeholders. To this end, standard approaches involving player experience questionnaires and interviews can be difficult, particularly when working with participants with cognitive impairments or physical impairments that impact their motor skills. Instead, it may be more suitable to work with a combination of carefully guided interviews and extensive observations that are made throughout the entire research process.

Particularly when working with groups of people, having the support of a second investigator can be invaluable in ensuring a smooth research process along with high-quality observations. Additionally, generous session scheduling should be considered so that buffer time is available to deal with unexpected situations and participants' needing more time to complete parts of the research. Finally, we would like to emphasize the responsibility that researchers generally bear when working with human participants, and which is particularly important when working with vulnerable audiences. In many of the case studies presented in this chapter, there were instances where accommodating participants' needs meant adapting our research process, possibly negatively impacting the quality of data (e.g., changing the research protocol for one of the groups in our work on older adults' long-term engagement with games). Therefore, we recommend flexible research approaches that leave room to accommodate participant needs; to this end, qualitative approaches are recommended, as they offer opportunities to address and explore issues that emerge throughout the research process.

27.6.3 Game-related considerations

The case studies also demonstrate the importance that considering player abilities throughout the design and development process has for GUR. As games need to find the right level of challenge to provide a positive player experience, it is important to keep in mind that early prototypes bear the risk of overwhelming players, possibly leading to a frustrating experience that exposes vulnerability. To this end, we recommend that even at early stages, games need to be flexible in terms of adapting to player abilities. Alternatively, researchers need to make a range of games available to participants that cater to different abilities.

Likewise, challenge is a complex consideration in projects that aim to deliver therapy through gameplay. Therapeutic games present two different types of challenge to players. Each has the potential to cause frustration and disengagement to players and must be carefully considered and investigated through the design process. Firstly, game-related challenges provide a frame for the action in the game. Players work to overcome challenges. They must take some actions in order to progress through the game and receive rewards. Games that are too easy or too difficult do not motivate players to keep playing. Secondly, therapy-related challenges are inherent in these games. Players are recommended to play the game because they cannot do the task that the game asks of them—in physical therapy, this may be a specific upper arm movement; in vision therapy, it may be the searching of visual fields. To further complicate matters, these two types of challenge may require contradictory design solutions. Physical requirements of therapy may need to progress at regular intervals regardless of success, or lack thereof, with game challenges.

27.6.4 Considerations regarding the research setting

With respect to the research setting, two main aspects need to be considered. Firstly, while testing games in a focus-group setting can generally provide valuable insights that emerge from discussion between participants, the social context of a group setting can be hard to navigate for players with special needs. Particularly when working with older adults, there were several instances where we observed that participants lacked confidence in their abilities and were apprehensive to expose themselves in social play, which could have created instances of vulnerability. We saw similar tendencies when working with young people using wheelchairs, where a pair of players developed their skills at different speeds and direct comparison with another person introduced risk of frustration as a result of different physical abilities. To this end, researchers need to be ready to moderate the process, and, if necessary, adapt the research context to allow players to engage with games in a safe environment. Secondly, when carrying out GUR in the field (e.g., school or community centre) rather than in the lab, researchers need to be prepared to appropriately manage other attendees who do not participate in the research. For example, when working with children with disabilities, communicating to them that not everyone will be part of the research project may be difficult, and alternative activities should be considered.

In general, these considerations show that GUR with players who have special needs can be challenging, but are essential in the development of engaging playful experiences. We hope that our case studies and considerations can aid others in establishing accessible GUR processes that are flexible, consider the needs of participants at all stages, and allow them to share their insights and opinions in a respectful, encouraging environment.

27.7 Ethical approval and guidelines

In academic GUR work, ethical clearance is required for any research that involves people. This is in particular the case for any work focusing on people with disabilities or children. For anyone new to working with these audiences, it is strongly recommended to investigate the rules and regulations of university ethics boards, which are often freely available online, or by simply reaching out to the research board in question.

Here, Case Study 1 was approved by the University of Saskatchewan Behavioural Ethics Research Board as well as by the Saskatoon Health Region. We gathered written consent from all participants. Case Study 2 was approved by the same two bodies. Case Study 3 was approved by the University of Lincoln School of Psychology Research Ethics Committee, as well as by the WESC Foundation research ethics committee. Case Study 4 was approved by the University of Lincoln College of Science ethics board. For further guidance, the Canadian Panel on Research Ethics provides a comprehensive overview of requirements when working with human research participants which is available at http://www.pre.ethics.gc.ca/eng/policy-politique/initiatives/tcps2-eptc2/Default/.

27.8 Conclusion: considering the special needs audience

While GUR often looks to improve the experience of the average player, the common methodologies can be difficult to utilize when designing for audiences with special needs, or just for broader-than-normal audiences. Particularly when designing for players with little technology experience or people with disabilities, efforts in GUR should not just focus on the experience of most or the 'typical' players, but also ensure that engagement with games does not harm, and comes easily to, those who require more support to be able to play. To this end, researchers and developers bear the responsibility of ensuring that games are appropriate, enjoyable, and empowering for all players. We hope that the case studies and considerations of this chapter can contribute to the work of those wishing to create positive gaming experiences for broad audiences.

Takeaways

- This chapter is intended to provide guidance for game developers and researchers intending to co-design and evaluate interactive experiences with populations such as young children and people with cognitive disabilities.
- We provide four case studies of projects that investigated the process of GUR with audiences with special needs, for example, older adults in long-term care, and young people with disabilities.

- The chapter includes recommendations for constructively and respectfully involving special populations in GUR.
- We identify specific cognitive, physical, emotional, and social considerations relevant for both the organization of the design process and the functionality of the designed artefacts.
- We discuss the broad problem of designing challenging yet enjoyable games for populations that already face significant challenges.

References and further reading

Note: some of these references are academic publications and locked behind publisher paywalls. They can be accessed via one-off purchases; however, your nearest university library will be likely able to provide free access, and some are available without a fee via repositories maintained by the authors' institutions—please see http://eprints.lincoln.ac.uk/ and http://hci.usask.ca.

Benton, L., Vasalou, A., Khaled, R., Johnson, H., Gooch, D. (2014). Diversity for design: a framework for involving neurodiverse children in the technology design process. In Proceedings of the 2014 CHI Conference on Human Factors in Computing Systems. Toronto, ON: ACM.

Fisk, A., Rogers, W., Charness, N., Czaja, S., Sharit, J. Designing for older adults: principles and creative human factors approaches. Boca Raton, FL: CRC Press.

Folstein, M. F., Folstein, S. E., McHugh, P. R. (1975). 'Mini-Mental State'—a practical method for grading the cognitive state of patients for the clinician. Journal of Psychiatric Research, 12, 189–198.

Gerling, K., Linehan, C., Kirman, B., Kalyn, M., Evans, A., Hicks, K. (2016). Creating wheelchair-controlled video games: challenges and opportunities when involving young people with mobility impairments and game design experts. International Journal of Human-Computer Studies, 94, 64–73.

Gerling, K., Mandryk, R., Linehan, C. (2015). Long-term use of motion-based video games in care home settings. In Proceedings of the 2015 CHI Conference on Human Factors in Computing Systems. Seoul, South Korea: ACM.

Waddington, J., Linehan, C., Gerling, K., Hicks, K., Hodgson, T. (2015). Participatory design of therapeutic video games for young people with neurological vision impairment. In Proceedings of the 2015 CHI Conference on Human Factors in Computing Systems. Seoul, South Korea: ACM.

Gerling, K., Livingston, I., Nacke, L., Mandryk, R. (2012). Full-body motion-based game interaction for older adults. In Proceedings of the 30th International Conference on Human Factors in Computing Systems. Austin, TX: ACM.

Watson, D., Clark, L. A., Tellegen, A. (1988). Development and validation of brief measures of positive and negative affect: the PANAS scales. Journal of Personality and Social Psychology, 56(6), 1063–1070.

Pauwels, L. (2010). Visual sociology reframed: an analytical synthesis and discussion of visual methods in social and cultural research. Sociological Methods & Research, 38(4), 545–581.

CHAPTER 28

Gamer motivation profiling: uses and applications

NICK YEE, *Quantic Foundry*

NICOLAS DUCHENEAUT, *Quantic Foundry*

Highlights

Gamers are not a monolithic group; gaming preferences and motivations vary in important ways among gamers. An empirical, validated model of gaming motivations provides a crucial methodological bridge between player preferences and their in-game behaviours, and, more importantly, engagement and retention outcomes. Instead of simply seeing on a key performance indicator (KPI) dashboard that a certain percentage of gamers are leaving, a motivation model allows us to pinpoint why those gamers are leaving.

28.1 Introduction

The heterogeneity of gamers necessitates investigation into their preferences and motivations, to inform and provide tailored and customized game experiences to attract a wide range of players (Hilgard et al., 2013; Vandenberghe, 2012; Yee, 2006). Under the motivation factors action, social, mastery, achievement, immersion, and creativity, our motivation model allows for the exploration of

Games User Research, Anders Drachen, Pejman Mirza-Babaei, Lennart E. Nacke (Eds).
© Oxford University Press 2018. Published 2018 by Oxford University Press

player motivations, thematic relationships between games, and the identification of distinct player segments. Here, we also explore some applications of our motivation model in the context of some of our previous work.

28.2 Motivation frameworks streamline game development

Adopting a validated motivation framework streamlines game development within a game company in multiple ways. Firstly, it provides a standardized taxonomy and vocabulary across designers, marketers, and user experience researchers, thereby reducing the friction of collaborations across different teams that might otherwise develop their own folk taxonomies. Secondly, by identifying how motivations do and do not cluster together, these motivation frameworks generate guidelines on which game features complement each other—for example, do gamers who enjoy competition tend to like or dislike collaboration? Finally, validated models provide an empirical basis (via a survey inventory) to test hypotheses and benchmark outcomes. For example, which gaming motivations vary between gamers from different retention cohorts?

The large amount of behavioural data that can be tracked in-game and the ability to segment gamers based on their in-game behaviours are not, in and of themselves, a more effective way of achieving these goals. After all, a game cannot track the behavioural preferences that it does not cater to, no matter how good the telemetry is otherwise. In this sense, motivational frameworks and in-game tracking cover each other's blind spots.

28.3 An overview of the Gamer Motivation Profile

In the remainder of this chapter, we will describe the Gamer Motivation Profile that we have developed at Quantic Foundry (Yee, 2015). Instead of focusing on the model itself, we will focus on how we are applying our large data set around gaming motivations to inform decisions in game development.

Starting with a literature review of motivation taxonomies that have been proposed in academia and the game industry, we used an iterative approach to collect data and develop a motivation model via factor analysis. We developed an online app where gamers could take a 5-minute survey, receive their

Action "Boom!"	Social "Let's Play Together"	Mastery "Let Me Think"	Achievement "I Want More"	Immersion "Once Upon a Time"	Creativity "What If?"
Destruction Guns. Explosives. Chaos. Mayhem.	**Competition** Duels. Matches. High on Ranking.	**Challenge** Practice. High Difficulty. Challenges.	**Completion** Get All Collectibles. Complete All Missions.	**Fantasy** Being someone else. somewhere else.	**Design** Expression. Customization.
Excitement Fast-Paces. Action. Surprises. Thrills.	**Community** Being on Team. Chatting. Interaction.	**Strategy** Thinking Ahead. Making Decisions.	**Power** Powerful Character. Powerful Equipment.	**Story** Elaborate plots. Interesting characters.	**Discovery** Explore. Tinker. Experiment.

Figure 28.1 Quantic Foundry's Gamer Motivation Model

personalized profile report, and share their results via social media. As more and more gamers submitted their data, we tested new inventory items, re-ran the factor analysis, and revised the underlying model and norms.

Our current motivation model, based on data from over 250,000 gamers worldwide, is presented in Figure 28.1. The motivation factors in the same columns are highly correlated, while factors in different columns are relatively independent from each other. In the survey, alongside the motivation inventory and basic demographic questions, gamers were asked to list their favourite games as well as recent games they have enjoyed playing. Thus, our data set allows us to pivot between gamer demographics, motivation profiles, and specific game titles and franchises.

28.4 Applications of the gamer audience data

The large data set provides us with robust population norms and benchmarks across game titles and genres, and allows us to compare and pivot on game audiences in a variety of ways that inform common production and marketing questions in game development.

28.4.1 Prioritize game features

We can use these audience profiles to identify the most and least important motivations for the audience of a specific game title, franchise, or genre. We do this by sampling the relevant subset of gamers and then generating an aggregate motivation profile of that sample. We have worked with game companies in the early stages of game development as well as with those who are working on a franchise's next entry to help them prioritize the development of their game's features. This has been particularly helpful for companies working on relatively new or blended genres, such as our work in identifying the profile of idle clicker gamers (Yee, 2016).

28.4.2 Game space mapping

We can also use our audience data to visualize the competitive landscape around a specific game title or franchise. By ranking the odds ratios of other game titles within a specific audience's data, we can surface the games that are most closely related to a given audience. We can then apply factor analysis on the motivations of these gamers to identify the two primary motivation axes (i.e. combinations of motivations) for this audience space. The resulting graph (Figure 28.2) visualizes the proximity of game audiences and the motivational dimensions on which they vary. By overlaying the audience density on this map, we have helped

Figure 28.2 Game space mapping example of open-world action-adventure games

game companies distinguish game spaces that are underserved from those that are overcrowded.

28.3.3 Player segment analysis

Game audiences are never perfectly homogenous. We can use our gamer data to identify distinct player segments within a game title, franchise, or genre. We achieve this by applying cluster analysis on the relevant gamers and clustering based on their demographic and motivation data. The lists of disproportionately popular games for each segment add further context. We have used these empirically derived player segments to help game producers and marketers target their audience and tailor their messages more effectively.

In the games research space, a great deal of effort and attention has been directed at developing taxonomies of gamer motivations. While adopting a standardized model benefits the game development process, a surprising amount of analytical value can be derived from a large data set on gamer motivations across game titles.

28.5 Takeaways

The Gamer Motivation Profile that we have developed at Quantic Foundry allows us to elucidate players' motivations, understand how other games relate with respect to a game title or franchise, and allows for the identification of smaller player segments within the population that plays any specific game, franchise, or genre (for additional perspectives see e.g. chapter 29 which focuses on social network analysis in GUR, or chapter 19 which introduces large-scale analytics tools for e.g. player profiling). These tools facilitate a rich understanding of the constellation of gamers' preferences and motivations, and the application of this knowledge allows one to prioritize game features during future development, understand how game elements relate to each other in the current gaming market, and effectively target subsections of their player base.

References

Hilgard, J., Engelhardt, C., Bartholow, B. (2013). Individual differences in motives, preferences, and pathology in video games: the Gaming Attitudes, Motives, and Experiences Scales (GAMES). Frontiers in Psychology, 4. https://www.ncbi.nlm.nih.gov/pmc/articles/PMC3766857/

Vandenberghe, J. (2012). The 5 domains of play: applying psychology's Big 5 motivation domains to games. Presented at the GDC 2012. http://www.gdcvault.com/play/1015364/the-5-Domains-of-Play

Yee, N. (2006). Motivations of play in online games. Journal of CyberPsychology and Behavior, 9, 772–775.

Yee, N. (2015). The Gamer Motivation Profile: model and findings. Presented at the GDC 2016. http://www.gdcvault.com/play/1023242/the-Gamer-Motivation-Profile-Model

Yee, N. (2016). The surprising profile of idle clicker gamers. http://quanticfoundry.com/2016/07/06/idle-clickers/

CHAPTER 29

Social Network Analysis in Games User Research

JOHANNA PIRKER, *Graz University of Technology*

Highlights

This chapter is an introduction to Social Network Analysis (SNA) with a focus on the context of player and in-game data. An overview of the key elements for network analysis is presented along with a discussion of the possibilities that can be realized through the use of networks and advice on using networks for Games User Research (GUR) to understand player behaviour in a social context.

29.1 Introduction: social networks in games—focus on the player

In multiplayer and social network games, the social interactions—competition or collaboration—between players are an important factor for player engagement and retention. Thus, it is a crucial but challenging endeavour to understand better the social structures, dynamics, and interactions between players. One method to investigate the relationship between players is the use of *Social Network Analysis* (SNA), which in recent years has become an important tool to understand user behaviour in social media networks such as Twitter, Facebook, and LinkedIn.

Social networks are graphs of individuals represented as nodes and their relationships and interactions represented as links between these nodes

Games User Research, Anders Drachen, Pejman Mirza-Babaei, Lennart E. Nacke (Eds).
© Oxford University Press 2018. Published 2018 by Oxford University Press

(Figure 29.1). They serve as a medium for information about behaviour, dynamics, and influences in these social structures (Zheng et al., 2012). Social networks are used to study how individuals are connected to and interact with other individuals. Social network analysis is described as the process of investigating social structures with methodologies from network and graph theory (Otte, 2002). SNA became extremely popular as a tool to analyse social media networks such as Twitter and Facebook, with a focus on user relations, the dynamics of the relationships (e.g., how users build relationships or form groups), and the relevance of single users in those networks.

Network analysis in the domain of games can be used to analyse, visualize, and investigate structures and relationships among players, geographical points, or other in-game elements, which can be represented as mathematical nodes in a graph structure. These networks can be investigated with different concepts inspired by graph theory. In *social* network analysis, the focus is on the social interactions between users or players.

In GUR, the analysis of player networks allows us to remotely investigate the players' behaviour and issues in player collaboration and communication. Doing so allows us to use this information for relating multi-user information to aspects such as player performance and engagement (e.g., to find weak ties and keep those players engaged). In multiplayer games, social connections are an

Figure 29.1 Example network with about 70 nodes connected through about 230 edges. Larger nodes represent users with more connections

important aspect of the user experience. By building networks between players in competitive or collaborative frameworks we can get a deeper understanding of how players interact and how these interactions influence their play and play style. This information can be used to analyse small but also large-scale player data sets. SNA as a part of GUR allows us to investigate player connections, collaborations, and missing connections in active multi-user games to identify important or weak connections between players, strengthen recommender systems, and keep players engaged and playing the game.

Typical questions we can answer with such concepts include the following:

- Analysing individuals:
  - Who are well connected/important players in a network?
  - What is the influence of individuals?
  - Who is the player with the largest reach?
  - Who are the players connecting different player groups?

- Analysing groups and communities:
  - How can we identify groups and communities?
  - How are players connected with each other?
  - Are players more engaged by playing alone or together?
  - Are players in groups performing better than players playing on their own?
  - Do connected players share common interests?

- Analysing social dynamics:
  - How do players connect to other players?
  - How do players build guilds?
  - When a player gets an interesting item to share with other players, how far will it get transmitted?
  - How can we recommend players in PVP matches?

In the literature, different examples of SNA in games are described. Ducheneaut et al. (2006), for instance, investigated guilds in World of Warcraft as social environments and built social networks within guilds to assess their potential for sociability and to measure the number of social activities. Bovenkamp et al. (2014) investigated different social structures and interaction types to build social networks in Defense of the Ancients, StarCraft, and World of Tanks. Rattinger et al. (2016) looked at various networks based on match data in Destiny and combined it with behavioural profiling. By combining network data about players playing either with or against the same people, the authors were able to show that strong social connections correlate with high performance. Top-performing players have strong social connections and play with and against the same people repeatedly. Playing with or against the same team repeatedly increases the player's overall performance. Additionally, clan membership correlates with performance.

In this chapter, a brief introduction of selected topics from SNA in the context of games is given. While network analysis without the social focus could be also used to illustrate relationships between in-game places, items, and other elements that could be connected through links, the focus of this chapter is SNA between players.

29.2 Social networks in games—essentials

The goal of SNA in games is to obtain information about relationships between players, identify interesting networks, and map connections to interesting features. Typical steps of SNA are (1) mining the data (information about the players), (2) identifying interesting networks (through identifying different relationships), and (3) analysing and mapping network data. In the next sections, an overview of the process of identifying player networks and how to analyse the networks is given.

29.2.1 Building player networks

To build social networks between players, graph structures are used. Players are represented as *nodes* (v). Relationships between players are represented as *edges* (e) between the nodes (Zafarani et al., 2014). Different forms of interactions and social behaviour connect friends, player groups, and similar players. To build these links, different forms of interactions can be used.

- *Direct relationships:* Direct (explicit) interactions between players are identified and used (e.g., in-game messaging, friendships, clan memberships).
- *Indirect relationships:* Relationships also can be identified through indirect (implicit) interactions (playing in same matches or opponent matches, same playing time, same in-game location).

In literature, we find different examples of relationship information used to create player networks. Rattinger et al. (2016) built networks between players based on different match interactions: playing matches together, playing matches on the same team, or on opponent teams. Ducheneaut et al. (2006) built the networks based on overlapping online time and/or same playing-zone of players connected through guilds. Szell et al. (2010) used positive (friendship, communication, trade) or negative (enmity, armed aggression, punishment) interactions to build player networks.

Links can be undirected (connected both ways), directed (connection only one way), or weighted (e.g., by a number indicating the number of interactions).

For a simple classification, we can identify three different network structures based on properties of links:

- undirected networks (links are undirected)
- directed networks (links are directed)
- weighted networks (links are weighted)

Figure 29.2 gives an overview of different graph types. Figure 29.2a represents an undirected graph: all three players are connected with each other. Figure 29.2b illustrates a directed graph, in which only the relationship between Player A and Player B is bidirectional and all connections to Player C are only one-way (e.g., Player A and Player B are following updates of Player C, but not vice versa). Figure 29.2c additionally contains weights, which could be used to illustrate the number of interactions (e.g., number of matches played together, numbers of messages sent).

The resulting networks can be then used to analyse the relationships, identify key players and weak players, or find sub-graphs and communities. The mathematical representation of a network is an adjacency matrix correlating the links to the nodes.

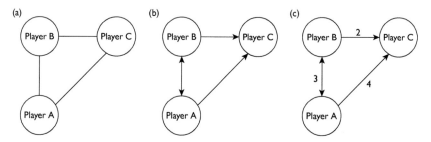

Figure 29.2 (a) Undirected graph (b) directed graph (c) directed weighted graph

29.2.2 Analysing player networks

There are different metrics from graph theory to analyse and investigate networks. In this section, the most important metrics are briefly described to give a first overview of the possibilities of graphs. Further details and the mathematical background can be found in Zafarani et al. (2014). These metrics can be used, for instance, to identify weak or key players, which are important for the existence and the robustness of the network. Game designers and operators can then try to include elements to motivate these players.

The *degree* (d) of a node (player) represents the number of links to other nodes (players). A high degree represents a high number of friends, interactions, or matches played together. In directed graphs, additionally *in-degrees* (edges towards node) and *out-degrees* (edges away from node) are described. To measure the *centrality* of players, different metrics can be used including various features. The degree *centrality* measures the number of connections of players based on the degree. Looking at directed graphs, the in-degree centrality describes the prestige or level of activeness of the player (many interactions with others) and the out-degree centrality describes the gregariousness. Other forms of centrality measures consider, for example, the number of friends of friends (e.g., PageRank).

To measure the *closeness* (distance) in graphs between two nodes, the number of paths (links) between nodes is counted. This information is important to analyse how fast information would spread between two players or how likely they will befriend. If two people in the network are connected through a common friend, the chances that these players are also starting to interact is higher (Rapoport, 1953). To measure the centrality of players in terms of 'being close to all other players', the *closeness centrality* is used.

To identify the *connectivity* between nodes, the links are investigated: weak links are links connecting sub-graphs. These links are often very important to connect different groups with each other. A link is described as a *bridge* if it connects sub-graphs—the removal of such a link would disconnect the sub-graphs. Even though players in a bridge connection might not have essentially a lot of connections, they are still considered an important part of the graph in the sense of connecting groups (Easley and Kleinberg, 2010). It is crucial to identify and motivate such players to keep the social connection between subgroups. This measure is described as *betweenness centrality*.

Another way to look at graphs is to look at sub-graphs, also known as communities, clusters, or groups. In player research, this is an important aspect to identify groups of players strongly connected to each other. When playing games, players form groups based on interests, playing habits, playing times, geographical zones, and the like. These groups are not essentially related to in-game clans, or official groups, and therefore also not explicitly visible. The identification of such groups could be used, for instance, for recommendation systems or player classification.

The nodes and edges of the networks can be mapped to supplementary in-game information, such as playing behaviour, in-game performance, weapon or tool preference, and demographical data. Mapping such information to social network metrics can help identifying motivators, issues, or influences on in-game performance or behaviour.

29.3 Conclusion and next steps

In multiplayer games, one of the most important motivators for players is the social aspect. The use of networks in the domain of GUR can give valuable insights into social interactions, structures, and dynamics within the game. Based on different forms of interactions, various sorts of networks can be created. Typically, social networks give game designer and operators insights into social aspects such as key or weak individuals in a group or community, which are essential for the robustness and the connectivity between players and different player groups. The identification of such players can help to introduce additional motivators to strengthen the network. However, networks can be used not only to look closer at individual players but also to identify entire player groups. For matchmaking and recommendation systems, the use of social networks can, for instance, help to identify indirect or implicit communities to engage social playing.

In this chapter, only a first very brief overview of SNA in the context of GUR and player behaviour analysis was given (chapters 19 and 20 focus on analytics in general and form a supplement to this introduction). SNA is a broad and complex topic and this chapter was designed only as an introduction.

To get more information on this topic, readers are advised to study further books on social network mining and analysis such as Scott (2000) or Zafarani et al. (2014), and try social analysis tools such as Gephi.

Next steps

Aggarwal, C. C. (2011). An introduction to social network data analytics. In Social network data analytics (pp. 1–15). New York: Springer.

Gephi—open source software to visualize and analyse networks. https://gephi.org/

Scott, J. (2000). Social network analysis: a handbook (2nd ed.). London: Sage Publications.

Zafarani, R., Abbasi, M. A., Liu, H. (2014). Social media mining: an introduction. Cambridge, UK: Cambridge University Press.

References and further reading

Aggarwal, C. C. (2011). An introduction to social network data analytics. In Social network data analytics (pp. 1–15). New York: Springer.

Ducheneaut, N., Yee, N., Nickell, E., Moore, R. J. (2006). Alone together? Exploring the social dynamics of massively multiplayer online games. In Proceedings of the SIGCHI Conference on Human Factors in Computing Systems (pp. 407–416). New York: ACM.

Easley, D., Kleinberg, J. (2010). Networks, crowds, and markets: reasoning about a highly connected world. Cambridge, UK: Cambridge University Press.

Jia, A. L., Shen, S., Bovenkamp, R. V. D., Iosup, A., Kuipers, F., Epema, D. H. (2015). Socializing by gaming: revealing social relationships in multiplayer online games. ACM Transactions on Knowledge Discovery from Data (TKDD),10(2), 11.

Otte, E., Rousseau, R. (2002). Social network analysis: a powerful strategy, also for the information sciences. Journal of Information Science, 28(6), 441–453.

Rapoport, A. (1953). Spread of information through a population with socio-structural bias: I. Assumption of transitivity. The Bulletin of Mathematical Biophysics, 15(4), 523–533.

Rattinger, A., Wallner, G., Drachen, A., Pirker, J., Sifa, R. (2016, September). Integrating and inspecting combined behavioural profiling and social network models in Destiny. 15th International Conference on Entertainment Computing.

Scott, J. (2000). Social network analysis: a handbook (2nd ed.). London: Sage Publications.

Szell, M., Lambiotte, R., Thurner, S. (2010). Multirelational organization of large-scale social networks in an online world. Proceedings of the National Academy of Sciences, 107(31), 13636–13641.

van de Bovenkamp, R., Shen, S., Iosup, A., Kuipers, F. (2013, January). Understanding and recommending play relationships in online social gaming. In 2013 Fifth International Conference on Communication Systems and Networks (COMSNETS) (pp. 1–10). IEEE.

van de Bovenkamp, R., Shen, S., Jia, A. L., Kuipers, F. (2014). Analyzing implicit social networks in multiplayer online games. IEEE Internet Computing, 18(3), 36–44.

Zafarani, R., Abbasi, M. A., Liu, H. (2014). Social media mining: an introduction. Cambridge, UK: Cambridge University Press.

Zheng, X., Zhong, Y., Zeng, D., Wang, F. (2012). Social influence and spread dynamics in social networks. Frontiers of Computer Science, 6, 611–620.

CHAPTER 30

A short guide to user testing for simulation sickness in Virtual Reality

BEN LEWIS-EVANS, *Epic Games*

Highlights

The increased interest in Virtual Reality (VR) has yielded a lot of studies and development in both research and game design. Simulation sickness is an issue experienced by a significant subset of players in VR. This chapter focuses on the challenges this issue poses for user research, and suggests practical considerations for researchers to minimize legal and ethical risks.

30.1 Introduction

With the current renewed interest in Virtual Reality (VR) has come a need to carry out user research on VR projects. In addition to the normal usability and player experience issues, VR magnifies the issue of simulation sickness. VR magnifies this issue because simulation sickness is an accessibility issue with non-VR digital experiences as well. As such, many of the learnings related to preventing simulation sickness can also be used in traditional games (e.g., offering settings to turn off motion blur, weapon and head bob/swap, and altering the field of view can often be the difference between someone being able to play a first-person shooter or not).

Games User Research, Anders Drachen, Pejman Mirza-Babaei, Lennart E. Nacke (Eds).
© Oxford University Press 2018. Published 2018 by Oxford University Press

Simulation sickness in general is a syndrome that can result in eyestrain, headaches, problems standing up (postural instability), sweating, disorientation, vertigo, loss of colour to the skin, nausea, and, in extreme cases, vomiting. It is similar to motion sickness, and is often called such, but is technically classified as its own syndrome.

Given that simulation sickness is unpleasant (to say the least), detecting and reducing it can be an important part of user research for games. However, like other areas of research, detecting and testing for simulation sickness comes with its own challenges.

30.2 Challenges

30.2.1 Traditional usability sample sizes may not be useful

There is often a desire in Games User Research (GUR) to get everything done with a small sample. This desire is often driven by commercial pressures and can be reasonably successful when assessing task-based usability issues. However, much like the actual subjective player experience, simulation sickness is a fundamentally individual issue related to player biology and life experience. It cannot be detected and fixed with traditional usability-focused small samples. The common-practice $N = 5$ methodology for usability testing makes the assumption that individual differences are not significant. This is not the case for physiological issues such as simulation sickness that only impact a (significant) minority unless the VR hardware and/or software is designed poorly.

30.2.2 What can be done?

Given that traditional recruited usability samples cannot be relied on, what can you do? The best answer is to use large samples and assess simulation sickness, but if that is cost prohibitive (in time and money) there are some potential alternatives.

30.2.2.1 EXPERT ANALYSIS

The game design factors that can lead to simulation sickness are relatively well known thanks to research and military simulators. As such, when assessing a game for possible simulation sickness, issues to watch out for include the following:

- Inconsistent frame rate and poor latency. The game should maintain a consistently high frame rate and latency. At least 90 fps is good and the latency between action and the display updating should be stable and less than 20 ms.
- Motion blur and blurry scenes in general.
- Flickering or flashing lighting effects.
- Rolling motions and/or a moving horizon.
- Movement that does not match the affordances of the head-mounted display (i.e. the camera should operate like a head does).
- Any camera movement that is not in the control of the player (e.g., no taking away of camera control for death animations/cutscenes/anything).
- Zooming the camera in and out is likely to increase simulation sickness.
- Camera height. The lower to the ground, the faster the perception of motion, and therefore the increased likelihood of simulation sickness. However, particularly high cameras or putting players in high places may induce feelings of vertigo.
- Any artificial (e.g., not one-to-one movement related to a room-scale experience) movement through a scene that involves a sensation of acceleration or deceleration. Basically most feelings of acceleration (vection) can result in simulation sickness.
  - A common solution to this is teleportation or to have players inside an enclosed vehicle of some sort (although this is less successful than teleportation).
- Experiences that would make people sick in real life (e.g., being in a weightless environment or on a rollercoaster). VR feels more real, therefore if someone would get sick in reality in a situation, then they are likely to get sick in a simulation of that situation.
- Uncomfortably positioned UI or game elements that result in excessive, large, and rapid head or eye movements.

The foregoing are just a few things to consider and a chapter much longer than this could be filled going into more detail. However, thankfully there are many guides and talks online that cover these points and others in more detail that you can read and share with others. Oculus, for example has a great best-practices guide that you can find online (see Further Reading).

30.2.2.2 RECRUIT VULNERABLE POPULATIONS

If you are trying to test for simulation sickness, you can try to do so with smaller numbers by recruiting vulnerable populations. That is, try to get people who suffer from simulation sickness (or if you cannot find them, motion sickness sufferers, although there is not always a strong correlation between simulation sickness sensitivity and motion sickness sensitivity) to test out the game. You can recruit such people by simply asking them, by having them fill in a form such as the Simulator Sickness Questionnaire and then recruiting people across the scale of simulation sickness risk, and by trying to recruit older people and people who do not play many first-person games (both factors that may be associated with increased sensitivity simulation sickness).

30.2.2.3 RECRUIT MORE THAN YOU THINK YOU WILL NEED

When testing for simulation sickness, some people will get sick. In terms of research impact, this means they will not be able to continue. If you need to see a certain amount of play time for usability and/or player experience, you will not get that information from sick players. As such, consider adding an extra 10% at least to your sample size numbers.

30.3 Additional practical considerations

Some practical considerations should be discussed that people may not usually consider when assessing simulation sickness. You are testing to see if people are going to get dizzy, fall over, and throw up. Are you ethically, legally, and practically ready for this? For example:

- Is your testing space a safe place? Could people hurt themselves if they fell over?
- Have you asked players to tell you immediately if they feel uncomfortable and are you ready to assist them to quickly remove the headset if they need to?
- Have you made it totally clear that if participants want to stop they can and will get the full amount of compensation? If not, you may have people trying to tough out simulation sickness and skewing your results (or spewing all over your testing space).
- Players are likely to be wearing headphones in addition to a VR headset. Do you have a quick and easy way to communicate with them? Consider using voice chat either via the game or a third-party app.

- Does your non-disclosure agreement (Non-Disclosure Agreement, NDA)/permission form cover the fact that players may feel ill? What do the local laws say about this?
- Do you have a quiet, cool, and safe space where players who do feel ill can be monitored and recover?
- How do players get to your testing location? Do they drive? Simulation sickness can, in extreme cases, last for hours. What are your responsibilities in this case and are you prepared to look after someone for that long?
- Be aware that observing what someone is seeing in VR can also cause simulation sickness in observers. Observers may need to take breaks, sit further away from screens than normal, and need some time to acclimatize themselves to observing VR footage.
- Be upfront with players. This may cause expectancy problems, where people expect to get sick and therefore are more likely to do so. However, this will let you be conservative in your assessments of simulation sickness, and also means that players will be less likely to be scared off coming to test in the future.
- Be upfront with developers as well. Communicate the challenges and additional considerations of testing for simulation sickness and why it may differ from the user testing they could be used to seeing.

The preceding list should not be seen as attempt to scare off Games User Researchers, but rather as an incentive to think about the challenges. Testing games is a highly desirable activity for many people; getting sick is not so desirable. Make sure you are ready to look after your players.

30.4 Takeaways

With the increase in games using VR, researchers should be mindful of the distinct challenges this technology can hold. It is also important to follow best practices and guidelines to pre-emptively avoid issues shown to induce simulation sickness, being aware that some scenarios are prone to cause these symptoms. In terms of recruiting participants, researchers should include users that suffer from simulation sickness or motion sickness and, when possible, include older people and people that have not played first-person games. Finally, researchers should take care to ensure risk to players and observers is minimized during playtesting sessions.

Further reading

Kennedy, R. S., et al. (1993). Simulator Sickness Questionnaire: an enhanced method for quantifying simulator sickness. The International Journal of Aviation Psychology 3(3), 203–220.

Oculus VR, LLC. Oculus Best Practices. Retrieved 4 May 2017 from https://developer.oculus.com/documentation/

The Future of Games User Research

CHAPTER 31

Frontlines in Games User Research

ANDERS DRACHEN, *Digital Creativity Labs, University of York*

PEJMAN MIRZA-BABAEI, *UXR Lab, University of Ontario Institute of Technology*

LENNART E. NACKE, *University of Waterloo*

Highlights

Games User Research (GUR) methods and principles are evolving rapidly in keeping pace with the innovation rates in games. Every day brings new insights and practices, and new technologies keep expanding the boundaries of GUR. In this conclusion, we briefly outline some of the areas where innovations are being made or the front lines expanding in GUR, from new contexts to special topics such as telemetry, virtual reality, and physiological measures.

31.1 Introduction

When considering the chapters of this book and the recent work in GUR across industry and academia, an image emerges of a field in rapid development where new front lines are constantly opening up—for example, virtual reality (VR) (Chapter 30) and augmented reality games. At the same time, new methods, tools, and ideas are presented daily—for example, automated, AI-driven

Games User Research, Anders Drachen, Pejman Mirza-Babaei, Lennart E. Nacke (Eds).
© Oxford University Press 2018. Published 2018 by Oxford University Press

testing—and while GUR today has a well-defined role to play in game development and in several academic research areas, this does not mean the innovation rate has slowed down.

GUR has come a long way, as demonstrated by industry visionary Michael Medlock's review of the decades-long history of the field at the GUR Summit 2015, a yearly event held by the GUR community in San Francisco. Michael outlined how GUR has evolved from initial interest in how the players actually experienced games all the way through a scientific, evidence-building process that is deeply integrated into the production of games, big and small, worldwide (chapters 2–4). From this history, it is also apparent that many of the fundamental challenges in GUR are as important today as they have always been—for example, how to actually measure user experience in a practical way, or how to effectively communicate user testing findings to a diverse stakeholder audience.

GUR as a community also faces a variety of challenges, notably related to knowledge dissemination, exchange, and preservation. GUR is inherently a multidisciplinary field, stretching across academia and research, and this makes knowledge migration challenging. In a domain with rapid emergence of new knowledge and high innovation rates, but a fragmented infrastructure to communicate the knowledge, tracking existing and emerging knowledge is difficult. There is, however, an excellent tradition for collaboration across and within industry and academia, and people arriving to the field generally report feeling welcomed and inspired by the active GUR community. These are people who are passionate about games.

In this chapter we briefly outline the core areas of critical interest and development. For example, the reintroduction of VR, the maturing of techniques for behavioural and physiological tracking, attempts to measure player experience, new contexts of play, the evaluation of learning, and ongoing efforts to broaden the target audience of games all present new opportunities and challenges for GUR work in industry and academia. It is only natural that these front-line areas are discussed in the chapters of this book, and we therefore link them to chapters for easy reference.

31.2 Front lines and flagship areas

While we are not claiming the following list to be comprehensive, four areas—technologies, contexts, methods, and challenges—are topics that are much discussed in the GUR community and which all hold interesting challenges for

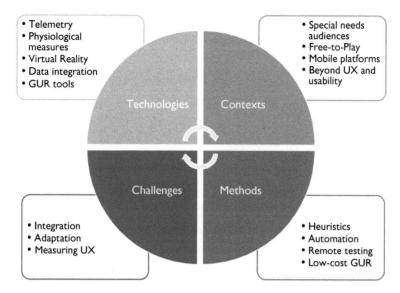

- Telemetry
- Physiological measures
- Virtual Reality
- Data integration
- GUR tools

- Special needs audiences
- Free-to-Play
- Mobile platforms
- Beyond UX and usability

Technologies
Contexts

Challenges
Methods

- Integration
- Adaptation
- Measuring UX

- Heuristics
- Automation
- Remote testing
- Low-cost GUR

Figure 31.1 Flagship areas in GUR: areas that are currently forming some of the frontline topics in the field, or which form potential future areas of innovation. These topics are heavily interrelated; advances in one area tend to bring others forward as well

innovation in theory and practice (Figure 31.1). (We are expecting many 'But why are you ignoring problem X, which is incredibly important to GUR!', and will update future editions of this chapter accordingly! We are also planning a blog series on 'the lost chapters' which will be published on the book's website www.gurbook.com.) We call these 'flagship areas', which essentially means a topic or issue that has either garnered critical interest from professionals, or which is emerging as a new trend with the potential to reshape the roadmap in GUR. They are all interrelated and dependent on each other in various ways. For example, the adaption of behavioural telemetry in user testing is related to the use of mobile gaming platforms.

31.2.1 Technologies

In recent years substantial advances have been made in the application of various technologies to academic and industry-based GUR work. These notably fall within the domains of psychophysiological sensors, VR, and behavioural telemetry. While the technologies are well known in GUR, they have gained substantially in maturity within the past few years.

31.2.1.1 PHYSIOLOGICAL MEASUREMENTS

GUR approaches have been around for a decade that make use of physiological data. These approaches still remain to be explored for their actual usefulness in game development. Physiological measures may provide important information on change in a player's emotion that is complementary, or even contradictory, to that provided by self-report or observation measures. They are often regarded as more objective compared to self-reports; they may also provide information on a player's feelings that, for some reason (e.g., subtle nature of the responses, repression) are not available to the players' conscious awareness. However, to provide context (or ground truth) to sensitive physiological measures, they are usually used in conjunction with other user research methods. Through the use of game logs/behavioural telemetry (or other indexing approaches) that pinpoint exactly when game events were happening, we are able to contextualize physiological reactions of players. Overall, physiological-based evaluation has been used with two general aims: (a) to look for correlations between collected physiological measures (event-based analysis or session-average analysis) and self-report measures as a means of validating the quantitative values captured for summative evaluation; (b) formative evaluation, to use changes in a player's physiological state as an indexing tool to structure post-session interviews or observations. While physiological methods have been around for many years, there is a way to go in terms of making them more accessible and resource-efficient before they are ready for truly widespread adoption in GUR.

Physiological measures—also referred to as biometrics—and their current use in GUR is introduced by Lennart Nacke in Chapter 16, and further elaborated on by Pierre Chalfoun and Jonathan Dankoff in Chapter 17, where biometrics are put into a practical development context.

31.2.1.2 VIRTUAL REALITY

Virtual reality (VR) technology has in the past years seen a widespread resurgence in games and elsewhere, but mass adoption has still not occurred. With the introduction of companies who have started prototyping a new generation of VR technology, embodied VR games are already happening. The potential for the game industry and the larger creative industries in the area is tremendous; however, embodied VR technology comes with a set of associated new challenges for user testing, such as the difficulty of running think-aloud testing with participants wearing head-mounted displays. There is thus a need for new research and development for GUR methods able to handle the unique situation these new immersive technologies provide.

VR and the new challenges this opens up for GUR is discussed by Ben Lewis-Evans in Chapter 30.

31.2.1.3 BEHAVIOURAL TELEMETRY

The application of telemetry tracking to obtain data about in-game and associated behaviour from game players has gained substantial traction in both the industry and academic sectors. Behavioural telemetry offers high-resolution, precise data about how users interact with games that traditional GUR methods are hard-pressed to produce. Since the early days of applying behavioural telemetry in GUR, the advent of free-to-play (F2P) business models and mobile technologies have seen a rapid adoption of game analytics techniques in the industry (see also chapters 19–21). However, telemetry is not always integrated with user testing. While recent years have seen excellent progress on this topic, a current and future challenge lies in making telemetry analysis available to, notably, small-to-medium-sized developers, and developing tools and techniques for integrating telemetry with existing GUR frameworks, as well for visualizing behavioural telemetry to make it actionable alongside other user testing results.

Shawn Connor and Anders Drachen in Chapter 19 describe the current state of the art of how behavioural telemetry is used in the incredibly fast-paced area of game analytics, and how the strengths of analytics and GUR combined provide unprecedented insights into player behaviour. In Chapter 20, Lysiane Charest focuses on how analytics can be performed on a budget, and Pejman Mirza-Babaei and Thomas Galati (in Chapter 21) further drive home the point that GUR and game analytics are the best of friends.

31.2.1.4 MULTICHANNEL DATA INTEGRATION AND COMMUNICATION

User research can produce substantial and complex data sets. Consider the combination of surveys, interviews, behavioural telemetry, screen capture, recording of facial expressions, physiological measures, and post-session discussions described in this book. While in practice all of these are rarely combined—as the information gathered might be amazing, but the resource cost horrendous—several systems have been described over the past few years for handling some of these. Indeed, several major developers have presented systems for integrating different sources of data, for example, behavioural telemetry, screen capture, surveys, and face tracking. There are, however, substantial challenges remaining with figuring out the best ways of meshing qualitative and quantitative data, aligning data recorded at varying frequencies, and handling complex multichannel data sets to make them actionable.

The different classes of core GUR methods are described in several chapters in this book. Industry visionaries Michael Medlock and Graham McAllister provide an overview of GUR methods and a framework for player research in Chapters 7 and 8, respectively. Florian Brühlmann and Elisa Mekler dive into survey techniques in Chapter 9, and Steve Bromley covers interviews in Chapter 10. The observation family of techniques is described by Mirweis Sangin in Chapter 11 and the immensely popular and flexible think-aloud protocol by Tom Knoll in Chapter 12. In Chapter 13, Michael Medlock rounds off these chapters by describing the RITE framework for linking GUR methods in an iterative testing framework.

31.2.2 Contexts

Games do not get played in a vacuum, and there are many different kinds of games and delivery vehicles for games. The contextual impact on game user experience is recognized as being highly important, and in recent years more attention has been given to adapting GUR methods to different situations. At the same time, our knowledge of what we do *not* know has broadened.

31.2.2.1 GUR METHODS FOR SPECIAL NEEDS AUDIENCES

Providing access to games for all people can be a major challenge—but one that can be addressed in GUR. A main problem for the group of disabled users identifying themselves as able gamers is an extended controller support and adherence to multisensory types of feedback (e.g., extending visual feedback to other modalities like audio cues for blind players), since they often cannot operate a standard controller or need special gesture input. In addition, younger kids and older adults are becoming increasingly interested in playing games on different devices and often bring with them special needs regarding the comprehensibility of the interface and controls. As part of an inclusive GUR, we need to be able to provide testing for these special populations.

In Chapter 27, Kathrin Gerling, Conor Linehan, and Regan Mandryk discuss the challenges and opportunities in creating games for audiences with special needs and how to user test with a diversity of audiences.

31.2.2.2 FREE-TO-PLAY: GUR FOR RETENTION, ENGAGEMENT, AND MONETIZATION

Free-to-play (F2P) and similar revenue strategies based on the Freemium business models have necessitated the adoption of business analytics methods to monitor and predict user behaviour via the collection of behavioural telemetry. For example, the adoption of techniques such as split-testing (A/B testing or multilevel testing) and the introduction of machine learning techniques for classifying and predicting player behaviour. These goals move outside of the traditional areas of GUR to cover user spending patterns. There has been some debate as to whether game analytics is also GUR, but there is at least an overlap between game analytics and GUR. As a new area, there is a substantial room for new theories, methods, and techniques that focus on monetization, or investigate monetization in parallel with user experience and design.

While not a major topic of this book, the combination of user testing in mobile F2P and casual games and game analytics is an exciting frontier that is currently evolving rapidly as the traditionally analytics-driven mobile game sector is exploring the integration of GUR.

31.2.2.3 MOBILE AND OTHER NEW PLATFORMS

The video games industry is experiencing changes in how players interact with games. New platforms provide, for example, intuitive motion-sensitive controllers and less complex games designed to be accessible to non-gamers. On the other side, the increasing computing power of mobile devices provide increased competition with consoles. These new platforms and ways of interacting with games increases the breath of user research and invites innovative methods to capture and analyse experiences (Steven Schirra and Brooke White cover the in and out of user testing on mobile platforms in Chapter 26).

31.2.2.4 TESTING OUTSIDE USABILITY AND UX

While the GUR tool set allows testing concepts around usability and player experience, games have left traditional settings and are increasingly used in so-called gamified applications, serious games, and learning games. Here the goal is often to test how effective a behavioural change or a learning effect is. Novel GUR methods are promising for getting insights into learning and decision making in games. However, GUR still needs to establish a standardized tool set and methods for this separate market where the goal of the game is not to play, but to learn something or motivate a behaviour.

The topic of motivation specifically is addressed in Chapter 28 by Nick Yee and Nicholas Ducheneaut. In Chapter 29, Johanna Pirker provides a brief overview of what we can gain learn from integrating the social context around players into GUR work.

31.2.3 Methods

The methods used for GUR have matured immensely over the past decade. There is more refinement, and more specialized models are available today than ever before. A lot of detailed methodological knowledge is also available, although highly fragmented and not always easily accessible or adoptable. Technological innovations have specifically opened up the opportunity in the future to bring GUR more out of the lab and into the wild. This has many challenges and benefits, but significantly means it is getting easier to assess players and their experience in their natural environments, outside the user testing lab.

31.2.3.1 PLAY HEURISTICS

Although heuristic evaluation promises to be a low-cost usability evaluation method, it suffers significantly with problems concerning evaluators' subjective interpretations. To answer this limitation, researchers have aimed to develop sets of heuristics that are specific to particular genres or situations—for example, to fit 2D platformers, or taking into account a problem's frequency, impact, and persistence. Heuristics are a great tool in GUR as the principles can be picked up and applied by non-experts, and adaptable to suit different situations.

Heuristics as a foundational method and tool for GUR are described in detail and with great examples by Heather Desurvire and Dennis Wixon in Chapter 14, and further elaborated on by Janne Paavilainen and colleagues in Chapter 15.

31.2.3.2 AUTOMATED TESTING

Lab-based testing, data collection, and analysis done in an automated fashion. Different testing scenarios bring different experimental requirements with them. For certain GUR testing approaches, a lab-based environment is paramount to rule out any confounding factors (e.g., environmental influences that can affect volatile physiological measures). For other approaches, automated data collection and analysis is preferable. Automation of in-game data collection and triggering is always better when there are large amounts of data to collect. The rule here seems to be that higher density data is extremely hard to analyse and cross-correlate with other GUR measures manually, so automated markup and processing of the data is desirable. Protocols are currently being established, but so far every researcher and many industrial GURs are building their own solutions, which is justified as there might be specific needs for a particular team. Furthermore, recent innovations in AI-supported testing, automated and manual, indicate the future availability of automated GUR testing that is highly responsive to player input and behaviours.

31.2.3.3 REMOTE TESTING

Remote testing in the context of GUR describes the application of techniques for obtaining information about user behaviour and user experience over a distance. Remote testing has gained traction recently thanks to the introduction of behavioural telemetry tracking and associated analytics, but remains a relatively underdeveloped area of GUR beyond the capture of player behaviour. For example, remote surveying and video capture provide the ability to capture user information at a distance, or in contexts where laboratory-based methods are not ideal. The potential for new tools and methods in this area is substantial, opening up larger sample sizes and cheap alternatives to laboratory testing. However, there is a costs-benefit balance, as remote testing requires the flexibility to work in conditions where there is less control than in the laboratory. Remote testing is likely an area of substantial innovation in the future of GUR.

31.2.3.4 LOW-COST TESTING

Although conducting 'formal' GUR studies as part of video games development cycle has become more popular over the last decade, apart from cases from large developers and publishers, there are not many reports of smaller-to-midsize studies that have fully applied these measures. Barriers towards adapting GUR studies—such as that personnel need to be trained extensively in interpreting and correlating multiple data sources—may seem out of scope for small-to-midsize development companies. One step towards making GUR studies more available for larger game developer communities is to develop low-cost testing methods (methodological optimizations suitable for small-scale GUR studies). This would have a direct impact on including GUR in the development process and on return on investment.

Sebastian Long deals with lab set-ups on any budget in Chapter 6, and in Chapter 22 Guillaume Louvel focuses on the ecological validity of user testing. Johan Dorell and Björn Marklund in Chapter 25 join forces with Julien Huguenin in Chapter 24 to discuss how small studios or others on a shoestring budget can gain value from GUR. Lysiane Charest (Chapter 20) and Pejman Mirza-Babaei and Thomas Galati (Chapter 21) also discuss how small studios (with arguably smaller budgets) can leverage data-driven user research in their game development.

31.2.4 Challenges

There are many open challenges in GUR, but what is perhaps most striking is that the foundational challenges of how to actually measure player experience and how to integrate user research in game development remain far from solved. Fortunately, a substantial part of this challenge relates to the happy circumstance that games and game development keeps changing, and thus GUR has to adapt with it and address new and specific situations.

31.2.4.1 INTEGRATING GUR IN ITERATIVE DEVELOPMENT

A substantial number of presentations and discussions in the past few years at GUR-focused events, as well as industry-wide events such as the annual Game Developers' Conference, have focused on the challenge of integrating GUR in iterative game development. This central challenge is how to obtain valid and generalizable information from playtesters in a way that is financially viable, flexible with respect to a variety of play contexts and goals (e.g., feedback on gameplay, art/graphics, mechanics, narrative), capable of delivering actionable insights, and fast enough that it can be integrated in a rapid iterative development process. This is not a new challenge, but rather one of the fundamental issues that underlies GUR work. The vast majority of the innovation in this area is being driven by large studios with the capacity to build in-house test labs and hire experts. Less work has been focused on developing solutions for small-to-medium-sized developers. Regardless, the introduction of new technologies, business models, and play contexts means that the practical challenge of user testing games is getting progressively more complex.

The process of GUR and how it can be integrated in production is covered in depth in Section 1 of this book, by Veronica Zammitto in Chapter 2, David Tisserand in Chapter 3, Ian Livingston in Chapter 4, and Graham McAllister in Chapter 5. James Berg provides a great case study in Chapter 23, while Pejman Mirza-Babaei discusses how to report GUR findings to development teams in Chapter 18.

31.2.4.2 MEASURING PLAYER EXPERIENCE

One of the largest challenges that the GUR community is currently facing is the development of good player experience models that can be used in game design and GUR. The challenge of measuring player experience is that some aspects like enjoyment cannot be measured as solidly by more objective measures as they can be by self-report measures. The major challenge for GUR remains to find a good combination of measures that can identify a valuable player experience holistically, efficiently, and cheaply.

31.3 Conclusion

GUR is still maturing, and as a field that focuses directly on the crucial user experience of games, it is not likely to stop maturing any time soon, if not for other reasons simply because games are not likely to stop breaking new ground any time soon. Many new technologies have emerged and gained maturity in recent years, all of which have carried with them new challenges and opportunities for user research. At the same time, the target audience for games has diversified, as have the contexts of play, which means that user testing has to accommodate these scenarios.

On a final note, it is worth iterating that the flagship areas outlined here do not exist independently. For example, the emergence of new mobile platforms and expansion of the target audience for games, combined with F2P business models and behavioural tracking, creates a need for GUR techniques to handle large-scale user data, combine in-house testing with remotely captured data, and integrate all of this with the iterative rhythm of game development. We are not claiming to have put forward the definitive list—indeed, there was much agonizing about what to include and exclude, and we again thank the advisory board for their invaluable input to the book—but the foregoing forms a synthesis of much discussion in the GUR and Game UX community and a starting point for future discussion about the intersection between players, user experience, development, technology, and games.

INDEX